Gamify Your Classroom

Colin Lankshear and Michele Knobel
General Editors

Vol. 77

The New Literacies and Digital Epistemologies series
is part of the Peter Lang Education list.
Every volume is peer reviewed and meets
the highest quality standards for content and production.

PETER LANG
New York • Bern • Frankfurt • Berlin
Brussels • Vienna • Oxford • Warsaw

Matthew Farber

Gamify Your Classroom

A Field Guide to Game-Based Learning

REVISED EDITION

PETER LANG
New York • Bern • Frankfurt • Berlin
Brussels • Vienna • Oxford • Warsaw

Library of Congress Cataloging-in-Publication Data
Names: Farber, Matthew, author.
Title: Gamify your classroom: a field guide to
game-based learning / Matthew Farber.
Description: Revised Edition. | New York: Peter Lang, 2017. | Previous edition: 2014.
Series: New Literacies and Digital Epistemologies; vol. 77 | ISSN 1523-9543
Includes bibliographical references and index.
Identifiers: LCCN 2016040486 | ISBN 978-1-4331-3502-6 (paperback: alk. paper)
ISBN 978-1-4331-3882-9 (ebook pdf) | ISBN 978-1-4331-3883-6 (epub)
ISBN 978-1-4331-3884-3 (Mobi)
Subjects: LCSH: Educational games. | Educational technology.
Learning. | Lesson planning.
Classification: LCC LB1029.G3 F37 2017 | DDC 371.33/7—dc23
LC record available at https://lccn.loc.gov/2016040486

Bibliographic information published by **Die Deutsche Nationalbibliothek**.
Die Deutsche Nationalbibliothek lists this publication in the "Deutsche
Nationalbibliografie"; detailed bibliographic data are available
on the Internet at http://dnb.d-nb.de/.

The paper in this book meets the guidelines for permanence and durability
of the Committee on Production Guidelines for Book Longevity
of the Council of Library Resources.

© 2017 Peter Lang Publishing, Inc., New York
29 Broadway, 18th floor, New York, NY 10006
www.peterlang.com

Printed in the United States of America

CONTENTS

FOREWORD

I've covered education for most of the past 15 years, and I've come away with several rather cynical ideas about our schools. The most significant of these is this: We must never underestimate the ability of a group of people to mess up a good thing.

Again and again, I've seen instances where seemingly simple, straightforward ideas turn to dust amid the fraught politics and bizarre incentive structures of our education system.

Matthew Farber's book does a lot of things, but what I'm hoping it will do most effectively is provide a kind of booster shot—or maybe it's an actual vaccination—against future mess-ups. I really hope this book wards off the misuse of a potentially transformative tool: smart, well-designed games that get children and teachers excited about learning. We need them badly, and if anyone is going to show us how to get it right, it's Farber.

Again and again while reading this book, I was struck by the breadth of his research. The last time I saw him, I told him he seems to know—and have scored an interview—with everyone in this business. But just as important is the depth and thoughtfulness that he brings to the enterprise, his ability to look at games through a teacher's problem-solving lens.

Remarkably—though I suppose I shouldn't be surprised—he has the true practitioner's ability to see the folks doing amazing things not as competitors, but as a community of practice, a group of enthusiasts who understand that they must support one another and celebrate one another's successes.

As he points out, many of these folks are friends who play together too, a "tribe" that has developed organically as more and more teachers come to appreciate the charms of good learning games. In that regard, I almost see these folks as I would jazz musicians who, when they get together, naturally play music, or as chefs who in their spare time swap recipes and stories—and eat good food.

That, more than anything else, is what our schools need: people who love and care so deeply about their job that they do it when no one's looking.

Actually, food may be the best analogy by which to understand this world. In the book, Farber quotes learning games pioneer James Paul Gee, who says that learning, like play, is "an appetite" that we must satisfy. "When you put it in school and make it boring and decontaminated, then of course you kill that appetite. It's like when you give people bad food. The fact of the matter is that when you trigger the human instinct of learning—and this is true of adults, not just children—you're triggering a deeply satisfying thing."

One of the great pleasures I took while reporting my 2015 book on games and learning was the opportunity it afforded me to see that in action. I was, for just a little while, able to get away from the endless, often pointless debates on policy that seldom affect what happens in actual classrooms.

I was thrilled to be able to spend time—sometimes hours or even days on end—in the presence of energetic, creative teachers who were searching for ways to feed the appetite of which Gee writes. They'd spent enough time puzzling over this world to know the difference between a good game and "dressed up flashcards." They saw that great games make learning central to the task at hand, not a formality that must be endured so the fun can begin.

They weren't afraid to take big risks or to turn their backs on what was taking place elsewhere in their school. I used to joke with Peggy Sheehy (who appears in these pages) that every time I wrote about her classroom, I somehow ended up describing it the same way: the door was shut, the curtains were drawn, and the lights were out.

If you think that's transgressive, just you wait: Farber's account of Paul Darvasi's big, month-long "pervasive games" in Chapter 12 will change your mind forever about what's possible in the classroom.

But here's the thing: commitments like these, while remarkable, are not required. There's room in this tribe for all kinds of enthusiasts, even those who don't much care for video games, avatars, dungeons, dragons, or even digital technology.

Actually, most of the teachers I met while doing research got into this discipline not because they love games, but because they love children and want something better for them. After a while, I stopped counting the number of times that someone leaned in and told me, "I am *not* a big gamer."

Farber writes, "My hope is that you will integrate games for learning, and not be overwhelmed by 'the next big thing.'" I could hardly agree more. When I speak to teachers, parents and policymakers, I admit that, even though I wrote a book about this stuff, I hope games never become "the next big thing." I hope they always remain "the next small thing," because the next big thing rarely lasts very long.

I sometimes say that I want teachers to look at games as just another tool, like a pencil sharpener. Think about every classroom you've ever visited— you'll soon realize that they all have two pencil sharpeners: the school-issued one on the wall that chews up pencils … and the one on the teacher's desk that actually works. Chances are the teacher saw one of these pencil sharpeners in a colleague's classroom and bought one herself, probably with her own money. It endures not because anybody forces her and her students to use it, but because it works. Everyone can see that.

I spent four years exploring this world and could only offer a flyover, a kind of cursory introduction, a simple instruction manual for the pencil sharpener. Farber offers an actual, detailed, deeply reported "field guide." Use it like a naturalist.

—Greg Toppo, national education writer for *USA TODAY*, and author of
The Game Believes in You: How Digital Play Can Make Our Kids Smarter (2015)

ACKNOWLEDGMENTS

This book would not have been possible without the support of many people. I would like to express my gratitude to the New Jersey City University Educational Technology Department. I am grateful to my series editors, Michele Knobel and Colin Lankshear, for their faith in my vision. Thanks also go to the staff and administration at Valleyview Middle School and the Denville Township Board of Education, as well as my student playtesters. This journey would not have been possible without the support of my community of practice: "The Tribe." On a more personal note, I would like to thank my wife, Laura, for her patience throughout the duration of this research; my curious son, Spencer; and our playful dog, Lizzie. A special thank-you is extended to my parents, Gary and Judith Farber. And thanks to my wife's parents, Virginia Fisher and Frank Fisher.

INTRODUCTION

Most people in my community of practice of game-based learning educators know Marianne Malmstrom as "Knowclue Kid," her onscreen gamertag. Malmstrom is a veteran classroom teacher, and "follow the learning" is her mantra. The phrase came from a situation back when she began integrating more technology into her classroom. "With no map, I looked to see how the kids were using tech," Malmstrom recalled, when we spoke in April 2016. "Kids were making movies with iMovie, so I built a multimedia program around that. Similarly, I look at games to see what they teach me about learning."

About a decade ago, the virtual world of Second Life changed how Malmstrom taught. It also affected her best friend Peggy Sheehy's pedagogy. Back in 2005, Sheehy launched the first school in the Teen Grid section of Second Life (Toppo, 2015, p. 119). Sheehy now teaches using the massive multiplayer online game *World of Warcraft*, which I observed during dissertation research. Her 6th grade humanities students played *World of Warcraft* as they read J. R. R. Tolkien's *The Hobbit* (1937). The unit was all framed around Joseph Campbell's book *Hero with a Thousand Faces* (1939), which famously proposed the monomyth, the hero's journey that mythological protagonists take. Sheehy's students play the game, read the book, and then draw connections from the game and the novel to their own hero's journey in adolescence.

Like Sheehy, Malmstrom started teaching in Second Life's virtual world a decade ago. Then she started using the massive multiplayer online role-playing game *LEGO Universe* (2010) in an afterschool club to teach digital citizenship. "It was phenomenal," she recalled. "They saw their avatars and that others had avatars." Students could see the consequences of their online actions. "It's hard to then sit kids down after that experience and teach them PowerPoint. Games gave me the space to look at that in a way I hadn't understood before." Malmstrom next shared how virtual worlds led her to "follow the learning." She said:

> The play children engaged in was far more interesting than the lessons I was planning. The more space I made for kids to play and hang out in, the more I saw how sophisticated they were with networking skills. I changed my own approach to what I was doing in the classroom. It's been this crazy wonderful journey. It's not intuitive for teachers to do. We are paid to teach, so to go into a classroom not having all answers and to experiment with kids is scary. But agency and choice is paramount.

As in some classrooms today, 100 years ago students sat in rows listening to direct instruction from a lecturing teacher. Game-based learning challenges this factory model of schools. Games present players with optimally challenging, meaningful choices in a situated context (Gee, 2007; Salen & Zimmerman, 2003). Active learning, rather than passive sit-and-get education, seems possible due to digital technology. What's more, computers can be used to create personalized learning environments that adapt to student ability. Student engagement and an increase in learning outcomes are part of the many promises of game-based learning.

Some proponents of educational reform have turned to game-based learning as a way to transform schools the way Uber disrupted taxi transportation. After all, the skills in the P21 Framework for 21st-Century Learning can be mapped to align with current game-based learning research (King, 2011). The P21 Framework includes the necessary skills students should possess to be able to compete in today's global economy, which includes critical thinking, problem-solving, communication, collaboration, creativity, and innovation ("Framework for 21st-Century Learning," 2015). Aside from 21st-century learning standards, many games can deliver instruction and assess learning outcomes seamlessly.

Any experienced teacher knows that there are no simple and elegant, silver bullet solutions to problems in modern education. Like designing a game, the practice of teaching is iterative, constantly being modified and fine-tuned.

Malmstrom's fear is that games can become "school-ified"—the use the games will only serve to enhance content curriculum. Her vision is to look at games and ask, what can they teach us about learning? "The agility to make stuff, to play games, is so critical," she said.

Welcome to Our Tribe

Peggy Sheehy affectionately dubbed our community of practice of game-using teachers "The Tribe." Toronto-based teacher Paul Darvasi defines The Tribe as a "community of practice of game-based learning teachers that supports one another." Sheehy elaborated when we spoke in late 2015. "The Tribe shares a philosophy about virtual worlds, games, new technologies, new environments, new approaches to learning," she said. "They very often attend the same conferences, they tweet each other. Each member is a conference compatriot."

My dissertation work pertained to three teachers in The Tribe—the aforementioned Sheehy and Darvasi, as well as Steve Isaacs. I studied how they, as high-end users, teach with games. Aside from their depth of knowledge, each was a leader in the movement to bring more quality games, and playful learning, to students. I observed each deliver a keynote address at the Games in Education Symposium, an annual professional development conference in upstate New York. They spoke about their experiences using game-based learning as a teaching approach.

A few years ago, Steve Isaacs was "initiated" into The Tribe as a community of practice. He shared the story when we spoke in April 2016. "I came down for breakfast at the hotel [while attending the Games for Education Symposium]. I saw an open seat at a table. I was asked to sit down and was immediately welcomed. Eating at that table was Sheehy, Malmstorm [*World of Warcraft in Schools* co-creator], Lucas Gillispie, and [Rezzly co-founder] Chris Haskell." Isaacs continued:

> Over the years we became dear friends. There is nothing I love more than interacting with people who are passionate about game-based learning. When I travel to conferences, the best part is connecting with my tribe. These are the people I want to surround myself with. We are an extensive support system of affirmations, guidance, and feedback. If I have a question about something, I throw it out there to them. Also, these people tend to be outside of my school because I do something very different. I'm immersed in games in the classroom. Most of what I learned is the "outside" community of practice, and this has led to deep friendships. We play together and laugh together. I wouldn't be nearly as inspired or excited without this community to interact with.

This book is here to help guide you along the exciting field of game-based learning. So what exactly is game-based learning? Well, that can be difficult to define. It can mean different things to different people: teaching curriculum like a game, using parts of a game in nongame contexts (gamification), actually playing a game, or making games. What is important is that each variant is "gameful"—what your students do should feel like a game. Game-based learning expert Bron Stuckey prefers the term "game-inspired learning." "It was because there was backlash about gamification in education," she said, when we spoke in April 2016. "[The word] gamification comes with a lot of baggage. Teachers think gamifying means designing a game." She elaborated:

> There are different spaces for gameful learning in schools, one of which is game-based learning. Game-based learning is not game design or gamification. They are three different practices. Game-inspired gets the gamification message across better. If you're game-inspired, you know the lesson is not going to be exactly that [to be literally designed like a game]—but it will have hints in it, and tributes of it, in the design.

Stuckey recommends that teachers create their own local tribes of game using teachers. She suggests starting with a community of practice *in* your school—not just on social media outlets, like Twitter. "Get two people to implement games in the school," she said. For you, this may mean sharing this book and its resources with a colleague. Or having teachers observe your use of games. Stuckey continued:

> A professional learning community is needed in a school so other teachers will take notice—especially if it is across grade levels or disciplines. Otherwise, the game-based learning teacher is seen as a "Lone Ranger teacher." Others may write off the use of games from that teacher as just being part of his or her passions and interests, just as other teachers may be interested in Shakespeare.

Nebraska-based English teacher Melissa Pilakowski is a "Lone Ranger" game-using teacher at her school. She started as a novice and now leads the #Games4Ed Twitter chat, an active community of practice. "I'm probably known as the biggest game teacher in my school," she said, when we spoke in May 2016. "The history teacher next door does a lot of games and simulation. But if you asked who the game teacher was, it would be me."

Like many teachers I spoke with researching this book, Pilakowski has autonomy to use games in her classroom. Her view of games is similar to that of educational technology integration in general. "With technology, once teachers start doing something, others take note," she stated. "It's organic, and I'd like to see it continue that way."

Book Overview

I wrote this book to share what I have learned about using games as an educational tool as a "boots-on-the-ground" classroom teacher. This book draws on my experiences implementing games with my students, as well as shared stories from teachers in the field. Research brought me several times to the game-based school Quest to Learn, the offices of BrainPOP, Schell Games, and Filament Games, and to the Games for Change Festival, the Serious Play Conference, and the Games + Learning + Society Conference.

Like a game, this book edition represents iteration. It is a "field guide" to help you navigate best practices in game-based learning. I have included practical advice on game implementation, no matter what level of experience you have. Each chapter is divided into sections and concludes with lesson plan ideas, games to play, and additional Internet resources. The point is to create as useful a book as possible. I have tried my best to assure that the links in this book are as up to date as possible. Of course, the Internet changes rapidly, and some links may not remain active after this book's publication date. Nonetheless, I encourage you to learn by doing, exploring as much as possible, online and from other texts.

Just about every lesson plan idea can be aligned to a state's standards or Common Core State Standards. Because some games are tools, not just content-drivers, I did not always specify standards. For example, the building-block game *Minecraft* can meet a variety of math, science, and social studies standards, depending on what the student is learning in the environment. I also share links from online lesson plans, many of which contain specific state and Common Core standards. My hope is that you will integrate games for learning, and not be overwhelmed by "the next big thing." Start by adding in a few per games year. After time, you will see an engaged student population intrinsically motivated to learn. So, welcome to The Tribe! Now let's follow the learning!

· 1 ·

GAMES FOR LEARNING

Learning with video games dates back to the 1970s. Digital games entered schools around the same time as desktop computers. I fondly remember playing *Oregon Trail* on an Apple II computer in 7th grade. Over the years, computer games grew in sophistication. To understand how we got to where we are today, it helps to review the successes and misfires of the past.

Recently, several educational versions of commercial games have entered the market. *SimCityEDU: Pollution Challenge!* is the systems thinking game about city management. There is also *Words with Friends EDU, CivilizationEDU*, and *Minecraft: Education Edition*. Comparatively, there aren't EDU novels in classrooms. Why? Is the information delivered in a game different than with other media? I didn't read *Call of the Wild EDU* to learn about Jack London's usages of literary devices. Do books need teacher dashboards that report data analytics on chapters read? Do EDU versions of games imply distrust in the ability of a teacher to use games as high quality curriculum, the way off-the-shelf books are used? I asked Tanner Higgin, the Director of Education Editorial Strategy at Common Sense Education, in March 2016. He said:

> It gets to this issue of play that's always been central to learning. Teachers always knew that [play] is the mechanism to facilitate learning. It is one of the essential

qualities of human beings. We're going to continually get caught in this cycle, where certain interests try to colonize play and make money off of it by narrowing its possibilities, because play is a little bit dangerous. We're in a moment like in the 1990s in which there is a "good kind of play"—serious play. We'll allow that in the classroom. Everything else goes right out.

Higgin, like other proponents of game-based learning I spoke to, imagines a future where this cycle stops happening, and play is embraced in all classrooms. Play is always going to be the facilitator of learning; however, it is, by its very nature, risky and unpredictable. "It's a battle we have to win to make that reality happen or the edutainment era will never end, it'll just keep continuing," Higgin concluded.

James Paul Gee is the Presidential Professor of Literacy Studies at Arizona State University. In 2003, Gee published *What Video Games Have to Teach Us About Learning and Literacy*. The book included a set of "Learning Principles" about what digital games can teach. For example, the "Probing Principle" connected the trial and error one does while exploring a virtual environment to the methodology of scientific experimentation (2007, p. 105). Gee's research and findings have been very influential in game-based learning circles, and are cited throughout this book. I highly recommend reading further into Gee's research, including his article "Good Video Games and Good Learning" (2005).

I first spoke with Gee in April 2014. He often leads talks to the game-based learning community at large, some of which are self-described rants. I asked him what ways games have expanded into learning spaces. "The area has expanded [more] than anything anyone could have predicted," he said. He explained how he led a group from the University of Wisconsin when they attended an American Education Research Association (AERA) conference. At the time, it was the only presentation on game-based learning. Now there are dozens. Gee continued:

> The expansion of it has been surprising. To me it has expanded in two ways. A lot of people want to rush out games for school simply to be able to make a profit. They design their games for the schools we have: skill and drill and teacher accountability to tests. They design their games to be standalone things, by themselves. None of that was what I proposed. What I proposed was not to put games in school, but to put the type of learning and teaching games do in school—with games, and with everything else. I wanted to create a new paradigm of learning in school. I wanted to change the way school works. I don't want to stress skill and drill—I want to stress problem-solving, complex and critical thinking.

Gee is describing two different interpretations of game-based learning. One is content driven, supporting the current culture of high-stakes assessment and rote learning. The second interpretation uses games to present authentic problem sets for children to collaborate on and reason out together, often by taking multiple approaches. Solving a math problem to kill a zombie is drill-and-skill rote learning. Having a conversation of physics concepts such as velocity in the slingshot game *Angry Birds* can promote higher-level discussions.

From *Mancala* to *Kriegspiel*

Developmental psychologist Jean Piaget based his theories of constructivism ("learn by doing") on his observations of children playing marbles. Learning theorist Lev Vygotsky and educator Maria Montessori also wrote about childhood games. The rules and structure of a game is like a wrapper; playing takes place within. And play creates the zone of proximal development—the space where learning occurs (Vygotsky, 1978).

Games have been entertaining and teaching humans for thousands of years. It is hardly a trend! People are finally connecting the dots from play to learning. Many classic board games have roots hundreds—if not thousands—of years old. Ancient games were used to reinforce belief systems, strategize, and apply a practical use of mathematics. I use board game history as a talking point when teaching middle school world history. The study of "what dead people did" seems more relatable when you picture people playing and interacting together, not just signing famous documents and saying really important things. Think about classic games such as China's *go!* and *mahjong*, Japan's *shogi*, as well as parlor games including *chess, checkers, poker,* and *bridge*. Why they are still popular in today's digital age?

Jane McGonigal's best-selling book *Reality Is Broken: Why Games Make Us Better and How They Change the World* (2011) detailed the ancient Greeks' fascination with *Mancala*, a game that used sheep's knuckles as dice, which provided a diversion to Herodotus's people during long periods of starvation (McGonigal, 2011, pp. 5–6). *Mancala's* objective was to capture the opponent's game pieces across the board. It was also played throughout the Middle East region. Versions can still be purchased at most toy stores today.

Senet is one of the earliest games on record. It was discovered within the tombs of the Egyptian pharaohs buried thousands of years ago (Piccione, 1980). The name *Senet*, or "passing," referred to death, when one meets the sun god Ra. Paintings showed the game on a checkered board with small moveable pieces. It was played both for skill and to reinforce religious beliefs (Piccione, 1980). King Tut was buried with four game sets (Piccione, 1980). Perhaps the boy king needed something to do in the afterlife!

Snakes and Ladders—better known to Americans as Hasbro Gaming's *Chutes and Ladders*—originated in India several hundred years ago. It reinforced tenets of Jainism such as karma. The board was often decorated with more snakes than ladders to subtly illustrate that it is more difficult to do good than evil. *Snakes and Ladders* was eventually brought to England in the Victorian Age. Its appeal and popularity transcends world cultures, probably because the game board is heavy on illustrations and contains little text. It is now so ingrained in Western culture that it is often parodied in the cartoon *SpongeBob Squarepants*, renamed "Eels and Escalators."

Strategic board games were popular across Europe, too. The simplest may have been *Nine Men's Morris*, a precursor to *Tic-Tac-Toe* (Boyle, 2013). Digital versions can be found in Apple's App Store or online, and even as a "mini-game" in *Assassin's Creed III*. One of the more complicated games to emanate from Europe was *Kriegspiel*. Basically a 19th-century variation on *chess*, it was "devised as an educational game for military schools in the eighteenth century" (Poundstone, 1992, pp. 37–38). One could argue that it was a precursor to modern-day war simulations, more advanced than the board games *Risk* and *Stratego*. The Prussian army obsessively played it (Poundstone, 1992, pp. 37–38). Some battles in the Russo-Japanese War and World War I were attributed to tactics from the game (Poundstone, 1992, pp. 37–38). *Kriegspiel* and *poker* eventually inspired mathematician John von Neumann to devise game theory (detailed further in Chapter 3).

Video Game Mania!

Many of the earliest video games were made by academics to entertain other academics—the few who had access to large, mainframe computers. In the 1950s, computers with cathode ray displays were programmed to play simple games. Alexander S. Douglas created OXO (1952), a simple *Tic-Tac-Toe* game, and William Higinbotham, at the Brookhaven National Laboratory, made *Tennis for Two* (1958). The first popular video game, which spread on college campuses throughout the 1960s, was the spaceship game *Spacewar* (1961).

The first commercially successful video game is considered to be *Pong* (1972). Basically a simple paddle-and-ball tennis emulator, *Pong* was an instant success. It marked the first time televisions became interactive, "transforming viewers into players, permitting them not to just watch a media image, but to play with it" (Salen & Zimmerman, 2003, p. xiv). It was originally created for the Magnavox Odyssey home gaming system in 1972 and then was ported to coin-operated arcade machines.

Similar to pinball, early video games often were played in public places. The hardware and monitors were stored in wood cabinets and the games usually cost a quarter to play. This time period, from 1979 to 1983, is often regarded as the classic era of arcade video gaming. Early games were designed to entertain and turn a profit. Arcade games were played in short bursts, with little to no instructions required (Dunniway & Novak, 2007, p. 30). Simply pop in a quarter and click the buttons until the game ends. Then, repeat. Popular titles included *Space Invaders* (1978), *Pac-Man* (1980), and *Donkey Kong* (1981).

The goal of the immensely popular *Pac-Man* was to navigate a maze, eating white dots while being chased by ghosts. *Pac-Man's* significance extends beyond its status as a cultural phenomenon. It was also among the first games to feature a "cut scene," or short, narrative sequence between completed levels. Cut scenes serve as a reward, as badges and achievements do in today's games. They also give players a moment of reprieve and relaxation from non-stop action. *Donkey Kong* pushed game storytelling further. Exploits of Mario's quest to save the princess have been copied innumerable times, even today. The popularity of the documentary *King of Kong* (2007), about the high-scoring champions of *Donkey King,* and Disney's animated *Wreck-It Ralph* (2012), attest to the nostalgia arcade games elicit.

After the video arcade revolution, console games found a place in our homes. Console home video game systems refer to the external box and controllers that hook up to a television. Modern examples include the Nintendo Wii, the Sony PlayStation, and the Microsoft Xbox. Engineer Ralph Baer is credited with inventing the console system in 1968. His "Brown Box" used a set of transistors and could play multiple games (Baer, 2005). In 1970, Magnavox purchased the rights to sell the device, and encased it in plastic. The original version does not look all that different from the so-called "next-gen" (next-generation) systems of today. Baer went on to create other computer-based toys and inventions, including the electronic memory toy *Simon* still sold today.

While not the first home system, Nolan Bushnell's Atari 2600 (1977) brought console gaming to most of America's living rooms. (Apple's Steve Jobs began his career as one of Bushnell's early employees.) The Atari 2600 could plug into any television; the game cartridges were sold separately. Activision, founded in 1979 by former Atari programmers, became one of the first video game software companies. To this day, Activision (*Guitar Hero, Call of Duty*) and Electronic Arts (*Madden NFL, Mass Effect*) are two of the biggest publishers of third-party gaming content. (Former Apple employee Trip Hawkins founded Electronic Arts in 1982.) Nowadays, smaller studios often design and develop games, and then larger publishers such as Activision and Electronic Arts distribute them.

Due to a crowded market and lackluster sales of titles that were rushed to market, the video game business crashed in 1983. Atari reportedly filled a landfill with unsold *E.T.: The Extra Terrestrial* game cartridges. (Excavating the landfill was the topic of a terrific 2014 documentary, *Atari: Game Over*.) The 1985 release of the Nintendo Entertainment System home console (known as Famicom in Japan) turned the industry around. This system featured a (then) cutting-edge 8-bit processor. Popular titles included *Super Mario Bros.* (1985), a classic "side-scrolling" adventure, and *The Legend of Zelda* (1987). Nintendo's legendary Shigeru Miyamoto created both. Nintendo positioned itself as rescuing the home video game market by enforcing strict standards such as its Nintendo Seal of Quality. Similar to Apple's business model, Nintendo created a walled garden of vetted games. In the early 1990s, competitor Sega released the 16-bit Genesis home console system. The competition between Nintendo's Mario and Sega's Sonic the Hedgehog—nicknamed the "console wars"—was fierce. Sega became Nintendo's chief competitor by targeting games for older children. The result was that consoles became less like toys and more a way for digital content providers (e.g., Sony) to enter people's living rooms. (The complete story of Nintendo and Sega is told in Blake J. Harris's 2014 book and documentary *Console Wars: Sega, Nintendo, and the Battle that Defined a Generation*.) The 1990s also saw the growth of handheld games devices such as Sega's Game Gear, Nintendo's GameBoy, and the PlayStation Portable.

Faster microchip processors led to console and PC games that featured more realistic graphics. First-person shooter games that arm the player with an array of violent weapons, including *Wolfenstein 3D* (1992) and *Doom* (1993), became instant bestsellers. Controversy followed soon after. (Interestingly, John Romero, one of the minds behind *Wolfenstein 3D* and *Doom* is now designing educational games like *Wuzzit Trouble*.) *Mortal Kombat* (1992) became notorious, outraging parents as children were encouraged to "finish" their opponents with final, gory deathblows. (The gore was tuned down in the Nintendo version; blood was displayed in grayscale.) *Super Mario 64* (1996) was less controversial. It was among the first games to feature a 3D world that let the player control the "camera"—the point of view that appeared on the screen (Dunniway & Novak, 2007, p. 22). Other 3D games followed, including *The Legend of Zelda: Ocarina of Time* (1998). As a result, today's console game controllers have two thumbsticks (small joysticks for your thumbs), one to move for the onscreen avatar and one to control the camera. PC games usually use the mouse or trackpad to control viewpoint; arrow keys or WASD keys control the game's action.

Violence in video games can be misunderstood. It is often a device intended to advance a storyline. Furthermore, violence isn't exclusive to games. It is prevalent in "traditional" media, too, from books to film. Senate hearings prompted by parental concerns occurred in the 1990s. This eventually led to the creation of the industry's self-regulating Entertainment Software Rating Board (ESRB). As with the introduction of film ratings in the early 1970s, the rating of video games led to an increase in content targeted to adults (e.g., the films *Midnight Cowboy* and *The Godfather,* and the game *Grand Theft Auto*). Mobile apps, such as those found in Apple's App Store, do not apply for ratings. Apple has its own parental warning system.

The new millennium enabled gamers to connect via Internet-ready consoles from Microsoft (Xbox) and Sony (PlayStation), as well as by personal computer. People could now play cooperatively, helping one other to advance. A new genre emerged—massively multiplayer online role-playing games (MMORPG), where players play in large groups via remote servers. Popular titles included *World of Warcraft* (2004) and *Star Wars: Knights of the Old Republic* (2003). New technology also meant that designers could create more immersive virtual worlds with high-definition graphics. The *Tomb Raider* series' female protagonist, Lara Croft, solved puzzles and explored exotic locales. So-called "open-world games" (e.g., the *Grand Theft Auto* series, the *Assassin's Creed* series) allowed users to explore and choose which "missions" to play. This type of story unfolds in a nonlinear, self-directed fashion, and is often from the third-person or over-the-shoulder perspective. The Internet enabled independent game publishers (or "indies") to join the marketplace via digital download distribution (e.g., Valve's Steam platform for PC and Mac, Xbox Arcade, PlayStation Network).

By 2007, video gaming had become quite complex, alienating new users. A case in point: the introduction of Sony's PlayStation 3 controller, with seventeen buttons! A game on Xbox or PlayStation can take up to 50 hours to fully complete. Enter the Nintendo Wii. It not only introduced the concept of motion-controlled gaming, but also brought casual gamers into the market. PlayStation next offered motion gaming via its Move controller. Microsoft further innovated by introducing the Kinect camera capture system, which turned the player into the controller—no buttons needed. Dance and workout games for each of these platforms became popular.

Mobile platforms such as Apple's iPhone and iPad, and Facebook, the social media giant, brought even more casual gamers into the fold. The prototypical touch screen game, or "killer app," was the physics-themed slingshot game *Angry Birds* (2009). Zynga popularized social gaming games with *Farmville* (2009) and *Words with Friends* (2009). Social games can be played asynchronously: Draw a picture with *Draw Something* (2012) and then check later in the day to see if your friend guessed what it was. Casual, social games do not always follow the "win, lose, or tie" paradigm of traditional, competitive games. People may play in a semicompetitive, virtual environment with the goal of simply "liking" other's actions rather than winning (Kim, 2012b). They may also seek only to collaborate with others (Kim, 2012b).

The Edutainment Era

For many of my students, the words "educational game" are equated with "boring." After all, educational games have a checkered reputation of being poorly designed, putting educational content ahead of game mechanics, or fun. Yes, fun. What's the point of a game if it's not fun to play! Playing a boring game is like watching a movie that is all exposition, with little conflict or entertainment value. You wouldn't give a student a boring novel to read, so why do the same with a learning game? To understand today's successful learning games such as *SimCityEDU* and *Mission US* (both discussed in later chapters), let's review more about the history of game-based learning. This period still casts a long shadow over learning games in schools.

Educational games began with *Oregon Trail*. It showed the promise of what an educational game could deliver—learning though meaningful play. Developed in 1971 and sold in 1974 by the Minnesota Educational Computing Consortium (MECC), it was one of the first games designed specifically for schools. The game used interactives and simulation to teach children about the hardships traveling cross-country in 19th-century America. The game was originally played on the Apple II computer. The fail state (what happens when you lose) displayed a message that has joined the popular lexicon: "You have died of dysentery." Iterations of *Oregon Trail* still exist on Facebook and on mobile devices. There is also a space-themed version from Schell Games, *Orion Trail* (2015).

Following the success of *Oregon Trail,* many other for-profit publishers began to design "edutainment" (a portmanteau of "education" and "entertainment") games. More computers in schools during the 1980s meant more educational games would come to market. In 1983, Electronic Arts published *M.U.L.E.,* an economic simulation game about colonial survival on a new planet. Beginning in 1985, Broderbund Software published *Where in the World Is Carmen Sandiego?* In this geography game, Carmen traveled the world solving mysteries. The Learning Company, founded by three teachers and a game designer from Atari, focused on language arts skills (Shuler, 2012). It published the *Reader Rabbit* series. *Math Blaster,* basically *Space Invaders* meets arithmetic problems, came next. This is the classic "chocolate-covered broccoli" game, where the mechanics (shooting spaceships) had nothing to do with the concept it was delivering (math). Other edutainment titles evolved over the years, including *Mavis Beacon Teaches Typing* (1987) and games found on *Fun Brain.* Many of these games relied on simple, "drill-and-skill" mechanisms adapted from early arcade game design principles, such as pattern recognition and hand-eye coordination. Corporate consolidations by Mattel and Vivendi, coupled with changes in consumer demand, eventually ended the era around the turn of the millennium (Shuler, 2012).

Serious Games

Serious games are used to teach or train in schools or in professional development classes. They may involve a simulation of a problem in a workplace scenario. Clark Abt first coined the term "serious game" in his 1970 book, *Serious Games.* He wrote about strategy board games used by the military. As mentioned earlier in this chapter, the Prussians played *Kriegspiel,* a *chess* variation, to train for the battlefield. One of the most played modern military games of all time is *America's Army* (2002). Businesses use serious games, too. For example, *Everest Manager* (2013) teaches team building.

As the name implies, the Serious Games Association aggregates educational serious games. It curates titles for kindergarten through grade 12, higher education, business, the health care sector, and government institutions. I first interviewed Serious Games Association founder and president Sue Bohle in April 2014. Since then I have given talks on game-based learning at the Serious Play Conference. The conference, which launched in 2011, is a forum for stakeholders to come together. It takes place at different university campuses nationwide, including the University of Southern California, Carnegie Mellon University, and the University of North Carolina-Chapel Hill. Many people interviewed in this book are also regular speakers and attendees.

Bohle started in the video game business in the 1980s, with Atari—just before its business model imploded. A decade ago, specialized organizations emerged, such as Games for Health, founded by Ben Sawyer. The Game Development Conference (GDC), for commercial developers, included "serious games," but it took a "stepchild approach" to them in comparison with its bread-and-butter business—entertainment games. Bohle explained that there was a push for serious games to have its own conference. As a result, the Serious Play Conference was started. It is a favorite of mine to attend each year, as it brings together thought-leaders from across the field.

Because serious games are designed to teach and train, I wondered how game play could potentially interfere with the delivery of content. I asked Google's Noah Falstein, because serious games were part of his design background. We spoke in May 2014. He also was a keynote speaker at the 2014 Serious Play Conference. Falstein had worked for 17 years at LucasArts, 3DO, and DreamWorks Interactive. His credits included *Indiana Jones and the Fate of Atlantis*. Following LucasArts, he grew interested in serious games, or, as Falstein called them, "games with purposes beyond entertainment." As a consequence, he worked on a lot of educational titles, including *Hungry Red Planet,* a children's nutrition game funded by a National Institutes of Health (NIH) grant. Falstein shared an experience about a game that encouraged children to continue chemotherapy treatments. His example is valuable when considering how to construct game-based lessons. Falstein explained:

> There was a game I did with Hope Lab called *Re-Mission*. It helped kids with cancer understand their treatment. It used the fiction of a little nanorobot in your bloodstream fighting cancer cells. At first they [NIH] wanted to make everything look realistic. One of the problems is that, on microscopic level, healthy cells and cancer cells don't look different at all. Only the nucleus may be different. Accuracy is important, but we weren't teaching microbiology. We were teaching teenagers why

they should care about chemotherapy. The concept was more important than the literal depiction. A study eventually showed that the game encouraged people take their chemotherapy.

Falstein's point is that sometimes it can be acceptable for serious games to sacrifice details when delivering a message. "What's critical from a designer's standpoint is a clear way to distinguish what is factual and what is part of a game fantasy," he continued. "Effective games have some of both. People can pick up the information later once you get them interested, but you can't get them interested by dry information alone." This is another important take-away from an experienced, serious game designer. Falstein uses games as a starting point for learning. In other words, students shouldn't just play serious games; the activity requires teacher-led reflection to enable real-world connections.

New Media Literacy and Games

As opposed to more "traditional" media, such as books or the theater, games are "new media." I spoke to digital media scholar Henry Jenkins in May 2014 about where games as new media fit into the context of school. Among other organizations, Jenkins cofounded MIT's Education Arcade, with Kurt Squire, to "prototype how games could be used in learning." He has published several books on new media literacy, including *Textual Poachers: Television Fans & Participatory Culture* (1992), *From Barbie to Mortal Kombat: Gender and Computer Games* (1998), and *Convergence Culture: Where Old and New Media Collide* (2006), as well as white papers for the MacArthur Foundation. Jenkins has also been featured on PBS's *Digital Nation*, and even testified in front of Congress about the misunderstandings about violence in video games.

It is helpful to remember that movies, cable television, Google Apps, You-Tube, and other technologies that now are used for teaching also have had their educational validity questioned. Jenkins was prompted to write a blog post in 2006 about misunderstandings about video games, "Reality Bytes: Eight Myths About Video Games Debunked." Common misconceptions included:

1. The availability of video games has led to an epidemic of youth violence.
2. Scientific evidence links violent gameplay with youth aggression.
3. Children are the primary market for video games.

4. Almost no girls play computer games.
5. Because games are used to train soldiers to kill, they have the same impact on the kids who play them.
6. Video games are not a meaningful form of expression.
7. Video game play is socially isolating.
8. Video game play is desensitizing. (Jenkins, 2006b)

Data supported Jenkins's points about who actually plays video games. The proliferation of casual gaming on smartphones (e.g., *Angry Birds, Candy Crush Saga*) diversified the population of digital game players. Furthermore, social media has made the act highly participatory (e.g., *Farmville, Words with Friends*). The Entertainment Software Association, the lobbyist organization that runs the ESRB (the rating agency for games), reported that today's gamers are, on average, 35 years old and have been playing for 13 years (Essential Facts About the Computer and Video Game Industry, 2016). Forty-one percent of players are female (Essential Facts About the Computer and Video Game Industry, 2016). I asked Jenkins about what has changed since his "Eight Myths" post. He stated that the blog post took just minutes to write and has lingered on longer than he had expected. Often it comes up in the discourse, especially when senseless tragedies such as the Sandy Hook Elementary School shooting in 2012 are blamed on gaming (in that case, Wayne LaPierre, the head of the National Rifle Association, pointed the finger at the gaming sector). Almost all children play video games, many of which contain violence. But correlation does not imply causation. Jenkins continued:

> Every time we have a Sandy Hook we're back to the debate about game violence. On the gender front, there is probably greater equity from girls and boys playing games, especially if you factor in casual games, but the stereotypes culturally around female players still persist as a very active problem. I think we've made some progress in educators getting to play games and see it as valuable in their classroom, thanks in part to the MacArthur Foundation's Digital Media and Learning initiative, and a few other things. When I talk to teachers, the kneejerk response is that children should be doing homework and not playing games. These myths are not as deeply rooted in the culture, but we still revert back to them when pushed on questions. They're questions we must engage with closely and critically moving forward.

Game-based learning scholar James Paul Gee wrote an online article about *Grand Theft Auto* demonstrating new media bias. He stated, "In a mission, the player must sneak into a parking lot and, unseen, plant a bomb in the trunk of a car and leave the scene without doing damage to the getaway car. Our intuition about content-driven media tells us that this is about a crime but the task could be changed to placing flowers in a loved one's car without being discovered, and the problem and its difficulty would be the same" (Gee, 2010). In other words, gamers care more about mechanics of play than the narrative thread. In *Theory of Fun for Game Design*, Raph Koster shared a similar view. He wrote that players do not see actions as morally wrong; rather, "they see a power-up" (2005, p. 85). A simple solution to alleviating new media bias is for parents to play video games with their children.

The Art of the Game

There was a time when photography ("anyone can take a picture!"), movies, comic books, and television weren't considered artistic mediums. In 1961, Newton Mino, Chairman of the Federal Communications Commission, famously called television "a vast wasteland." I think viewers of *Game of Thrones* or *House of Cards* would disagree. The debate may stem from the growing pains of being an immature medium that struggles to be taken more seriously. Like traditional media (novels, film, theater), games evoke emotions. The most obvious feelings players have are fun, happiness, or frustration. But can games make us cry? Are games—like books, theater, music, and photography—art?

Like video games today, comic books and graphic novels were once thought to corrupt young minds. This changed after Art Spiegelman published *Maus*, a graphic novel depicting Nazis as cats and Jewish people as mice. In a 2011 *New York Times* article, Spiegelman recounted being asked by a reporter in 1987, "Don't you think that a comic book about the Holocaust is in bad taste?" In response, Spiegelman said, "No, I thought Auschwitz was in bad taste" (Garner, 2011, para. 17). In 1992, *Maus* became the first graphic novel to win a Pulitzer Prize. Will video games mature as a medium to reach the same critical acclaim?

Shortly before his death, film critic Roger Ebert took a hardline stance that games could never be elevated to be art, like film. After all, he considered movies to be "the most powerful empathy machine in all the arts" (Ebert, 2005). How can games evoke empathy the way movies can? A few years later, Ebert wrote a controversial blog post, which stated, "The difference between art and games is that you can win a game" (Ebert, 2010). Of course, not all games have a win-state, or necessarily a goal. You can't "win" *Minecraft*. You don't win by playing through the nonlinear, story-based game like *Gone Home* (2013) or *Her Story* (2015) either.

At the time, critics of Ebert suggested that he play the video game *Flower* (2009), designed by Jenova Chen. *Flower* is told from the point of view of a dreaming flower. Others recommended Kellee Santiago's TED Talk about art and games (see the link at the end of this chapter; Santiago worked with Chen at Thatgamecompany). Ebert still did not agree. I asked Tracy Fullerton, Chen and Santiago's graduate professor, about games as art. When we spoke in March 2014, she called Ebert's view "too rigid." (Fullerton collaborated with artist Bill Viola on his art installation *The Night Journey*.) In his book *Video Games and Learning*, Kurt Squire also disagreed with Ebert. He wrote, "Independent games like *Flower* show that games are capable of expressing a range of emotions, but developers may need to go around the mainstream to do it" (2011, p. 216).

Brenda Brathwaite's *Train* (2010) is an example of a game as an artistic expression. *Train* was part of her *Mechanic is the Message* series. (Now known as Brenda Romero, she is married to *Doom* cocreator John Romero. Both lead talks on game-based learning worldwide.) Like *Monopoly*, *Train* was packaged in a box. The difference was that there were broken shards of glass mixed in with the yellow pegs, cards, and pieces. The cards, called Terminus, represented concentration camp locations. The game's objective was not revealed until midway during play. She told *The Daily Beast* that she intended to "make a game about complicity, and so the rules drop the player not in the shoes of a Holocaust victim but a train conductor who helped make the Nazi system run" (Crair, 2010).

Mary Flanagan, of the Tiltfactor studio at Dartmouth University, considers games to be both art and science. She has written about the differences between games made for commercial consumption and socially critical games in her book *Critical Play: Radical Game Design* (2009). "The sweet spot is to work at something transformative," she said when we spoke in April 2016. Flanagan continued:

> Games aren't really a story medium. Games are a fictional universe made of symbolic representations. Look at a deck of playing cards. It's not a grand story. But when you add the mechanic, the rules, they can use story—but they are not a big storytelling medium. It's not narrative versus game.

Games *may* interrelate narrative, sounds, and imagery—but you don't necessarily need any of those other things to have a game. Games don't have to tell a story to be effective to change people's minds and hearts, either. "They are a high-level, primal construct for expression," Flanagan said. "Therefore, it makes no sense to use games as a storytelling medium, or to model things. Games allow choice and allow great things, but games for change [games intended to affect social change] have to embrace that abstractness."

Using Giacometti as an example, Flanagan talked about how artists sometimes look at problems systemically. Aside from his post-World War II sculptures, Giacometti designed games impossible to win as a form of political commentary. His games were like Braithwaite's *Train*: an artistic statement. "Games like these are intellectual exercises," Flanagan said.

Like other art forms, games "make meaning" for players. Common Sense Education's Tanner Higgin explained how video games potentially could do this in schools. Higgin explained:

> Like any other art, what games can bring to a classroom is [a way] to understand meaning in the world. You play a game and you understand some kind of system, then you can take that into the world and see reflections of it. It provides new lenses to see the world through. Like experiencing a great novel that imparts a theme on you, a game—the system you experience—provides a framework for you to critique the world at large. You get kids thinking about the world in a whole different way. You see those light bulbs pop up when students understand game logic, and mechanics, and a little about code. They not only understand computational culture, but also see how it's in the world around them, in a profound way.

Higgin explained Common Sense Media's mission to help parents and teachers learn about the appropriateness of media use. Common Sense Media is a nonprofit, non-biased website. Graphite is its vetted, educator community, and it reviews games based on three different scores: engagement, pedagogy, and support. By support, they look for experiences that are supportive of different learners' needs, as well as the teachers' needs. To Graphite, a good game is somewhere in between those things, and they do those things well. "We saw this need and opportunity to help teachers connect with tools, many of which are games," he explained. "That has evolved over time to not just connect with great tools but to connect with great practice. Games have been a fundamental part of that the entire time."

Every year, there seems to be a new study that comes out about the positive or negative effects of media, and then another that counters it. "The specter is that there is something special about games that can connect people in a deeper, more visceral level," Higgin continued. "Even if the game doesn't have violence, there's a perception that the game will have a greater effect than a book would have. Any kind of content that's in a game gets amplified because of its perceived severity."

There is a certain expectation parents have about what will be in a book compared to a game. Every new media has gone through this cycle, including Westerns, murder mystery novels, comic books, film, and television. "The uproar eventually settles and gets transformed," Higgin said. "TV is going through that right now—people are starting to take TV as seriously as they do movies. Games will get there, and it'll take time with the work of educators showing interesting things that are happening."

We may be getting close to that moment. In January 2016, the emotional and poignant final episode of the story-based game *Life is Strange* was released. *Life is Strange* is a coming-of-age story set at an art school; sort of *Mean Girls* meets *Catcher in the Rye*. Players make choices that are either innocuous (what to order for lunch at the diner) or difficult (do I alter the past to save my friend?). Regarding *Life is Strange*, *The Washington Post* proclaimed that the "Spielberg test" was met. In 2006, film director Steven Spielberg quipped, "The real indicator that games have become a storytelling art form will be when somebody confesses that they cried at level 17." *The Washington Post* continued, "If such is your litmus test, I direct you to the subreddit [discussion forum] thread 'Life is Strange Episode 5: Did you cry?'" (Byrd, 2016). As I played through *Life is Strange* myself, I was similarly moved.

Getting Good Games into Classrooms

In May 2016, co.lab shuttered. Partnered with the NewSchools Venture Fund and Zynga.org, co.lab accelerated innovative from new educational technology companies, including Edmodo, BrainQuake, and Nearpod. However, after four years of cohorts, it ceased operations. Executive Director Esteban Sosnik wrote a blog post on Medium citing several obstacles its start-ups encountered. One included the barrier to school-wide adoption. He cited Tynker's summer camp programs and BrainPOP's platform as companies that have stood the test of time. He continued, stressing how technology and educational games should have "consumer-driven design" (Sosnik, 2016). Nevertheless, he held out hope. Sosnick wrote:

> We believe that a cultural shift will happen sooner rather than later. Just like we once started recycling (and now composting) our garbage and eating organic foods, we

believe parents will soon happily supply their children with quality educational apps and pay for them. (Sosnick, 2016, para. 7)

Although there is over a half of a century of research regarding games and learning, significant barriers to adoption still persist. Most of the people I interviewed expressed a "disconnect" between game developers and classroom implementation. Textbooks and educational websites continue to refer to review quizzes as games. Dan White, cofounder of Filament Games, explained to me in 2014, "There are too many interactives that try to pass themselves off as learning games; they are really dressed up flashcards." As a result, teachers become confused about which games (if any) to implement. White pointed out a "literacy gap with teachers who cannot discriminate between the 'drill and kill' and quality gameplay delivery."

When I spoke with researcher Jessica Millstone in January 2014, she said, "We find that teachers don't know what is a game. Teachers have trouble distinguishing a game and an interactive. Our research is on how teachers choose a game, where they go to find out about games, and the logistics about the way a game changes a classroom. How do you take a beginner to the next step, iterating it to make it better and better?" Issues linger regarding how to bring games into formal teacher education (both preservice and graduate-level), professional development, and workshops. Much needs to be done to make game-based learning more embedded in the training of teachers.

To that end, the Joan Ganz Cooney Center at Sesame Workshop launched *GamesandLearning.org*, funded with help from the Bill & Melinda Gates Foundation. The site features original stories, as well as aggregated news. The purpose is to provide a centralized place for investors and developers to find out about educational games. "It's hard for game makers to know what's happening in the classroom because the classroom is a closed environment," Millstone said. "We need to have a bridge between the two worlds."

Whereas commercial video games are targeted at children, learning games must be appealing to both teachers and students as end users. Looking at a teacher-inclusive model, it becomes obvious that the teacher needs to be engaged in the ideas of games in the classroom. To scale games for school use, there must be teacher demand, as well as professional development training and support. Millstone shared a story about attending the Games for Change Festival several years ago. Impactful games were introduced; however, no one mentioned the teacher's role. Millstone told attendees, "You're not getting it into the classroom unless you go through the teacher. The teacher is the bridge."

Kurt Squire was among the first to bridge games with the curriculum. His influential case study of *Civilization III* took place in "one class of marginalized students in Boston" (Squire, 2011, p. 109). *Civilization III*, and its subsequent sequels, is a game in which players manage historical nations. Squire's (2011) study provides an early glimpse into how a game-based learning classroom looks. The study, which took place in 2006, was in an urban setting.

Rather than reading about history from the traditional Western European perspective, like that found in a textbook, Squire's students were offered the chance to rewrite history. One group of students played as the Bantu people, thus shifting how history was usually taught from a European perspective. Squire noted an increase in student engagement as well as learning outcomes. After each lesson, students were debriefed using whole class discussions to unpack knowledge (Squire, 2011). As a result of this case study, Squire (2011) formulated teaching strategies for using games in the classroom:

- *Know thy game.* It is imperative that teachers know the game.
- *Game play drives learning.* Managing failure and frustration was a constant challenge, and facilitating students' learning as players minimized these challenges.
- *Just-in-time lectures.* Lectures helped students understand the game's model.
- *Supporting game communities.* Participating in a community transformed students' experience from focusing on their game, to studying games, to understanding the game model.
- *Facilitating inquiry.* The most useful teaching activities encouraged community by compiling data across games and comparing emergent patterns. (pp. 138–139)

In February 2014, I asked Institute of Play cofounder Katie Salen about why games are still considered an afterthought in teachers' colleges and kindergarten through grade 12 classrooms. She offered a hopeful response. "The interesting thing to me about the field is that it is moving forward really fast in terms of the changing of people's attitudes," she said. "Eight years ago was a totally different state of mind. Even last year people had assumptions that they don't anymore, like you can never bring a console game onto the classroom. Nowadays, it's okay. The speed of time a person's mind can be changed can be rapid." Nonetheless, bringing games into classrooms can still be seen as tacked on, similar to how other educational technologies are sometimes misappropriated. Salen elaborated, "The add-on thing is really interesting when it is not the central experience, like a novel. It's always an exception to play a game."

One way to get games to students is to partner with textbook publishers. Publishing giant Houghton Mifflin Harcourt's HMH Marketplace partnered with Muzzy Lane, a game design studio in Massachusetts. "They have a system where they have a template for different game mechanics," Muzzy Lane's Bert Snow told me in March 2016. "The idea is to grow the set of templates, each of which aims at a teacher's learning objectives." In addition to Houghton Mifflin Harcourt, Muzzy Lane produces content for McGraw Hill, Pearson, National Geographic, and PBS. Muzzy Lane also works with schools by licensing their platform, called Muzzy Lane Author. In 2015, it won a grant from the Library of Congress to create a series of game-based learning "episodes" for younger children, using primary sources.

Conclusions and Takeaways

People have been learning with games for thousands of years. Gaming, both paper-based and digital, has endured and become ingrained in popular culture. Like any new media, it has its growing pains, which itself is a teachable moment. Bringing effective games to students has many barriers. Teachers may see play as frivolous, while students may be biased against learning games in school. The business world embraces serious games and simulations.

Lesson Plan Ideas

Digital Compass, a choice-based digital citizenship game from Common Sense Media. Educator guide and lesson plans are available—https://www.common-sensemedia.org/educators/digital-compass

Games

America's Army, the U.S. Army's serious recruitment game—http://www.americasarmy.com

Everest Manager, corporate team-building serious game. Works as a classroom icebreaker activity, too—http://www.everestmanager.com

The Fiscal Ship, from 1st Playable Productions (lead sponsor of the Games in Education Symposium) comes a game about solving the nation's fiscal crisis. It won a Gold at the 2016 Serious Play Awards, and is free to play—http://fiscalship.org

Game Dr. is a set of science games from researcher Carla Brown—http://gamedrlimited.com/games

Government in Action, a serious civics game—http://www.mhpractice.com/products/GinA

Life is Strange is a story-driven experience that takes place over five episodes. It is a deeply emotional game in which the protagonist can rewind time and change decisions, resulting in a butterfly-effect chain of consequences. The story has echoes of *Catcher in the Rye* and can be close read like a book. There is some coarse language, as well as themes of bullying, so preview first. Consider its use with older students, or play yourself to see the potential of games as an artistic medium—http://www.lifeisstrange.com

Night of the Living Debt, a serious financial literacy game—http://apps.nmsu.edu/livingdebt

Oregon Trail, the original and in many ways quintessential educational video game—http://www.oregontrail.com

Orion Trail is sort of *Star Trek* meets the *Oregon Trail*. It was developed by Schell Games, whose founder, Jesse Schell, is interviewed throughout this book—http://oriontrail.schellgames.com

Pac-Man, one of the games that ushered in the "golden age" of arcade video games—http://www.thepcmanwebsite.com/media/pacman_flash

Pong, the simple tennis game that started the video game revolution—http://www.ponggame.org

Squinky (AKA Dietrich Squinkifier) is a game designer and performance artist—http://squinky.me

Spacewar, emulator of the first video game, playable in a computer browser—http://www.masswerk.at/spacewar

Vital Signs: Emergency Department is an award-winning serious game about being an ER doctor—http://www.breakawaygames.com/vitalsigns

Resources

Are Video Games Art?, Kellee Santiago's TED Talk—http://youtu.be/ K9y6MYDSAww

Art of Video Games exhibit at the Smithsonian American Art Museum— http://americanart.si.edu/exhibitions/archive/2012/games

Common Sense Media, a web portal to advise parents on appropriate digital media—https://www.commonsensemedia.org

Cooney Center at Sesame Workshop—http://www.joanganzcooneycenter.org

EK Theater mixes video games and live theater to retell classics, from Shakespeare to Poe—http://www.ektheater.com

District Game-Based Learning Implementation Guide from Filament Games: http://bit.ly/FG_GBL_Guide

Entertainment Software Association (ESA), the game industry's lobbyist organization. It also hosts the annual E3 Conference and manages the ESRB Ratings System—http://www.theesa.com

Essential Facts about the Computer and Video Game Industry—http://essential-facts.theesa.com/Essential-Facts-2016.pdf

GamesandLearning.org—http://www.gamesandlearning.org

Gamasutra, the online magazine about trends in game development, including in education. Every year *Gamasutra* hosts the Game Developer Conference (GDC)—http://www.gamasutra.com

Game Informer magazine, popular game magazine at a surprisingly high reading level—http://www.gameinformer.com

Game-based learning blogs on Edutopia—http://www.edutopia.org/blogs/ beat/game-based-learning

Gaming Can Make a Better World, Jane McGonigal's TED Talk—http://www.ted.com/talks/jane_mcgonigal_gaming_can_make_a_better_world

Gaming for Understanding, Brenda Brathwaite's TED Talk—http://www.ted.com/talks/brenda_brathwaite_gaming_for_understanding.html

James Paul Gee's *Good Video Games and Good Learning*—http://dmlcentral.net/wp-content/uploads/files/GoodVideoGamesLearning.pdf

Life is Strange passes the Spielberg test for video game as artform—http://wpo.st/HsfY1

Polygon, online magazine that covers the gaming industry, as well as the designers, players, and related conferences—http://www.polygon.com

Serious Games Market blog—http://seriousgamesmarket.blogspot.com

Serious Play Conference—http://seriousplayconf.com

Serious Games Industry—https://seriousgamesindustry.com

· 2 ·

WHAT ARE GAMES?

There are several competing definitions for what a game actually is. As mentioned in Chapter 1, games have been used to teach people's shared cultural history for thousands of years. Modern research about play and games dates back to the early 20th-century alongside the emerging fields of child psychology and human behaviorism. Almost all of the modern-day discussions of games are rooted in the essays and observations from Johan Huizinga and Roger Caillois. Both were among the first to connect the significance of structured play to childhood development.

This chapter breaks down how games function as interconnected systems. The approach, known as "systems thinking," is ingrained in the mission of Quest to Learn, a school that included the Institute of Play as its founding partner. Games model real-world systems, which can help make learning concepts more relatable. The ability to discern how parts interplay—like characters in a novel, weather patterns, or cause-and-effect patterns in history—is a 21st-century workforce skill. The section includes strategies and tips to implement systems thinking in your classroom.

Defining Games

In 1938, Johan Huizinga published *Homo Ludens* (Gr., "Man the Player"). Huizinga, a Dutch historian, wrote about play as a competitive act, as well as how play promotes socialization. He recognized that humans—like other animals—engage in playful activities. For example, cats hunt toys around people's homes as practice for tracking down live prey; moose battle one another with their antlers to practice combat skills. His treatise was more philosophical than psychological, discussing the process more than the need for play.

Huizinga introduced the concept of the "magic circle"—the place where play occurs. Sometimes known as a playspace, the magic circle is where people engage together in games. Basically, it is "where the game takes place" (Salen & Zimmerman, 2003, p. 95). It can be a game board, a field, a bridge table, or even a multiuser virtual environment. In *Apples to Apples*, the magic circle is the "Table Talk," when players argue their case to the game's judge for which combinations make the better fit. Game tokens, from the thimble in *Monopoly* to video game avatars, serve to draw the player into the magic circle (Salen & Zimmerman, 2003, p. 96). The magic circle remains significant to developers of virtual worlds, discussion forums, and massive open online courses. Huizinga wrote:

> The arena, the card-table, the magic circle, the temple, the stage, the screen, the tennis court, the court of justice, etc., are all in form and function playgrounds, i.e. forbidden spots, isolated, hedged round, hallowed, within which special rules obtain. All are temporary worlds within the ordinary world, dedicated to the performance of an act apart. (1938/1955, p. 10)

In 1961, French anthropologist Roger Caillois published *Man, Play, and Games*. In it he defined four types of games: *agon*, representing pure competition; *alea*, where the player choice depends on random variables or luck; *mimicry*, for acting, singing, and role-playing; and *ilinx*, the thrill from being in motion (My 6-year-old son loves spinning around endlessly around in circles!). Caillois described his four domains of play by drawing on everyday examples. He wrote, "One *plays* football, billiards, or chess (*agon*); roulette or a lottery (*alea*); pirate, Nero, or Hamlet (*mimicry*); or one produces in oneself, by a rapid whirling or falling movement, a state of dizziness or disorder (*ilinx*)" (1961/2001, p. 12). In 1990, psychologist Mihaly Csikszentmihalyi posited that each of Caillois's sets of game activities serves to keep people happy, fulfilled, and positively balanced. As we will see in the following chapter, Csikszentmihalyi's theory of optimal psychology is very influential in game—and learning—design.

In the book *Reality Is Broken* (2011), Jane McGonigal defined games as those that share four overlapping components. All games have four interconnected parts: a) a goal, b) rules, c) a feedback system, and d) voluntary participation (2011, p. 21). Just about all games adhere to this definition. Take bowling, for example: There is an achievable goal (anyone, even a novice, can throw a strike); rules (two throws per turn; the play is turn-based); feedback (a leaderboard is displayed in tabulating everyone's scores); and the unspoken agreement to participate and follow the rules. With my social studies students, I connect games to the election process. You run for office (the goal to becoming president is 270 electoral college votes), and there are rules to follow (the media is watching!), feedback (polling), and, of course, participation—our government is a participatory democracy. The magic circle is the United States map, with each state worth different amount of points, based on population. The presidential election is a winner-take-all, red-state-vs.-blue-state, zero-sum game.

Games create structures in which expectations from play exist (Walther, 2003). A game can also be defined as "a system in which players engage in an artificial conflict, defined by rules, that results in a quantifiable outcome" (Salen & Zimmerman, 2003, p. 80). What players do in a game is dictated by the rules (Björk & Holopainen, 2006). The outcome, therefore, is dependent on the rules (Suits, 2006). Rules "add *meaning* and *enable actions* by setting up *differences* between potential moves and events" (Juul, 2003, "Conclusion"). Thus, the play experience in a game requires experiential learning to figure out the designed system—"part of the challenge is to figure out what is to be done, and how" (Norman, 2013, p. 256).

Massive multiplayer online (MMO) games, from *World of Warcraft* to *Minecraft*, do not necessarily have a win or loss state (Salen & Zimmerman, 2003). The player "never reaches a final outcome but only a temporary one when logging out of the game" (Juul, 2003, "After the Classic Game Model"). In *Minecraft* a child may build a house on an iPad and then, when dinner is ready, pause his or her action. Other players in the game, however, may continue interacting. Games like these are set in persistent virtual worlds, in which events continually occur—even when a player is not actively playing (Sheldon, 2012). These games never end. They lack a quantifiable outcome, thus changing "the classic game model by removing the goals, or more specifically, by *not* describing some possible outcomes as better than others" (Juul, 2003, "After the Classic Game Model").

Designed Experiences and Meaningful Play

Sid Meier, creator of the *Civilization* series, remarked that a game is a series of interesting choices. In other words, aside from rules and goals, at its core, players solve problems that are meaningful. The choices players make have consequences that intrinsically matter to them (Salen & Zimmerman, 2003). Video games are "designed experiences" in which players solve a series of well-ordered problems (Gee, 2007, p. 41; Squire, 2006). Player agency describes the "knowing actions taken by the player that result in significant changes within the world" (Gibbs, 2011, para. 4).

During play, one must exercise metacognition—learning about the design constraints of the game as a system—in order to best maneuver through it (Gee, 2007; Squire, 2006). When I play a video game like *Assassin's Creed* and I enter a building protected by soldiers, I lose. This forces me to think about what the designers want me to do. I then change my strategy sand sneak through bushes into the building. Exploring the game's virtual environment by trial-and-error mirrors the methodology of scientific experimentation (Gee, 2007). Through the cycle of play and iteration, I learned what I can and cannot do, as prescribed by the constraints of the game's—in this case, *Assassin's Creed's*—system (Gee, 2007; Norman, 2014).

Voluntary Participation

Games require voluntary participation, in which "everyone knowingly and willingly" accepts the conditions of play (McGonigal, 2011, p. 21). Can a child be required by a teacher to play a game? Play is, at its core, "voluntary" (Huizinga, 1938/1955, p. 28). Assigning children to play removes agency. If a child is assigned to the dramatic play corner, it is no longer a playful activity. To achieve play in a classroom, teachers can create situations that invite role-play and student choice (Bodrova & Leong, 2003). As we shall see, to effectively implement play in the classroom, a degree of freedom must exist.

Bernie DeKoven is one of the foremost experts of play. He wrote several books on the topic, including the highly influential *The Well-Designed Game* (1978). His writing was significant to the "new games movement" in the 1970s (he was also quoted several times in Salen & Zimmerman's *Rules of Play*). When I spoke to DeKoven in April 2014, I asked him whether teachers could assign play and games for learning. I got a terse response: "No." He then elaborated, "Game-based learning goes against that [play]. Play-based learning says, 'Do what's fun for you,' which means kids may not be learning what's on the curriculum or directly relating to the curriculum." Allowing children to discover through play, especially in today's high-stakes testing environment, is a tough sell for schools that adhere to a standards-based curriculum. DeKoven believes that teacher-led (or top-down) games curtail the natural learning that play delivers. "If it [game-based learning] is prescribed and kids have to do it, you won't get the kind of play you need for kids to learn from it," DeKoven continued. "The best, most effective way is if kids want to play the games on their own free will. For me, play is freedom."

In March 2014, I asked Richard Bartle whether students could effectively play a game if they are obligated to do so. Bartle is a game design professor at the University of Essex in the United Kingdom. He explained that engaging with a game doesn't mean that the participant is necessarily playing. "[Students] have a choice whether to 'play it' or whether to 'work it,'" he said. "If the game is fun they'll play it. If it's not fun, then they'll work it, so you do have a choice." Bartle used a disconcerting game of *chess* as an example, just to drive his point home. He said, "If a person likes *chess*, it wouldn't matter if he or she were forced to play—even at gunpoint." As an extreme, think about how children "tributes" were forced to compete in Suzanne Collins's *Hunger Games* books. "If you get a group of people together and they don't want to play [a game], they'll work it," Bartle continued. "Any advantage of the gainfulness and of the playfulness is gone." He proposed a straightforward solution: Teachers should look for games that are fun for everyone to play. The component of putting fun first is natural for game designers, but not for teachers. If the goal is to engage learners, then educators should take notice to what drives game design.

My quest to understand playing games in a compulsory educational setting led me to game scholar James Paul Gee. When we spoke in April 2014, he gave me a detailed and lengthy response. Because his response mirrors much of my intended vision for this book, it is worthwhile quoting in its entirety. He said:

> Good games set up learning and how to teach. We want to take those principles. To me, it's not game-based learning or game-inspired learning. It is taking principles from games and extending them across multiple platforms, multiple tools, and

multiple forms of participation—one of which happens to be games. I know it's been a fetish for people who try to find the definition of games. Many of these people are inspired by a notion of play, or play is the magic circle, and if you add any external goals you've destroyed the play. I don't believe in the magic circle. What I believe is, if the child is motivated enough—motivated intrinsically—then it [the activity] becomes like play. He is not doing it for the external factors; he's not doing it for extrinsic reward piece. [When] children and animals are playing, they are learning. And when they are learning, they are playing. Learning is an appetite for human beings. When you put it in school and make it boring and decontaminated, then of course you kill that appetite. It's like when you give people bad food. The fact of the matter is that when you trigger the human instinct of learning—and this is true of adults, not just children—you're triggering a deeply satisfying thing. When people learn something new and they gain mastery, they are profoundly satisfied. The issue is how do we get engagement by an affiliation, not whether we call it play or call it a game.

Gee wrote *What Video Games Have to Teach Us About Learning and Literacy* (2007) to examine what educators can learn from effective, well-designed games. This book intends to continue that conversation. Yes, free play is important. Sometimes, using games in the classroom is appropriate. Creating fun and engaging, student-centered activities should be the goal of every teacher. Keep in mind that not every concept needs to be taught with a game; rather, adopt the techniques that games do well. Like stories, games are better at teaching whole concepts; do not use games to just teach dates, facts, or other rote information.

Designing Game-Like Lessons

Joe Bisz, a professor at the City University of New York's (CUNY) Game Network, classified simple and complex game mechanics. Bisz's webpage (referenced under "Resources" at the end of this chapter) illustrates how to apply game mechanics in teaching. He linked activities to Gee's Learning Principles, as well as futurist Marc Prensky's Engagement Principles (Prensky popularized the terms "digital native" and "digital immigrant"). Examples of complex mechanics that work in school included Challenge-and-Switch, in which students answer questions incorrectly, and then trade to see who can figure out what went wrong, and Collecting-and-Creation, a mechanic that involves dissecting and trading words and sentences (Bisz, n.d.). Other mechanics pertained to role-play. Complex mechanics can be applied to studying, too. Rather than flashcards, Bisz recommends *Concentration*, the memory matching game, *Classify the Pieces*, a sorting game (the mechanic is present in BrainPOP's *Sortify*), *Cut-Ups*, using scissors to scramble information, and *Find-the-Clue*, an inquiry-based discussion activity (Bisz, n.d.). For more ways to integrate game mechanics to teaching, I highly recommending purchasing a deck of cards Bisz created called *What's Your Game Plan?* It can be used by one person or with a roomful of teachers at a workshop to help educators brainstorm ideas. (See the link under "Games" at the end of the chapter; there are free downloadables as well.)

Game design is really about the player's experience. If you feel frustrated or pressured by time in a game, it was likely intended to trigger that emotion. In March 2014, I asked Carnegie Mellon's Jesse Schell about mechanics that work best for educational settings. He first recommended reading *New Traditional Games for Learning: A Case Book* (2013), research from teachers who used nondigital games in the classroom. The book covers studies of what did and didn't work, including how live-action role-playing (LARPing) games can be used to engage students.

Schell said that he hesitated to use competitive situations in the classroom. "It rewards people who need the least help and punished those that need the most help," he said. Instead, Schell recommended using a narrative to frame authentic learning, emphasizing intriguing stories. Schell's gave me a teamwork example about firefighters in an emergency situation simulation. "People like solving problems together. Cooperative challenges with a point work the best." If this sounds to you like problem-based learning, you are right! Schell continued:

> One of the biggest things a teacher may overlook—one of the greatest powers of games in the classroom—is the ability of a game to introduce a teachable moment. A lot of game designers are creating educational games that are striving to replace the educator. What they should be doing is augmenting the educator. Games are great at creating teachable moments. Games are terrible at knowing they have successfully delivered the teachable moment and then filling in the right information at the right time. But instructors are great at that!

One of the objectives of Schell's firefighter simulation was to usually set up a situation where students would fail. Upon failure, the instructor could then say, "You failed because you didn't use this simple four-step methodology. Let's talk about what you should have done." According to Schell, the biggest power of games in education is to create that conversation. "When you've done the game right, students ask questions in their minds," he concluded. "That means they want to learn."

In my practice, I have found that it is essential to integrate game mechanics in almost all student projects and activities. Match a mechanic with a learning objective. Not every activity I teach is a game; however, every lesson attempts to involve a game-like mechanic. I also bring students into the equation, asking them which mechanics I employed in a particular lesson—and why. This is another way to employ "game-inspired" learning in an activity that is not quite a game.

When I spoke to Google's Noah Falstein, in May 2014, I asked him to me give an example of how mechanics can drive instruction. "As a consultant it drove me crazy," he said. "People would want the wrong things. They would say they wanted a game teaching the history of the American Revolution. Then they would say, 'My son loves *World of Warcraft*, so we can use that and put in some American Revolution content in there?'" In Falstein's opinion, teaching with games only works when it is matched with other traditional methodologies. He continued, "It is a bit of an art and a science to match the mechanic to the subject of what you are trying to teach. Games are not good at teaching lists of facts. I'm not sure there is any good way; it's dry and rote. They are good at teaching about relationships, allowing people to step into the shoes of another experience." Falstein recalled learning from playing simulation games. He said:

> I remember playing a version of *Civilization* when resources were first added. I had a big country and we were at the point where we just discovered oil. Oil deposits showed up on my map, but there weren't any in my country. But there was a big one in a small country adjacent to mine. I was ignoring this country because it was small and innocuous. I was thinking, "It's small and I can put together an army and go and grab it; the other countries will get angry, but I'm wealthy enough and I can give some money and appease them." All of a sudden, I realized that this is what Saddam Hussein was thinking about Kuwait. It's an eerie feeling running this country, and I found myself rationalizing why I would expand my country. Would the country I took over want to be part of my country? It gave me the feeling of how leaders of countries can talk themselves into missteps or things seen as either infamous mistakes or great, bold moves that unify the country.

Any experienced educator will tell you that there is no universal single way to teach everything. Falstein recommended a "combined arms approach," using games, traditional lectures, and books. Kurt Squire's research, where he used the game *Civilization III* combined with class discussions about the book *Guns, Germs, & Steel* (1999), recommended the same approach. Falstein found this model to be equitable, as well. "It is a good tripod to discuss the rise and fall of civilizations," he said. Matching game mechanics with learning objectives, while mixing in books and teacher-led reflection, is a key to effective game-based learning.

Rules and Constraints

As designed experiences, games have affordances, signifiers, and constraints in which players interact. Affordances are invitations to a person about an object—in the virtual or real world—that result in an interaction (Norman, 2014). A steering wheel affords (or invites) spinning from the driver. In a video game, an affordance may be a vine on a wall, which suggests climbing. A signifier is more overt in messaging, indicating with imagery actions to be taken (Norman, 2014). Signifiers may be flashing arrows on a screen, signaling what action should be taken in the game's designed space. Constraints are the boundaries of the game's space (Norman, 2014; Salen & Zimmerman, 2003). They limit play to the structure of the game.

In a video game, the rules and goals of play are revealed as the game is played (Bogost, 2008). Playing with affordances and constraints becomes part of the game experience (Bogost, 2008). To learn a game, one must be free to "explore the possibility space its rules afford by manipulating the symbolic systems the game provides" (Bogost, 2008, p. 121). For example, the player learns during, not before play that *Pac-Man* cannot touch pink ghosts, but can eat blue ghosts. This is the essence of constructivist learning. Some (or most, depending on who you ask) students tune out when teachers review directions. Children are used to learning constructively by playing games, whether on the playground or on a tablet. Perhaps lessons should reveal themselves the same way.

Constraints breed creativity. Poetry is an example. To write a poem, like a Haiku, limitations inspire word choice. Twitter is another example. Users discovered that hashtags filter tweets, which gave rise to Twitter chats. Similarly, the design constraints on a game present players with a safe space to hypothesize and experiment with creative solutions to problems.

Games as Interconnected Systems

Systems thinking is a way of viewing the world as a series of interlocking connections. It is the study of how components interconnect, as well as how those relationships fit within other systems (Senge, 2006). James Paul Gee wrote that games offer something unique, because they "encourage players to think about relationships, not isolated events, facts, and skills" (2005, p. 36). The game is a system: The goal, rules, feedback, and participation all interconnect. Change one element and the entire dynamic is different. Weather is another example of a system. It is composed of evaporating water, rain clouds, and precipitation.

Plague, Inc. is a commercially successful, systems thinking game. I initially learned about it from a sixth grader back in 2015. To play, you take on that role of a lethal pathogen. The "magic circle" is a map of the entire world. I interviewed James Vaughan, the game's designer, for an article for MindShift in early 2015. Vaughan is a London-based economist and his game is really an economic modeler, of sorts. "The world is your Petri dish, and you are in there, tweaking the variables," he explained.

When I played *Plague, Inc.* for the first time, I took the role of a deadly strain of bacteria borne in the United States. My thinking was that developed and industrialized nations have active ports and outgoing flights, which could spread the disease farther and faster. I lost. When I told the student, who was 11 years old, he said that I should have started in a less developed nation. Poor counties have an insufficient infrastructure, in which diseases can thrive. And wealthier nations often manufacture goods in poorer countries. As a result, diseases traveled on shipping lanes, from poor countries to developed nations. His strategy indicated that he was a systems thinker!

The version of *Plague, Inc.* I played was on iPad. There is also a computer and console version, *Plague, Inc.: Evolved*, which is far more robust. Released in 2015, players can design their own "diseases." Here, the world-as-model becomes an effective teaching tool. What if parts of the world were "infected" with democracy? Or free speech? Or Christmas cheer?

Reflections about decisions are a powerful indicator of student understanding. Students that play *Plague, Inc.* can write about how and why they won or lost. To go one step further, teachers can extend the role outside of the game's magic circle. Ask students what would happen if a deadly virus grew so lethal that all hosts die out? The answer, of course, parallels historic pandemics, like the Black Death. Too many fatal hosts means that the disease has no more places to live.

Feedback Loops

Feedback loops are the most basic element of a system. Veteran game designer David Cook (2006) described the interactions of games as being based on feedback loops built into an interconnected system. In a blog post, Cook (2006) wrote:

- The player starts with a mental model that prompts them to …
- Apply an action to …
- The game system and in return …
- Receives feedback that …
- Updates the mental model and starts the loop all over again. Or kicks off a new loop. (Cook, 2006, "Feedback Loops")

When I visited New York City's game-based Quest to Learn school, I saw feedback loop diagrams posted around in the hallways. One sign read, "Taking the Stairs" and "Healthy Body," with arrows pointing to each phrase. Above the arrows were plus symbols indicating a positive flow. Systems thinkers attempt to break the habit of thinking linearly; life happens in cycles (Senge, 2006). Games, therefore, can be used to serve as a microcosm of real-world systems, in which every action has an effect.

Does it work? Were students at Quest to Learn making the connection from playing games to systems thinking concepts? A study was conducted in 2012 to evaluate students' competency in systems thinking skills. Topics included the interconnectedness of sleep and being tired, as well as causal loops showing the peer pressure competition to wear and collect Silly Bandz (animal-shaped rubber bands) (Shute, Ventura & Torres, 2013). Although the population size was relatively small (one school), the study suggested that students, with teacher facilitation and support, were thinking less linearly and more in causal loops. The findings suggested that after 20 months, "Students who started at Quest to Learn as sixth graders when the school opened in September 2009 significantly improved on their overall systems thinking skills" (Shute, Ventura & Torres, 2013, p. 61).

As a social studies teacher, I am accustomed to teaching cause and effect. The world is composed of complex and dynamic systems (Senge, 2006, p. 70). If one person—or nation—takes an action, it has a consequential effect; other events are set in motion. When I teach about Japan's surprise attack on Pearl Harbor, I discuss that the United States first had an oil embargo on the island nation as a response to its invasion of China. The 2006 update of Peter Senge's 1990 book *The Fifth Discipline* used terrorism as an example of systems thinking in action. He argued that military retribution in response to a terrorist attack exemplifies a "linear" approach to thinking. It doesn't account for other points of view, including the terrorist's (Senge, 2006,

p. 70). When events are drawn together as a loop, one can see that responsive military attacks make the United States more threatening to its enemies, thus causing an insurgence of more terrorists (Senge, 2006, p. 70). Linear thinking presents an incomplete reality; systems thinkers view interconnections as causal loops, in which one cause has an effect which then leads into another cause, and so on.

In the classroom, it can be helpful to break interconnections down into smaller parts. Concept mapping, or mind mapping, can be used to connect parts of a whole. Teachers and students can use poster boards, sticky notes, or interactive whiteboards to examine feedback loops in systems. The idea is to list ideas and then draw lines and loops connecting related ideas. Educational software includes Kidspiration and the browser-based Popplet. Mind Meister offers live, collaborative publishing options. It features an intuitive drag-and-drop interface that works seamlessly across multiple devices. Students can work simultaneously, on iPads or laptops. The result can be seen in real time when projected onto an interactive whiteboard. Many of these applications offer deep educator discounts.

Computer-based systems modeling, such as those found on ISEE System's STELLA Modeler, are loosely based on a bathtub faucet analogy originally described in Peter Senge's *The Fifth Discipline* (1990/2006). Whatever is being measured—from predator/prey relationships to money—flows from the faucet. It is then collected in "stock," pictured in models as a square. Connectors and converters, which are diagrammed to look like plumbing equipment, complete a systems model. Creative Learning Exchange offers educators an easy-to-read document on simulation terminology and tips on implementation. Modeling software helps business leaders to visualize the interrelations between causal loops so they can make better predictions. The overall goal of modeling simulators is to create a learning organization that reflects on past practices and grows together as a community (Senge, 2006).

Before creating models, feedback loops, and causal loop diagrams, have students plot graphs. An example would be plotting weight loss over time on an x-, y-axis. Next, put weight loss over time together to create a causal loop diagram. This will illustrate how multiple feedback loops (e.g., eating less junk food, exercising) interconnect. Exercise may make you energetic (one feedback loop), but also thirsty (on offshoot feedback loop). The goal is for students to move from "describing the 'what' of the system's behavior to the 'why' of its behavior" (Creative Learning Exchange, 2013). Every simulation is based on positive and negative feedback.

The power of teaching systems thinking with games is in its authenticity. Simulations of war can be better illustrated by playing *Rock-Paper-Scissors* than by running through a role-playing military drill. The two-player version of the classic children's game is a system of interlocking rules (e.g., paper covers rock, etc.; everyone "throws" their hand in simultaneously), a goal (one winner per round), and voluntary participation (it is a zero-sum game—one winner, one loser). If you change one part of the system (rock covers paper?), or add in more rules (best out of three rounds), the game's system changes. Therefore, games can be seen as a microcosm of reality.

Playing a game that has systems management as an objective can reinforce the competency. *SimCityEDU: Pollution Challenge!* tasks players with balancing a virtual city's systems, including school bus stops, pollution, and employment. GlassLab's former Lead Designer Erin Hoffman-John explained to me how it works. "When an action is made, there are multiple consequences," she said. "If one piece of the system is modified, it can have surprising or unpredictable effects farther down the line because of the connections between all of the parts of the system."

Reach for the Sun, designed by Filament Games, is another systems thinking game. Played from the point of view of a flowering plant, the objective is to gather soil nutrients, sunlight, and even bees, in order to survive. Each element, including sunlight, pollination, and water, is part of the plant's interconnected system. Master the plant's survival and you have mastered the system. Just about all Filament Games have a system that engages the player. The system doesn't even have to be that complex. Filament's Dan White told me, "It's not about the complexity of the system, but whether it delivers it with an appropriate amount of fidelity." In other words, in a game, every action taken has a consequence to the system as a whole.

Conclusions and Takeaways

There are several competing definitions of what games are. Interestingly, although most are based in developmental psychology and stem from observing children's games, still it seems frivolous to play in school. Games are not just interactive; they are systems. Systems can be modeled with games. Mathematicians and economists also use games to analyze human behavior, which is a cross-curricular activity.

Lesson Plan Ideas

Collaborative Brainstorming: Use *Mindmeister, Bubbl.us,* or *Popplet* with students to brainstorm in real time. Standards depend on the discipline and content area.

Feedback Loop Exit Tickets: Students can diagram simple causal loops in any discipline. Be sure to include plus and minus signs to illustrate positive or negative relationships. Standards depend on the discipline and content area.

Game Kit: Challenges that require little to no technology. Have small groups try each challenge. Standards depend on the discipline and content area— http://beta.gamek.it

Mansa Musa: Inflation Then and Now: Auction lesson from the Council for Economic Education. Standards met include social studies (economics) and Common Core State Standards for mathematics. This link includes a PowerPoint presentation and a handout to drive home lessons about purchasing power, inflation, and currency devaluation—http://msh.councilforeconed. org/lessons.php?lid=68371

Modeling Hamlet: Use *Forio Simulate* to run systems models to see how Shakespeare's *Hamlet* looks to a mathematician or a scientist. Standards met include Common Core State Standards for English language arts—http://forio.com/ simulate/netsim/virtual-hamlet/run

Systems Thinking: How to Create a Digital World: Standards depend on the discipline and content area. Lesson plan from Scholastic—http://www.scho-lastic.com/browse/lessonplan.jsp?id=1418

Games

Diplomacy, the classic strategy game of consequential actions, playable online—http://www.playdiplomacy.com

Mekorama is a puzzle game for mobile devices that includes a level editor. My 6-year-old son makes puzzles with obstacles and a goal, similar to those in

Monument Valley, a more elegant game. *Mekorama* is rare because players can design and share creations—http://www.mekorama.com

Power Grid is a systems thinking board game in which players build an electric grid for a country—http://riograndegames.com/games.html?id=5

Re-Mission, cancer treatment game—http://www.re-mission.net

Ticket to Ride is a systems thinking tabletop game. The goal is to claim railway networks across America. There are other game boards, too, like Europe, India, Asia, and Africa, and there is a mobile version too!—https://www.daysofwonder.com/tickettoride/en/usa/

What's Your Game Plan, a deck of cards created by Joe Bisz. "Suits" include Lesson, Game, Mechanic, and Action. It is very useful to help brainstorm about how to bring game mechanics into teaching—http://joebisz.com/whatsyourgameplan

Resources

Board Game Mechanics—http://www.boardgamegeek.com/browse/boardgamemechanic

Creative Learning Exchange, systems thinking resources for kindergarten through grade 12—http://clexchange.org

ISEE systems thinking tools—http://www.iseesystems.com

Kidspiration, school-focused mind-mapping tools—http://www.inspiration.com/Kidspiration

Mind Meister, real-time, collaborative mind-mapping tool—http://www.mindmeister.com

Popplet is a browser-based and mobile mind-mapping tool. It works great with interactive whiteboards, too!—http://popplet.com

Prisoners' Dilemma as taught by the Khan Academy—https://www.khanacademy.org/economics-finance-domain/microeconomics/nash-equilibrium-tutorial/nash-eq-tutorial/v/prisoners--dilemma-and-nash-equilibrium

Institute of Play's *Systems Thinking Q Pack* helps integrate systems thinking across the curriculum—http://www.instituteofplay.org/work/projects/q-design-packs/q-systems-thinking-design-pack

Waters Foundation, featuring systems thinking for schools and free downloads—http://watersfoundation.org

· 3 ·

PLAYER TYPES AND MOTIVATION

One of the most influential papers to affect modern video game design came from Richard Bartle. His Player Type Model first described in *Hearts, Clubs, Diamonds, Spades: Players Who Suit MUDs* (1996), transformed how games were designed. Bartle's observations still reverberate today—especially in gamification's approach to engagement (adding game elements in spaces that are otherwise not games, such as websites and exercise programs). Bartle graciously granted me an interview, and in it he puts an educational spin on his now famous Player Types Model. Designing games should put the gamers' experience first and foremost. Shouldn't learning design do the same? It is as important to understand the work of Bartle when integrating game-based learning as it is to learn about Howard Gardner when planning to teach students using a variety of intelligence modalities.

Much of the current research I found on game design came from behaviorists and designers, not programmers or computer nerds. Game designers Jane McGonigal and Amy Jo Kim, for example, have PhDs in the field of behavioral psychology. It is common for school districts to have a child psychologist and/or a behaviorist on staff. Most of their days are spent with students who exhibit social or emotional problems. It would be unusual for a school to hire a behaviorist to ensure that the general population is having a happy and ful-filling learning experience.

This chapter compares and contrasts intrinsic and extrinsic motivational factors as they pertain to student engagement. I will also review the field of positive psychology, including the concept of "flow." In the "flow channel," people feel fulfilled because they are so involved in an experience (Csiksz-entmihalyi, 1990). Applied to games, the flow channel is used to describe the environment where the skill and the difficulty increase just enough to ensure that an experience is neither frustrating nor boring (Lazzaro, 2009, p. 13; McGonigal, 2011, p. 49). This chapter also covers the emotion of fun. If something—even the most serious topic—doesn't have an element of fun, then there is little chance for engagement. Even the most somber of books and movies still put entertainment first. Failure to do so would mean disen-gaged readers and bored viewers.

Lastly, this chapter reviews the basics of game theory and its applica-tions to game outcomes, as well as modern economic theory. Mathematicians during the Cold War used games to model human behavior. In what came to be known as game theory, researchers created scenarios to interpolate how nations would react in standoffs. John von Neumann and John Forbes Nash (famously portrayed by Russell Crowe in the movie A *Beautiful Mind*) both consulted for the RAND Corporation during the height of tension between the United States and the Soviet Union.

Bartle's Player Type Model

Game design has a lot in common with learning design. In a game, systems are created and then set into motion by its core mechanics. The result trig-gers an emotion in the player. Like education, game design has its models. Bartle's Player Type Model (1996) has had a significant influence on how games are made. The innovation was to create—or design—games for oth-ers to play. People play games for different reasons, aside from the rules and objectives. Friends may gather to play cards every week in a setting to chat or gossip. Others may play to win. Bartle's realization was that game designers must keep different personality types in mind. As a teacher, you may recognize components of Howard Gardner's Multiple Intelligence Theory, where people learn visually, kinetically, musically, or simply by listening. Creating games for different player types also has commonalities with differentiated instruction, teaching each learner to his or her strengths.

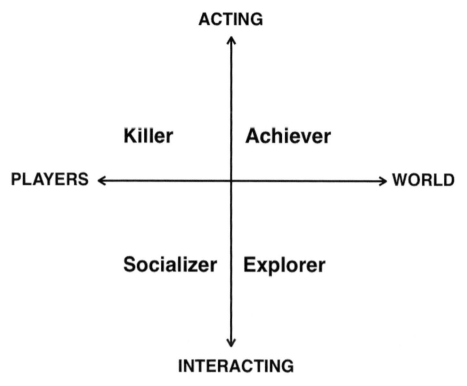

Figure 1. Bartle's Player Type Model.

Bartle, a professor specializing in artificial intelligence and virtual worlds, wrote *Hearts, Clubs, Diamonds, Spades: Players Who Suit MUDs* in the mid-1990s to explain how players interact differently when participating in multiplayer environments. (MUDs are multiuser dungeons, or text-based virtual worlds.) Plotted on an x-, y-axis, Bartle compared player actions, or interactions, of multiplayers in game worlds (Bartle, 1996). The model, also known as Bartle's Player Types, classified four types of players:

- Killers—those who act on, or against, other game players
- Achievers—those who build up their in-game status
- Explorers—those who gather artifacts and look around
- Socializers—those who build friendships. (Bartle, 1996)

I have had some spirited discussions about Player Types with students. In school, lessons can be designed to encourage young explorers to explore. Personally, I prefer games that engage me in exploring, such as the *Tomb Raider* series. In the book *The Multiplayer Classroom* (2012), Lee Sheldon hypothesized that he was an Explorer Type because he enjoys writing. He researches facts and assembles them into stories, and sometimes into the TV episodes he wrote. Achievers pursue goals (not just extrinsic ones, such as grades). These include class "power-ups" or points from games on a class leaderboard. Socializers enjoy connections made from being with other people. They are the students who want to work together in cooperative groups. Killers obviously shouldn't be as aggressive in a classroom; I find that appropriate outlets for this type are structured debates or the lead roles in skits.

Bartle's model has been widely adopted by designers and is part of virtually every game design course. It seems obvious now that games should be designed for the variety of people that play them. I spoke to Bartle in March 2014. As mentioned in Chapter 2, he is a game design professor at the University of Essex.

Bartle has always been making games. I've noticed this trait in several game designers I interviewed—their minds are constantly thinking how the world can be modeled as a game. "When I was a kid used to make games," Bartle recalled. "I played games the whole time, games are one of those things that you did." Whether it was word games or simply running around, many of his childhood games involved simulation and role play. "I was particularly interested in the world-building thing," Bartle recalled. "The real world sucked. If you were a working-class boy living in a derelict seaside town, there were no prospects of anything because of how you spoke or what your parents did. I really wanted a world where you could be free. That's why I wrote *Ultima* [the classic text-based adventure]. Building imaginary worlds was a way to change the real world. That's why I did it."

I was curious about how Bartle came up with the idea of Player Types. He explained that at that time, in the mid-1990s, designers were making games that they personally wanted to play. He wanted to show that they should be making games that *everyone* would want to play. Bartle made several analogies in our conversation. "If you're a brewer, you don't necessarily make beer you want to drink," he said. "You make beer for other people to drink. You might not even like beer yourself!" In other words, the designer is someone who should enjoy designing. It is not a prerequisite for someone who makes games to necessarily enjoy playing what he or she creates. What I find fun is not necessarily what a 12-year-old middle school student finds fun to do. It is easy to lose sight of what others may find fun. This is why game designers rely on playtesters.

If you focus on just one of the Player Types, such as the Achiever type, the designer is doing the game a disservice; only competitive people will play, turning away Socializers or Explorers. "People want to play games for lots of different reasons," Bartle continued. The game, therefore, isn't as effective as it could be. "I really expected the paper and the Player Types [Model] to not last very long, maybe 6 months or so," he continued. "I waited for people to come up with a better set. The point I was making was that there are different reasons people play games."

A persistent question on my mind was how to effectively design an educational game. "Games are designed for purposes. In war games, like the Prussians did (with *Kriegspiel*), it wasn't necessarily fun—but it taught them things," Bartle explained. In my classroom, I use games as a metaphor for historical conflict. I also use simulations to teach empathy. Bartle suggested starting with subject matter that is interesting to children, "like dinosaurs, pirates, or French musketeers." Next, add the learning objective onto the system. Then, right there on the spot, Bartle designed a game to test people's propensity to xenophobia. He explained:

> You design a game about your company, which is a large company, and it just bought up another company, which is a small company. The small company is closing down offices, and the people from that company come to work in your company. They have different practices and ways of doing things, and there are far fewer of them. Should you take their best parts and practices and adapt them to you, or should you bring them into your existing system which you know works, try to spread them around, keep them in one section?

Bartle's example is a "serious" business game masking what is really being studied: xenophobia. The trick is to make sure that the systems underneath, essentially the game's architecture, are compatible. Learning must be deeply embedded in an educational game. Games, however, cannot teach everything. A flaw in using games to assess behavior pertains to *how* people take on roles, player agency. Players may be just exploring an aspect of their personality through the game. Stealing cars in *Grand Theft Auto* doesn't turn thousands of people into carjackers. You can't always rely on game data, but if it is well crafted, it can be more reliable than questionnaires and role-playing scenarios. If you want to find out people's attitudes toward immigrants you can just give them a survey, but their answers may be dishonest because people don't want to sound racist.

People learn from games if the game is about something they are interested in; the other facts are just things they pick up that make it easier for them to play. The content both at the surface level and at the gameplay level is why people play. What comes with it is actually what you want to teach. Bartle explained, "That's the vehicle that you attach your educational payload. If you wanted to teach a particular thing, find something where knowing that particular thing will help you, and not knowing it wouldn't hinder you, but it would slow you down a bit. That's how I recommend it from a game designer's point of view." The classic mistake occurs when educators make games and don't know anything about game design. Conversely, the mistake you get from game designers is that they don't know anything about education. This is why edutainment has a poor track record and why "educational" games can make a student cringe. There really isn't a common language—at least, not yet.

Bartle told me that he could name every country in Europe because he plays games. Because of the setting of *Assassin's Creed III*, I have had students who were quite proficient in detailing battles of the American Revolution. "Likewise, I know the geography of the Caribbean because I played so many pirate games," Bartle said. "There are a lot of things you can pick up from just playing—when the actual game involves higher-order problem solving things, like how to figure out how to do certain things. How to solve (problems); games are very good at that. The trouble is the stuff in the middle. If you want to teach people how to integrate an equation or differentiate an equation there's probably a better way than using games to do that."

Bartle has spoken at conferences about how his model is used—and misused. The biggest abuse of Bartle's Player Type Model is when people take all of the types and make content for each one as if each everyone was an Achiever. He explained to me:

> What do Explorers like doing? They like exploring. So, you explore enough, you get a badge. Wait a minute! A badge is something an Achiever wants. Why would you give a badge to an Explorer? They don't want a badge—they want more things to explore. That's for Achievers. Here's another misuse: If you get 15 friends, you get a special pet. Why would someone who wants friends want a special pet? Achievers might want pets. They like collecting pets. Collecting is an Achiever thing. That's where people read the Player Types and create content all for the same Player Type, which is typically just for Achievers. That's one area that I see a lot of.

The Player Type Model was not designed to put customers on a journey, or to engage learners in a classroom. It was created to improve the experience of players in multiuser virtual worlds. Bartle gave me an analogy of a novelist who wrote a successful book. Would an author add math problems to a text and ask the reader to track the money spent by a character? The problem is that these add-ons take away from the intended experience of the novel. "People read a story because it's fun," Bartle said.

Bartle's Player Types is worth knowing because it is a common starting point for gamifying learning. In a game, there are the core mechanics, or actions of play, like guessing or running. And then there is the aesthetic framework, which can be the game's board or an immersive virtual world. "Games might have a fictional framework. That's what supports what's fun about the game," Bartle continued. "Once you turn it the other way around, having the game support the fictional framework, you're talking about a different beast." Is the setting of *Assassin's Creed: Revelation* the best way to teach about Byzantium? Would you show *Saving Private Ryan* to teach French geography?

Teachers should play games for learning prior to integrating them. Bartle gave me advice on this topic. He said, "Make sure you know what it is you want to teach, and find a game that it isn't about. Because if the students think the game is about what the teacher wants taught, they won't engage with it. Introduce a game about math that has a mechanic of adding and students may become suspicious of how fun it is before they even start. What would be fun is exploring an undersea world and, in order to get over there, I need to get some fuel. You learn math because you need to get fuel and know how long it's going to last. You're not concerned about fuel; you're concerned about submarine exploration." Learning theorists call this a "felt need." For this to occur, use authentic projects connected to real-world situations. Also, keep in mind that if a game is crafted well, then it will be fun. If you don't think it's fun, the student is not going to think it's fun.

Social Engagement

Richard Bartle told me that his model appears in all sorts of unintended places. He spoke highly of one particular modification of his model: Amy Jo Kim's Social Action Matrix. "If you're going to adapt a model, that's how you do it, instead of wholesale apply it," he said. "She looked around for different things, and that's what shined best for her."

Kim updated the Player Type Model to better align with social interactions. She replaced the "Killer" type with "Express"—a much more friendly descriptor. Completing her axes, "Compete" took the place of "Achiever," "Explore" replaced "Explorer," and "Collaborate" replaced "Cooperate" (Kim, 2012b). Kim extended her matrix by adding Social Engagement Verbs. Games—like learning objectives—are designed with verbs. These include "build, design, customize, challenge, curate, and share" (Kim, 2012b). Social Engagement Verbs are reminiscent of Bloom's Taxonomy of Higher-Order Thinking Verbs ("Identify" is a lower-order, or skill and drill, verb; "Compare" or "Create" are higher-order). Of course, no model is perfect. Like Bartle, Kim recommends modifying her version to fit a product (in this case content, skills, or, better yet, a love of the learning process) or an intended audience (students).

Do all of Kim's descriptors sound familiar? Don't I already do this by having students engage cooperatively? The answer, of course, is: Yes! Social engagement works best in non–zero-sum games, which are cooperative. In a non–zero-sum game, there is competition; however, everyone is on the same team trying to achieve the same goal.

Offering student choice is a smart idea to boost engagement in a class-room. Explorers would enjoy peer feedback and collecting images from Google. Helping one another iterate on work is a positive and social experi-ence. Competitors may like the idea of class museums that put culminating projects on display. Displaying side-by-side work is a win-win competition. Collaborative work should already take place in a student-centered classroom. There are many Internet tools, from wikis to Google Drive, enabling students to collaborate together. Incorporating social meaning to a student's learning environment personalizes the journey or quest.

Rewards and Motivation

Behavioral sciences date back to the theories of classical and operant condi-tioning from Ivan Pavlov and B. F. Skinner. Pavlov is often associated with classical conditioning. His famous dogs drooled at the sound of a bell after they learned that a ringing bell was followed by a reward of food. Eventu-ally, Pavlov removed the food and discovered that dogs still salivated just at hearing the bell. Positive and negative reinforcement, in the form of rewards or punishments, is at the heart of Skinner's research. The Skinner Box was a rat-in-a-box contraption with a food lever as a positive reinforcer and an elec-trical charge as a negative reinforcer. Do people need the promise of food or fear of electrocution in order to learn? Should school be set up like a Skinner Box? Does the proverbial kick in the butt lead to success? Modern research has shown otherwise. While external rewards work in the short term, they do not create satisfied people who enjoy their work.

In the 1990s, Alfie Kohn wrote about the trappings of reward systems. *Punished by Rewards: The Trouble with Gold Stars, Incentive Plans, A's, Praise, and Other Bribes* (1999) is one of his more notable books. The proverbial carrot at the end of the stick can often demotivate people. Kohn's criticism was not directed at all reward systems, but those that focus on extrinsic motivation as an incentive. Most of the early behavioral research came from only animal testing (e.g., Pavlov's dogs), not from humans (1997, p. 15). The end result—paychecks, time off, semester grades, student-of-the-month, merit pay, or trophies—may not be enough of a motivator (Kohn, 1997, p. 15). Working toward your vacation days will not make you want to rush into the office; report card grades and summative assessments can have the same (lack of) effect on students. I often make an analogy about cooking: If making dinner or baking cookies is something you find fun to do, then it has an intrinsic reward. That may extend to watching others eat what you cook, another source of satisfaction. If the goal is just to eat, then it is extrinsic. In the long run, extrinsic rewards can discourage performance. Kohn wrote a "framework" describing the trappings of extrinsic reward systems. He wrote:

1. Pay is not a motivator
2. Rewards punish
3. Rewards rupture relationships
4. Rewards ignore reasons
5. Rewards discourage risk-taking
6. Rewards undermine interest. (Kohn, 1997, pp. 18–23)

There are clear parallels to mastery learning and level design in video games. Students should grow intellectually from schooling after mastering a standards-based curriculum. Each is related to the psychological theory popularly known as the *growth mindset*, proposed by Dweck (2015), who posited that when people have a growth mindset in which intelligence can be increased, they achieve more than people who have a fixed mindset. A growth mindset is based on the belief that "your basic qualities are things you can cultivate through your efforts" (Dweck, 2006, p. 7). Students are praised for effort, not necessarily for their achieved successes (Dweck, 2006). Facilitating children to grow based on challenges has met with some criticism. When a growth mindset becomes a label or a behavioral goal, it can become an extrinsic motivator, like grades on report cards (Kohn, 2015). Dweck (2015) clarified how educators should apply a growth mindset, stating that teachers should

encourage students to have a growth mindset and not simply label those who
do not.

Intrinsic rewards are the opposite of extrinsic motivators. They are internal-
ized and often represent satisfaction one feels from an accomplishment. These
rewards are similar to the self-satisfaction gained from finishing a great book,
enjoying a day golfing, the thrill of discovering a secret room in *Tomb Raider*,
or defeating a dragon with guild members in *World of Warcraft*. According to
Jane McGonigal, intrinsic motivation includes "satisfying work, the experience, or at least the hope, of being successful, social connection, and meaning"
(2011, p. 49). These are the reasons that so many people play so many hours
of games outside of their school and work days. In front of a computer, players
are empowered and feel in control. Amy Jo Kim wrote that video games are
"*pleasurable learning engines*—they offer up skills to master, and reward you with
greater challenges and opportunities" (Kim, 2012a; emphasis in original). The
fun is in the experience of play, not the score. Do you remember how much
money you've earned playing *Monopoly*, or the triple word score you got in
Scrabble? If nothing else, game design can teach teachers how intrinsic satisfaction should come before grades and other extrinsic motivators.

Pleasant Frustration and the Flow Channel

On its surface, game-based learning may seem to be following a trend of just
doing what kids like to do; the proverbial tail wagging the dog. The psychology of how it works actually runs deeper. Games can focus people into a state
of mind called "flow." Psychologist Mihaly Csikszentmihalyi first described the
concept. You can see it in the faces of Olympic athletes, Zen Buddhist monks,
and, of course, gamers.

Flow represents intrinsic satisfaction. It can best be described as "the
way people describe their state of mind when consciousness is harmoni-
ously ordered, and they want to pursue whatever they are doing for its sake"
(Csikszentmihalyi, 1990, p. 6). Csikszentmihalyi created a model, known as the
"flow channel," to describe the environment where skill and difficulty increase
just enough that an experience is neither frustrating nor boring. As shown in
the diagram reprinted below, he plotted the "flow channel" between the two
axes of "Challenge" and "Skills" (Csikszentmihalyi, 1990, p. 74). The flow
channel is where people feel fulfilled because they are so involved in an experience. In the illustration, "A" represents anxiety. The goal of a well-crafted game
is to keep the play within the flow channel (McGonigal, 2011, p. 49).

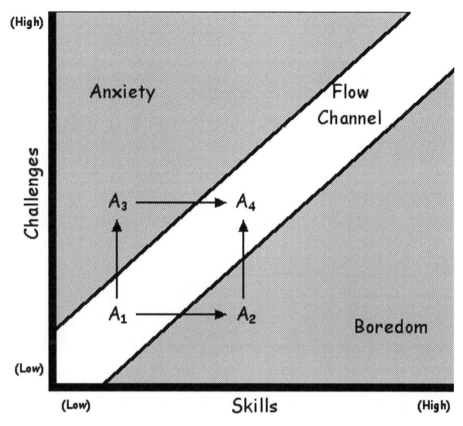

Figure 2. The Flow Channel.
Illustration from p. 74 from *Flow: The Psychology of Optimal Experience* by Mihaly Csikszent-mihalyi. Copyright © 1990 by Mihaly Csikszentmihalyi. Reprinted by permission of Harper-Collins Publishers.

Flow activities create enjoyment (Csikszentmihalyi, 1990, p. 72). James Gee called this "pleasant frustration," where the challenge is just difficult enough to promote replay and eventual mastery (2005). Csikszentmihalyi considered each set of Caillois's games (discussed in the Chapter 2: *agon, alea, ilinx,* and *mimicry*) to be a flow activity (1990, p. 74). Because of a game's design, "participants and spectators achieve an ordered state of mind" (Csikszentmihalyi, 1990, p. 72). *Agon* games are competitive, thereby motivating participants to win challenges. *Alea* games involve randomness, such as the throwing of dice; the feeling of anticipation is the flow. *Ilinx* is thrill-seeking: It is hard to think of anything else while on a rollercoaster. Finally, *mimicry* involves "being in the moment." Karaoke and dance games may be popular because they tap into this part of human behavior. About games, Csikszentmihalyi wrote, "Whether it [a game] involved chance, or any other dimension of experience, [it] had this in common: It provided a sense of discovery, a creative feeling of transporting the person to a new reality" (Csikszentmihalyi, 1990, p. 74).

Like Bartle's Player Types and Kohn's observations, Csikszentmihalyi's work was read by game designers in the 1990s and incorporated into design. Video games even use adaptive engines to ramp up difficulty. Schools have lagged behind. The flow channel is like the zone of proximal development, psychologist Lev Vygotsky's space where learning scaffolds on previous knowledge. The problem in schools is that the feedback loop is much slower than that which video games provide.

Game challenges do not necessarily need to get more difficult in a linear fashion. Designer Jesse Schell suggested that it is appropriate to level off the anxiety with breaks in the action (2008). Video games let players relax between levels and missions by showing animated sequences to move along the storyline. There may also be time to explore the virtual environment and collect and gather hidden rewards. In fact, it can be considered poor design to just put a player linearly in the flow channel, leveling up difficulty with each mission. The takeaway for teachers is that relief from constant challenge is an acceptable design choice.

Game designer Jenova Chen (his company made critical hits *Journey* and *Flower*) tested whether a player can self-sustain in the flow channel without a computer automatically scaling up challenges. He designed *flOw* (2006) for his master's thesis. In it, the player can increase or decrease his or her own difficulty of play. The result was an unexpected hit on Sony's PlayStation Network. *flOw* is an aesthetically hypnotic experience, with calming electronic music and visuals that resemble organisms under a microscope. Game mechanics are simple: Move your organism and consume smaller life forms. The more you eat, the bigger you grow. That's it. No score, no badges, no leaderboard. If you grow too big and can't handle the challenges, then you simply reduce in size. The result was strangely addictive. A lesson from Chen was that students might prefer to fine-tune their own learning difficulties. If you observe a child build in *Minecraft* or with LEGO bricks, you will see the same self-regulating behavior. The mechanics of *flOw* are also in the online game *Agar.io* (2015).

A classroom of active learners is the goal of every teacher. Think of all the activities that immerse your students. Those activities may lend themselves to a game-like context because they already are engaging. In my classroom, flow activities usually include opportunities for students to tweak projects they find personally interesting. These include editing in iMovie, coding with *Scratch*, or building in *Minecraft*. I can tell informally that the class is in a flow state when no one asks to leave to use the bathroom, and I have to ask the class several times to clean up when the bell rings.

Fun and Engagement

In 2005, Raph Koster's book *A Theory of Fun for Game Design* was published. Although targeted at the game designer community, it reads like a textbook for teachers. For example, Koster discussed Howard Gardner's Multiple Intelligence Theory and how games scaffold skills until mastery level is achieved (2005). According to Koster, the goal of an activity may be sufficient to make it fun. It's the hope of achieving success that engages players. Once mastery is reached, fun ceases. In other words, "fun is contextual" (Koster, 2005, p. 96). His words ring true for educators just as they do for game designers. Koster wrote, "Fun is primarily about practicing and learning, not about exercising mastery" (2005, p. 96). Fun quickly turns into boredom once a game—or a lesson—is mastered.

The excitement of overcoming an obstacle in a game should entice you to further play. In 2004, Hunicke, LeBlanc, and Zubek wrote a paper that described a taxonomy of fun, "game pleasures." The reference to "pleasure" wasn't a coincidence; it was a referring to Maslow's 1943 Hierarchy of Needs Theory, which includes food, shelter, and clothing. The act of engaging in a "fun" activity is, after all, what pleasure seekers do. That is why people visit Disney's theme parks, watch 3D movies, and skydive. Pleasures derived from games include:

1. Sensation—Game as sense-pleasure
2. Fantasy—Game as make-believe
3. Narrative—Game as unfolding story
4. Challenge—Game as obstacle course
5. Fellowship—Game as social framework
6. Discovery—Game as uncharted territory
7. Expression—Game as soap box
8. Submission—Game as mindless pastime. (Hunicke, LeBlanc, & Zubek, 2004)

School, certainly, can't be a "mindless pastime." It can, however, be enjoyable on other levels. Discovery learning, popularized by Maria Montessori, can be as fun in school as it is in a game. A well-conceived classroom presentation—where students can discuss and connect a topic to something they are interested in—is "Expression" pleasure. Clearly, you can't put a Ferris wheel in your classroom, but you can role play. Games provide spaces for people to socialize with others who share the same interests. Working cooperatively in a problem-based learning activity is also pleasurable—if deployed correctly and if it is designed well.

Part of the allure of gaming is the emotional satisfaction players receive. If the intent is to use a game to deliver learning, then it must be fun. "If the game is not fun, it won't achieve what you want it to achieve," explained Shula Ehrlich, formerly of the Institute of Play. We spoke in January 2014. To Ehrlich, there is no special key or magical ingredient, as long as the game mechanic works. Some are intrinsically fun, such as bluffing in the board game *Apples to Apples*. English language arts and social studies games should allow a student to give his or her opinion, followed up with opportunities to judge and persuade others.

4 Keys 2 Fun

Nicole Lazzaro, creator of the first motion-controlled iPhone game, *Tilt World*, proposed the "4 Keys 2 Fun" model. Her firm, XEODesign, used facial data to analyze player emotion (Lazzaro, 2009, p. 9). Teachers can learn from her findings. Researchers hooked up gamers to electrodes to measure eye movement and sweating during play (Lazzaro, 2009, pp. 10–11). This research helped game designers better pinpoint when fun occurs and how the flow channel functions. Game publisher Valve (*Portal, Half-Life 2*) also employs a full-time experimental psychologist to measure physiological responses to gameplay (Takahashi, 2013).

Using facial data to gauge emotional responses isn't new at all—or unique to gaming. Paul Ekman, a psychologist who pioneered the field, created a range of psychometrics to measure emotions (Lazzaro, 2009, pp. 9–10). This is another case of game design applying behavioral research ahead of other disciplines—such as education. Obviously, the goal of a teacher is not to elicit emotions from students ... or is it? If boredom is an emotion, then perhaps some schools need to pay more attention to who is learning. You can't force students to love learning. They must associate the act with positive emotions.

XEODesign published a white paper detailing player emotions during play. As a game progresses through the flow channel, the "newbie" player is given more information and increasingly complex tasks until mastery level is reached. Succeeding at the "boss level"—where all in-game skills get applied to a challenge—gives the player the feeling of *fiero*, the Italian word that describes what one feels after overcoming a difficult challenge (Lazzaro, 2009, p. 23). *Fiero*—not the high score—is the ultimate intrinsic reward for accomplishment. It is triggered after defeating the Joker in *Batman: Arkham Asylum* or scoring a home run in baseball. Quest to Learn's 3-week-long boss levels are designed to give students feelings of accomplishment from a great challenge. *Fiero* is the "epic win." (Conversely, games that are too difficult to play may cause players to "rage quit.")

How to get students to experience *fiero* in school is complicated. In many video games it takes several persistent tries—and fails—to win the boss level and give the player glowing pride. The culture of never failing in school can stifle *fiero*, pulling the emotional satisfaction from accomplishment away from the learner. I have witnessed students feeling *fiero* after succeeding in the final mission of *SimCityEDU: Pollution Challenge!* At the end of the game, all of the city's systems required balancing. (This part of the original version of the game was deemed too difficult in the beta test my students tried. The difficulty was eventually scaled back for the game's final release.)

It can be argued that creating *fiero* *requires* student failure. Failing and quickly recovering fosters grit and persistence. Providing relief from frustration is a game mechanic. It works so well that mobile games have made millions of dollars from selling in-game cheats to enable players to succeed. According to XEODesign, some emotions triggered during play include:

- Fear—Threat of harm, object moving quickly to hit player, sudden fall or loss of support, possibility of pain.
- Surprise—Sudden change. Briefest of all emotions, does not feel good or bad, after interpreting event this emotion merges into fear, relief, etc.
- Disgust—Rejection as food or outside norms. The strongest triggers are body products such as feces, vomit, urine, mucus, saliva, and blood.
- Naches/Kvell (Yiddish)—Pleasure or pride at the accomplishment of a child or mentee.
- Fiero (Italian)—Personal triumph over adversity. The ultimate game emotion. Overcoming difficult obstacles, players raise their arms over their heads. They do not need to experience anger prior to success, but it does require effort.

- Schadenfreude (German)—Gloat over misfortune of a rival. Competitive players enjoy beating each other, especially a long-term rival. Boasts are made about player prowess and ranking.
- Wonder—Overwhelming improbability. Curious items amaze players at their unusualness, unlikelihood, and improbability without breaking out of realm of possibilities. (Lazzaro, 2004)

There are certain "keys" that can unlock the emotions in the above list. People feel different levels of fun during different types of play, depending on the action. Designers, therefore, can customize an experience best suited to unlock certain feelings. Game-based lesson plans should include fun descriptors and goals, similar to how Bloom's Taxonomy of Higher Order Thinking verbs are integrated into learning.

Of course, not all school is fun. Not all websites are fun, either. When I bank online, I don't expect the same experience as playing a video game. I certainly don't want a surprise at the ATM! Nonetheless, more of our lives are becoming gamified. XEODesign research proposed a four-domain model of emotional responses, some of which are appropriate to lesson planning. The 4 Keys 2 Fun are:

- Hard Fun—Challenge, strategy, and problem-solving, frequently generates emotions and experiences of frustration, and fiero
- Easy Fun—Intrigue and curiosity generate emotions and experiences of wonder, awe, and mystery
- Altered States—The internal experiences in reaction to the visceral, behavior, cognitive, and social properties
- The People Factor—Players use games as mechanisms for social experiences. (Lazzaro, 2004)

Design is about the experience the person has interacting with something (a lesson plan, a game, an object, a device, etc.). "Serious games" are designed with fun as a starting point. Lesson plans should have some measure of fun, whether it is Hard Fun, Easy Fun, or the People Factor. (Altered States, such as the thrill of skydiving or rollercoasters, is clearly not attainable in a school setting, although it can be in the educational game *Rollercoaster Tycoon*.) Try teasing information to hook students (Easy Fun), then introducing an authentic, problem-based learning task (Hard Fun).

People Fun is clearly social and is a straightforward application of gamification in face-to-face or online learning environments. Lazzaro described

People Fun mechanics as "high score boards, profile pages, avatars, gifting, emotes, and chat" (2009, pp. 42–46). Each can be applied to the context of school. High score boards, or leaderboards, can challenge students or teams to improve. Many learning management system applications, including Moodle, Blackboard, and Edmodo, have user profile pages to give students a space to express themselves. Avatars, or digital representations, can range from profiles in social media to animated characters, such as those on Voki, the talking avatar tool. Gifting in social constructs includes liking Facebook posts or clicking the heart icon on Instagram. Each is a game-like act of kindness. Emojis are also common with both students and adults, who often pepper online and text messages with smiley faces.

The Tyranny of Fun

I asked play expert Bernie DeKoven about where "fun" fits in play-based activities. When we spoke in 2014, he said, "Find people who have fun in their discipline, find what's fun for them in that discipline, and then share that with the kids." He had students invent new rules for elementary school science. He explained, "Kids had fun playing with measurements, I felt the kids were really catching fire." It wasn't the task of measuring things that was fun; rather, students began to internalize what drives scientific theory out of their own sense of play. He began to let students create new mathematical symbols. Parents 45 years ago didn't understand his vision. "The problem was, it didn't prepare the kids to take tests in 5th and 6th grade," DeKoven recalled. "Parents were really worried that their kids wouldn't be prepared to pass the state test. I tried to give something long-term, like a love for the discipline."

Common Sense Media's Tanner Higgin had a grounded take on fun. When we spoke in March 2016, he posited that a good learning game is really dependent on the objectives of that game. "There are games about isolating some sort of learning goal, and getting students to understand them conceptually," he explained. "And there is something like [the game] *Journey*, which is just as valuable, but doesn't have that explicit goal." Regarding fun and engagement from games, Higgin continued:

> We think something that's going to be good for the classroom needs to grip the students in some way, it doesn't have to be fun—it has to be absorbing. Fun is one of the most annoying things in game-based learning. I call it the "tyranny of fun." It is a bad measurement for what makes a game good [*laughs*] and we need to get away from it, desperately! It's about attention and absorption. Take something like *Papers, Please*

[the serious game, in which you play as a Soviet-era passport agent], which isn't fun at all, but it is definitely affecting. You may not want to play it very long, but when you do, you are dialed in to what this is trying to tell you.

Play theorist Brian Sutton-Smith included a quote from researchers Apter and Kerr (1991) in his seminal book *The Ambiguity of Play* (1997). In it he wrote, "Golf is not necessarily play and research is not necessarily work" (Apter & Kerr, 1991, p. 14, as cited in Sutton-Smith, 1997, p. 174). Writing this book may not be "fun" in a traditional sense; however, writing is fulfilling to me. I often lose track of time staring at my computer's screen.

For media scholar Henry Jenkins, play is also not just about fun; it's about engagement. When we spoke, in May 2014, he told me, "As faculty we are engaged in our favorite area of research. We are committed to working long hours with difficult materials. It doesn't mean that it's all fun and games, that it's not challenging and difficult. The goal is to create an environment where engagement drives learning. For engagement to drive learning, you have to have relative freedom with what you're engaged with."

Researcher Jeremiah (Remi) Kalir embarked on a project about just that: play in research settings. He is a professor at the University of Colorado-Denver, and he ponders the possibility for "flash mobs," seemingly spontaneous, yet coordinated, assemblies of web annotators. Kalir is leading the Playful Annotation with Hypothesis Studying Interactive Text (PAHSIT) research study (linked under Resources in this chapter). The study is reviewing how the collaborative tool, Hypothes.is, enables researchers to playfully annotate documents together, in real time. One of PAHSIT's research questions is, "Under what conditions is the collaborative and networked practice of open web annotation playful?"

Game Theory

"Game theory" refers to the mathematical result obtained when two or more "rational" people play a game. This book is concerned with game design and its value as an instructional delivery method, not an analysis of combinations and permutations that can result from games. Games are not pure luck, like flipping a coin. Hitting a baseball or throwing rock, paper, or scissors has a human component (people play to win). Because of that, game theory is considered to be more than a branch of mathematics; it's a social science.

In 1928, John von Neumann wrote "Theory of Parlor Games." He attempted to link *how* people play games such as *poker*. As it turned out, parlor games had a lot in common with economic theories such as supply and demand (Chen, Lu & Vekhter, n.d.). To von Neumann, a game was defined as "a conflict situation where one must make a choice knowing that others are making choices, too, and the outcome of the conflict will be determined in some prescribed way by all the choices made" (Poundstone, 1992, p. 6). In 1944, he published the book *Theory of Games and Economic Behavior*. His theory, known as minimax, focused on two-player, zero-sum games such as *Rock-Paper-Scissors*. Zero-sum means that there is one absolute winner and one loser.

John Forbes Nash built on von Neumann's work. Nash eventually won a Nobel Prize in economics for his contribution: mixed-strategy Nash equilibria. Unlike von Neumann, Nash's research was about games with multiple players. Nash's troubled life was depicted in the Academy Award-winning film *A Beautiful Mind* (2001), starring Russell Crowe. According to biographer Sylvia Nasar, Nash equilibrium is the moment when each player follows his or her "best strategy assuming that the other players will follow their best strategy" (Nasar, 1998, p. 119).

For the purpose of game-based learning, it can be helpful to review some of the basics of game theory. A zero-sum game is when there is one absolute winner and one loser. The 1982 movie *War Games*, about a computer modeling global thermonuclear war gone awry, is essentially a morality tale of the dangers of zero-sum games. The popular film compared all-out winning (or, equally, completely losing) global thermal nuclear war to the game *Tic-Tac-Toe*. We (or they) attack first, then they (or we) retaliate, both reducing each nation to rubble. Conversely to games such as *Tic-Tac-Toe*, non–zero-sum games, as the name implies, aren't win-lose, but rather win-win. Cooperative games in learning should, of course, be non–zero sum. I recommend having students view the BrainPOP video on game theory, which effectively frames how games can be used as models for real life interactions.

In the 1950s, the RAND Corporation, a California-based think tank, studied game theory. Nash and von Neumann were hired as consultants to model and analyze Cold War strategies. At RAND, Merrill Flood, Melvin Dresher, and, later, Albert W. Tucker proposed a parable, popularly known as the Prisoners' Dilemma, to illustrate how Cold War military standoffs work. The dilemma, or difficult choice, is described below by Nash biographer Sylvia Nasar. She wrote:

The police arrest two suspects and question them in two separate rooms. Each one is given the choice of confessing, implicating the other, or keeping silent. The central feature of the game is that no matter what the other suspect does, each (considered alone) would be better off if he confessed. If the other confesses, the suspect in question ought to do the same and thereby avoid an equally harsh penalty for holding out. If the other remains silent, he can get especially lenient treatment for turning state's witness. Confession is the dominant strategy. The irony is that both prisoners (considered together) would be better off if neither confessed—that is, if they cooperated—but since each is aware of the other's incentive to confess, it is "rational" for both to confess. (Nasar, 1998, p. 118)

The Prisoners' Dilemma led to subsequent research papers that dealt with subjects other than war. Teaching the basics of game theory is good practice because it integrates social studies (economics, causal loops due to scarcity and power) and practical math applications applicable to the business world. People don't just act out, there are always motivating factors; incentives and rewards must be considered. Therefore, one can look at the dilemma as a mathematical game. Mathematicians analyze game outcomes by creating a matrix, already common in math classes such as algebra and statistics. A matrix is a chart of rows and columns where possible outcomes are listed. Another mathematical method for illustrating game theory is to draw decision trees, which have possible answers branching out from the proposed problem.

Nash's observations extended to how auctions work, too. Perhaps you have heard of online auctions that start bidding at extremely low prices, sometimes at a penny. Conventional wisdom would dictate that bidding should start high to ensure a high final price, but when tested, it turns out that auctions that start with very low bids actually tend to end much higher. This is because humans are innately competitive and enjoy a feeding frenzy. This drives up prices—sometimes substantially—on low-bid (or unique-bid) auctions. Because people can't see the previous bids, they consistently assume they were high and therefore drive the price up even higher. William Vickery was credited with this finding. He was posthumously awarded a Nobel Prize for his paper on the subject, "Counterspeculation, Auctions, and Competitive Sealed Tenders."

In my 6th grade social studies class, I teach game theory in a simulation lesson with paper clips used as currency. The lesson is from the Council for Economic Education, and it illustrates Mansa Musa's pilgrimage from Mali, through Egypt, on his way to Mecca. First, I give each student a small and unequal number of paperclips. Next, I auction off items such as crackers or candy. For round 2, I hand out handfuls of paper clips to every student and

PLAYER TYPES AND MOTIVATION

run the auction again. The prices skyrocket, illustrating that printing more currency actually devalues money. Like any game, the teachable moment is that purchasing power is dependent on the scarcity of money.

Conclusions and Takeaways

Game designers have theories and models about players just as teachers have about students. Bartle's Player Type Model is not just a fun discussion point with students, but also a way to gauge teacher-created projects and activities. Bartle warns not to expect his model to be one-size-fits-all; however, if it works, then great!

Many game designers have backgrounds in behavioral psychology. Teachers can integrate intrinsic rewards into lessons to keep students engaged. The flow channel should be the sweet spot for student learning. Another factor for engagement is fun, at least in hooking the student into learning. There are many modalities of fun, including *fiero*, relief from frustration, and social interactions. These theories all support cooperative group learning. In order to achieve some levels of fun, students need to fail and then quickly iterate.

Lesson Plan Ideas

Bartle Test: I have used multiple intelligence quizzes as an icebreaker activity. How about trying the Bartle Test? This is an icebreaker; no standards apply— http://4you2learn.com/bartle

Darfur Is Dying: Role-playing, running, and hiding are "fun" mechanics in this very serious game. Ask: Why do you think this game is so hard to play? Students can make the connections about struggling as a refugee in Darfur because the mechanics are perfectly aligned with the message. This can lead into a discussion of problems in modern African nations. Extending this globally, have students list current problems and try to create difficult mechanics that illustrate the message. Standards met are primarily for social studies— http://www.darfurisdying.com

Flappy Bird lesson on Code.org, which is a game that plays on frustration in the flow channel—https://studio.code.org/flappy/1

Game Theory Dilemma: Have students engage in argumentative writing using dilemmas such as the Prisoners' Dilemma. Start by showing the BrainPOP video on game theory. English language arts classes can write a play or short story describing the situation. Decision trees and mind maps should be used as a prewriting tool. Social studies can relate it to how cultural and economic interactions play out. Math can attempt to solve the problem using a matrix, as well as a decision tree. Probability outcomes can be analyzed, too. Science can look at the game as a simulation model with predicted results. Standards met include Common Core State Standards for mathematics.

Kriegspiel: A free digital download for Mac and PC from Alex Galloway of New York University—http://www.r-s-g.org/kriegspiel. This game can be used to meet social studies standards, including the Russo-Japanese War and World War I.

Games

Agar.io—http://agar.io

Jenova Chen's *flOw*, playable for free on a computer browser—http://interactive.usc.edu/projects/cloud/flowing

QWOP, a nearly impossible track and field game—http://www.foddy.net/Athletics.html

Resources

Richard Bartle's *Hearts, Clubs, Diamonds, Spades: Players Who Suit MUDs* (1996)—http://www.mud.co.uk/richard/hcds.htm

Richard Bartle on *Player Type Theory: Uses & Abuses*—https://youtu.be/ZIzLbE-93nc

4 Keys 2 Fun, a high-quality, full-color image; helpful when lesson planning—http://xeodesign.com/assets/images/4k2f.jpg

Flow, the Secret to Happiness, Mihaly Csikszentmihalyi's TED Talk—http://www.ted.com/talks/mihaly_csikszentmihalyi_on_flow

The Future of Work Is Play, Nicole Lazzaro's TEDx Talk—https://youtu.be/X_3KyV31iqg

Hypothes.is is a free playful and collaborative academic research tool. It is available as a Google Chrome Extension, thus enabling users to mark up documents right from a web browser—https://hypothes.is

B.F. Skinner discussing his "Teaching Machine," a Skinner Box for students—http://youtu.be/jTH3ob1IRFo

Playful Annotation with Hypothesis Studying Interactive Text (PAHSIT) is the research study led by Remi Kalir about annotation tools, specifically Hypothes.is—http://pahsit.com

A Theory of Fun, by Raph Koster—http://www.theoryoffun.com

XEODesign's research on games and emotions—http://xeodesign.com/whyweplaygames.html

· 4 ·

BALANCED DESIGN DIGITAL GAMES

Jordan Shapiro is the Senior Fellow at the Joan Ganz Cooney Center, a *Forbes* contributor on topics about global education, and an international thought leader on game-based learning. In late 2014, he coauthored the *MindShift Guide to Digital Games + Learning* (the free PDF download is linked at the end of this chapter). Most of Shapiro's work pertains to learning through digital play. Because of this, I asked him what teachers should look for in a good learning game. "Make sure the mechanics themselves—even the user interface itself—is the subject matter," he said, when we spoke in May 2016. "The game shouldn't be a platformer [like *Super Mario Bros.*] that has math problems. The game has to be an instrument of the subject you are talking about. It's not a game that rewards you for reading; it's a game that makes you understand how reading works."

Similarly, game-based learning scholar James Paul Gee told me in 2014 that he advocates "getting really beautiful games—where the content and mechanic are well married—into some sort of learning system." When bringing educational games to your classroom, look for balanced design. Balanced design are games "where the learning goals, game mechanics and judgments about learner play and performance are aligned" (Beall, Clarke-Midura, Groff, Owen, & Rosenheck, 2015, p. 7). What the student does in the game is what the teacher needs him or her to learn. Balanced design games are often single session, content delivery games. Students play a game that focuses on one curricular content strand, which can be played in a short time period. "The problem is that there are very few good content delivery games," Shapiro concluded.

This chapter features a "behind-the-scenes" look at the few good quality balanced games in the market. Teaching with balanced design games can personalize student instruction, teaching each child at his or her zone of proximal development through play. Because core mechanics with learning outcomes, this chapter concludes with game-based assessment models.

Avoiding Chocolate-Covered Broccoli

Free to play and aimed (pun intended!) at math classrooms, *Line Shoot* is part of the Sheppard Software's "Shoot Geometry" arcade series. To play, you shoot (by clicking the mouse) on a floating the line segment or vectors. Get 10 correct and you win! But what does shooting lines have to do with the properties of lines?

An unbalanced game is "chocolate-covered broccoli"—the mechanic doesn't fit the learning objective. They can be derivative in nature, with learning content sprinkled in. They may be engaging for a few minutes here and there, but not long term. In many "edutainment" games, the learning is presented as an obstacle for students to solve in order to progress. While seemingly educational, the actions one takes in *Line Game* have nothing or do with geometry. The mechanic of target shooting is literally interrupted with a question about identifying (lower order thinking in Bloom's Taxonomy, by the way) what a line segment is. *Line Game* is actually a simplified take on *Math Blaster*, a classic chocolate-covered broccoli game. *Math Blaster* plays like the arcade game *Space Invaders*—with math problems. Chocolate-covered broccoli turns the fun act of learning into something the student has to—rather than wants to—do. "The verbs have to match to an activity, and the activity is what you do in the game," Gee reiterated.

Core mechanics are "the essential play activity performed again and again in a game" (Salen & Zimmerman, 2003, p. 316). In baseball, core mechanics include hitting, running, throwing, and catching. In *Angry Birds*, the mechanic of angles occurs when a player's finger pulls back on the slingshot. Eating dots is the mechanic in *Pac-Man*. Core mechanics includes "anything a player can do in a game, such as moving, jumping, shooting, fighting, or driving" (Dunniway & Novak, 2007, p. 5). Other core mechanics are judging, arguing, voting, trading, guessing, contending with time constraints, and engaging in role-play simulation.

In a balanced design game, when you master the core mechanics, you master the learning goal it is trying to teach. One example is *The Land of Venn: Geometric Defense*. The game's strategy is to defend a tower from hordes of oncoming invaders, which look like points floating in space, approaching the tower. The core mechanic of drawing points, lines, and shapes directly correlates with the game's goal.

Tapping the points on the tablet's screen, and then drawing lines between them, connects points to make lines and shapes. When my son was four years old, I observed him connecting three points to draw open shapes and isosceles triangles. Through actions of play, or core mechanics, players gain an understanding of the properties and characteristics of shapes. His experience playing *The Land of Venn* added meaning to abstract geometric concepts.

DragonBox

Like *The Land of Venn*, *DragonBox Algebra 5+* is a balanced design game. The goal is to drag cards from one box to another, thus isolating one of the cards. Some of the images are called *night-cards*, which represent negative integers (*day-cards* represent positive integers). An additional rule is introduced in a subsequent level: adding cards into one side of the box means that the same card must be added to the other side. Eventually, all of the night-cards and day-cards are replaced with letters, such as -c or x, representing unknown variables or numbers.

The Common Core State Standards for algebraic thinking begin at grade 1; solving linear equations is a grade 8 standard ("Common Core," 2015). Designed for children in kindergarten, "83% of children learn the basics of algebra in an hour" after playing the game ("We Want To Know," 2016). Rather than explaining algebraic concepts, players of *DragonBox Algebra 5+* simply have the opportunity to engage and play with the material (Toppo, 2015).

Gee (2013) praised *DragonBox Algebra 5+* as one of his "favorite" educational games because it shows "some of the core 'game mechanics' behind algebra" (para. 7). He discussed the balanced game mechanics and learning goals of *DragonBox Algebra 5+* in an interview with Patrick Miller, the Game Developer Conference's Director of Online Community. Gee (2013) stated:

> The game mechanic is centered on cancelling and balancing the images on two sides of a box. The game mechanic is integral to the content (balancing equations) and brings out some deep and aesthetic properties of the rules by which algebra manipulates equations. In fact, it is not until the middle of the game that players realize they are doing algebra. (para. 14)

Core mechanics, like Bloom's Taxonomy of Higher Order Thinking, are designed using action verbs. Gee explained the "design grammar" of core mechanics to me in 2014. "Games are built on verbs, not nouns," he said. "That's what a game mechanic is, depending on the action you take." In a game, you are doing something. You are taking an action that has consequences to the system and to other players. He continued:

> The power of a game is matching the mechanic to the content. When you get a beautiful mechanic that fits perfectly with the problems you are solving, it's genius. A good example is *DragonBox*. It's teaching algebra, and the mechanic is balance and the content is solving equations. It fits perfectly. It's not a matter of picking the perfect mechanics. It's how do we get really good marriages between the mechanic and the problem solving set. That's an art.

DragonBox Numbers (2015) is a game to teach children about number sense, the abstract concept of associating numerical symbols with mathematical values. I spoke with Jean-Baptiste Huynh, DragonBox's founder and designer, in October 2015. He explained how *DragonBox Numbers* was "inspired by Cuisenaire and Montessori rods," which are hands-on mathematical manipulatives. In the game, young children interact with "nooms"—colorful cartoonish characters of differing lengths—that can be combined together or sliced apart, thus illustrating the actions of addition or subtraction. Players "explore patterns" about how numbers fit together.

Huynh is a former teacher who envisions teachers using his games in class by "working from behind students," facilitating knowledge transfer after experiential play. "Students should play the game first; then the teacher should gather the students and talk about the experience," he said. Here, the role of teachers would be "to create that moment where students want to share their experience." When my son plays *DragonBox Numbers* he sometimes draws pictures of the noom characters, labeled with accompanying numbers. I asked Jordan Shapiro about knowledge transfer from games. He said:

The hard part with content delivery things is transferability. My kids are masters of DragonBox; they've been playing it for a long time. But does that mean they can do algebra on paper? Can they transfer the skills out of DragonBox? Most of the evidence is that transferability has been poor so far—unless there is a teacher there. In that case, what's the point? Then games are great, but it becomes a novelty.

DragonBox's value becomes apparent after the teacher facilitates transfer. "We, as a nation, already know how to teach math," he continued. "The math issues in this county are socioeconomic. Rich kids have been learning math for a century excellently without any computers. We're not solving the problem of better quality math teaching. We're trying to figure out how to get more quality math teaching to more people." High quality math content delivery games like DragonBox, when paired with an excellent teacher, can bring equity to math education.

Filament Games

Filament Games is a Madison, Wisconsin-based development studio with a simple design philosophy: Learning itself is a fun act (unofficially, its motto is to make learning games "that don't suck"). If you master a Filament game, then you show mastery of the content it delivered. An example of Filament's approach is *Backyard Engineers*. It uses a catapult mechanic similar to *Angry Birds*. General education students who played Filament Games's Next Generation Science Standards-aligned game, *Backyard Engineers* showed a 20.9% increase in posttest scores ($n = 47$; "Backyard Engineers," 2015).

Filament Games co-founder and chief executive officer Dan White has a deep connection with the games and learning space. I first spoke with him in January 2014 to learn more about his and his company's philosophy (we have spoken regularly at game-based learning conferences, including Games for Change and Serious Play). White's journey began as an undergraduate student at Cornell University. He used a National Science Foundation grant to create an online virtual museum. The project was called *Active World*. "It was very primitive compared to *Second Life*," he said. *Active World* was initially playtested with the local 4H and Boys & Girls Clubs. White recalled, "I was taken with how kids engaged with it, even though [it was] primitive." After the project, White earned his master's degree in educational technology. Kurt Squire was one of his advisors; James Paul Gee funded the project. He then parlayed his project-based thesis into a prototype of an ocean science game.

Filament Games came next. "Game technology should be authentic, constructivist, inquiry-based—not flash card–based—because learning is inherently fun," White explained. "Don't take something that sucks and sugarcoat it with sparkles." His philosophy lets players "inhabit new identities and interact with systems, to learn the subject matter." White wants to move education to constructivist, project-based learning. Filament's games, therefore, are authentic spaces of learning.

In *Gamasutra*, a game industry magazine, White compared the process of getting games into schools to the rigors of rock climbing (White, 2014). Games get created, and then rewritten to integrate teaching styles, the Common Core State Standards, and other modifications (2014). These demands can distract from the designed core mechanic (2014). White proposed playtesting with teachers to bring the end users into the process (2014). Filament tests its games teachers and students in the design phase.

Filament uses several metrics for measuring a game's success, including user downloads and industry recognition. iCivics games have had millions of plays. This indicates that teachers derive value from its games. *Reach for Sun* was a critical hit, winning the Best Gameplay award at Games for Change in 2013. It is a life science game that puts the player in the role of a growing plant. The mechanic is systems thinking: Balance the plant's life cycle system to win. Overall, Filament uses five metrics to measure learning outcomes. Rather than a pre- and posttest, each are constantly checked during gameplay. The learning metrics used by Filament are:

1. Elegant Design
2. Adaptive Difficulty
3. Multi-part Problems
4. Big Data
5. Emergent Gameplay (Calendar, 2016)

Including teachers in the design phase generates useful feedback. The result is a better product. There is an advisory panel comprised of half a dozen teachers. Filament has teachers in residence and a learning specialist, too. Carry Ray-Hill, a former classroom teacher, is the resident educator from iCivics at Filament. In 2015, she assisted the designers in updating political topics in *Win the White House* to be more relevant for the 2016 presidential election. Most of its civics-themed games can be found on the iCivics platform, covered in the following chapter.

Filament Games also develops science games for textbook giant McGraw-Hill. Rather than gamifying an entire STEM curriculum, Filament focused on a few single content strands. One such game is *Pinball Energy Challenge* (2015). To play, students align objects and then fire off a virtual pinball. The resulting physics—kinetic energy, for example—are recorded on a bar graph on the side of the screen. White demonstrated the difficulty of the game at the 2016 Serious Play Conference. Hard to master, students iterate on hypothesized solutions over and over.

Along with her close friend Peggy Sheehy, Marianne Malmstrom was a Filament teacher fellow in 2015. She recalled the experience, when we spoke in April 2016. "That was really, really interesting," Malmstrom recalled. "I was surprised they entertained me as a fellow because I've been outspoken against educational games." Malmstrom put her opinions aside as she learned from the Filament team. "I thought it would be interesting working for three months for a studio that made educational games," she said. She now counts Filament, along with BrainPOP, as one of the few educational gaming companies she respects. She continued:

> They are really trying to figure it out. Filament wants to be a really good game company, to make more than just shoot 'em up games. They want to make games that help people learn. For me, it was good to be in that environment. They brought Peggy and me in to push their envelope and have more diverse voices. The young people at Filament work so hard. The schedule was intense. As a teacher who uses games and teaches game design, I loved seeing the process.

In the summer of 2015, Filament moved to a new studio in downtown Madison. Filament has hosted open house events that coincided with the Games + Learning + Society Conference, formerly held nearby at the University of Wisconsin-Madison. It is evident that Filament is passionate, with a goal to bring high quality learning experiences to students. For more on Filament's games, follow the links at the end of this chapter.

Wuzzit Trouble

Wuzzit Trouble, designed by California-based BrainQuake, has a natural, learner-friendly interface that breaks the symbol barrier of mathematics. To play, children turn clock-like gears with the goal of releasing cute Wuzzit creatures that are trapped inside. The game "invites players to pick a series of locks by spinning little number dials that add, subtract, or multiply increasingly complex number combinations, all without any of the calculation symbols present in math exercises" (Toppo, 2015, p. 87). And like DragonBox's games, math is never discussed; you simply play with the rules. "Our point of departure was that the real problem is math's interface—its symbols and syntax, the symbol barrier," BrainQuake's co-founder Randy Weiner explained to me in early 2016.

After children play, teachers can choose to discuss solutions with students. "We didn't want this to be an excellent product that was impossible to use in the classroom," Weiner stated. "*Wuzzit* can fit into many different ways of teaching. It's simply a matter of practice." It can be assigned at home, used in a station rotation, assigned as individual work, or in a whole class lesson.

Wuzzit Trouble is BrainQuake's signature game and Weiner has been involved in education and technology for his entire career. About five years ago, he co-founded the Urban Montessori Charter School in Oakland, California. "We serve a population as diverse as Oakland," he stated. Weiner served as chairperson on the board of directors until the time when BrainQuake was founded.

Increased student engagement is one of the promises of game-based learning; however, increased engagement does not necessarily correlate with an increase in learning outcomes. And with games, engagement does not imply learning. Tapping to uncover hidden objects on a tablet's screen may be engaging, but it is not necessarily educational. Using an adaptive learning engine can remediate that. The engine can apply data analytics and then adjust the puzzle challenges to suit the needs of the learner. As a result, BrainQuake launched an adaptive learning engine, which was built using Small Business Innovation Research (SBIR) grant-awarded funds. This version adapts challenges to meet the player's zone of proximal development. Weiner explained:

> The adaptive engine represents a lot of changes to the app, at least under the hood. We certainly know from doing work with our adaptive engine that we could absolutely engage children with puzzles that are way beyond their ZPD [zone of proximal development]. They [children] were happy playing these puzzles; they did not want to stop. They chose to play these puzzles outside their ZPD, which is virtually unheard of in math. We measure time on task and see how that time is being spent on inefficient solution paths. This demonstrates that the child has no idea what they are doing. Our adaptive engine takes this into account.

BrainQuake's marketing approach is similar to Netflix—*Wuzzit Trouble* can be played on iOS, Chromebook, the Web, Kindle, and Windows. It can be accessed on platforms, like GlassLab's portal, as well as BrainPOP and Brain-POP, Jr. *Wuzzit* is literally everywhere! I recommend getting it for your smart-phone and playing yourself, for fun. Yes, play a math puzzle game for fun!

Schell Games

Shortly after the first edition of this book was published, I received an e-mail from Jesse Schell. He sent along images of his writings from a school newspa-per, *The Valleyviewer*, and a picture of him wearing a Valleyview Vikings hat. As it turned out, he was looking at the back cover of my book and discov-ered that I teach at Valleyview Middle School, in Denville, New Jersey—his alma mater! Schell learned to program the BASIC computer language on a Radio Shack TRS-80 (affectionately nicknamed the Trash-80 by many) in our school's computer lab (the computers have been since updated!). His computer teacher at the time later became our building principal. And he was the principal who hired me to be a social studies teacher, back in 2008, based on my educational technology background. (The principal, who has since retired, remembered having Schell as a student. In 2015, I reunited them via e-mail.)

In the summer of 2015, along with my family, I visited Schell Games's stu-dio on the Pittsburgh, Pennsylvania riverfront. The company hosted an open house for participants of that summer's Serious Play Conference. My family attended, and our son was thrilled! He played several games, including the systems thinking puzzle game *Water Bears*. The goal is to combine PVC-style pipe connectors to shower microscopic water bears with water. Unlike the iPad version he plays at home, he used an HTC Vive virtual reality headset, literally putting him in the game's world.

Schell Games has a diverse portfolio, beyond educational titles. The team designed Disney's Toy Story Mania ride, as well as attractions at other theme parks. (Jesse Schell had once been a Disney Imagineer). It released *Daniel Tiger's Stop & Go Potty* app for PBS Kids, as well as *The World of Lexica*, a suite of interconnected English language arts games playable on tablets. In *Lexica*, there are quests in which students can interact with characters from their favorite books. Designed by Schell Games and published by Thames & Cosmos, *Happy Atoms* is a hands-on kit of interlocking, molecules that can be scanned with a mobile app. Players can experiment with molecules combi-nations and then use a tablet to see the results. A child in grade 5 can piece together two hydrogen molecules with an oxygen, hold the tablet camera to it, and view the model become water on the device's screen.

Jesse Schell is also a professor of entertainment technology at nearby Carnegie Mellon University. He was always interested in games and entertainment. He began at the Walt Disney Company's virtual reality studio (hence his continued affinity for virtual reality; in 2016, he led keynote talks on the topic at Games for Change and the Serious Play Conference). Schell moved up the ranks at Disney from computer programmer to Creative Director. Then he came to Carnegie Mellon, drafted by fellow Disney employee Randy Pausch (famous to many for his memoir and video *The Last Lecture*. Pausch's Carnegie Mellon team created the digital animation tool *Alice*). "Randy Pausch and I started working at Disney in '95," Schell recalled, when we spoke in March 2014. "We stayed in touch and he brought me to Carnegie Mellon. I teach his classes now."

Jesse Schell's textbook *The Art of Game Design: A Book of Lenses* is now in its second edition. It is widely adopted in game design courses. There is also an accompanying mobile app, called *A Deck of Lenses*, which is worth checking out (it's free and linked at the end of this chapter). The deck in the app is useful to me when I want to bring game mechanics to everyday teaching.

Entertainment can fit into an educational setting. "All entertainment works when it has found a way to make you care about something," Schell said. "Education is the same way. You've got to find a way to make people care. If I don't care about doing these math problems, some fake thing about saving the princess may not work." Check out the entertaining, educational games from Schell Games at the conclusion of this chapter. They are all high quality, balanced games that are also very fun to play.

Words with Friends EDU

Words with Friends EDU is the first project Zynga.org has been a lead developer on. It is free and web-based. Zynga.org is the nonprofit part of Zynga, the maker of casual social games, like *Farmville*, *Draw Something*, and, of course, *Words with Friends*. My students playtested *Words with Friends EDU* during the 2015–16 school year. I spoke with Abby Speight, Zynga.org's Senior Product Manager in April 2016. We talked regularly during the playtest period of *Words with Friends EDU*.

Like *Scrabble*, there is a clear pedagogy associated with *Words with Friends*. It is inherently educational. "A lot of the interest came from players, many of which were parents and teachers," Speight said. "We heard anecdotally that it could have a great benefit in a classroom, and it had a lot of educational potential." Speight pointed to past studies about playing the *Scrabble* led to positive cognitive outcomes. "There was an opportunity to reimagine the game by adding kid friendly features to further unlock the educational potential."

The whole user interface of *Words with Friends EDU* looks and feels like the commercial version; however, it was made to be more kid-friendly. Students can design their own avatars and can unlock badges as they keep playing. Another added feature is a system of incentives that rewards students for playing "high value academic words," what the game calls "Power Words." The Power Words list was added so students could bring meaning to the words played in the game. "Those are words that help students succeed in school," Speight said. "They show up in places like assessments and textbooks." To that end, Zynga.org partnered with Dictionary.com. "The dictionary part is a bigger part of *Words with Friends EDU* than its commercial counterpart," she continued. "Players earn bonus points if they know the meaning of a word."

GlassLab Games built the teacher dashboard and classroom management tool. Teachers can then administrate their students' account, and check on what each student is learning. Zynga.org also partnered with WestEd, an educational research firm, to develop the Power Word list and lesson plans. The beta-test teachers also worked on lesson plans. "Lesson plans focus on helping teachers easily get this into their curriculum, to get the most out of the learning potential of the game right away," Speight said.

Because it is a turn-based game, it is possible for students to play throughout the school day—and even afterward. My students were playing as many as six games at once! The casual game can turn any down time in a school day into a pocket for game-based learning. Speight told me that the average play session Zynga.org observed was between 10 and 20 minutes. In fact, a parent could play along too. Theoretically, a parent could create an account and play with his or her child while at work, at home, or even in line at the grocery store.

Game-Based Assessments

Because digital games are incredibly adept at providing data, their usefulness as an assessment tool becomes increasingly apparent. The physics sandbox

Newton's Playground included "stealth assessments" embedded into its code. I contacted Val Shute, cocreator of *Newton's Playground* and author of the concept of stealth assessments in February 2014. She explained that the purpose is to blur the distinction between learning and assessment. Unlike a pre- and posttest, with content delivery in the middle, players are assessed without a break in the action. Shute said:

> In a nutshell, stealth assessments are a methodology that uses evidence-centered design in order to bury the assessment deep into the code of the game. It determines what you want to capture and analyze, with a log file. It's automatic. At any time and at any grain size, I know how well you are doing. For example, creativity in general, or some aspect of creativity, like cognitive flexibility versus your divergent thinking. I know about all those things by virtue of what you are doing in the environment. Then I can pull out certain data from play to make meaning to certain constructs.

Digital game journalist and educator Jordan Shapiro looks to the day when games can deliver content practice, instruction, and assessment simultaneously. "Hopefully we can turn some of the mediocre teachers into great teachers, because the screens do some of the heavy lifting for them," he said, when we spoke in 2016. Good teachers conduct stealth assessments all the time, throughout a lesson. This is something Shapiro does when he teaches, adjusting delivery on the fly to meet student needs. "As a teacher myself, the biggest difference between the good teachers and the mediocre ones is the intuitive ability to do formative assessment while you're going through the classroom. While you teach you make a million assessments at every moment."

Illinois-based teacher Zack Gilbert spoke to me in May 2016 about how he uses game-based assessments. He teaches with games designed by Filament, as well as commercial off-the-shelf games, like *Civilization* and *Minecraft*. "Any assessment data I can get is useful," Gilbert said. "My job is to assess what students know. I will use whatever tool I can, which could be a game. I think teacher dashboards can give us some insight at certain times."

Gilbert started using Filament's teacher dashboard because it led his students to discussions. He also uses topics in the nation-building game *Civilization* for discussions. Formative assessment data becomes a talking point to have with students. "The game gives you a score and I ask kids what does that mean? Then I ask, well let's look into that. And then we look at the reports."

In games, failure presents a chance to iterate, to experiment, and try again. When Gilbert's students play the Charlemagne scenario in *Civilization IV*, he knows they will fail at first. "They play it and are failing, and it's tough," he said. "The farther you go, the more you learn, and then you make adjustments. It's that process. What decisions did they make? If they play it a second time, why did you change? The process of looking at it is meaningful."

When playing *SimCityEDU: Pollution Challenge!*, my students discovered that certain businesses tend to catch fire more frequently than others. For fun, some zone for fire-prone industries near each other just to experiment and see what happens. Because my learning goal is systems thinking, I am fine with this. After all, there is a feedback loop at work, even when the result is failure.

Teachers who teach with educational games can track learning gains from games via dashboard features populated with their students. They may also use traditional formative tools, such as graphic organizers or quizzes, written to assess learning from games (Fishman, Plass, Riconscente, Snider, & Tsai, 2014b, p. 5). The Analyzing Games for Assessment in Math, ELA/Social Studies, and Science (A-GAMES) Study reported on how teachers use the assessment reports in balanced design digital games, like the ones described earlier in this chapter. Its case study survey looked at "how teachers understand and make use of game features that support formative assessment" (Fishman, Plass, Riconscente, Snider, & Tsai, 2014a, p. 3). Grades 5–8 teachers in New York City ($n = 30$) indicated that teachers could not easily identify a link from the rewards in the system of the game to learning goals (Fishman et al., 2014b).

The A-GAMES Study surveyed teachers in 2013. They were asked why they used games, and how they measured students' learning from play ($n = 488$). Teachers of K12 students were included in the study. There was a relationship between how teachers use games and the formative assessments provided from the game (Fishman et al., 2014a). Specifically, Fishman et al. (2014a) found the following:

1. Game use is related to how teachers conduct formative assessment.
2. Game use is related to how teachers use formative assessment information.
3. Game use is related to the barriers teachers report to conducting formative assessment. (pp. 5–6)

I spoke with Barry Fishman in March 2016 about the findings. He is a professor at the University of Michigan, and was one of the A-GAMES Study's coauthors. He said, "There's a general desire for people to get answers to questions like: Are games good for formative assessments? What are the best ways to do formative assessments with games? But those aren't the right questions to ask. The answer is almost always: It depends."

This led the research team to conduct an exploratory study. They next formed a partnership with BrainPOP to study games that were easily accessible and usable in classrooms. One part was a survey that tried to "get a handle of what the backdrop was." As it happened, at that time the Joan Ganz Cooney Center was also conducting a survey, similar in nature: the Level Up Learning Report. Both research teams decided to collaborate, contributing demographic and population questions. "It was encouraging that the findings synced up," Fishman recalled.

For Fishman, the number one takeaway from A-GAMES was that games "have potential, but they're really handicapped in some ways." He cited the lack of communication between game designers and the teachers who use games. He also pointed to the lack of coordination across game designers. "In particular we focused on the games you find on BrainPOP," he said. "It's curated—BrainPOP has already done the legwork to see if it [the game] meets learning goals. If students play it, then students will learn the thing that the game purports to teach. It's much better than a Google search for a game on a particular topic."

Most games have a scoring system to indicate progress in the game. Obviously that progress will tell you how you're doing in the game, which should be related to telling you what you're learning in the game. "But there was just something missing that would have made it super useful," Fishman said. "Teachers were put in the position of putting in a lot of workarounds that were local to their particular assessment needs." The A-GAMES study did show promise in the features that were embedded into the games as formative assessments. Fishman continued:

> Very few games translate that progress into learning outcomes that are translatable to instructional goals. What does 85 points and two stars [earned in a game] worth? What does being on level 7 mean? In general that was a limitation. The second problem is that the score isn't always stored anywhere. At the end of a level, unless the teacher was looking over that kid's shoulder, there was no way of knowing how he or she was progressing.

There are competing models about how to assess learning outcomes from games. One is to use qualitative data, asking students to write about and explain what they did in the game. BrainPOP's SnapThought tool is useful in this regard. It enables students to screenshot where they are in the game and then write a response, which can be sent to the teacher. Fishman explained how the innovation of using SnapThought emanated from BrainPOP, not the games' designers on its platform. "We argue the value of aggregators like BrainPOP," he continued. "It creates a tool like SnapThought that works across multiple games. BrainPOP needed cooperation from game designers to do that."

GlassLab has been attempting to think about what it looks like from a teachers' perspective, and it works with multiple games. "You don't use 120 different gradebooks," Fishman said. "You want the dashboard you use for any game you use in classrooms." In fact, GlassLab built evidence-centered design assessments into *SimCityEDU: Pollution Challenge!* It seamlessly measures student mastery of systems thinking tasks. This style of assessment differs from chocolate-covered broccoli, which measures responses after play, by adding in problems and puzzles. Evidence-centered design is measured during the game, gathering data from player choices. GlassLab partnered with the Educational Testing Service to utilize the evidence-centered design assessment approach formalized by Robert Mislevy, Linda Steinberg, and Russell Almond in the late 1990s. This technique works "well for skills, competencies, and attributes that are difficult to assess" (DeBarger, Dornsife, Rosier, Shechtman, & Yarnall, 2013).

After each student plays a mission in *SimCityEDU*, the teacher receives data based on evidence collected pertaining to successes and challenges in the virtual city. These are "actionable analytics" provided by the dashboard. Fishman noted that to have value to the teacher, actionable analytics should be based on progress, and then inform what the learner should do next. The dashboard should recommend an intervention. The technology to do that is not quite here.

There needs to be a standard about what data are coming from games. "After all, teachers aren't trained data scientists," Fishman said. "But they do need data to make decisions." Regarding personalized learning, the dashboard needs to do the background work for the teacher. Dashboards need to show a teacher who is struggling, and, more specifically, who is struggling in the same ways. Then that student can be grouped with others so they can learn in different ways. "That's what we need dashboards to do and we're nowhere near that yet," Fishman concluded.

Conclusions and Takeaways

Mechanics must match the learning objective to be most effective. When successful, a game's mechanic can become the message, driving home content. Students should also understand game mechanics as a form of literacy, in the same way they are taught to deconstruct novels. Teachers should borrow mechanics and match them with learning objectives. Developer websites are an excellent resource for learning games, research, and lesson plans. There is a renaissance in educational game design, with a lot of developers trying to create truly innovative experiences.

Lesson Plan Ideas

DragonBox educator plans—http://dragonbox.com/educators

Planet Mechanic curriculum, tied to the Filament-produced game—https://www.filamentgames.com/teacher-guides/teacher-guide-planet-mechanic

Water Bears lesson plans and teacher dashboard—https://www.glasslabgames.org/games/WPLUS

Words with Friends EDU lesson plans—https://wordswithfriendsedu.com/instructors

Wuzzit Trouble lesson plans and teacher dashboard—https://www.glasslabgames.org/games/WT

Games

Daniel Tiger's Stop & Go Potty app, published by PBS Kids, designed by Schell Games—http://pbskids.org/apps/daniel-tigers-stop--go-potty.html

DragonBox—http://dragonbox.com

Filament Games can be purchased with single use licenses in 1:1 classrooms, or with fewer accounts in a learning center, which would fit a station rotation activity—https://www.filamentlearning.com/products#all

Happy Atoms, from Schell Games, which blends physical molecular models with an augmented reality tablet app. It also has a *Pokémon* "gotta catch 'em all" mechanic, to challenge players to collect matter—http://www.happyatoms.com

The Land of Venn: Numeric Storms—https://appsto.re/i6YW3BH

Pinball Energy Challenge is a science game published McGraw-Hill School Education Group, and developed by Filament Games—https://appsto.re/us/VIBL9.i

Science-themed card games with balance mechanics. Build DNA strands and link ions, molecules, and proteins using decks of cards—http://gotgenius-games.com

ST Math—http://www.mindresearch.org/stmath

That's Your Right, a free, digital multiplayer Bill of Rights card game, which is hosted on the Annenberg Classroom—http://www.annenbergclassroom.org/page/thats-your-right

Twelve a Dozen mobile math game, which is balanced in design—http://www.bossastudios.com/games/twelve

Words with Friends EDU—https://wordswithfriendsedu.com

Resources

Abby's Wish, the moving story of a girl whose Make-a-Wish was to be in a video game. Filament Games and McGraw-Hill Education helped grant that wish—http://www.mheducation.com/prek-12/explore/abbys-wish.html

Alice, from Carnegie Mellon University, teaches coding in a 3D virtual environment—http://www.alice.org

The Art of Game Design: a Deck of Lenses app—https://appsto.re/i6Yc7bC

Better Learning in Games: A Balanced Design Lens for a New Generation of learning Games—http://education.mit.edu/wp-content/uploads/2015/07/Balanced-DesignGuide2015.pdf

Peggy Sheehy's blog post about being a teacher fellow at Filament—https://www.filamentgames.com/blog/getting-schooled-filament-games

Filament Games—https://www.filamentgames.com

MindShift Guide to Digital Games + Learning—http://www.kqed.org/assets/pdf/
news/MindShift-GuidetoDigitalGamesandLearning.pdf

Schell Games—http://www.schellgames.com

Water Bears—http://waterbearsgame.com

Words with Friends EDU field study showing increased learning outcomes—
https://wordswithfriendsedu.com/assets/WWF_EDU_Field_Study.pdf

· 5 ·

PLATFORMS WITH LEARNING GAMES

Apple's App Store and Android apps on Google Play offer digital distribution; however, the categories of games can be overwhelming and confusing. A search for "math" in the App Store may yield chocolate-covered broccoli games, as well as rote flashcard apps right next to the innovative games like *DragonBox Algebra 5+*. It is daunting to aggregate good digital games for your students.

Solutions are emerging, including learning game platforms. They vet games for classroom use, have a single student login for multiple games, include lesson plan ideas, and report analytics on learning outcomes. This chapter includes a review of three leading platforms for learning games—BrainPOP, iCivics, and GlassLab Games—as well as conversations with the creative minds working from behind the scenes.

BrainPOP and The Meaning of Beep

Many of the games in this book are playable on BrainPOP's GameUp platform. The first time I visited the New York City headquarters was back in May 2014, along with my then 3-year-old son, Spencer. When we arrived in the lobby he complained, "This isn't BrainPOP. This is an office!" It took some convincing to assure him that we were, in fact, at BrainPOP! Eventually, we were led into a game room, a kid-friendly space for my interview. As it happened, the company was hosting an office celebration that day: The 100th game had been added to GameUp.

BrainPOP is a well-respected brand for teachers and parents. Started in 1999 by pediatrician Avraham Kadar, it is now in about 20% of American schools. The first video was created to help Dr. Kadar explain asthma to his young patients. Now BrainPOP has more than 1,000 short, educational videos featuring Moby, the beeping robot, and Tim. BrainPOP, Jr., the early elementary portal, features Moby and Annie. Late 2015 saw the redesign of the main website, which gave the same user experience (UX) on a mobile browser as on a computer. And early 2017 brought the same UX to BrainPOP, Jr.— including the mobile-friendly "write about it" and "draw about it" assessment features, as well as a wordplay game.

In 2014, I first met with Karina Linch, Senior Vice President of Product Management, Allisyn Levy, Vice President of GameUp, Scott Price, the Games and Education Project Manager and Katya Hott, the UX Researcher. Hott visits classrooms (including mine in 2014) to see how BrainPOP and BrainPOP, Jr. is used in the field. Hott and Price formerly worked at E-Line Media developing *Gamestar Mechanic*. BrainPOP designs for the classroom experiences; the team is cognizant that play occurs while there are other students physically located in a room.

Since this meeting, I have become a Certified BrainPOP Educator (see link at the Resources at the end of the chapter to learn how to become a Certified BrainPOP Educator yourself!). I have also worked on the Moveable Game Jam initiative with Kevin Miklasz, the Director of Data and Assessment. And, in early 2017, BrainPOP added a Make-a-Movie authoring tool. Students can now write their own letters to Tim and Moby, and then add BrainPOP art, narration, and animation. This adds a fun layer of content creation to the website.

The game room at BrainPOP is filled with hand-drawn pictures of Tim, Annie, and Moby that kids mail in. Many of these letters are answered in the animated videos. During our 2014 meeting, I discovered that Linch— who oversaw the launch of BrainPOP, Jr.—was also the voice of Annie in the Moby videos. She brought my son and I into the booth where all of the videos are recorded. While there, we screamed at the top of our lungs; after all, it was soundproof! In the animations, Moby has no voice, just a series of beeps. His background remains a mystery. Maybe he is an alien? Maybe he is

Figure 1. The character of Moby the robot is also a trademark of BrainPOP. ©2014 BrainPOP and/or its related companies. All rights reserved. Reprinted by permission.

just a robot? Linch explained that the original Moby videos, from about 15 years ago, were shorter in length due to the limited bandwidth schools had at that time. As a result, Tim, voiced by Creative Director Mike Watanabe, who started at BrainPOP when it launched in 1999, had to speak very fast. Moby's beeps were also a result of technical limitations; it used to be challenging to have multiple speaking characters in streaming videos. When technology improved, the team rerecorded Tim's dialogue and redid the accompanying quizzes. Interestingly, Moby still beeps. It turned out that children guess and infer his dialogue based on the pauses and perceived social cues. In 2016, these mysterious beeps became part of a guessing game developed by Brain-POP called *The Meaning of Beep!*

BrainPOP is fulfilling the need for a one-stop source for games, videos, teacher support, and ease of use. The dedicated digital game platform, GameUp, launched in 2011, is a collection of vetted learning games. You can play games related to science, math, social studies, health, English language arts, and technology. One of the "rules" with GameUp is that it has to be extremely easy for a teacher to implement—no downloads or installations required. Of course, this limits the games it can add. Nonetheless, it provides a trusted portal for teachers to sample learning games. BrainPOP includes research and lesson plan suggestions with games.

When you play a game on BrainPOP, you see connected topics on the bottom of the page. The idea is for teachers and students—who may be driven crazy with standardized assessments—to see where a game fits into the scheme of the class. It makes recommendations for related games within the Brain-POP "Educator" login and "Lesson Plan" pages. BrainPOP doesn't tell teachers what to do or how to implement the games. In the end, it is still the teacher's role to contextualize the games. Best practices and research are also freely available. The opinion is that teachers want to know the best ways to implement games, and prefer not to be told what to do.

Unlike teacher dashboards for games that provide quantitative analytics, BrainPOP's games have a qualitative reflection tool, called SnapThought, as its game-based formative assessment. Students can take a screenshot of gameplay and answer a question about why they made certain decisions. An example of a self-reflection question relating to a game could be: What's one method you used to solve that problem? The games also feature a quiz about what was learned, and lesson plan ideas for implementation, all aligned to Common Core State Standards.

Playful Assessments

According to a 2016 webinar led by Kevin Miklasz, the goal of an assessment is to measure a student's ability on a task. This can depend on three things: 1) content knowledge; 2) grit or persistence; and 3) interest in a task. "Playful assessments" are continuous and seamless. As discussed at the end of Chapter 4, they go by different names, such as stealth assessments and evidence-centered design, "something between a game and a quiz." The learning and assessment happen at multiple points. This differs than the pre- and posttest assessment model, in which there is an intervention or event—like playing a game or reading a book—between testing. "Playful assessments have task specific content that tends to be fun," Miklasz said. "Fun sparks interest to keep going and persist on a task so students do their best. Playful assessments give students agency, multiple ways to play and to be simultaneously assessed."

One playful assessment is *Make-a-Map,* a concept mapping tool created for BrainPOP by Ideaphora. Students can make "nodes" about its Moby movies. Nodes have a play button with an accompanying BrainPOP movie clip.

Make-a-Map is open-ended; each constructed knowledge map is different. In May 2016, templates for *Make-a-Map* were added, giving a predefined structure for students to use. When my students make BrainPOP-related concept maps, I also ask them to also include a short reflection about why their maps look the way they do.

Sortify is another playful assessment. To play, students choose a topic, label bins or baskets, and then sort out image-adorned icons to where they belong. It looks like a game: there is a score and points with each bin. And it feels game-like. When my students sorted the American Revolution and the Constitution, they click "Submit to teacher," and I was able to instantly review how each student performed on my teacher dashboard. Other topics include parts of speech, the Constitution, natural resources, and musical instruments. The assessments are stealth, or invisible. Submitting the bin is the feedback, not quite a traditional graded assessment. Because it is playful, there is a replay button, which enables students to persist. There is also a downloadable document for students to create and play their own paper-based versions.

In 2014, Scott Price and Katya Hott tested a timeline history game with my students. One of my class periods played the paper-based version, which featured a blank timeline and cards with historical events. The other period played a digital mock-up. One of the playtest feedback questions asked students to name the game. One of my students suggested Time Zone. When released in fall 2015, BrainPOP took his or her (it was an anonymous form) advice, naming it *Time Zone X*. Tested as multiplayer, it has been scaled to be a single-player game. *Time Zone X* is about cause and effect, which challenges the player to contextualize what was happening in time when something occurred. I have students play *before* I start a unit, which enables them to playfully learn history through trial-and-error.

One of the newest playful assessment games is *The Meaning of Beep*, a context clue game. First designed in 2013 by the Institute of Play, it was a paper-based game played by students at the Quest to Learn school. BrainPOP's Michael Gi helped design the digital version, which was released in 2016. Like Hott and Price, Gi worked at E-Line Media, creating the game *Never Alone (Kisima Ingitchuna)* (described in Chapter 17).

To play *The Meaning of Beep*, you guess what word best fits Moby's beep. As Certified BrainPOP Educator, I had the opportunity to test the game's mechanics early on. The idea was to ask teachers about the grade-level appropriateness of vocabulary. Then, at the 13th Annual Games for Change Festival, I watched the Institute of Play's Brendan Trombley and BrainPOP's Scott

Price walk-through the finished game. Trombley explained how difficult it became to ensure that this was, in fact, a game, and not a vocabulary quiz. He helped develop the paper-based version played at Quest to Learn. Extensive playtesting in classrooms revealed how to word the sentences. At the Games for Change talk, Trombley advised the crowd, "Target a skill, and support it with content." Price then likened the mechanics to the board game *Wits & Wagers*—without the wagering and betting part.

The learning transfer at Quest to Learn occurred when students designed their own paper versions of the context clue game. As a result, printable materials are included on BrainPOP's page. *Meaning of Beep* not only represents a successful partnership between two game design studios—it also showed how an educational game could take advantage of the affordances of both paper and digital play.

"Mom, All of School Should Be Like iCivics"

Civics education has not been well treated by the standardized testing regime. Enter iCivics, which began back in 2009, launched by Sandra Day O'Connor, three years after she retired from the Supreme Court. The iCivics platform hosts 19 civics-themed video games, as well as paper-based activities and lesson plans. In a *USA TODAY* interview, O'Connor said that she does not consider the Supreme Court decisions she wrote to be her legacy. Instead, in the interview, she stated, "I consider engaging the next generations of citizens to be my most important work yet and my legacy" (Toppo, 2015).

Originally known as OurCourts, it was later rebranded as iCivics in 2010. "Sandra Day O'Connor certainly didn't know about video games," Louise Dubé explained. Dubé is iCivics' executive director; we spoke in April 2016. "iCivics started with her [O'Connor's] clerk, Julie O'Sullivan and her son Danny." Like most kids, Danny was a gamer and he was at the critical age at that time: middle school. "He showed Justice O'Connor how powerful this could be," Dubé said.

Danny's mother incubated the idea at Georgetown Law School. Before fully committing to the game-based learning route, the team explored lots of different approaches. Board member and game-based learning scholar James Paul Gee reached out to different university contacts for assistance with the project. "It takes a real unusual set of folks who care about learning for its own sake," Dubé said. It had to be easy enough for a "line teacher" to understand, and it needed to have sound pedagogy baked into the design. Dubé continued:

They went down many avenues where that didn't work out. Finally they hit upon Gee's students—Dan White, Dan Norton, and Alex Stone who founded Filament Games. They had the combination of being practical developers, they had a strong engineering background, and they had the commitment to get things done on time and on budget.

Carrie Ray-Hill, iCivics' Director of Content, is embedded in Filament's office in Madison, Wisconsin. Ray-Hill was originally a middle school social studies teacher and she is the instructional designer for its games. I asked Dubé about how iCivics and Filament work together. She explained:

> We start with the learning standard. That's our number one thing. If we're trying to teach about the separation of powers, we start with that. Then Carrie will do her magic and see how she would have taught that in her classroom. Then she asks how would the best teacher in the world teach it. From there she goes to the Filament team—the game designers, the artists—and they brainstorm different contexts and ideas about how it could work. It's an agile methodology.

Since launch, iCivics has done some remarkable things. "We have a lot of adoption without spending marketing dollars," Dubé said. "What made iCivics popular has been teachers talking to other teachers. We are now at 3 million users a year, which is only the registered kids we count—there's probably more." Dubé said the site now has over 110,000 registered educators, and it is used by about half of all middle school social studies teachers. Almost a quarter of all high school government and history teachers use it, too. "There has been an unbelievably rapid growth, particularly in the past three years, which shows no abatement," she continued.

Dubé started her career as a lawyer based in Canada, and then later in the United States. She also worked in educational technology in the mid-1990s, "back when laser discs were used in schools." The idea was to use innovative technology to get students interested in different ways, including using games, simulations, and virtual environments. She also led a few companies that developed speech recognition software to be personalized reading tutors, as well as simulations that modeled earth science and interspecies interactions. Dubé saw the power of putting children at the center of the learning. "They try different things, they fail quickly, and yet, just at the zone of proximal development, they end up learning," she said. While in Boston, Dubé took a job at WGBH, the local PBS affiliate.

The first time Dubé realized the power of iCivics was when her son played *Do I Have a Right?* in 2012, while in the 4th grade. "I had never heard of iCivics," Dubé recounted. "He came home from playing *Do I Have a Right?* and said, Mom, all of school should be like iCivics. I'd worked in ed tech for

20 years and never heard that before. I really started paying attention." (Dubé told this story at an ISTE Conference panel we were on, and it also appears in Asi Burak and Laura Parker's (2017) book, *Power Play: How Video Games Can Save the World*.) A Dubé's son is really into the elections now, "and he's not political—he's just into the world. It really translated beyond the game." In 2014, Dubé had the opportunity to be iCivics's executive director. Her unique combination of educational technology and legal skills to the organization was desirable to the nonprofit. Of course, she said yes!

One of my favorite iCivics's lessons is not digital at all. *Separation of Powers: What's for Lunch?* is a simulation about how a bill becomes a law. Students are divided into groups and play five rounds in which they create the school lunch menu. The simulation puts students in the roles of Lead Chef, Menu Writer, and Nutrition Inspectors. Each round is led with prompts and a timer on our interactive whiteboard. After the final round, I debrief to see who can connect the dots to how the U.S. government is structured: The Lead Chef is the Executive Branch, the Menu Writer is the Legislative Branch, and the Nutrition Inspectors are the Judicial Branch. Some students seem confused as to why they were planning lunch in social studies. After I debrief, they realize why, and the learning "sticks." When I shared this story with Dubé, she said:

> Isn't that awesome! I love that lesson. There's a lot to that. I don't really care if the game is on technology or not. The key is the learning path for the student. That they have a puzzle that they can actively have agency, learn and fail, and collaborate with other students. The key is not online or paper. We have over 130 lesson plans written, all of them active, to some degree.

Do I Have a Right? is one of iCivics's most successful games. It is a perennial favorite of my social studies students. It is one of the few learning games they voluntarily play again from home! The objective is to run a law firm and make decisions based on the Bill of Rights. Rather than learning disconnected facts, my students learned their rights through experiential play. My findings are, of course, purely anecdotal. When I shared my observations with Gee back in April 2014, he said, "When you're incorporating games into a curriculum, you are encouraging people to play the game multiple times, to think of different ways to do better, to play collaboratively." Gee is still on iCivics' advisory board and continues to play a role. "Playing it to beat it is fine initially, but again, we want those experiences in school to go over to kid's thinking of the game as a designed object," he continued. This is Gee's Design Principle, in which "learning about and coming to appreciate design and design principles is core to the learning experience" (2007, p. 221).

Figure 2. Start screen for *Win the White House.* © 2016 iCivics.

Win the White House is its newest game. Actually, it is an update, retooled for the contentious 2016 presidential election season. The goal, as the title implies, is to successfully campaign and be elected president. I wondered how real-world politics, which can be divisive at times, is accounted for in the game. "We have a set of values we code in that are predisposed to create a set of outcomes," Dubé said. The game dings the player if an inflammatory or disrespectful choice is selected toward their virtual opponent. iCivics is a nonpartisan organization. It does not espouse anyone's point of view; rather, it exists to let students discover and think for themselves. "iCivics is about understanding how the government and rule of law works, and understanding how the government can work for you," Dubé said. "I want to make sure that kids understand that they have power and should use it in the right way. I want kids to think about issues on their own. They have to be able to think critically."

How people argue is the teaching goal. "Whether left wing, or right wing, or in the middle, you should be able to have a reasonable conversation without it being inflamed and start insulting each other. We are trying to teach kids this and these are exactly the kinds of values that Sandra Day O'Connor supports as well." There remains a sense that civics education is being abandoned. The Common Core relegates social studies to be in the position of supporting English language arts. Everyone else is assessed and taken seriously, social studies is not." Dubé explained:

> The kinds of kids you want are the kinds of kids who have studied social studies. They are good at making connections, taking different sources and challenging evidence, being media literate, and are good at working with other people of serious issues. That's what we want as workers, and yet we're not paying attention to that. That, to me is a travesty.

Next up on iCivics' radar is to increase high school adoption. "Most of civic education is taught in high school," she said. While iCivics has a full curriculum for middle school, its goal is to reach every single child in America. "We can't do that without high school." The goal is to go from 3 to 10 million student users. Dubé continued:

> That requires us to have a full high school curriculum. We went out and asked teachers what they were looking for. Teachers responded that they needed a little extra content; mostly what they needed was more depth (compared to middle school). We use the same games, but have more lesson plans, which are activities. They have more reading and writing activities, like Drafting Board and DBQuest. DBQuest is small now, but it's a great source for primary source reading, which we want to expand.

Education is, of course, really complicated. Games and technology are not going to solve every problem. "The only magic bullet is the teacher, and a good one at that," Dubé said. Good technology can help balance out what we get without games, or without the good technology. "That's the real key behind gaming and technology—the fact that kids actually want to do this. That overcomes a lot of barriers; otherwise, you can't reach some kids."

At the International Society for Technology in Education (ISTE) Conference in 2016, Dubé, Benjamin Stokes (one of the founders of Games for Change, discussed in Chapter 16), and myself tool part in a panel titled, *Games & Learning: First Person Shooters vs. First Person Learning.* Greg Toppo, *USA TODAY*'s national education writer, was the moderator. In particular, we discussed how games are simple, yet effective learning tools to build engaged citizens.

GlassLab Games

The Games, Learning, and Assessment Lab, or GlassLab, was founded in 2012 with a $10.3 million grant from the Bill & Melinda Gates Foundation and the John D. and Catherine T. MacArthur Foundation in partnership with the Entertainment Software Association and Electronic Arts. GlassLab became an independent studio in July 2014, focused on developing the next generation of learning games to support the development of academic and 21st-century skills. Alongside their game development work, they also advanced game design concepts by studying the impact games have on improving student outcomes. In spring 2015, they launched the GlassLab Games platform to give game developers the tools they need to build better learning games, lower barriers for educators, and make outcomes visible.

GlassLab is located on the campus of Electronic Arts in Redwood Shores, California. GlassLab also partnered with Pearson and The Educational Testing Service, who created the evidence-centered design model that is built into its original-content games. This brought together known quantities in the education space to help with assessment and telemetry. The GlassLab platform includes a teacher dashboard for each game that provides feedback on learning outcomes. Electronic Arts was GlassLab's first partner on the *SimCityEDU* project. Take-Two Interactive Software, parent company of Firaxis, is its latest content partner, as it develops *CivilizationEDU*, to be released in the second half of 2017.

GlassLab has since evolved, and is expected to merge into a new entity in 2016: Collective Shift. I had been an early adopter of GlassLab's games and the rapid pace of their work was making my head spin! I wanted to make sure that GlassLab's platform for game-based assessments would continue to grow and thrive. I decided to contact Paula Escuadra, LRNG's Head of Content Partnerships, to learn more. I have known Escuadra since she led the GlassLab Teacher Network.

When Escuadra and I spoke in April 2016, LRNG's platform was still being tested. Currently, she has three primary responsibilities. One is to secure content partnerships for Collective Shift. The second is to lead the strategy and implementation of Collective Shift's overall games and interactives portfolio. Lastly, she leads one of the user testing and co-development sites that LRNG has formed to validate youth engagement, which will inform the overall design process on a local-to-national scale.

LRNG

LRNG emerged from the Digital Media and Learning (DML) project the MacArthur Foundation has been funding for the past decade—including GlassLab. Collective Shift, a 501(c) (3) nonprofit organization, leads it. "Collective Shift serves to redesign learning for 21st-century so all youth will have an opportunity to succeed," Escuadra explained. "It is a social enterprise that brings together an ecosystem of learning that includes in-school, out-of-school, online and employer-based opportunities." Collective Shift will be the parent organization of GlassLab.

The MacArthur Foundation wanted to find out ways to use 21st-century technology to use GlassLab's model of next generation assessment more broadly. After all, GlassLab has a substantial, four-year body of work. "For me, this the next step for how game-based experiences and formative assessments can be used in real-world applications," Escuadra said. "There are learning events unique to individual games, but those competency models—and what students learn in virtual environments—have the capacity to be used in other environments in the long term. It's just a question of how."

The LRNG platform is intended to do just that. Youth participants can choose from a series of learning Playlists, similar to those found on music streaming services, like Spotify or iTunes. There are two types of Playlists. In participating LRNG cities, local organizations can create their own Playlists that incorporate learning opportunities throughout the community. LRNG is also creating national Playlists that can be accessed and completed by youth anywhere.

Each Playlist consists of at least two XPs (or learning experiences), and learners who complete a Playlist earn a digital badge that captures their learning outcomes. LRNG Playlists focus on digital, as well as live, learning experiences in participating cities. For example, someone might design an online game and then visit a museum for a game jam day. Each of those would constitute an XP. This summer, LRNG will debut a series of national Playlists codesigned with workforce and civic partners, including a game design Playlist in partnership with Electronic Arts, a workforce readiness Playlist codesigned with Gap, and a financial literacy Playlist in partnership with We.

LRNG Playlists "aim to create a tangible form of currency" for corporate employers and universities. Certain XPs and Playlists will be attached to real-world opportunities, like workshops, internships, and someday employment. "Youth can take learning experiences and artifacts and bring it to an employer or a university and say, 'this is my tenacity and perseverance,'" Escuadra said. "'I've navigated and created something that is not like what others have.' If youth like photography or design media, they can follow those pathways—or find new ones they'd never considered before. LRNG also will have mentors on a national level to the local level."

SOWONOW

GlassLab is still developing new games and content. The GlassLab Games platform is still primarily focused on games and interactive experiences that can assess more academic competencies aligned to Common Core and Next Generation Science Standards, among others. It is scaling its platform, alongside the LRNG platform.

GlassLab is a bit like iTunes. It is a publishing platform for its games, as well as titles from other developers, like BrainQuake (*Wuzzit Trouble*), Schell Games (*Water Bears*), and Filament (*Argument Wars*). One login from teachers and students is all that is needed to access several learning games. The teacher dashboard reports on actionable analytics on one easy-to-follow website. At any time, I can log into GlassLab on my laptop and check on my students' progress in a game. And because the games on its platform are balanced in design, I know that if a mechanic is mastered, so is a concept. "This has been particularly useful for teachers who play games, as well for those who don't," Escuadra explained. This will continue to be GlassLab's mission.

GlassLab has been refining the way they make game-based assessments over the past few years, and then validate those learning outcomes and engagement impacts. One of the sets of reports on GlassLab Games is internally nicknamed "SOWONOW"—an acronym for "Shout-out, Watch-out, and What now?"—the three types of reports on its teacher dashboard tool. In 2016, I took part in a research study from Educational Development Center aimed to refine how SOWONOW reports student progress.

It used to be a tricky process for GlassLab to onboard partners to its publishing platform. "It's especially difficult when you are also developing an analytics system dashboard," Escuadra said. Apps submitted by developers for iPad, for example, are coded at the onset to comply with Apple's system. Games on GlassLab's platform are often already commercially available and must be retrofitted.

In order to scale effectively, GlassLab Games is working to make its platform easier to access and easier to use. "The telemetry tools required a manual hook from a dedicated engineer for weeks at a time," Escuadra continued. "In February 2016, we made available a beta version of developer toolset." This toolset enables developers a greater level of control regarding their own reporting rules and game pages, and provides a more easily accessible snapshot of student behavior.

At the 13th Annual Games for Change Festival, which took place in 2016, *CivilizationEDU* was announced. It represents a partnership between Take-Two Interactive Software, 2K and Firaxis Games. *CivilizationEDU* will be a modification of 2010's *Civilization V* (for those keeping track, *Civilization VI* was released in fall 2016). Like other games on GlassLab's platform, *CivilizationEDU* will include a teacher dashboard and assessment tools to track skill mastery. Like other games on GlassLab, there will be standards-aligned lesson plans.

The next sections are about my students' experiences beta-testing *SimCityEDU: Pollution Challenge!* and *Mars Generation One: Argubot Academy*, GlassLab's first published games. Since then, it has brought to market other original games, including *Ratio Rancher* and *Battleground 538*.

SimCityEDU: Pollution Challenge!

SimCityEDU: Pollution Challenge! is a modification of the 2013 commercial release *SimCity*. GlassLab was given the actual source code and customized it by adding an educational focus on science, English language arts, and 21st-century standards. The experience put structured problems in a sandbox space (like creating challenges with LEGO bricks, rather than allowing children to freely play). In other words, GlassLab built the cities, and then transposed environmental impact challenges. The game assesses in real time during play. An assessment engine processes all player choices—from bulldozing power plants to zoning. Student competencies are reported to teachers, detailing how well students can make systems diagrams. "From a design standpoint, with a large sample, you get a lot of patterns," Lead Designer Erin Hoffman-John told me, in January 2014. "You can make correlations to data. If you see a behavior happening, you can pair it to other behaviors." *SimCityEDU* is pattern-based, and scaffolds skills. The seemingly simple system of virtual city planning quickly becomes complex.

My students took part in playtesting the prerelease version. It is to be the first in a series of *SimCity*-modified games. Students assume the role of the mayor and must balance a city's systems. We joined the beta in August 2013;

the release was scheduled for early November 2013. I deployed the game in early September, making the activity double as an icebreaker for the new school year.

The final release featured six missions. Missions are further divided into "Gameplay" and "Challenges." Gameplay involved balancing a virtual city's systems. Some challenges are mind maps that reinforce systems thinking concepts from missions. Other challenges are text-based—words are clicked and dragged from paragraphs onto a systems map. Each mission levels up in difficulty to encourage mastery. The first mission, Parktown, tests player strategy in placing bus stops throughout the city. Too many bus stops are inefficient; too few will not transport enough children to school. Students experimented by placing one bus stop in the center of the city, and then waited to see what would happen. The second mission, Little Alexandria, tasks the player with increasing the number of jobs in the city. Later missions are pollution-related, specifically, coal versus solar. The final mission is the boss level. Coal creates jobs, but also increases pollution. Players must decide how to boost employment without harming the city's environment. It is a difficult challenge and involves many overlapping causal loops. Students must apply all that they learned to overcome the hardest challenge. (This mission was actually deemed too challenging in the beta version, and was scaled back in difficulty.)

Psychometricians embedded evidence-centered design assessments into the game (Bauer et al., 2014; Gushta et al., 2010). Data collected reports on player mastery of positive and negative relationships in interconnected systems. The assessment reports mastery of systems thinking—a 21st-century skill—without pausing the actions of play (Almond et al., 2003; Bauer et al., 2014; "Framework for 21st-Century Learning," 2015). In addition to the embedded formative assessments, lesson plans for the missions end with self-reflection writing prompts. When I run the game in class, I print out prompts and give to students in a packet. They know from the onset that the grade is dependent on reflection, not a win-state. Other options for summative assessments can include putting the questions on a Google Doc and asking students to include screenshot from parts of the game as evidence.

Mars Generation One: Argubot Academy

In August 2013, a few months before *SimCityEDU*'s release, Hoffman-John stepped off and led the concept of GlassLab's first original game. She was running tests for a product code-named *Hiro*. It was initially prototyped as a text-based, interactive fiction game, before graphical elements were added. At the time of my initial interview with Hoffman-John, it was called *Argubot Attacks*. It was eventually released as *Mars Generation One: Argubot Academy* in the spring of 2014. A tablet game that teaches argumentation evidence as part of the Common Core State Standards, the objective is to teach students how to evaluate and create an argument by connecting data and evidence to support a claim.

GlassLab worked with NASA to ensure the authenticity of a Martian setting. The player is part of the first generation of a human city on Mars. Their society resolves conflict using argument robots. Players equip their robot with an argumentation claim, and then evidence, and eventually other dimensions of arguments. In the tutorial, you argue about ice cream flavors. The dispute is settled by dragging a claim, along with supporting evidence, to the robot. Both pieces interlock as a completed puzzle. Some evidence is off-topic, which can cause defeat in battle.

Argumentation is a commonly used game mechanic, especially in board games such as *Apples to Apples* and *Taboo*. When arguing, there are particular kinds of emotions one experiences from participating. There is actually a dramatic feeling in an argument. The game, therefore, must capture the essence of the interpersonal drama one feels from arguing.

The challenge was to match the game mechanic with the competency of argumentative thinking. Herein lies the trap of "edutainment," or chocolate-covered broccoli. Hoffman-John's solution was to "find the fun within the competency itself." The team started with a competency map. "I dove into the mechanics of argumentation, how it's being taught, the difficulties of how it's taught, and then I associated the competencies with proven game mechanics," Hoffman-John said. GlassLab's Learning Director recommended the pedagogy of Stephen Toulmin. This methodology states that there really is no such thing as a false argument; rather, there are different schemes appropriate to an argument. If you have a scheme, or argument, and if it can stand up to critical question attacks—such as experts agreeing or other supporting evidence—then the argument is valid.

Hoffman-John realized that Toulmin's argument schemes were similar to those at play in the trading card game *Pokémon*. Because each Pokémon has a different ability, the player needs to strategize about how to duel with his or her opponent. She explained, "You have to determine the scheme, what the appropriate attacks are for that scheme, then what attack you're using in your

Pokémon/argumentative scheme. There were a lot of parallels so we developed the game structures that connected the core feeling of the competency itself of the game mechanic we knew would work with kids."

After playing *Mars Generation One: Argubot Academy*, students showed "as much as one year of learning gains in key aspects of argumentation" (*Field Study Results: Mars*, 2015, p. 3). Of the students tested, 65% improved from pretest to posttest after playing for 2 hours (*Field Study Results: Mars*, 2015). Like *SimCityEDU*, *Argubot* has a features links to game-based research and lesson plans. Teachers can import student lists and track student progress on the dashboard. Tablets simply need a student name with a log-on code—no e-mails are necessary.

In my class, I have students play the game for three consecutive days early in the school year. Because I teach social students, and not science, I ignore the content and focus on the skills it teaches through play: argumentation claim schemes. On day four, I introduce documents from Stanford History Education Groups' Reading Like a Historian curriculum, a free resource of primary sources, which includes overarching questions that have no "right" answer. Two opposing views are often given, and students are asked why an event happened, not when or how. When students complete the reading and questions, I then ask which argubot they would use to craft an argument and why. As game-using teachers, it is important to facilitate knowledge transfer from the game to other areas. Other similar assessments could include journal writing, from the perspective of Zodiac, the game's protagonist. I have also used the game to lead up to face-to-face debates, like the Institute of Play's *Socratic Smackdown*. As students prepare to argue, I remind them of what they mastered in *Argubot Academy*.

Conclusions and Takeaways

Many vetted learning games are available to play on platforms. They can offer a single sign-on (SSO) for students and teachers alike. Aside from lesson plans, platforms frequently report analytics of progress and learning outcomes to a teacher dashboard. BrainPOP, iCivics, and GlassLab Games are leading platforms for learning games. Each company is trusted in the field of educational technology, and publishes research to support the games supported. Using a platform is a simple, yet meaningful way to dip your toes into game-based learning.

Lesson Plan Ideas

Compare and Contrast as a Trading Card Game: Students will create trading cards, along with evidence and claim cards. To create trading cards, try the *Trading Cards* app or draw cards by hand. Students will make at least one claim card per trading card; each claim card needs two or three accompanying evidence cards. Evidence cards are student-ranked from 1 to 3, 1 being the least important (similar to how battle cards are numbered in *Magic: The Gathering*). Students play in groups of five: Two students "duel," and three students judge and keep score. The game begins with drawing a card to see with whom they are battling in the duel. If players draw the same card—or if a card is from the same point of view—that card is returned to the deck. Students next put down their claims and evidence, one at a time, to "attack" each other's claim. The judges vote on whether the attack is effective.

Design Your Own Meaning of Beep: Materials for teachers—and better yet, students—to make a paper-based *Meaning of Beep* game are here—https://www. brainpop.com/pages/dyo

Separation of Powers: What's for Lunch? iCivics's paper-based, cooperative game about how laws are written. Standards are posted on iCivics, along with the entire lesson—https://www.icivics.org/teachers/lesson-plans/separation-powers-whats-lunch

SimCityEDU: Pollution Challenge!: I used GlassLab's reflection questions and writing prompts to create a project with a culminating deliverable: a student portfolio. This style of grading can work for any long-form video game. (Of course, students can download it and play from home, too, to replay missions!) Because the only way to unlock the next mission is to complete current challenges, performance in the game need not be graded. What should be graded is the portfolio of written work that accompanies the game. Standards for the game, which include Next Generation Science Standards and Common Core State Standards, are available—https://www.glasslabgames. org/games/SC

Sortify Game: This is the printable, design your own lesson plan from Brain-POP. Standards vary, depending on the discipline or content area—http:// www.brainpop.com/educators/community/printable/sortify-design-game

Games

BrainPOP's GameUp, the platform to play many well-designed learning games in a browser, complete with lesson plans and teacher support—http://www.brainpop.com/games

iCivics, featuring lesson plans and learning games, both digital and paper-based—https://www.icivics.org

Poptropica game platform—http://www.poptropica.com

The Meaning of Beep from BrainPOP—https://www.brainpop.com/games/themeaningofbeep

Sortify from BrainPOP—http://www.brainpop.com/games/sortify

Time Zone X from BrainPOP—https://www.brainpop.com/games/timezonex

Touch http://www.touchpressgames.com

Trading Cards, authoring tool for tablets, published by the International Reading Association. Free for iPad—https://appsto.re/i6gP5VS and Android—http://goo.gl/YJB5KQ

Touch Press Games, which acquired the educational mobile games originally on Amplify's platform—http://www.touchpressgames.com

Wits & Wagers board game—http://www.northstargames.com/products/wits-wagers-family-1

Resources

Become a Certified BrainPOP Educator—https://educators.brainpop.com/certified-brainpop-educator-program

BrainPOP's SnapThought photo reflection tool enables students to take a screenshot and then submit an open-ended response to the teacher—http://www.brainpop.com/educators/community/video/snapthought-aphoto-reflection-tool

Filament Games has its own platform, too—https://www.filamentlearning. com/gbl-program

Legends of Learning game platform—http://www.legendsoflearning.com

LRNG—http://about.lrng.org, and a short video explaining the LRNG Youth Platform Orientation—https://vimeo.com/172463133/b952567d67

LRNG National Playlist Practitioner Guide—http://about.lrng.org/wp-content/uploads/2016/06/LRNG-Overview_v1b-1.pdf

The Meaning of Beep blog post by the Institute of Play's Brendan Trombley—http://www.instituteofplay.org/2016/06/the-meaning-of-beep

Ideaphora concept mapping—http://www.ideaphora.com

Stephen Toulmin's argument methodology, a major influence in GlassLab's approach to its argumentation game *Mars Generation One: Argubot Academy*—http://www-rohan.sdsu.edu/~digger/305/toulmin_model.htm

Stanford History Education Groups' Reading Like a Historian curriculum—https://sheg.stanford.edu/rlh

· 6 ·

PLAY AND LEARNING

To play expert Bernie DeKoven, the philosophy of play is simple: Given enough freedom, and people will play. "Freedom is an absolute necessity for the play to be meaningful and for the learning to be something the kids could truly internalize," he said, when we spoke in 2014. Games should give students freedom to play. Too much structure in a game, or game-like activity, and learning becomes stifled. Play in a game describes "the free space of movement within a more rigid structure" (Salen & Zimmerman, 2003, p. 475).

Humans are hardwired to play (Gray, 2014). It is so ingrained in our genetic code that limiting play can be detrimental to development (Gray, 2014). This chapter reviews the educational and psychological history of play and games. I consulted several experts on play, and where play fits into informal and formal learning environments. First, I review play theories, which help frame the psychology of why games should be used in teaching. Next, I discuss where play fits into spaces like museums, cities, and school. There are many takeaways for you to bring playful experience—like those in this chapter—to your students.

Theories of Play

Play is inherently difficult to define—it is ambiguous (Sutton-Smith, 1997). Experiences of play are as diverse as are the players themselves that take on agency, as performers of the roles of play (Sutton-Smith, 1997). Brian Sutton-Smith (1997) wrote about seven "rhetorics," or cultural lenses, that describe play. To Sutton-Smith, the hazy line that characterizes play may change based on whether one is a psychologist, a sociologist, or otherwise (1997). His seminal work serves as a critique of the exactness of defining the boundaries of play. Sutton-Smith's (1997) rhetorics of play are the result of several years and hundreds of observations of children at play. The rhetorics of play are:

1. *Progress*—how people grow and learn from playing;
2. *Fate*—luck and chance in contests;
3. *Power*—competition to be the hero in a game or sport;
4. *Identity*—playing together at social events, including family gatherings;
5. *Imagination*—creative play;
6. *Self*—hobbies and personal activities; and
7. *Frivolity*—silly or foolish play. (Sutton-Smith, 1997)

The *American Journal of Play*, the academic publication from the Strong Museum of Play in Rochester, New York, has a similar definition to that of Sutton-Smith's. It shares six overlapping elements: (a) anticipation, (b) surprise, (c) pleasure, (d) understanding, (e) strength, and (f) poise (Eberle, 2014). Categories of play do not unfold "linearly" on a continuum (Eberle, 2014, p. 222). Here, play is cyclical, organized in a way that also helps to enforce, or regulate, social skills (Eberle, 2014).

The zone of proximal development exists because of play (Bodrova, Germeroth, & Leong, 2013; Vygotsky, 1978). Play enables a child to be "a head taller than himself" (Vygotsky, 1978, p. 102). In other words, learning is scaffolded, a process in which new skills and concepts are mastered by moving in the zone of proximal development. New knowledge is built, or scaffolded, onto what is already known. Scaffolding builds to mastery. Similarly, in a video game, a player starts at level 1 and moves up to a "boss level"—where all skills and knowledge are tested. A game's level design—where challenges are progressively increased—has clear commonalities with moving through the zone of proximal development. Effective learning games use this philosophy;

mastering the game represents content or skill mastery. This is an example of James Paul Gee's Learning Principle of "Achievement," in which "there are intrinsic rewards from the beginning, customized to each learner's level, effort, and growing mastery and signaling the learner's ongoing achievement" (2007, p. 223).

The social constructs of play teach self-regulation of behavior to children (Vygotsky, 1978). Self-regulation refers to how children adjust behavior to compensate for others in social spaces of inquiry. A child may be more risky in a strategy board game than in a roomful of children sitting in rows of desks. The system of a game makes it safe from the child actualizing real-life "material consequences" from actions (Huizinga, 1938/1955, p. 10).

To Swiss psychologist Jean Piaget (1962), children play three types of games: *practice games*, *symbolic games*, and *games with rules*. Practice games, which are not rule-based, are observable in young children as well as in the animal kingdom (De Lisi, 2015; Piaget, 1962). Rough-and-tumble play is an example. From ages 2 through 6, children begin to play symbolic games (De Lisi, 2015; Piaget, 1962). Symbolic games have three stages, moving from imaginative fantasy to role-play reenactments (De Lisi, 2015; Piaget, 1962). Piaget observed children with dolls, and then used it as an example of symbolic play; dolls come to life based on the imagination of a child. The frequency of symbolic games diminishes with age because games with more than one person "may give rise to rules, so games of make-believe may become games with rules" (Piaget, 1962, p. 145). Games with rules occur later in childhood. They are more structured, having an agreed-upon codified rule set and a goal (Piaget, 1962). Games with rules are social and rule-dependent. Some rule sets, like the game of marbles, are passed down from older to younger children. Others are "spontaneous," designed by the participants (Piaget, 1962, p. 143). Games with rules are the most common in middle childhood and are "almost the only ones that persist at the adult stage" (Piaget, 1962, p. 146).

Today's standards-based curriculum model can make playing in school seem ancillary—a sidetrack to "serious" learning. Montessori (1912/2012) believed otherwise. She wrote that children have an innate ability, and appetite, to learn. The Montessori method is a teaching strategy that pertains to how children learn from playing freely. It is "a model of what a game-based learning system should look like" (Squire, 2011, p. 49). Through uninterrupted play, children discover new information. The Montessori method is a hands-on approach to learning (Montessori, 1912/2012).

In a student-centered classroom that uses Montessorian principles, give as little direct instruction as possible. Learning occurs when "overt telling is kept to a well-thought-out minimum, allowing opportunity for the learner to experiment and make discoveries" (Gee, 2007, p. 226). Let students figure out how things work. When I use a Web 2.0 tool like the talking avatar creator Voki, I only give out login instructions. Figuring out how to customize the characters is completely up to my students. I literally announce, "I won't help you. This was designed for you to be messed around with." (Of course I do assist children who are in need; the point is to promote self-directed learning.) Similarly, in my dissertation research I observed Peggy Sheehy tell students to figure things out for themselves. After all, designers of good games and apps took time to create an intuitive user environment. No one taught me how to play *Pokémon GO* with my smartphone. My iPad didn't come with an instruction book!

To make your classroom more playful, try adding in Sutton-Smith's rhetorics or one or more from the *American Journal of Play*'s list. Use games that have affordances that invite playfulness. Give little direct instruction to how to play the game during rollout, loosening structures typified in a school setting. After all, learning occurs from freedom to play, not from the game.

Teaching is a design science. Envision the lenses your students view in a lesson. Better yet, collect feedback from students. What would make a lesson more playful? Frivolity in unexpected places is a good start. Add in a randomness mechanic to lessons and see what happens when students let dice decide how their projects unfold. Or try having students act out themes of an essay without speaking out loud. Doing so will demonstrate how play drives learning. Oh, and it's fun!

Risky Play

It is theorized that play prepares people for events that previously faced humans in their hunter/gatherer past (Heft 1988; Sandseter, 2009). Risky play enables children to be "future ready" by creating a safe space to practice and learning from behavior (Gray, 2014). When free to play, young children who are not directly supervised in recess environments gravitate to risky play affordances, depending on the current environment (Sandseter, 2009).

Much of the research pertaining to risky play affordances falls within the taxonomy first proposed by Heft (1988). These affordances invite playfulness, such as rough-and-tumble play, chasing, and hiding. Risky play affordances include the following:

- Climbable features;
- Jump-down-off-able features;
- Balance-on-able features;
- Flat, relatively smooth surfaces;
- Slopes and slides;
- Swing-on-able features;
- Graspable/detached objects; and
- Dangerous tools. (Heft, 1988; Kyttä, 2004; Sandseter, 2009)

The above list may explain why children love amusement parks, hiding in clothing racks at department stores, running fast, and climbing trees. The video game series *Assassin's Creed* smartly weaves risky play into its game mechanics—all experienced from the safety of your couch! To "sync" to the map in *Assassin's Creed*, which reveals locations on a map, you must climb a very tall building, then dive off into a conveniently placed haystack. Players also run and chase enemies, hide in bushes, fight (rough and tumble), and use an array of weapons. No wonder Ubisoft keeps publishing sequels! The gameplay is fun and timeless.

Students can play educational games that involve risk. One ingenious example is *Darfur Is Dying*, the free, flash-based game from 2006. The objective is to forage for water without getting caught. Players take on the role of a refugee. You can choose to be a child, who can run fast but carry very little, or an older character, who moves more slowly but can carry more. You can hide, or attempt to outrun the enemy militia. In May 2014, I spoke to Google's Chief Game Designer, Noah Falstein, about *Darfur Is Dying* and how hiding and chasing deliver its social awareness message. He explained:

> Every so often people say, "Why do you make so many violent games? Why can't you just make happy games about people collecting flowers?" People do make games like that. With entertainment in general, there are often life-and-death situations presented. Deciding who to mate, who to date—it is also very Darwinian. We're hardwired to be fascinated by those things and not quite so fascinated by things like picking flowers. I think *Darfur Is Dying* is a brilliant example of a very simple game that puts you into life-and-death situations, which was more like real life. It helped me identify more with people in Darfur than any of the articles I read until that point.

In my world history class, the game's tension provided a compelling experience for my students. They are in the flow channel, focused on getting water
without getting caught. The lesson concludes with an exit ticket asking,
"Why do you think this game was so hard to play?" Here, students can make
the connection about struggling as a refugee in Darfur, because the mechanics
are perfectly aligned with the message. Falstein continued, "*Darfur Is Dying*
is a great example of a very simple game that doesn't take a lot of graphics or
depth of gameplay to give you the sense of how helpless you can feel being
hunted down in barren landscapes when all you're trying to do is get water.
It's very direct that way." His view is that games give humans an evolutionary
advantage. "Play is a safe way for people to prepare for survival in the real
world," he concluded.

Explorable Explanations

Explorable explanations are websites with playful interactions. They are
reactive documents that "allow the reader to play with the author's assumptions and analyses, and see the consequences" (Victor, 2011). One example
is the iPad book, *Earth: A Primer*. Perusing its virtual pages, readers can
create volcanoes and sandstorms simply by dragging their finger on the
pages. The *New York Times* article, *Is It Better to Rent or Buy?* (http://nyti.
ms/1han05C), is playable, embedded with a sliding mortgage and tax simulator. *Parable of the Polygons* (http://ncase.me/polygons) is a Games for Change
award-nominated explorable explanation. About segregation and discrim-
ination, authors Nicky Case and Vi Hart interspersed text and drag-and-
drop interactives to drive the message home. To "play" the blog, you drag
unhappy polygons to the happy polygons. To learn more about explorable
explanations, check out the resources and games at the end of this chapter.
Follow the link to *Up and Down the Ladder of Abstraction* in Resources to see
how it all works.

Making playable websites is a meaningful game-like project for students.
In your class, consider having students use Glogster to have students create interactive digital posters around a theme. Another option is Sway, free
from Microsoft. Both platforms provide a canvas that can be populated with
embedded media, which stand in for clickable interactions. What's more,
Glogster and Sway projects are published online for an authentic audience
to play.

Play at Museums

Barry Joseph is the Associate Director for Digital Learning at the American Museum of Natural History, in New York City. He has a highly resourceful blog with an amusing name: Moosha Moosha Mooshme (linked at the end of this chapter). When I inquired, Joseph told me that his blog's name was how his place of employment once sounded to his young son. We spoke several times throughout 2015 and 2016.

Joseph first became interested in games and learning 15 years ago. He had read an article in *Wired* about how video games exceeded the revenue grossed from Hollywood films. Around that time, he observed how three children played Nintendo's *Super Smash Brothers* video game together. In the game, all of the Nintendo game characters battle one another. Joseph was blown away when observing how children could play together by selecting avatars that gave them powers and abilities that were each developmentally appropriate for their vastly different ages. He also observed a powerful gaming literacy—each child effortlessly played the game, which Joseph could hardly follow as an outside observer.

Museums need patrons to not linger in front of exhibits. They need to keep crowds moving along. "You can only go so deep at one spot," he said, in early 2016. "A game lets you go deep." In other words, games let patrons continue their learning experiences from home. The astronaut ice cream souvenir I buy for my son in a museum gift shop serves to extend our visit, deepening our experience.

One example of a souvenir that lets patrons extend learning after the visit is *Pterosaurs, The Card Game*. Codesigned by Joseph, along with Nick Fortugno and youth learners in the Museum education programs, it is a trading card game about flying reptiles that lived in the time of the dinosaurs. Games can enable learners to "go deep" before a visit, too. Prior to seeing the 2016 exhibit, *The Secret World Inside You*, students can play the Museum's game *Gutsy*. Available for free from the museum's website, it is print-and-play (also linked at the end of the chapter). Like the exhibit, the game is about the importance of biodiversity in gut microbes. The goal is to get six different microbes in your gut, all while avoiding pathogens. The game includes "event cards," too. For example, pull a family reunion card and then all players have to mix up their decks. Kissing event cards means you trade microbe cards. When a dog card is drawn, players share microbes.

Location-Based Play

Pokémon GO is, perhaps, the most popular location-based game. It was code-signed by The Pokémon Company and Niantic, Inc., a lab spun off from Google. The game creates an overlay on Google Earth, and uses augmented reality to simulate *Pokémon* characters on a smartphone screen. Prior to the *Pokémon GO* phenomenon, Niantic, Inc. developed *Ingress*, a team-based game that takes place in the real world.

Location-based games work well in informal learning spaces—like museums and libraries—where people already gather and congregate. That's why the "poké stops" and "gyms" in *Pokémon GO* are often in parks. Similarly, the "portals" that players "hack" in *Ingress* are in public locations. This, of course, presents a challenge to a teacher who wants to bring location-based game play into school. Students don't typically wander outdoor spaces, or even the grounds of a school campus, during the school day. But, of course, learning doesn't stop when the bell rings and children go home.

In March 2016, I spoke with Kellian Adams-Pletcher, cofounder of Green Door Labs, a small and innovative, Boston-based studio, about location-based games. Unlike *Pokémon GO* and *Ingress*, its location-based games are designed so players look up from their phones when they arrive at a location. The idea is to interact with the location, not the device. *Murder at the Met* was its first and most famous game, primarily because it took place at New York City's Metropolitan Museum of Art. The game challenged patrons to solve a murder by wandering the galleries of the museum. The clues were in the artworks.

Adams-Pletcher then walked me through a game called *Escape in Time*. It is a four-player game literally set on Boston's Freedom Trail, the walk around historic locations from the time of the American Revolution. The game has two pathways across town and includes a walkie-talkie feature over smartphone. While venturing on the Freedom Trail, players solve clues, challenges and puzzles. The goal is to disable a "temporal device." Players begin at the Old State Meeting House and then move to locations, like Faneuil Hall.

Green Door Labs built a location-based game for soldiers training at the Quartermaster Museum in Fort Lee, Virginia. For past 23 years, the base had trouble getting its new recruits into the museum to learn about the history of quartermaster troops. As part of the training curriculum, it was often boring: a lecture followed by a quiz. Adams-Pletcher and her team devised a game, which starts with a brief history of the quartermaster troops. Then recruits are given a website link to access with their smartphones. "You then interact with goofy little pieces and artifacts," Adams-Pletcher said. "It's not the game that goes deep, it's the objects that go deep." For example, one object prompt reads, "There is a ghost bell you have to find and find out why. What used to wear this ghost bell that was found in South Carolina?" The answer is a camel. Yes, there were camels imported into the pre-Civil War south! Adams-Pletcher continued:

> The thinking was that it might be a useful way to move troops around. Camels don't need a lot of water, and there is hot terrain. But it was a total disaster—a camel disaster! No one could make it work. Many of the soldiers were terrified of the camels and were unwilling to work with them. Then there was a story of a soldier who went AWOL and was later caught. He was tied to the camel and was sent out to the wilderness, where he died on this camel. People would randomly see this camel walking around with the dead body, and it wore a bell.

Eventually, all of the camels were let go, into the wild, wearing bells. Because trained camels cannot survive in the wild, they quickly died out. It is this legacy of interesting stories that drives engagement. "The stories are behind the objects," Adams-Pletcher said. "A bell? Why a camel? Why a ghost? The soldiers learn the information because they are at the museum. The digital prompt makes you explore the physical."

Developed in response to museums needing to build flexible content, Green Door Labs launched Edventure Builder, its platform to create location-based content. Museums have used it for children to build games when they stayed overnight with camps. Edventure Builder has also been used at university libraries, for first year student orientation. "Most of the engagement you want to be off-screen," Adams-Pletcher explained. "You want a prompt to get people engaged with the environment and the people around them. It's up to the player to see how deep they go with the content."

Play and School

Is it realistic to have a strictly play-based classroom, devoid of structure? In April 2014, James Paul Gee expressed to me the struggle between free play and teacher-directed instruction, using "liberal" to describe the free play argument and "conservative" for structured learning. Like most things in life, strive for moderation. There must be a balance for learning to realistically occur. Gee explained:

> The liberals are interested in projects. They say, "Let's just turn them loose, and be in a rich environment, and back off with the teaching." That doesn't work. Good

project-based learning still requires a teacher to mentor you to know what to pay attention to, to give you information when you need it—just in time and on-demand [Gee's Explicit Information On-Demand and Just In Time Principle], to constrain the experience so it doesn't get out of hand and you know what to pay attention to. Sometimes these labels by liberals mean to turn the kids loose, that they don't like instruction. Then conservatives say, "All you should have is instruction." But good learning is instruction of all different types: mentoring, telling, and just in time and on-demand modeling.

When I interviewed digital media expert Henry Jenkins about play and learning in May 2014, he echoed Gray's observations (and others I interviewed, including Google's Noah Falstein). He felt that play, in many ways, is more useful for thinking about education than games. Jenkins said, "People in a hunting society play with bows and arrows; people in an information society play with information."

The issue, of course, is that school tends to see play as a disruption. "Games are rule-driven and play is not," Jenkins continued. "It is much easier to bring games into the classroom, into an institution, than play. We tend to view play as the disruption of the class clown, rather than the innovation of the really creative, probing student. I think we have to value that before we bring play into schools."

I spoke with Sujata Bhatt in March 2016 about play in formal settings, specifically school. Bhatt founded the Incubator School in Los Angeles, California (she moved on from the school to new opportunities shortly after, in June 2016). When the topic of play came up, she explained that a mission of her school is to create more student-directed pathways. Game-based learning can sometimes tend to be teacher-structured. "I think of play as a stance towards exploration, more than anything," she said. "Whenever you get something new, you try it out. Play is a form of curiosity. That's embedded in the structure of the classroom."

At the Incubator School, whenever a topic comes up in class, like an ancient civilization to explore, Bhatt explained that teachers use it as a design constraint for students. She continued, "The students then go play, explore, and test out research questions [about the civilization]. There is a playfulness towards knowledge."

Institute of Play and Quest to Learn

The Institute of Play's mission is to transform education through play. The Institute was the founding partner of the Quest to Learn school, in New York City. In a May 2016 email correspondence I had with Rebecca Rufo-Tepper, she explained about the Institute's relationship with the school, and where play fits into learning. Rufo-Tepper is the director of programs, professional development, and teacher training. "Our role in the very beginning was to design the school, and build capacity within the school to continue the design process we helped start," she began. Rufo-Tepper continued:

> We had a team of game designers and learning designers who worked in Mission Lab full-time while the school was still growing and adding a new grade every year. One result of our deep collaboration with teachers was developing the teachers' capacity to design games and game-like units, and mentor other teachers in doing so. So now Mission Lab is a space for collaboration between teachers, and Institute of Play is focused on supporting the school and its leadership through ongoing professional development, as well as spreading Quest to Learn's approach to other schools.

Quest to Learn opened in 2009. Initially for just the 6th grade, it has since extended through the 9th grade. It teaches the same Common Core State Standards as a typical school and it participates in state standardized testing. In fact, it is a public school. The difference is in its approach. Quest has an "approach to pedagogy that connects game design and systems thinking across a standards-based curriculum" (Rufo-Tepper, Salen, Shapiro, Torres, & Wolozin, 2011, p. 49). Seven "Principles of Game-like Learning" guide it:

1. *Everyone is a participant*—A shared culture and practice exists where everyone contributes, which may mean that different students contribute different types of expertise.
2. *Challenge is constant*—A "need to know" challenges students to solve a problem whose resources have been placed just out of reach.
3. *Learning happens by doing*—Learning is active and experiential. Students learn by proposing, testing, playing with, and validating theories about the world.
4. *Feedback is immediate and ongoing*—Students receive ongoing feedback on their progress against learning and assessment goals.
5. *Failure is reframed as iteration*—Opportunities exist for students and teachers to learn through failure. All learning experiences should embrace a process of testing and iteration.
6. *Everything is interconnected*—Students can share their work, skill, and knowledge with others across networks, groups, and communities.
7. *It kind of feels like play*—Learning experiences are engaging, learner-centered, and organized to support inquiry and creativity. (Q Design Pack Games and Learning, 2013, p. 49)

Quest to Learn teachers attempt to include each of the principles in classroom lessons. Many of these lessons implement paper-based, "unabashed rip-offs of existing titles or modifications of games they've created for other lessons" (Toppo, 2015, p. 108). Game-like lessons also match with learning outcomes, which align to the Common Core State Standards (Rufo-Tepper et al., 2011). According to Rufo-Tepper et al. (2011),

> Students learn about the way systems work and how they can be modified or changed. Through designing play, they learn to think analytically and holistically, to experiment and test out theories, and to consider other people as part of the systems they create and inhabit. Game design serves as the pedagogy underlying this work. (p. 56)

Games played and designed at Quest serve the purpose of teaching how interconnected systems in the world function (Rufo-Tepper et al., 2011). When students are using games for learning, they "pay explicit attention to the status of games as dynamic learning systems, as rule-based models supporting specific ways of knowing and doing" (Rufo-Tepper et al., 2011, p. 85). Katie Salen explained how she went from cowriting the influential game design book *Rules of Play: Game Design Fundamentals* to helping to launch Quest to Learn. When we spoke in February 2014, she said:

> I think games can teach us so much about how to design other things. I actually wrote the book [*Rules of Play*] to help people understand how games work so they can apply those principles to design things that weren't games. Quest to Learn was a by-product of that thinking. It didn't faze me that the choice of what we could design was a school and not a game. Writing *Rules of Play* was an exercise to help people literally understand how games work. Doing that set up the whole theoretical foundation for what became Quest to Learn. It's not a one-to-one mapping, but that book was all about systems. At Quest, that was one of the founding ideas. If you really want to make a change, you have to think at a systemic level. You cannot just design a game, or a piece of curriculum, or just work with teachers; you have to think of the design of the entire system, which was, in this case, an entire school. That's the connection.

Quest to Learn is quest-driven (hence the name). Learning trajectories are housed in a mission and quest structure. Missions are weeks long, while quests have goals that are achievable in 1 or 2 days. Quests take place within missions, lasting a day or two. Students also take part in "boss levels," the culminating task to apply all that was taught. The missions and quests are similar to those found in video games because they include opportunities to "level up" until the final level. Leveling up in challenge is similar to Vygotsky's zone of proximal development in which new knowledge is scaffolded on what learners already know. More skills are learned until mastery is achieved. It is the flow channel at work, and it translates well into school settings.

At Quest to Learn, the boss level week is when students "bring all of their skills to bear throughout a design process: brainstorming, prototyping, testing, iterating, and finally, publicly sharing their solutions with family, friends and classmates" (Parker, 2013). All of the gained skills and knowledge are applied to overcome a final challenging task. Activities include building a Rube Goldberg machine, video creations, and robotics, and developing ideas to end the systemic problem of bullying (Parker, 2013). The boss level asks students to "work together to make something that they do not yet know how to make" ("Boss Level at Quest to Learn," n.d.). The notion of a culminating activity in a project is not quite the same. Boss levels ask students to apply what they have learned. During boss level weeks, Quest to Learn actually adjusts the school schedule and even the physical classroom layouts. The result is a noisy and excited classroom filled with active learners. When I reach a boss level in a video game, *I expect to fail.* If the challenge is too easy, I assume that the rest of the game will be that way. Sometimes it can take dozens of tries to win a match. If the goal is to increase tenacity and persistence, try adding boss levels to your culminating activities.

At Quest, a mission is a curriculum unit housed in a larger framework, with a game-like narrative. The mechanic involves a student solving a problem. A teacher can add a narrative frame around projects with a mission/quest structure. An example is the 6th grade cell biology science mission, *The Way Things Work*. Introduced in the second trimester, the goal is to help Dr. Smallz, a doctor who has shrunk himself and journeyed into a human body to cure a disease. Smallz has lost his memory and knowledge and now can't get out. As students learn about body systems, the doctor begins to send hints, such as, "I see long red strings, where am I?" Quests build knowledge and skills with smaller challenges to get to a larger, overarching goal.

TeacherQuest is the Institute's professional development program, which Rufo-Tepper leads for educators of all grade levels and subject areas. Educators learn to use games, design games, and to master the art of student-centered teaching. Rufo-Tepper explained:

> Over 600 educators in 20 states and 13 countries have participated in TeacherQuest to date, through face-to-face and online programs. A lot of the research about barriers to widespread implementation of game-based learning cites the lack of professional development. TeacherQuest aims to support implementation, but also increase the impact, and use games and play to catalyze a lasting change in teacher practice.

There are several different types of TeacherQuest programs: short pop-up workshops, longer face-to-face courses, or online courses. Some programs are open to educators from anywhere. "For others, we will partner on a customized program with a school or district or professional group," Rufo-Tepper explained. "We also have some programs that are targeted to a specific content domain [like STEMQuest, and HistoryQuest], as well as interdisciplinary programs that bring teams of teachers of different domains together."

Conclusions and Takeaways

A degree of freedom must exist for play to thrive. Humans are evolutionarily hardwired to seek "risky play." Play happens in structured games. Free play can be sustained digitally in the classroom by using digital sandboxes and open-ended toys. Game mechanics can also be simulated. Because of its open-ended nature, it can be difficult to assess play. Be sure to keep the learning objective focused and apparent to the student, and loosen up the reigns on the path the child takes to achieve it.

Lesson Plan Ideas

Caterpillar Game: Math board game created by Alicia Iannucci (Quest to Learn)—http://www.edutopia.org/blog/caterpillar-game-real-world-math-alicia-iannucci

Food Chains: In a station rotation, use *Phylo* or *Ptersosaurs: The Game,* alongside other high quality curricular resources, like BrainPOP videos, and books. Include a station in which students make a food web on a concept map website. Both card games are printable from their websites—http://phylogame.org and http://www.amnh.org/ology/features/pterosaurs_card_game/index.php

Galactic Mappers: Paper-based geography game for 6th grade with embedded assessments, from C. Ross Flatt from Quest to Learn. Social studies standards apply—http://www.edutopia.org/made-with-play-game-based-learning-assessment-video

EduCaching has a location-based GPS curriculum, many of which are game-like—http://educaching.com

Everyone's a Critic: A free, downloadable non-digital museum game from the Institute of Play. It was part of its collaboration with the Museum of Modern Art in New York City. This activity works well outside of museums, including in student museum displays. Standards vary, depending on discipline and content—http://www.moma.org/pdfs/docs/learn/moma_everyones-a-critic.pdf

GlogsterEDU, to make playful digital posters   https://edu.glogster.com

Institute of Play Mission Pack: Dr. Smallz (The Way Things Work) science unit—http://www.instituteofplay.org/work/projects/quest-curriculum/mission-pack-dr-smallz

Institute of Play Mission Pack: I Spy Greece, world history curriculum—http://www.instituteofplay.org/work/projects/quest-curriculum/mission-pack-i-spy-greece

Institute of Play Mission Pack: Shark Tank, math and financial literacy presented in an authentic game-like structure—http://www.instituteofplay.org/work/projects/quest-curriculum/mission-pack-shark-tank

Institute of Play Mission Pack: Self on a Stand, English language arts unit—http://www.instituteofplay.org/work/projects/quest-curriculum/mission-pack-self-on-the-stand

Games

Disaster Detector is a science-themed game from the Smithsonian Institute—https://ssec.si.edu/disaster-detector

Emoji Simulator from Nicky Case, is an explorable explanation with has a simple drag-and-drop interface. Move trees, lightening, and fire emojis—http://ncase.me/emoji-prototype

Extreme Event is a free, large group, disaster survival game from Koshland Science Museum—https://www.koshland-science-museum.org/explore-the-science/extreme-event/plan-your-game

FreshAiR is a location-based game and authoring tool—http://www.playfreshair.com

Firewatch is a beautiful open world game in which you are a national park ranger—http://www.firewatchgame.com

Getty Images museum game—http://www.getty.edu/games/switch

Goose Chase is an app to create location-based scavenger hunts—https://www. goosechase.com/solutions/k12

Gutsy, the print-and-play gut microbe game—http://www.amnh.org/ology/ features/gutsy_microbiome_card_game/

Ingress is a live, location-based game—https://www.ingress.com

The League of Extraordinary Bloggers, location-based game for the Boston Children's Museum and the Freeman Foundation Asian Exhibit Series—www.lxb-game.com

List of explorable explanations—https://github.com/explorableexplanations/ explorableexplanations.github.io/wiki/List-of-Explorable-Explanations

MicroRangers game, from the American Museum of Natural History—http:// www.amnh.org/learn-teach/families/microrangers

Parable of the Polygons is an explorable explanation that was nominated for a Games for Change award—http://ncase.me/polygons

Phylo, the printable trading card game from Nick Fortugno, about life sciences—http://phylogame.org

Pokémon: GO is from The Pokémon Company and Niantic, Inc., maker of the mobile, location-based game *Ingress*. To play, use your iOS or android phone to catch *Pokémon* in the real world—http://pokemongo.nianticlabs.com/en

Pterosaurs: The Card Game—http://www.amnh.org/ology/features/pterosaurs_ card_game/index.php

The Quartermaster Game—http://www.edventurebuilder.com/quartermaster

Taleblazers is a tool to make augmented reality, location-based games using smartphones—http://taleblazer.org

Resources

Adventure Playground, in Berkeley, California—http://www.ci.berkeley.ca.us/adventureplayground

Come Out & Play is an annual festival in New York City—http://www.comeoutandplay.org

DeepFUN, Bernie DeKoven's website, featuring several games and activities—http://www.deepfun.com

Edventure Builder for University Libraries, location-based games to help freshmen learn library literacy—http://www.greendoorlabs.com/for-libraries

Earth: A Primer is an interactive explorable explanation iPad book—http://www.earthprimer.com

Explorable explanations blog posts about how it all works—http://www.maartenlambrechts.be/the-rise-of-explorable-explanations and http://blog.ncase.me/explorable-explanations

Exploratorium, a hands-on science museum in San Francisco, featuring an interactive website and apps—http://www.exploratorium.edu

Gigantic Mechanic is a New York-based studio that specializes in playful experiences—http://www.giganticmechanic.com

Peter Gray's blog on play—http://www.psychologytoday.com/blog/freedom-learn

Barry Joseph's American Museum of Natural History blog—http://www.mooshme.org

Strong American Museum of Play, in Rochester, NY—http://www.museumofplay.org

Museum Games wiki—http://museumgames.pbworks.com/w/page/38863237/FrontPage

Now I Get It Jam was an explorable explanation-themed transformational game jam held at Carnegie Mellon University. Click the "What Happened?"

link to see the results of playable pages created by game designers and educators—http://www.nowigetitjam.com

Quest to Learn Curriculum Exemplar, featuring postmortem reflection questions—http://www.instituteofplay.org/wp-content/uploads/2013/09/IOP_QDesignPack_Curriculum_Exemplar_1.1.pdf

Q Design Packs, from the Institute of Play. Free resources, or "packs," for teachers and schools interested in adopting games and learning—http://www.instituteofplay.org/work/projects/q-design-packs

Quest to Learn: Developing the School for Digital Kids—http://dmlcentral.net/sites/dmlcentral/files/resource_files/Quest_to_LearnMacfoundReport.pdf

Quest Learning in Action from Institute of Play video series, video for each of the Seven Game-Like Principles—http://vimeo.com/channels/qla

Up and Down the Ladder of Abstraction is an explorable explanation using a road and car to illustrate algorithms—http://worrydream.com/LadderOfAbstraction

· 7 ·

PUZZLES, GAMES, AND DIGITAL TOYS

Back in 1994 Will Wright was interviewed by *Wired* magazine about an upcoming project he called "Doll House." Wright had trepidations about his game because it wasn't really a game at all. Playing with dolls, after all, is not like playing *Twister* or *Monopoly*. He told interviewer Kevin Kelly, "I have in mind a game I want to call 'Doll House.' It gives grown-ups some tools to design what is basically a dollhouse. But a dollhouse for adults may not be very marketable" (1994). The digital dolls in Wright's Doll House were eventually released under a different name: *The Sims*. The name refers to "simulation," as in a simulated version of real life. Wright's toy—or game—was success-ful because it tapped into a psychological need for symbolic play. It has also spawned an entire genre of games, where the player controls a fishbowl-like world. *Civilization* and *Clash of Clans* are examples. In April 2014, I spoke to James Paul Gee about digital toys such as *The Sims*. He said:

> The best-selling game in history is *The Sims*; people say it is not a game. Who gives a damn? It's good interactivity. We're producing interactivity that's engaging and relates to real learning. Whether or not the thing is a pure game, whether everything in it is a game, is quite irrelevant.

Henry Jenkins shared an anecdote with me in May 2014 about his interview with Wright. Teachers inquired about fitting *The Sims* into the disciplines they taught in school. For example, characters and avatars that vote could teach civics. This conversation lingers today with other open-ended games, like *Minecraft*. Wright told Jenkins that what's valuable about *The Sims* is that the learning environment is undisciplined—the world is open-ended and, out of that, a variety of different types of learning take place.

Digital toys, like *The Sims*, now reside on smartphones and tablets. Formerly tools for adults, computers are part of the toy industry. "Kids are playing and learning in different platforms that we never imagined," Sandbox Summit conference cofounder Wendy Smolen explained to me in 2014. Claire Greene, the Summit's other founder, continued, "Just because there is a sound or a light didn't mean it was teaching anything. Push 'A-B-C' or '1-2-3' and then ring a bell has no cause and effect, like the centuries before of traditional toys and games."

Smolen and Greene shared mutual concerns about digital toys and games: What are we teaching? What's happening to play? Are digital toys creating a generation of children merely adept at pushing buttons? "The research is an important component," Greene continued. "Teachers want to know: Does this work? Does gamification help disenfranchised learners? We help percolate these ideas. Technology is here; let's harness its power for good."

This chapter stems from conversations I had with some of the makers of innovative toys and games. The first section includes a profile of ThinkFun and a conversation with its cofounder. ThinkFun makes non-digital learning games for both children and adults. Next, I speak with Toca Boca's play designer and research manager, Tiggly's chief learning officer, and Originator's cofounder. I also chat with people from *Bloxels*, both a tactile toy and a mobile game design engine. This chapter concludes with the Diversity in Apps initiative, and its Diverse and Inclusive Growth (DIG) Toolkit.

Aside from gaining a deeper understanding about each toy and game company, each conversation discusses the design process which can be replicated in a classroom. For example, Toca Boca and Tiggly use children's play patterns when each makes a design decision. ThinkFun thoughtfully considers both play and learning in its games. As a game-based learning teacher, the same principles should apply to your classroom.

ThinkFun

Bill Ritchie grew up thinking that all households had science puzzles and brainteasers at home. After all, his mother kept bringing them home for him and his brother to play. Ritchie's father was an executive at Bell Labs, the innovative research and development branch of the (at the time) telephone giant, AT&T. One of his dad's colleagues and close friends, William (Bill) Keister used to visit and bring along games he invented. Since the early 1930s, Keister invented small mechanical puzzles, usually based on binary arithmetic and Boolean algebra. When asked what he did at Bell Labs, Keister would hand over a puzzle and say, "This kind of stuff!"

Ritchie later attended junior high school with Scot Osterweil, a brilliant mind in computers who went on to be a research director at MIT, as well as the designer of the game *Zoombinis* (more on *Zoombinis* in Chapter 9!). Ritchie's older brother, Dennis, was also scientific minded. Years later, Dennis created the C programming language, and cocreated the UNIX operating system. "I didn't get his [Dennis's] brains, but I did get this notion early on that there were some really smart people out there and it's really fun to talk to them!" Ritchie recalled, when we spoke in April 2016.

In the mid-1980s, Ritchie and his wife, Andrea Barthello, started a small toy and puzzle company. They wanted to bring puzzles like Keister's to market. This was at a time when toy companies weren't selling a lot of "heady inventor's toys." Seeing this market opening, ThinkFun, first known as Binary Arts, was founded in 1985. "Our broader mission was to bring the craziest ideas from the wackiest mathematician and inventors to the world, distilled down to toys and games for boys and girls," Ritchie said. Headquartered in Alexandria, Virginia, ThinkFun is still a family business. Ritchie is its president, and Barthello is the chief operating officer.

As it turned out, the 1980s was "a terrible time" to start a puzzle and game company. Toys R' Us was in its ascendency, as specialty toy stores left the market. What's more, the Rubik's Cube fad crashed, leaving retailers with enormous inventories of the cubed puzzle. "We persevered," Ritchie recalled. Then, after the 1989 recession, new modern indoor malls began to open across the American landscape. Upscale retailers like Sharper Image and the Nature Company grew nationwide "proving out that there was a market for intellectual toys and puzzles."

After the dot-com bubble in the early 2000s, many stores and companies went bankrupt. Ritchie began to wonder where it was all going. It was around this time that Ritchie's son entered middle school. "They used to drag me in as the go-to math and thinky parent," Ritchie recalled. In 6th grade, his son Sam invented *Math Dice*, which "teaches math facts in a fun way." Ritchie decided that he wanted to take the concept of puzzles and games and "do a more explicit intentional job of educating kids."

In 2007, Ritchie tried to find if teachers were using games in schools. He checked with groups like Gathering for Gardner (a mathematics puzzle conference named in honor of *Scientific American* contributor Martin Gardner) and other similar conferences. He was looking for kindred spirits. He found few teachers using games in practice; however, "we found northern California, near and around Silicon Valley, seemed to be a hotbed." There was a dearth of people using games and puzzles used for creative thinking.

Ritchie decided to create his own set of learning standards for Think-Fun games, rather than worry about meeting other people's standards. He refined games and worked on new ones. When *Chocolate Fix* was developed around 2003, he had a friend develop a "logical deduction engine" that could be played into the puzzle. "We did things like create a program to present selected challenges and show the tree graph structure of the puzzle system," Ritchie explained. "Then we asked students to explain the different kinds of contradictions. Why didn't those branches work out?" In other words, players found a graphical way to demonstrate a mathematical proof; it was "proof by contradiction." To that end, ThinkFun turned the lesson into an online course, which also featured videos.

At the University of California-Berkeley, Sylvia Bunge began an independent study of the effects games and learning. She conducted MRI brain studies and used some of ThinkFun's puzzles. "They used games, including ours, and got a measurable increase in IQ scores," Ritchie explained. And then *Newsweek* published an article about the results. The article included ThinkFun's *Rush Hour* and *Chocolate Fix*, and suggested that playing games could build people's intelligence (Bronson & Merryman, 2009). It seemed that the market and research was catching up to Ritchie's vision.

ThinkFun has found recent success with a series of maze games: *Laser Maze*, *Gravity Maze*, and its newest, *Circuit Maze*. To play *Laser Maze*, players use small mirrors to guide a laser pointer through a maze to its target: a light beacon. *Gravity Maze* is similar, using stackable cubes and a marble, which should roll to its intended target. *Circuit Maze* uses a maze mechanic to teach electrical circuitry. Players choose from one of 60 challenge cards and then place game tokens (parts of the circuit) from the battery source to a beacon, causing it to light up. I played it at the 2016 New York Toy Fair. I saw how computational and logical thinking were deeply imbued in the design. As players learn the rules of the game, they learn the rules of electronic circuitry. The set includes switches, too, just like an actual circuit board. Using the switch interface alters the direction of the current in the maze.

How electricity works can be hard to explain. When the team at ThinkFun wrote *Circuit Maze*'s instruction manual, the first draft said that Ben Franklin was actually confused about how electricity worked. Ritchie explained how students often begin electronic circuitry classes without a mental model of the basic concepts. Ritchie explained:

> We decided not to explain electricity. Instead, we explain the rules of our maze game. You have these pieces form the game and a challenge, now go to it! The rules to our game match what the rules to electricity are. You learn the game you learn about electricity.

Learning the rules of *Circuit Maze* is the fun. "We're now bringing *Math Dice* back to schools, along with an online program to teach you how to get better at the game," Ritchie explained. He demonstrated it to me at Toy Fair. Admittedly, I struggled to keep up with the math at 9:00 am on a Saturday! *Math Dice* teaches exponents and orders of operations (PEMDAS, I'm talking to you!). Ritchie shared a story about playing *Math Dice* with his youngest son. "It took his son about 15 minutes to learn the concepts of exponents, because it's part of the game," he recalled. "After I rolled the dice, I explained the rule of the power of two. It was a game rule that made him get better." Explaining exponents as a rule of a simple game made it easy for Ritchie's son. "I realized that if you make something into a fun game that kids want to play, they want to get good and are enjoying it, things that seem complicated, simplify out."

At Toy Fair, Ritchie also demonstrated its new *Balance Beans* game. It is a simple-yet-challenging, non-digital math game. The set includes a seesaw, with nine gridded indentations on each side, and multicolored plastic beans. The beans are either single, double, or in groups of three. The seesaw's fulcrum indicates equality—when one side is tipped upward, that side is literally greater than the other. Moving the beans back a row on the seesaw grid visually and mathematically represents an increase in power. This abstract concept, as well as algebraic thinking, becomes meaningful through actions of play. The teeter-totter mechanic effectively illustrates what an equation actually is: balance on both sides of the equal sign, not an output. After having students play *Balance Beans*, a teacher can introduce mathematical expressions, thus facilitating knowledge transfer from skills learned through play.

ThinkFun launched the board game *Code Master* in 2015. The idea was that the rules of the game model computational thinking. To play, you use physical pieces that represent logic phrases. "Studies show that when students enter a computer science program with a mental model about how this kind of thing, they have a higher success rate in the program," Ritchie explained. "If we can create seeds about how to think about something, we get a generation of kids better equipped to deal with computer science."

Toca Boca and Digital Toys

My 6-year-old son loves Toca Boca's digital toy apps on his iPad! Not one of them—all of them! In fact, Toca Boca has developed dozens of high quality digital toys for children aged 2 through 9. *Toca Cars* is a virtual toy car set. *Toca House* features colorful characters that can perform household chores. Toca Boca is a digital toy company—not a video game studio. According to its support page:

> Toys don't have rules. Toys can be played with in any way and only your imagination sets those boundaries. In that sense, toys are more open-ended and can be played with in many different ways. Digital toys are the same, but even more versatile as you fit so many of them in one device. Games, however, have specific rules, a "right or wrong" way of playing, and often an emphasis on winning and losing. This is not necessarily a bad thing, but it *is* different. (Toca Boca, 2013)

The above statement shows Toca Boca's stance on play. In fact, in 2016, it launched the Stand for Play campaign, complete with poster giveaways (yes, I got one!) and a hashtag: #standforplay. To learn more, I spoke with Sweden-based Chris Lindgren, play designer and research manager at Toca Boca, in April 2016. Lindgren began her career as a programmer, but she soon desired to be more in charge of the content she created. Next, she pursued a bachelor's degree in children's culture at Stockholm University. Her rare combination of technical skills and background in children's culture enabled her to start her own company, which produced online content games that related to Sweden's public television. Then an opportunity opened up: the chance to work at a unique new digital company, Toca Boca.

Toca Boca was a division of Bonnier AB, a Swedish multimedia conglomerate, a major publisher of books, newspapers, and television content. Bonnier was seeking to expand its digital operations business. Björn Jeffery and Emil Overmar—employees working in the research and development division—had a unique idea: to develop digital toys, not games. At that time, in 2010, the App Store's children's content consisted mostly of educational apps and games. "There was not many apps just for play, for the sake of play, like what kids do all the time," Lindgren recalled.

Jeffrey and Overmar cofounded the Toca Boca division and added two more employees, one of which was Lindgren. She and Jens Peter de Pedro were hired on to be play designers. The team first decided on the toothy smile logo first. Someone had suggested "rainbow teeth" as a name, but it sounded too much like the Tom Clancy video game series *Rainbow Six*. Instead, they opted for the playful sounding Toca Boca, which roughly translates to "touch mouth" in "kind of Spanish," as Lindgren explained. Once the logo and name were settled, the team went to work creating apps that invited (or afforded) open-ended play.

This was the first time Lindgren worked with touch screen interfaces. She immediately saw how easily children could use tablet devices. *Toca Helicopter Taxi* was its first app. Then came *Toca Tea Party*, Lindgren's first app. (*Helicopter Taxi* was later removed from the App Store; it required too many instructions to play, unlike actual toys, which are driven by a child's imagination. Parental guidance is something Toca Boca does not want their apps to have.)

After about three years in, the team stepped back to analyze play themes in its digital toys. Specifically, the team reviewed what kinds of play worked best in their apps. They looked at ways of playing, which ranged from active play to role-play. Next, they looked at the commonalities and divided the play they observed into different types. The ideas of play types were charted. Three common concepts were charted. Importantly, each type of play also transferred well into a digital toy space.

The types of digital play in Toca Boca apps are: 1) role-play, 2) creative play, and 3) exploratory play. Role-play, or make-believe play, describes the apps that put most of the play outside the screen. "It starts a conversation," Lindgren explained. Examples include *Toca Tea Party* and *Toca Store*, in which two children can play on each side of a tablet playing together, and the *Toca Life*. "It's a doll house app," she continued. "It's you that makes it happen. There's no play in the app—it's tools for playing."

Creative play describes many of Toca Boca's other apps. *Hair Salon* is likely its most popular creative app. "It was designed for children from 3 to 6 years old, but the theme is so universal," Lindgren began. "Teenagers love it!" *Toca Blocks* is another of its creative apps. "You build things, make art, and build worlds for the characters." And finally there is exploratory play. *Toca Nature* is an example, which Lindgren calls "kind of magic." She's right. *Toca Nature* is a robust world building game that children can grow and explore. My son loves wandering the forest he creates, taking the occasional photo in his virtual nature walks.

All play types mix together, of course. The benefit of parsing them out is that the design team can now focus on one as primary, thus engaging children to play. Next, Lindgren explained the design process that follows. She said:

> We do a lot of testing, and then try to have kids discuss their play. They also play with actual toys that already exist. Then we digital prototype it to see if children act out the play themes we didn't think about, so we can support those. In *Toca Blocks*, for example, you can build abstract art, or a specific thing, like a house. A lot of kids wanted to do that. We decided to support that more by adding blocks to make that more specific, like a toilet block for the house.

What sets Toca Boca as unique is the overall diversity in the characters and the play space. The concept started as being a gender-neutral toy, which later expanded to encompass a full definition of diversity, including skin color, disability, and ethnicity. "In the Toca Life series, we want to support many ways of playing with the dollhouse," Lindgren said. She continued, explaining the gender neutrality of the apps. She said:

> Maybe it's because we're in Sweden, the unisex perspective came natural. I don't even think we talked about it. It was just in our minds not to do a concept just for boys or girls. When we [Toca Boca] got bigger, we had to talk about it. We wanted to make sure everyone was on the same page. We did a workshop and had a consultant come in and discuss why we want it to be that way. It is so all kids can meet together, and play together, and have the same references, regardless of being a boy or a girl. One aspect that came up was could we do all these and play types? The car theme is traditionally a boy theme. Do we do that, or do we avoid it? We decided we have a Toca Boca way of doing things. We do it with our approach and consider all the details carefully.

The language is also neutral; Toca Boca characters speak in a kind of whimsical gibberish. "We don't want kids to ask the parents for help with the app," Lingren said. "We want the kids to feel like it's made for them." That design decision is why Toca Boca apps have no written text, nor do they require instructions to play. This, too, was decided from the beginning. And its apps have been downloaded in over 200 countries.

One of Toca Boca's core design principles is "the everyday." Lindgren explained, "Kids play in their everyday environment. They play with everyday things, like cooking and having a tea party." Lindgren told me about a presentation she game at a conference recently. In one slide, she compared digital toys and games. She said:

Toys are open-ended. It's your imagination that sets the limits. On the game side, there are rules. We don't want rules. We don't want achievements. You do whatever you want, there is no right or wrong. You decide. No time limits either. Self-expression is on the toy side. We say we don't make educational apps, but of course in free play that's how kids learn. You learn about yourself, you try out different roles and sides of yourself.

So what is Toca Boca's secret and how can a teacher replicate it? Like other successful game companies, they test often. They have children test early in production design to see if particular parts of the app are intuitive. Is a child able to just pick up the app and immediately get it? "If kids try to do something we don't support, we remove that invitation to that action in the app," Lindgren explained. "On the other side, we try to support it if it's not there. For example, in *Toca Life* there was a kid who wanted to pick all of the flowers, but we had a limitation on how many could go in a basket." By the process of setting milestones in the production in process for testing, they can iterate on design. "The best tip is to plan and iterate, and to plan for changing the plans," Lindgren concluded.

It is evident from playing Toca Boca apps that the designers value play. Just weeks after Lindgren and I spoke, Toca Boca, and its Canadian-based sister digital toy company, Sago Mini, were sold to Spin Master, maker of family and party games, like *HedBanz*, and the popular toy Hatchimals. As of this writing, Jeffery remains as Toca Boca's CEO, leading the way for more high quality digital toys.

Tiggly Toys

Tiggly is a sold as three separate sets: Shapes, Words, and Math. Each box includes manipulative toys, made from silicone, that interact with its growing library of mobile games. Each set is both a tactile toy and a suite of digital apps. The Math set has different side rods that can be used to create virtual recipes or to build ladders in a platformer Tiggly game. The Shapes set has four geometric-shaped toys: a square, a triangle, a star, and a circle. Apps that interact with it include *Tiggly Stamp*. Tapping the tablet screen with a shape creates objects that can be moved around and recorded as a digital story. *Sesame Street Alphabet Kitchen* is a sight word game featuring Cookie Monster that works with Tiggly's Word set of vowels. In March 2016, Elmo was added to the app. In April that year, *Tiggly Shapes Got Talent*, a math storybook game, which uses its Shapes toys, was released. It was developed with Columbia University's Herbert Ginsburg, who, along with Carole Greenes and Robert Balfanz, developed the math curriculum, Big Math for Little Kids.

I spoke with Azadeh (Azi) Jamalian, cofounder and Chief Learning Officer of Tiggly, in March 2016. Tiggly toys can be purchased at Apple Stores, Target, and other major retailers. In addition to starting the company, Jamalian is also an adjunct assistant professor in Cognitive Studies in Education at Teachers College at Columbia University. Her interests pertain to how children learn. Later, Jamalian earned a master's degree in instructional technology, which focused on games, specifically, what the elements are of games that make users feel or think a certain way. Her cohort developed the smoking cessation mobile game *Lit2Quit*, which was funded by the National Science Foundation. Jamalian continued her doctoral studies at Teachers College at Columbia University, in New York. Her PhD was in cognitive studies in education, with a focus on children. In addition to game design, Jamalian brings her academic background of how children learn through Tiggly toys.

Jamalian recalled that she had been "bothered" by how gamification often works, taking point systems, badges and levels, and then putting it over another activity. Gamification in the early days was not often well integrated. Also, children may not grasp the value of points; young children do not yet understand number sense, the abstract concept of big numbers. During this time, she continued to ponder how game designers create experiences that make users feel a certain way. "It doesn't have to be humorous or happy; sometimes you want players or feel sad or concern for a cause," she said.

Tiggly brings playfulness, a context for teaching and learning, to its products. "What you want to see is kids creating content, not just sitting in front of a screen," Jamalian began. My son is 6 years old—the target demographic for all three sets—and he particularly enjoys the agency the apps encourage. He owns his actions. "You don't need to actually play games to give agency to kids," Jamalian continued. "You need to create a safe environment to explore, and to create a context for children to solve problems."

Tiggly started in 2013, when many children first started to play on tablets. At that time, educators and parents began to express concern about screen time. How much screen time is too much? Jamalian explained how there were, basically, two camps: one would say screen time is bad, while the other said that if screen time is designed to teach how children think, it could be beneficial to learning. "We brought the best elements of both worlds together," she recalled. "Tactile play brought into digital learning to transform their learning experience. An experience you couldn't duplicate with digital or toys or blocks alone." The silly name, Tiggly, was chosen because the founders wanted to evoke a sense of happiness. After brainstorming words, as well as certain vowel-consonant pairs and sounds, Tiggly was the winner. It is a combination of giggle and tickle.

Each Tiggly game encourages players to try new things, by experimentation and to not be afraid of failure. Children are afforded an opportunity to test different variations. For example, baking cookies for Cookie Monster in *Alphabet Kitchen* presents players with sight words that are missing vowels. The child then stamps a vowel on the screen to see if it makes a real word. If the sight word doesn't have a meaning, care is taken to ensure that the action doesn't feel like failure. "We use a lot of humor and characters chiming in to make the learning space a safe space to experiment," Jamalian explained. "This helps kids to be creative, to try new things and discover. We also believe in creating an environment that drives thinking about a certain concept and to create within certain limits. It helps [children] bring their own identity to what they create."

Each app that accompanies the tactile toy is set in a backdrop reminiscent of a play zone in a classroom. Jamalian explained to me how the design pulls forward teachable lessons in settings appropriate to young children's play. The team observes how kids play naturally, like in a kitchen area or make-believe dress-up area. She said:

> We use a familiar context, like cooking, stories, drawing, or playing doctor—the play patterns kids basically know and actually want to do. What we do is look into those play patterns and ask ourselves about what the math or literacy thinking that take place in those patterns. We try to highlight those and bring it up front. It's not a forced way, like solving math problems to chop things in a kitchen. Instead, we think about the math thinking that would be in a kitchen area, and bring those up front. When you do that, kids can relate to it, they learn math in a context they can understand.

According to Jamalian, one of the most important things Tiggly does is to "not get fooled by the technology." This is a trapping of some learning games in the App Store. The design team thinks about tactile gestures and experiences, like using shapes, counting with manipulatives, or using letters. Then they use the digital, mobile platform to incorporate a sense of silliness. Finally, they scaffold playfulness, which keeps children coming back to the apps to play, and to learn.

This also differs from so-called "accessory apps" (or "appcessories"), tie-ins to familiar television and movie characters. "When it comes to apps, unfortunately it often looks like that character but it doesn't bring any of the personalities or the essence of the show into the app," Jamalian explained. "It becomes an add-on, that has nothing to do with the app." When Tiggly partnered with Sesame, it worked closely with their design team and the writers of the show. Sesame's writers wrote all of Cookie Monster and Elmo's lines. "When you play the app, it feels like you are playing with Cookie Monster or Elmo, it feels like you're in the video, rather than passively watching a video," she said.

Although Tiggly is mostly played in homes, the company sees potential in classrooms. In summer 2015, at the International Society for Technology in Education (ISTE) Conference, classroom sets of Tiggly were launched. This came after a pilot study took place in 10 schools. They wanted to see how teachers integrate Tiggly's manipulatives and apps into existing curriculum, as well as with different settings, from 1:1 iPads, to shared devices, as well as classes with just one iPad. They looked into both how and why they used Tiggly, as part of the lesson or for free play. They combined the teacher feedback data into handbooks that are packaged with the class sets. There are also paper-based activity books, based on apps, with the same sense of playfulness. The idea is for teachers to facilitate knowledge transfer from the app to other contexts.

Building Games with *Bloxels*

Bloxels is a visually based game-design system from Pixel Press. The box includes 250 colored cubes, a square board with cube-sized cutouts, a link to a free app, and easy-to-follow instructions. To play, place the physical cubes anywhere on the board. Next, open the free app and capture the cubed arrangement with the camera. Each cube has a different assigned property: for example, blue cubes become water and red cubes turn into lava. There are templates available on the app, including different backgrounds, playable sprite characters, and animations. Rather than coding, children *build* games through tactile play—design thinking is part of the experience.

I first heard about Pixel Press, the maker of *Bloxels*, in spring 2015, at a game jam. Participants were drawing game levels on graph paper, and then they scanned in with an iPad. The app, *Floors*, is free and results in a playable video game. After the game jam, I started to follow Pixel Press on Twitter. I discovered that they had a Kickstarter crowdfunding campaign for the set that became known as *Bloxels*. I e-mailed Robin Rath, the cofounder, and inquired about bringing a prototype with me to the ISTE Conference. Within a few days, FedEx delivered a wooden board and a large Ziploc bag of colored cubes.

I spoke with Pixel Press cofounder Josh Stevens in June 2016. He shared the history of the company, which is based in St. Louis, Missouri. "*Floors* came about from what we [Stevens and Rath] did as kids," Stevens said. "We have been friends since age 5. When our mom and dad said no more video games or TV, we continued the experience by drawing games on paper." Then, about three years ago, Rath shared an idea with Stevens. At that time, Rath had been working at a company that was doing ocular recognition technology. His work led to an idea: Turn drawings of games into actual video games. Thus *Floors* was born. Next came the Kickstarter crowdfunding campaign. "It was a big hit. The media latched onto it," Stevens recalled. "There was also nostalgia from parents. People started sending in drawings of game levels from their childhood."

In addition to nostalgic crowdfunders, Cartoon Network caught the attention of the Kickstarter campaign. Rath and Stevens were approached by Cartoon Network to make *Adventure Time Game Wizard*, a tie-in from the cartoon to the *Floors* app. Rath and Stevens quit their day jobs and officially started the company in 2014. Although *Floors* and *Adventure Time Game Wizard* were successful, there remained challenges. The iPad camera was inaccurate interpreting the lines younger children drew. Enter *Bloxels*, which eliminated user error from hard-to-read drawings. "*Bloxels* blew up the art side of it," Stevens said. "Our number one request from kids using Floors was to desire to create characters. That can now be done with *Bloxels*, as can animations for the characters. Users can animate how enemies run, plus kids were already familiar with pixel art."

After a full year of work, sets of *Bloxels* were shipped in January 2016. And in September that year, Pixel Press announced a partnership with toy giant Mattel. Pixel Press continues to develop *Bloxels*, while Mattel handles the manufacturing and distribution.

New Jersey teacher Robert Kalman is the educator in residence for *Bloxels*. Now a middle school computer technology teacher, he had been a 5th grade teacher for 2 years. He began using *Floors* because his district was a 1:1 iPad. He used the app during an administrator observation. "It went well!" Kalman said, when we spoke in June 2016. Kalman was drawn to the concept that anyone could be a video game designer. "I loved the connection between the physical and digital," he said. "It pulls kids a little bit out of their devices and lets them be collaborative." As the educator in residence, he serves as lead ambassador to keep people informed about *Bloxels*. "Pixel Press didn't realize their tool would be so teacher-friendly. I help make connections from the kids using it on their own to teachers who want to use it."

The beauty of *Bloxels* is that it is so open-ended. You can be hands-on with the cubes, or digitally design in the app. Kalman has a class set for his middle school students. "My students used it for the past few months," he explained. "For some students, the hands-on component is incredible, as are the collaborative elements." Using a class set, Kalman has students work on parts of games that they want to. A few design pixel art characters, and the accompanying frame-by-frame animations. Another team plans out the level design. "There is flexibility and openness in the design of the tool."

The *Bloxels* website features lesson plans for different content areas and grade levels. "Teachers were already finding ways to wrap their curriculum around it," Stevens said. One elementary class took a picture book the class was reading and recreated it using *Bloxels*. Stevens told me about a lesson plan on its website called "Presidential Run." Using it, he observed a team who made a game about Ronald Reagan. The enemies were Brussels sprouts—Reagan's least favorite food. Students used white blocks to tell his story throughout the game. (White blocks are interactive conversations that are told with thought bubbles.) Another group made a game featuring William Howard Taft. The character was portrayed as a round. "He rolled, he didn't walk," Stevens recalled. He continued:

> The coins were changed to be biscuits and gravy. There was a bathtub, because Taft got stuck in a bathtub. The white block was where the narrative took place. Towards the end of the game was a gym for Taft, and the coins became carrots and broccoli. They told Taft's story using *Bloxels* as the medium.

User-generated games are posted on an Infinity Wall. To find a game, search Cartesian coordinate on an x, y plane (e.g., -100, 50). There are categories for featured art and games levels, which are updated weekly, and there are also user profiles for users. Also there is a system of virtual coins to purchase virtual items from the Infinity Wall. You can't buy a complete game, but you can buy the terrain art, the hero, or coin art. "Some users only create characters and animations and derive satisfaction from that economy," Stevens explained.

The Kids As Video Game Makers contest began in March 2016. The idea was to empower kids to be game designers. It took place at the Children's Creativity Museum, which is situated right next to the Game Developer Conference (GDC), celebrating games built by entrants as young as age 6. In addition to the group of approximately 80 people who attended, the three student winners also were at the event. Their games were highlighted, and attendees had an opportunity to play the game levels. "Since then, one of the kids e-mails me at least once a week," Stevens said. "He tells me about his creations. He's got *Galactic Hunter 1*, *Galactic Hunter 2*, and he keeps building on this storyline about this character that he generated."

Using *Bloxels* to build games exemplifies the design thinking process. "The goal is not to creating the perfect game; instead it's the process," Kalman said. "I think that has so much value in education. Some kids are used to getting beaten down in classes where the goal is perfection. But it's the process. It's not about creating the perfect game—it's about creating, testing, and improving."

Originator's Endless Apps

Endless Alphabet, a playful sight-reading game, has been an App Store "Editor's Choice" and continues to spin-off endless sequels (*Endless Alphabet*, *Endless Reader*, *Endless Numbers*). I contacted Rex Ishibashi, CEO of Originator back in January 2014. Based in Silicon Valley, the studio originally consisted of five of the core team members from Callaway Digital Arts. Callaway had focused on e-books with interactive elements that enrich the story experience. According to Ishibashi, Callaway's founder believed that e-book pages should be read sequentially, in order, for a cover-to-cover experience. Analytics showed otherwise: children were navigating directly to the table of contents to find their favorite interactions within the e-books and "played" just those pages. It wasn't the story that was compelling on those pages; rather, it was the interactions. Ishibashi told me about *Another Monster at the End of this Book*, a Sesame Workshop title. He explained that Callaway gathered data on page views. Children were navigating directly to the section where Grover was setting up a wall of blocks. They would play the blocks page for minutes on end. This realization led to *Endless Alphabet's* nonlinear interface.

Children's interactive books and mobile games are often played in short time spans. According to Ishibashi, about 60 to 65% of all of the interactions on its apps occurred on an iPad; about 35% were on an iPhone. A parent may hand over an iPhone to a child to play for just a few minutes. These devices can be "digital nannies." About half of Originator's interactions happened while a family was away from home or in a car. Ishibashi said, "We started orienting our games really around shorter experiences that can be enjoyed in five minutes, but can be expanded to 10, 15, 30 minutes."

Endless Alphabet features a carousel of letters. Although the team at Originator aren't Montessori-trained, the drag-and-drop puzzle interface bears many similarities to the teaching style. Pick a letter and a word appears, and then it gets scrambled when a silly monster runs through it. Completed puzzles trigger a fun animation as a reward. Endless puzzles have no "kill screen" (where the player loses), no points are aggregated, and levels aren't saved. Ishibashi told me that education is deeply rooted in *Endless Alphabet*, but ultimately there has to be a "fun factor," otherwise the child will lose interest.

Originator's team is passionate about delivering a high quality experience. Each of the five company members has children, but they make no claim to being expert educators. Ishibashi explained, "We're teaching preschoolers, trying to make the lessons that we feel are important to a 2- or 3-year-old. A lot of apps out there really pander to kids, simply doing what is already done. Part of what we're doing is using the interactivity and focusing the experience on short session times where they are learning something in a way the classroom can't accomplish."

My son enjoys dressing up Originator's virtual *Mr. Potato Head* more than the physical version of Hasbro's classic plastic toy. Originator was given full creative license to develop it. "Potato truly comes to life in fantastical variations not limited by the challenges of plastic manufacturing, retail, and the physical box," Ishibashi explained. The character can be dressed and then animated. The app was intended to be marketing support for the physical toy. Ishibashi amusedly recalled how a Hasbro executive said that he could see a day when the plastic toy becomes the marketing support for the app.

Diversity in Apps

Literacy Safari publishes children's apps like *Dentist Bird*, based on a West African folktale, and *HangArt*, a sight word digital storytelling game. Sandhya Nankani, its founder, is also one of the founding members of Diversity in Apps. Started in June 2015, Diversity in Apps began as a grassroots coalition of folks across different disciplines: media experts, librarians, app developers, and researchers. "They were interested in taking the silhouetted conversations they had in their professional settings to create more intentionally and mindfully diverse content for children," Nankani told me in June 2016. "They wanted to raise awareness and support the industry in achieving these goals. Also, they wanted to call out and identify products that do a great job at achieving this."

Diversity in Apps started with mobile apps and has since expanded to other sectors of the children's media industry. In November 2015, it hosted an event with the Children's Media Association, in New York City. "It became pretty clear that these conversations were happening everywhere," Nankani continued. "It became about apparent that beyond having conversations, the industry should have a tool that they could use." The definition of what it means to be a "diverse app" has been "evolving." When I asked Nankani, she messaged me their definition over Skype chat. She wrote that diverse apps have:

> Stories and characters that represent the cultural diversity we see in our classrooms and communities, including differences in ethnicity, income, families, gender, class, demographics, mental and physical ability, and education level; complex characters that have their own authentic stories, enabling race, ethnicity, gender to be the secondary story and helping to break down existing stereotypes; accurate information about cultures, race, religion, language and traditions that offer kids new ways to connect to our diverse and rich world; innovative ways to help kids learn to read in their home language and in other world languages.

The audience whom app makers serve is not monolithic or homogenous. "How can we mindfully and intentionally create for that?" Nankani wondered. She considers Toca Boca to be a wonderful example of a diverse app maker. "The imaginative character depictions represent diversity in terms of ethnicity and race, and also gender-neutral content."

Diversity in Apps partnered with the Cooney Center and its researchers to create a DIG Toolkit. The purpose is for content creators to utilize it throughout their development process. They reviewed rubrics that look at diversity and bias in product development. The result was a list of 12 criteria, or milestones, to guide products to be more diverse, equitable, and accessible. The Toolkit is like an activity book, modeled on an interactive children's workbook. A coloring book page asks: What does your team look like? What networks are you tapping into to create a diverse team at the outset? Do I have an advisory board with people who can assist in looking out for stereotypes? Case studies are also included. For more, see: https://youtu.be/qWp15v5rorM.

Nankani has worked in educational publishing for the past 15 years. She started in textbooks and classroom magazines, where she observed diversity as a top priority. She noticed that the kinds of apps that were easily discoverable in the App Store did not reflect the world that we live in. "You have to dig hard," she said. The digital marketplace did not match the standards of print media.

As a content creator, Nankani decided to approach the issue of diversity head-on. Her company's *Dentist Bird* is an interactive book with game-like elements (see link at the end of this chapter) that blends in cultural elements about life in Liberia. And 2016's *Grandma's Great Gourd* brings the South Asian folk tale to life. Beyond this, she wondered whether diversity was not just about a culturally specific topic. So she decided to integrate diversity into a storytelling product: *HangArt*. The idea came as Nankani's daughter learned to read and write. She was intrigued seeing the pieces all come together. *HangArt* integrates pictures and storytelling with sight words. Instead of the hangman on a noose (not the most appropriate theme for a young child!), her game has a man hanging on a trapeze. When you win, he falls—but he can get back up. The sight words focused on Kindergarten through 3rd grade word lists. "The words needed to work for storytelling and for kids to be able to draw them," Nankani explained. "The mindful, intentional approach was baked in early. The palette for how to draw and represent yourself included many options for skin tones."

Conclusions and Takeaways

The toys and games in this chapter engender a sense of playfulness, often blending a digital with tactile experience. Each gives freedom for children to engage in open-ended play. Consider planning lessons and activities—at all grade levels—that are modeled on children's natural play patterns (e.g., Tiggly and pretend cooking, which children already tend to do in make-believe play). Observe your students' play patterns, and be mindful that experiences are gender neutral and free of culture bias.

Lesson Plan Ideas

Bring Your Own Book is a party game published that is excellent for English language arts classrooms. As the title suggests, you bring a book. Then pick category cards and skim through the book to find a sentence that fits the particular category. It is a fun and social way to having students engage together. Up to eight students at a time can play, and the game takes about 20 minutes, which works great in a learning center. It is commercially sold, or printable here—http://www.bringyourownbook.com

Design a Retro Game in Bloxels—Use *Bloxels* to make a game with a story. Lesson plans are here: http://www.bloxelsbuilder.com/lesson-plans. Exemplar work is here: http://www.bloxelsbuilder.com/kvgm2016, from the *Kids as Video Game Makers* competition, which was conducted in collaboration with the Children's Creativity Museum in San Francisco.

Grandma's Great Gourd activity guide—http://www.grandmasgourd.com/grownupguide

HangArt "grown-up guide" lesson plans—http://www.hangart.co/grownups

Games

Activate Games for Learning American English: Board Games—https://americanenglish.state.gov/resources/activate-board-games#child-1482

Adventure Time Game Wizard to draw video games based on the Cartoon Network show—http://www.projectpixelpress.com/adventure-time-game-wizard

Bananagrams is a fun wordplay game about anagrams—http://www.bananagrams.com

Bluebee Pals are plush dolls that connect via Bluetooth to its tablet apps—https://bluebeepals.com

Bring Your Own Book social, party game that uses books as components—http://bit.ly/1Z8eVFl

Carcassonne is a classic "Euro-style" board game set in medieval France—http://www.zmangames.com/store/p38/Carcassonne.html

Dentist Bird interactive West African folktale app—http://www.dentistbird.com

Dash and Dot coding robot—https://www.makewonder.com

Floors, draw a video game level—http://www.projectpixelpress.com/floors

Hang Art is a storytelling tool from Literacy Safari—http://www.hangart.co

HEXBUG are sets of low-cost robotic insects—https://www.hexbug.com

Love Letter is a card game in which a token, representing the love letter, gets passed from servants to the intended nobility. Look for *The Hobbit* and *Lord of the Rings* editions, which brings Tolkien's classic books to life. The game is light, inexpensive, and playable in minutes—https://www.alderac.com/loveletter

Osmo blends the mobile screen with the real world—https://www.playosmo.com

Spot-it is a pattern recognition game for young children, available everywhere—https://www.asmodee.us/en/games/spot-it

Storied Myth, children's adventure books that interact with the real world—https://appsto.re/i6Yn6pq

Super Mario Maker—http://supermariomaker.nintendo.com

Sushi Go card passing game for pattern recognition, for children as young as 5, with a grown-up—http://bit.ly/1XJYd0x

ThinkFun games—http://www.thinkfun.com

Tiggly toys—https://www.tiggly.com

Tinybop are apps for young children to design video games—https://tinybop.com

Toca Boca digital toys—http://tocaboca.com

Triqqy is a website to play tabletop games online—http://triqqy.com

Tsuro: The Game of the Path teaches multiple solutions to problems, for children as young as 5, with a grown-up—http://www.calliopegames.com/read/45/tsuro

Qixels are a toy to make pixel art—http://qixelsworld.com

Qwirkle is a Mensa-select game that is like dominoes mashed up with Scrabble. It teaches pattern recognition and logic—http://www.mindware.com/qwirkle-a2-32016.fltr

World Rescue Game—http://worldrescuegame.com

Resources

Bunge Lab—http://bungelab.berkeley.edu

Diversity in Apps—http://diversityinapps.com

From Books to Apps: Yes, Virginia, Diversity Does Matter When It Comes to Kids' Digital Diets, by Sandhya Nankani—http://bit.ly/1XpVAQV

Major Fun is an award founded by Bernie DeKoven. The team recognizes excellence in toys and games—http://www.majorfun.com

New Research: $13 Christmas gifts = 13 point gain in kids' IQ, from Po Brinson and Ashley Merryman—http://www.nurtureshock.com/IQLeaps.pdf

Originator—http://www.originatorkids.com

Sandbox Summit—http://sandboxsummit.org

The Sims 4 Expands Gender Customization Options—https://www.thesims.com/news/new-cas-update

Tap, Click, Read is a book from Lisa Guernsey and Michael Levine, of the Cooney Center—http://www.tapclickread.org

Teachers with Apps is a terrific blog created by a retired teacher. Consider following on social media—http://www.teacherswithapps.com

What Toy Makers Are Doing About Gender and Diversity, Cooney Center blog by Sandhya Nankani—http://www.joanganzcooneycenter.org/2016/05/10/what-toy-makers-are-doing-about-gender-and-diversity

· 8 ·

TEACHING WITH *MINECRAFT*

Markus "Notch" Persson, a Swedish computer programmer, developed *Minecraft* in 2009. The game now boasts hundred million of active users that either destroy (mine) or build (craft) in its blocky, virtual world. It was an independent release by Persson's company, Mojang (a nonsensical Swedish word). Rather than iterating the *Minecraft* game with nonstop sequels as most game publishers have (e.g., *Assassin's Creed III*, *Fallout IV*), Mojang pushes out content updates to the growing world. It can be played on PCs, consoles, tablets, and smartphones.

In March 2014, I spoke to game design professor Richard Bartle about *Minecraft*'s popularity. *Minecraft* empowers users by giving everyone a canvas to build their own virtual world. He compared it to the timeless success of LEGO. He said, "It's the great construction set, and you can build what you like in the sandbox mode." Bartle elaborated:

> As for what you use *Minecraft* for [in education]—the question is, what are the learning outcomes, which tend to be expressed in much blander terms. Are your students more creative than when they went in? The teaching profession acts as a brake on that type of thing. Personally, I like that, because when people play, they explore not just what they are playing with, but also their own play processes.

Steve Isaacs is an outspoken proponent of student choice and voice, as well as co-learning, in the classroom. When we spoke in April 2016, he shared how *Minecraft* transformed his teaching. "What is most powerful is for me is that it draws on students as the experts," he said. "It changed my approach to teaching and learning. Something spoke to me because of kids' excitement."

Minecraft can be played in two modes: creative or survival. Creative mode is when players make, or craft items. In survival mode, you gather resources, and then you have to create or craft using what you collect. "Each of those items has a recipe behind them," Isaacs explained. "The player has to figure out the recipes. Often they go to a wiki. To make a furnace you need to place cobblestone on a crafting table in a particular configuration."

One of the things that attracted Isaacs to *Minecraft* was the community of practice that players participate in. There are scores of websites and wikis devoted to explaining how to play and craft items. Perusing YouTube with my son, I discovered that when I stack one pumpkin head block on top of two snow blocks, the whole thing springs to life as a "snow golem." Soon after, my son found out that at night, snow golems throw snowballs at oncoming hordes of creepers (enemies). "The game has no instruction manual, which I love," Isaacs continued. "All of the content that explains anything about the game, or even how to play, is user-generated. This is an allure as a teaching and learning tool. Kids learn in a constructivist manner, learning from peers."

YouTube influences the way children learn about *Minecraft*. "Kids go out and learn what they need from others," Isaacs said. "Aside from watching content, they now want to create and share content, too." His students use a tool called SnapGuide to author step-by-step screenshot tutorials. "My students teach other kids how to build a furnace."

At first, Isaacs envisioned his students interacting in an adventure map he would create. "To me that made sense," he said. "Thanks to Marianne Malmstrom, I realized I didn't have to be in control of that part of it." The project's task eventually was simplified: Make a game in *Minecraft*. "I decided to keep the project open, like the game was intended to be."

Teacher Marianne Malmstrom is an advocate of partnering with kids. She does not advise coming up with a lesson to teach in *Minecraft*. "Kids are experts," she explained. "Have them help you set up a server. Engage kids with discussion of curricular goals. If you can take that leap of faith with your kids, you go on a journey." In other words, if the teacher creates the lesson in game, it becomes limited by the teacher—the learning can only go as far as what the teacher knows. "If the students are involved, the knowledge multiplies exponentially," she continued.

Malmstrom shared an example of a student-created lesson. One colleague at her former school wanted to teach a lesson on different types of government. She and the students developed the lesson together. The teacher told class that she wanted them to model different governments in the world, and the children made the rules. "It makes you think about pedagogy as a teacher," Malmstrom said. "You think about the ownership that comes alive when the kids get invested. It is because they study government in a very real, literal way. You can't read these lessons in a book!"

In June 2016, Microsoft rolled out *Minecraft: Education Edition*. Rather than turn it into an educational video game, the software giant decided to tap into the rich and diverse community of educators who were already adapting the game into their teaching. Several of the people profiled in this chapter attended the *Minecraft Summit*, at Microsoft's headquarters, in May 2016. Deirdre Quarnstrom, who is heading up the *Minecraft: Education Edition* team, met with me at the 13th Annual Games for Change Festival, in 2016. She explained the team's intentional design decision to let teachers take charge of student assessments. Quarnstrom shared how they opted for qualitative assessments using student screenshots. This means that students take charge of how to present their artifacts for grading. It also maintains the authenticity of the commercial version of *Minecraft*, and leaves the teaching to the teachers.

This chapter opens with the story Connected Camps, an out-of-school *Minecraft* program that is situated in the ethos of connected learning. Next, how the game is adapted into formal classrooms is reviewed. There are several ideas shared about how to best take advantage of the playful affordances *Minecraft* has to engage and teach students in several content areas. I speak with teachers who use it in Spanish class, math class, inclusive 5th grade class, and as a tool to design games.

Connected Camps

Connected Camps launched in 2015, using *Minecraft* for a virtual camp and afterschool program. The Institute of Play's Katie Salen, Connected Learning's Mizuko (Mimi) Ito, and Los Angeles Makerspace's Tara Tiger Brown are the founders. I spoke with Ito in April 2016 about how Connected Camps models digital citizenship in *Minecraft*. Ito has a background in cultural anthropology, and she is a professor of digital media and learning at the University of California-Irvine. Her main body of work pertains to researching how young people learn, as well as how they further their interests using new technologies, like mobile, games, and social media. Specifically, Ito focuses on learning in online affinity networks that pertain to gaming.

Ito found herself doing a series of case studies—"deep dives"—on high functioning learning in communities where there was "a really robust metagame and people are problem solving and learning together." This was around the time that Minecraft was getting more traction from both educators and parents. "I thought that Minecraft provided such an interesting opportunity to connect with young people around social, affinity-based, game-based learning," Ito said. "So we launched the start-up with Katie Salen and Tara Brown to mine this opportunity of social game-based learning through Minecraft."

Connected Camps runs a series of online learning programs in Minecraft that are staffed by high school and college counselors "that are Minecraft nerds themselves." The Institute of Play was a partner for the first summer, and remains a "close partner" in developing programming and counselor training. Brendan Trombley, game designer at the Institute, developed the camp's first coding program, and he trained many of the counselors. The counselors are trained to mediate griefing (harassing other players). "We don't exclude campers, we reform them," Ito explained. As a result, there is a strong code of conduct that is enforced by the counselors and community. "That we are really rigid about. To value player agency, you have to model the values of the community."

One of the interesting things about Minecraft is that it is so modifiable to so many learning goals. "The outcomes we're looking out are about digital literacy, agency, digital citizenship, collaboration skills, design thinking, problem solving," Ito explained. As a result, Ito looks for students to build social connections and social capital with peers. "Those are outcomes educators tend to think of more in the enrichment space. It's a natural fit." One enrichment space included the LA public library, which Connected Camps worked with in summer 2015.

The camp's model is centered on connected learning. "It is youth-driven, social, affinity-based, and informal learning," Ito said. The Connected Learning Model has three core principles: 1) shared purpose, 2) production or project-centered, and 3) an openly networked component. The idea is that the informal learning is in the real world, not in a "sequestered" learning environment. "If you have those three features you have an environment in which play is not just mucking around," Ito explained. "It's then about genuine inquiry and problem solving that is relevant and impactful in the world."

The focus has been in the enrichment and after-school space, as opposed to the classroom and curricular space. "This is not to say that we're not exploring partnership for class use, like coding, for example. Even with coding, it is youth-initiated project-based, not content-based learning." Connected Camps works with local educators who run their own local servers. These local servers are then connected to the camp's servers. "We're learning from each environment because the barriers and needs are different," Ito said. Connected Camps has piloted with smaller northern California communities, and in Chicago, too. LA Maker Space recently ran a Kickstarter crowdfunding campaign that enabled the camp to train library staff on how to use *Minecraft* using low-bandwidth settings.

Place-based programs in libraries and museums run for a short time for local kids and exhibits. As an online space, Connected Camps is longer term. "*Minecraft* is a safe space to develop interest-driven relationships that blossom into friendships," Ito said. "The friendships are based on interest and affinity, as opposed to place-based affiliation." Because of parental nervousness regarding safety, younger children often aren't afforded freedom to form those kinds of affiliations. I won't let my 5-year-old play at the park alone! The camp exists to "create an environment that is educator-sponsored, but is interest- and youth-driven to develop those forms of social capital development for kids."

Of course, not all households can afford *Minecraft*, and many more lack computers or high speed Internet. There is a gap—an economic divide—from families that play the game on mobile (*Minecraft: Pocket Edition*), on a console, or on a computer running its own server. Connected Camps is working to partner with non-profits that can help it serve lower income communities through free programs. "We've been doing active outreach in communities that serve for both the campers and counselor recruitment," Ito explained. "We feel it's important for non-dominant youth also have older peers that they have a sense of cultural affinity and social connection. It's been challenging, we're trying to remove the barriers."

There are several levels of participation in Connected Camps. There is an informal Kids Club in which its servers are open for a few hours each day. There is also a shared server in which children from all over the country are invited by counselors to share in collaborative builds, or to participate in scheduled club activities, like a book club or game club. Other campers participate in more structured program, and involve coding, building architecture, designing games, and playing in survival mode. "In those programs, there is more a structured curriculum with direct instruction up front," Ito said. "We have a design challenge for each session, which is about an hour-and-a-half every day for a week. It could also be after school for eight weeks, if it's in the after-school model." Of course, children can just wander off in *Minecraft* and free play. In summer, role-play in the game is even more self-initiated. The difference is that Connected Camps has counselors who moderate griefing and challenge the children to challenge themselves.

Minecraft in Schools

Up until 2016, TeacherGaming distributed the authorized educational modifications of *Minecraft*. It had been a partnership between Finnish educator Santeri Koivisto and New York City teacher Joel Levin. I interviewed Koivisto via Skype in February 2014. He was among the first to use the off-the-shelf version of *Minecraft* in his classroom. He had observed how students experimented by trial and error when building in the game. His inspiration also came from playing it personally. Then, when other teachers saw what he was doing, they inquired about emulating his success. It was then that Koivisto realized something was there—teachers wanted it too.

In April 2011, Koivisto met with representatives from Mojang at a local science fair. While there, Koivisto asked the team if he could become the exclusive Finnish distributor of *Minecraft* for schools. Serendipitously, in New York City, teacher Joel Levin published a blog post about his use of *Minecraft* in the classroom. Koivisto corresponded to Levin, which eventually led to a Skype chat. They decided to form a joint venture, known as TeacherGaming. Koivisto also met with Persson. They had a deep conversation about how to keep licenses secure in schools. Persson then said, "If we trust that most of our players won't pirate the game, why shouldn't we trust the schools?"

TeacherGaming offered a classroom and school discount on *Minecraft*, which is customized for student use. (It also licenses *KerbalEdu*, a rocket kit simulator, linked under Lesson Plans at the end of this chapter.) The safe-for-school version was called *MinecraftEdu*. Along with private servers, TeacherGaming featured lesson plans and adventure maps (premade worlds). Mojang, creator of *Minecraft*, wasn't directly involved with TeacherGaming's distribution. Mojang wanted to "concentrate on making fun and entertaining games," Koivisto explained.

With a PTA grant for eight licenses and a private server, I rolled out *MinecraftEdu* in my middle school classroom. I had a PTA grant for eight licensed accounts, and a private server. From my laptop, I could control whether students would be playing in daylight or nighttime, as well as where the multiplayer experience would be. This was around the time that the class was learning about the settlement of America. At first, students thought that they would be tasked with building forts. This would seem like how one would use *Minecraft* in a social studies class; however, it actually would miss the learning goals. It would be, as the Folger Shakespeare Library curriculum points out, like teaching *Romeo and Juliet* by having students build the Globe Theater out of Popsicle sticks! (Yes! That is a project in classrooms. Google Image it!) My learning goal, however, was to impart how difficult survival was in a strange land; this was not an architecture class. So I selected an island from *MinecraftEdu*'s world library that was geographically similar to the Jamestown Settlement. Then I had the class play in survival mode, in 8 teams.

I instructed students to build fortifications in this strange land. Some did, most did not. Because they were playing in peaceful mode, there was no fear of creepers (zombie-like monsters). But that was not to last long. I was a teacher in "god mode." Soon enough, I changed everyone's time to night, and then I ratcheted up the difficulty setting to hard. The class was audibly concerned, as zombie hordes emerged, attacking stranded players. Those who did build houses and forts were, of course, safe. They wondered why others had not listened. Then I paused everyone's game.

Minecraft became an effective tool for me to bring experiential learning to my students. The whole class discussion that followed, about why settlers needed to work together cooperatively, to fortify, to collect food, suddenly had meaning for students. I did not introduce anything about Jamestown until *after* this lesson. The class understood the lingering threat settlers felt in the strange land of the New World because they had a shared experience.

In 2014, Microsoft purchased Mojang. Then, in 2015, *Minecraft: Education Edition* was announced. *Minecraft: Education Edition* also extended the existing teacher community. Because a student's *Minecraft: Education Edition* account can be used at school and at home, homework might become something that a student might actually want to do. The Assessment of learning is put in the hands of the teacher and student—not from game analytics. *Minecraft: Education Edition* added a student portfolio feature, which is a qualitative assessment tool (more similar to BrainPOP's SnapThought than

GlassLab's teacher dashboards). The portfolio is intended for students to use when they collect in-game evidence of learning using a virtual camera. There are also non-playable characters (NPCs) in the education version, which can serve as digital tour guides, set up by the teacher. Digital chalkboards are in the game now, too, enabling teachers to guide along instruction.

It can be daunting for teachers not accustomed to game-based learning to bring an open-ended game like *Minecraft: Education Edition* into their class-rooms. To mediate this, Microsoft launched a free, online mentorship pro-gram. Steve Isaacs was one of the teachers around the world selected to lead the nascent program. In addition to reducing barriers to adoption, *Minecraft* mentors also provide support for teachers. To learn how to use *Minecraft*, a teacher first books time with a mentor. Isaacs often begins with a preliminary Skype call. "I talk about how it can be used in schools, comparing the stu-dent and educator experience," Isaacs said. Next, he leads a demonstration of the game by screensharing his computer with his mentees. Then he asks the educator to play the game, so they can enjoy and experience it the way kids learn it. "So much of the power of *Minecraft* is the learning experience," Isaacs continued. "Teachers should understand how kids learn it. They should know that it is okay to co-learn with students."

5th Grade in *Minecraft*

Mark Grundel, is the cofounder of the #MinecraftEDU Twitter chat, as well as a 5th grade teacher in New Jersey. Along with Isaacs, Grundel was invited to the *Minecraft Summit* at Microsoft's Seattle campus in late May 2016. When we spoke in April 2016, he explained how he integrated the game into his curriculum. It was very much of a DIY affair. "It's pretty crude," he confessed.

As it turned out, Grundel's school had been leasing computers. When the school transitioned to Chromebooks, he "claimed" four older computers the school owned outright. (Teacher Peggy Sheehy did the same thing. When her school switched over to Chromebooks, she requested all of the older Macs, so she could install and run *World of Warcraft* in her class.) Grundel's school technology department brought him a router, which connected the computers together. "Students use their accounts," he said. "Because of a Java issue, they can't collaborate in the same world—it must be single player."

As a 5th grade teacher, Grundel teaches all subjects. (In New Jersey mid-dle school is grades 5–8; however, many middle schools, like where I teach, start at grade 6). As a result, Grundel's students have an opportunity to use *Minecraft* in different content areas. When teaching English language arts, he had students study the setting in the novel *Tuck Everlasting*. As a project, two students created lead character Winnie Foster's house in *Minecraft*, as well as the town where she lived, and the gallows. "They do outside research to learn what gallows are, which becomes vocabulary," Grundel said.

In science Grundel students chose atoms from the periodic table, and then create it. "Kids used redstone [the *Minecraft* block that conducts virtual electricity] to make electrons fly around the atom," he said. "Other blocks were used for the nucleus and protons." In social studies, for the Westward Expansion unit, students recreated a Lakota Sioux village, and aspects of Lewis and Clark's expedition. In math, he put Dan Meyers' Three Act Math curriculum into the game. Three Act Math uses visuals, rather than numbers. Using blocks, the students make the problems. And for the lesson on volume, Grundel used Tinker Cad [used for 3D printer modeling] to import a diamond prism into *Minecraft*'s virtual environment.

Grundel teaches with games because it is engaging to him, as a teacher, and because it's what his students are doing at home. "It connects home and school," he said. Some students work for hours on end at home about atoms *because* they use *Minecraft* as a platform." *Minecraft* is on many platforms, including game consoles. When students play it on PlayStation at home, they bring their parents in to video their projects. Grundel can't get all parents to help students complete a math worksheet, but they will help by recording *Minecraft* videos. "It engages whole families," he continued. "Every kid and parent knows what *Minecraft* is."

Spanish Class in *Minecraft*

I spoke with Minnesota-based Spanish teacher, Glen Irvin, in March 2016, to learn about how he uses *Minecraft* in his teaching. I knew Irvin from *Minecraft* Twitter chats as @IrvSpanish. Teaching Spanish for 17 years, Irvin has been a gamer in his personal life for years. The inspiration to bring both worlds together came from educational technology professor Chris Haskell, at Boise State University (whom I interview about gamification in Chapter 11). Irvin was inspired after learning about gamification after taking online courses from Haskell.

"I thought they would throw me out of the meeting!" recalled Irvin. He thought the administration would immediately shoot down his request to purchase *MinecraftEdu* licenses. But he was wrong. Armed with research about games and learning, which were provided by Haskell, Irvin proposed his idea. To Irvin's delight, the administration agreed. The school ended up purchasing 24 user licenses, and a server for the computer lab. As part of the agreement, he would teach other teachers about *Minecraft* (Irvin is also the technology integrationist at his school.)

Irvin started with *Minecraft* at the "substitution level" of Ruben Puentedura's SAMR Model. SAMR is an acronym: substitution, augmentation, modification, and redefinition. It is intended to encourage educators to use technology that engages students in innovative ways. At the substitution level, Irvin used *Minecraft* as a platform. "Instead of creating a poster, they created it in 3D Minecraft world," he said. He soon realized, "We can go way beyond this!"

Next, Irvin put a business simulation lesson into *Minecraft*. Over the years, he had students discuss vocabulary and grammatical structures through face-to-face role-play. Irvin thought, why not run it inside of *Minecraft* and let students take on their own virtual businesses? He created a list of different occupations that students could be. He also created a monetary system, as well as a competitive atmosphere. The guiding rule was that text chats must be in Spanish. "I didn't know if it was going to work or if it would be a bust, but a week later, we were still playing [*laughs*]," he recalled. "It was supposed to be a two-day thing, but they wanted to keep doing it every day."

Engagement was at an all-time high level. What's more, students *wanted* to learn vocabulary words that were not yet presented in class lessons. They needed to learn beyond what was in the chapter they were in. As a result, the class created an in-game vocabulary list, consisting of Spanish phrases and words. This was the result of the intrinsic motivation to learn, not because there was an eventual test.

If you play in a multiplayer *Minecraft* game, you have many interactions. Besides your avatar in the game, you are having chats and conversations about what you are doing with other players. Irvin wanted to apply this kind of experiential learning to other situations, aside from business and commerce. In his Spanish II class, he offered students a choice: game-based learning or a "traditional route." About half chose game-based learning, which was run using a shared Google Doc. "Each week I sent global tasks, which are missions," Irvin explained. "They work together, by themselves, or with non-playable characters (NPCs)." He also set up on quests, which he does each week, letting students drive the vocabulary. He explained, "I figure that's the best, most authentic way to learn anything because it's driven by the student, not the teacher saying, 'We're in Chapter 7, let's learn about transportation.'"

Aside from Haskell's inspiration, Irvin is getting help from the *Minecraft* educator's community of practice. Garrett Zimmer, a *Minecraft* educational consultant (interviewed at the end of this chapter), has been assisting Irvin. Zimmer advised him to split his class into teams, and to situate the lessons into a storyline. Students became settlers who were given an opportunity to build a new civilization. Roving hordes of barbarians surround the settlements. Students then needed to work as teams in order to survive. "Everything I create—any lesson or ideas—he [Zimmer] breaks it down in the mind of a game designer," Irvin said. The story created an agency-based learning environment.

Irvin shares everything he and his students do on YouTube. "What I really like about *Minecraft* is that it is easily adaptable to whatever needs you have," he concluded. "While there are other game-based tools out there, *Minecraft* is what you want it to be."

Game Design Class in *Minecraft*

Building a game in *Minecraft*'s sandbox means that the game should be fully automated. If someone comes across an archery game that takes place on a moving roller coaster, the player should intuitively know what to do. Steve Isaacs uses *Minecraft* as a game design engine with his 8th grade video game design and development students. "Kids have to think this through. They design a preliminary build, get feedback from testing, and iterate. That process continues until they have a real playable prototype." After feedback, students publish their *Minecraft* maps online so others can download it and play.

Isaacs has many different *Minecraft* lessons, and all of which involve student choice. He begins the students' learning with a "watch it, build it" project. When we spoke in April 2016, Isaacs explained the process. "Kids find a YouTube video of something they want to create," he said. "Students learn by following the steps. My next step is to have students mod [modify] their creation, and then create something original."

Redstone are special blocks that enable players to create automated functions in the game. The blocks have virtual electric circuits. "Think of redstone like wires you connect," Isaacs explained. "The connection can be turned on or off to power things." On a simple level, one could power lights using redstone with a lever, which acts as a switch. More sophisticated programming concepts include using gates, where two switches have to be on to work. Roller coaster and railroads in *Minecraft* are powered by redstone.

Collaborative building in *Minecraft* is particularly compelling to Isaacs. It was the first game design engine that he has seen that can have collaborative groups of any size work together. "Most game design tools is one person on a computer one at a time," he said. "You can have 10 kids work on the same game, and diffuse responsibilities in which different kids bring their expert skills."

Isaacs' students also use command blocks, which allow players to code, or program, blocks (like a command prompt on a PC). Command blocks are especially useful because, in a game design engine, there is necessity to automate parts of the game. I tried using a command block once on a Sunday afternoon once with my son. He wanted to summon EnderDragon, a flying destructive dragon from the fictional Ender World. It was an involved experience that took me into *Minecraft's* vast community of practice. I went to YouTube and followed step-by-step directions from a video posted by an 11-year-old kid. To summon EnderDragon, a player places a command block, clicks it with the computer mouse, and then types: "/summon EnderDragon." Then you affix a lever to the command block. Once the lever is switched, the dragon emerges!

Isaacs has a bitCraft kit in his classroom. Made by littleBits, it is a set of interconnecting electronics. "Kids prototype electronic inventions," Isaacs explained. "They snap together circuits and pieces in the physical world." The Wi-Fi-enabled cloud bit can snap into the other littleBit components, like LED blinking lights. The cloud bit allows users to send signals into the game, as well as from *Minecraft* to the cloud bit. One way to use bitCraft is to set up a redstone circuit in *Minecraft* that is attached to a lever or a pressure plate. When a player switches the lever or steps on the pressure plate, a signal is sent to the real world. "You can create a train set in *Minecraft* that is powered with a switch in the real world," Isaacs said. "There are so many great opportunities for design challenges!"

MathCraft

Jim Pike teaches in southern California. Dubbed "MathCraft," Pike had his 5th grade students use the *Minecraft's* square meter blocks to illustrate math concepts (e.g., perimeter, area, volume). The curriculum was mapped to the Common Core State Standards. He self-reported an increase in learning outcomes, stating, "over a span of six months, my class' benchmark test scores shot up from 18% to 84% in math and from 24% to 81% in English" (Pike, 2015, para. 5).

I spoke in 2015 with Pike on a BAM Radio show I cohost. He spoke of the "instant buy-in" students had with *Minecraft*. "You have a math problem and the blocks are manipulatives," Pike explained. Going further, the blocks can represent algebraic expression. "I can teach the conceptual along with the procedural."

To keep the game fun, Pike has students design obstacle courses and puzzles that feature lava and monsters. His students use pencil and paper, too, in conjunction with the game, blending in academic rigor, technology, and fun. As a result, he reported that math-related arguments arise as the class debates where to place buildings. He also described as a "cultural shift" in his class— rather than leading the class, he is part of the class.

Like the official *Minecraft* mentor program, Pike takes on apprentice learners. He set up servers on his MathCraft professional learning community, so teachers can learn in multiplayer. New teachers can follow his curriculum in MathCraft, which levels up from simple to complex. For a new teacher, he recommends getting the game and then setting goals: first to learn how to mine, and then to craft. Next, try to survive on medium difficulty. "Start to play, be a kid again," he recommended. For more, check out Pike's community, the MathCraft PLC, in the resources of this chapter.

MineGage

For teachers new to *Minecraft* in the classroom, search the hashtag #MinecraftEDU or @PlayCraftLearn (the official *Minecraft Education* account) on Twitter. You don't need a Twitter account to be a lurker in the community, but you do to participate. Each week you will hear teachers share how they use *Minecraft* with students in different content areas, to teach design thinking, the growth mindset, assessment, and much more. Best of all, the chats are archived (see the end of this chapter)—if you miss the live feed, peruse it later, at your convenience. Glen Irvin and Mark Grundel, two teachers profiled earlier in this chapter, cofounded the chat. The third cofounder is Garrett Zimmer, an educational game developer. Zimmer is the CEO of MineGage, as well as a *Minecraft* YouTuber known as "PBJellyGames." I spoke to Zimmer in May 2016 to learn more about the intersection of gaming and teaching.

Zimmer's goal with MineGage is to build game-based learning environments that remain authentic to the game. It doesn't add in a gamification layer, like badges and leaderboards; rather, it advises teachers who seek to give their students a game to play in which learning also occurs. To do this, the company is creating "adventure maps," which are downloadable mods, games within the world of Minecraft. "Kids come in to an authentic Minecraft experience," Zimmer explained. "It is the same experience kids would get in a mini-game server, with mazes, competition, and collaborative teamwork." As a game designer, Zimmer lends his knowledge on Bartle's Player Types: people play games for different purposes. "We work with educators to make this a game that kids would actually want to play, not just because they are told to play."

The *Treasure of Thomas of Cavendish*, about the 16th-century explorer, it is one of MineGage's first educational adventure modules. Told over five chapters, it covers a second grade math curriculum—"at least what can be put into Minecraft! In geometry, it is difficult to make circles with blocks!" The map is not a series of rote math problems told with blocks. Instead, it follows an immersive story. "Kids are dragged into the adventure and they don't want to extricate themselves from it," Zimmer said. "Kids have an investment and relationship with the characters because it's part of the game. This is where I believe game-based learning has its true potential."

Open-ended games like *Minecraft* invite playfulness, but they are also unpredictable. This can seem unwieldy for a teacher new to *Minecraft*. "We recognize that kids will get distracted," Zimmer explained. In an open-world game (e.g., *Assassin's Creed*) players can continue the main mission and storyline, or they can play mini-games in the virtual world. This gives the illusion of freedom. "There are sidequests and opportunities for engagement in the open-world. You can develop your blacksmithing skills. You can develop archaeology skills. There are opportunities to step away from the main quest and do something different." Zimmer continued, explaining the teacher's role:

Some students may not have the attention span for the main quest. The goal of the main quest keeps them on task, as much as possible. Because it is adventure-based, they have to do what needs to be done to get to the end of the story. The teacher still has to be part of that process. A teacher will be responsible for checking quests and sidequests, corralling them back to main quest. The sidequests still do include light, and fun elements if mathematics education. You can't just go off and do whatever; you have to complete the quests.

One of the more positive attributes of *Minecraft* is the sense of community from educators, as well as gamers. "My advice to new teachers is to generate connections with the community," Zimmer recommended. "I know Bron Stuckey talks about it all the time. And Steve [Isaacs] and I talk about it all the time. There is a huge community of us who are experts that can help new teachers move forward."

Conclusions and Takeaways

Minecraft is designed to have affordances (invitations) to open-ended playfulness. Be mindful not to rob students of the experience of learning from play. Take Marianne Malmstrom's advice to follow the learning, and not be afraid to have students help lead lessons in *Minecraft*. There are now many supports out there for teachers, including Connected Camps for out-of-school time, and resources on the *Minecraft: Education Edition* website. Look into getting a mentor to show you the ropes, or just ask a kid!

Lesson Plan Ideas

Escape Rooms in *Minecraft*—Teacher Zack Gilbert challenged his students to make escape rooms in *Minecraft*. Students were grouped in threes and designed escape the room puzzles using redstone and command blocks.

Graphite, from Common Sense Education, curated *Minecraft* lesson plans in several content domains—https://www.graphite.org/blog/great-minecraft-lesson-plans

KerbalEdu is a rocket kit from TeacherGaming, the team that marketed *MinecraftEdu*. It is an educational version of the sandbox tool *Kerbal Space Program*, and there are STEM-aligned lesson plans on the site—http://www.kerbaledu.com

MathCraft PLC—http://minecraftplc.com/mathcraft-in-school

Writing fiction set in *Minecraft* by using *New York Times* Best Selling novelist Mark Cheverton's teacher resources. He is a retired teacher and he has helped my students their own publish books—http://markcheverton.com/resources-for-teachers

Games

Contraption Maker is a sandbox to teach physics by building Rube Goldberg machines. There are also curriculum-aligned lesson plans and educator resources—http://contraptionmaker.com

Eco from Strangeloop Games is *Minecraft*-like world in which ecological systems can be created. It is educationally friendly—http://www.strangeloopgames.com/eco

MineGage—Plug-and-play *Minecraft* educational games—http://www.minegage.com

Minecraft: Education Edition—http://education.minecraft.net

No Man's Sky is an expansive space exploration game—http://www.no-mans-sky.com

ROBLOX is a virtual world similar to *Minecraft*. There are many user-generated games to play, like dodgeball and capture the flag—https://www.roblox.com

Universe Sandbox puts the universe at your fingertips. You can manipulate planets, black holes, and star systems, play pool in zero gravity, or see what happens if the moon is moved closer to the earth—http://universesandbox.com

Resources

bitCraft from littleBits http://littlebits.cc/bitcraft

Glen Irvin's YouTube channel—https://www.youtube.com/c/Irvspanish

Grian's step-by-step *Minecraft* YouTube channel—https://www.youtube.com/user/Xelqua

Inspiring Young Writers with *Minecraft*—http://edut.to/2g9pUOg

Kid-friendly *Minecraft* YouTube channels—https://www.commonsensemedia.org/blog/the-12-best-kid-friendly-minecraft-channels-on-youtube

Amy Lee, on YouTube—https://www.youtube.com/user/amyleethirty3

MathCraft, a free webinar on how Jim Pike put the Common Core math curriculum into *Minecraft*—http://home.edweb.net/mathcraft-use-minecraft-teach-common-core-math

Miss Mousie Mouse, a popular YouTuber—https://www.youtube.com/user/MousieMouseMC

PopularMMOs is a kid-friendly YouTube channel by husband and wife Pat and Jen--https://www.youtube.com/user/PopularMMOs

SAMR Model—https://sites.google.com/a/msad60.org/technology-is-learning/samr-model

Stampy is a YouTube superstar, and he has wonderful instructional *Minecraft* videos—https://www.youtube.com/user/stampylonghead

Three Act Math, from Dan Meyer, which Mark Grundel integrated into *Minecraft*—http://blog.mrmeyer.com/2011/the-three-acts-of-a-mathematical-story

Tinkercad from Autodesk for *Minecraft* mods—https://www.tinkercad.com/Minecraft

Use Minecraft to Teach Math, a blog post from Jim Pike—https://www.iste.org/explore/articleDetail?articleid=558

Steve Isaacs' blog post, *Minecraft: Zen and the Art of Letting Go*—https://blogs.technet.microsoft.com/microsoft_in_education/2016/04/18/minecraft-zen-and-the-art-of-letting-go

Student-created *Minecraft* tutorial videos, from Steve Isaacs' students—https://www.pinterest.com/stevei2071

Sean Fay Wolfe wrote *The Elementia Chronicles* while in high school. Check out his educator resources—http://sfaywolfe.com/educators-zone

· 9 ·

GAME LABS

Research for this book brought me to a treasure trove of games that were both grounded in research and readily adaptable to my classroom. For example, the City University of New York (CUNY) Games Network has a portal entirely dedicated to teaching with games, as does Arizona State University, Teachers College at Columbia University, and American University. And the list goes on!

This chapter features interviews with several researchers in the games and learning community. First, I speak with Kurt Squire, formerly of the Games + Learning + Society (GLS) Center at the University of Wisconsin-Madison. The annual conference at Madison was widely attended by many in the game-based learning space. Next, I speak to the director of the Field Day Lab, also at the University of Wisconsin. Field Day specializes in augmented reality and interactive storytelling (ARIS), a location-based mobile game, authoring tool. The Games Research Lab at Teacher College, which is situated at Columbia University, in New York, follows. The lab, headed by Joey J. Lee, published *EcoChains: Arctic Crisis*, a commercially sold card game. Its core mechanics teach about the cause and effects of global climate change. In 2015, the Educational Gaming Environments Technical Education Research Center—or EdGE at TERC—relaunched *Zoombinis*, the lovable learning game from the 1990s. I speak with the executive director about *Zoombinis* and other free and low cost digital games on its site. Finally I share conversations with Alan Gershenfeld, cofounder of the Center for Games and Impact at Arizona State University, and researchers at the aforementioned Games and Innovation Lab, including Tracy Fullerton.

Games + Learning + Society Center

Much of today's games and learning research has been conducted at the University of Wisconsin-Madison. In 2003, husband and wife Kurt Squire and Constance Steinkuehler cofounded the GLS Center, which resided in the Wisconsin for Discovery. Each year—from 2003 until 2016—the Center hosted the GLS Conference. Many designers and researchers at Madison-based Filament Games have roots with the university. Prior to relocating to Arizona State University, James Paul Gee spent a decade as a professor at Madison.

Squire and Steinkuehler both led research on situated learning in games, describing how people learn informally in order to advance in a game. Their research has been supported by nearly $10 million in grants and gifts from the MacArthur Foundation, the National Science Foundation (NSF), the Gates Foundation, Microsoft, the Department of Education, the AMD Foundation, and the National Institutes of Health. Squire has directed several game-based learning projects, ranging from ARIS, a location-based, mobile app, to *ProgenitorX*, a game about harnessing stem cell technology in order to save the world from zombies. He is the author or editor of three books and more than 75 scholarly publications on learning with technology. Steinkuehler's work on *World of Warcraft* communities of practice is seminal, and she is the current president of the Higher Education Video Game Alliance (HEVGA). She also spent 2 years as the nation's video game "czar" for the Obama administration.

In July 2016, Squire and Steinkuehler announced their departure from the University of Wisconsin-Madison to join the University of California-Irvine Department of Informatics. Squire stated that the GLS Center would close in January 2017, and that the 2016 Conference would be their last (Lorenzsonn, 2016). Much of the research staff will remain at the University of Wisconsin-Madison; however, new directions would likely be pursued (Lorenzsonn, 2016). Steinkuehler pointed to the political climate in Wisconsin as a deciding factor for their departure. In an article in *Isthmus*, a local news source, she said, "The climate of the state of Wisconsin helped contribute to the feeling that it was time to leave. State government and state universities don't always align, but the way the conversations have gone lately—so disrespectful, so cantankerous—statesmanship has gone out the window" (Conklin, 2016, para. 3). In 2017, the Games Education and Research (GEAR) took the place of GLS. Unlike GLS, "the brunt of GEAR's work won't involve research. Instead, the focus will be on actually making and distributing games for learning" (Lorenzsonn, 2017, para. 6).

I interviewed Squire in January 2014, and we since spoke at the GLS Conference in 2015. He began his teaching career as a Montessori teacher, when he led a discovery-based learning classroom. He next became an instructional technologist. He wrote an influential dissertation about using the game *Civilization III* in an urban high school setting. This was back in 2004, when it was considered radical to play console-style games in school. To advance in the game, students were reading information from websites that were higher than their grade level (Squire, 2011).

In 2011, Squire published *Video Games and Learning: Teaching and Participatory Culture in the Digital Age*, featuring contributions from Henry Jenkins, with an introduction by James Paul Gee. Jenkins is an expert on participatory cultures, where content creators—and gamers—meet in a situated learning setting. The book and his coursework were integrated into a massive open online course hosted on Coursera in the fall of 2013. Along with others in the GLS research department, Gee was recruited to contribute videos about his Learning Principles from video games. Since publishing his book, Squire has continued his work on game-based learning research.

Unlike at commercial game companies, projects at GLS were built with the intent of being academic projects; however, some did get distributed to the general public. The development team mixed AAA (big budget) and indie (independent) designers, along with PhDs researching games and learning. This approach ensured that games created for research projects had balanced design mechanics. "As core developers we force ourselves to do a lot of play-testing, which is best practice, and then biweekly playtests and monthly builds with the target audience," Squire explained. "The goal is to get developers and academics working together. A shared office space keeps it culturally the same." The team also conducted outreach to schools.

The lab had developers working at the Learning Games Network, an off-spring of the MIT's Education Arcade and the GLS Center. It is "a non-profit institution trying to spark innovation in the design and use of learning games through promoting collaboration among scholars, teachers, developers, producers" (Squire, 2011, p. 217). One of the Learning Games Network's most recent projects was *Quandary*, a free online game that engages players in the ethical decision-making process of colonizing a new planet. Teachers can access *Quandary in the Classroom* to access Common Core-linked lesson plans. *Quandary* has won a Game of the Year award at the Games for Change Festival. Other Learning Games Network titles include the mathematics puzzler *Lure of the Labyrinth* and the English language game *Xenos*.

Squire explained that the barriers to game-based learning adoption were logistical, rather than teachers not wanting games in their classrooms. Perhaps it is generational, too. Younger teachers grew up playing games, especially *SimCity* and *Civilization*. Digital distribution—through platforms such as BrainPOP and iTunes—as well as teacher training and support can bring more games to students. So how should teachers use video games to extend learning? Squire suggested:

> Add games with interesting questions, a lot of enrichment, and high valued work. Games can then be used with academic value. One professor did something interesting, 16 weeks, 16 games; she got interesting results from a not very historically accurate game—*Age of Empires*. The professor then discussed what it does and what it doesn't do. It was used for a vehicle for interpretation and reflection, with writing prompts. That was really clever to me. There was also an ELA [English language arts] teacher who played *Skyrim*, in class, for 30 minutes and then did a whole writing unit afterwards.

The work of academics and nonprofits is being built upon and expanded. Squire remained cautiously optimistic. "One of the perennial challenges is not to care about games [themselves], but education, which games are a part of. We've done some work on that. We make sure that we have good models of how curriculum integration works. And, of course, empirical data."

Field Day Lab

Field Day Lab is a 2-year-old, interdisciplinary organization. Like the GLS Center, it is situated at the University of Wisconsin. I spoke with David Gagnon, who heads the lab, in April 2016. Gagnon has a background in computer science and educational theory. This is a natural fit for the lab—it develops new media from a learning science perspective. Field Day works closely with the GLS group, and the university's school of education. It builds free and open source science games, and conducts research and practice-related projects. "We want it to be free and open so it can be remixed and played with," Gagnon said.

Field Day develops open source ARIS software. Basically, ARIS enables any user to create a mobile app that can interact with a physical location. It is not very different than when you use your smartphone to "check-in" at a restaurant with Facebook or when you scan a QR code with a camera at a museum. Or catching Pokémon in *Pokémon GO*.

The idea for ARIS began just as the iPhone entered the market. "The mobile device blurred the line of what it means to be working with a computer," Gagnon said. Students in Kurt Squire's graduate school classroom wondered how they could leverage the sensors on a mobile device from a game-based standpoint. "What are the affordances of mobile media on video games and learning?" Gagnon recalled the team asking. The result was ARIS, which was a prototype "kicked out over a weekend." The team was awarded MacArthur Digital Medial Learning funding, around 2010. What resulted was the first version of the ARIS authoring tool.

ARIS now has about 50,000 projects published, ranging from children who are learning to build games to "high-end games and installations that have thousands of players a week." Called *Play the Past*, is about Minnesotan history, one project was for the Milwaukee Museum of Art. Another ARIS game is called *Dow Day*, a "situated documentary about a historic protest at the University of Wisconsin-Madison campus." Players take on the role of a newspaper reporter who interviews protesters, and the chancellor of the university, as events unfold in real time. "You run around the campus and find sources and video from the protests," Gagnon explained. Another is *Dilemma 1944*, which was created by Craig Brumwell, a teacher from Victoria, Canada. "It's an interactive narrative in which students decide if they would enroll for World War II or not." *Jewish Time Jump*, a game about Jewish labor in New York at the turn of the 20th-century, is a location-based game that was nominated for an award at Games for Change. A doctoral student from New York University, who also happened to be a rabbi, produced it.

Field Day has a large community of people building a diverse number of projects, from medical education to students making their own games. Gagnon shared with me an upcoming proposal for Wisconsin schools of nursing. Using ARIS as a platform, they plan to create 150 nursing simulations. On the simulated emergency room table there would be a mannequin affixed with scannable QR codes on its neck and wrist. The chair next to the mannequin would also have QR codes on it. Scanning the code with a smartphone would then trigger nurse-training videos.

Games Research Lab at Teachers College

The Games Research Lab at Teachers College, Columbia University, designs, develops, and studies games and game-like experiences for educational and social impact. Past projects include *Lit2Quit*, a smoking cessation app. One of the researchers on that project was Azadeh (Azi) Jamalian, who went on to cofound Tiggly, the interactive toy company covered in Chapter 5. Josh Larson, who was hired as *Lit2Quit's* graphic designer, helped develop the groundbreaking, emotional game *That Dragon, Cancer*, with Ryan and Amy Green (discussed in Chapter 16). For the past 6 years, much of the lab's work focused on innovative game-like experiences for climate change awareness.

Joey J. Lee is the director of the lab. We first met at the 2016 NJEDge Gamification Symposium; Lee was the keynote speaker. We spoke again later that month, in April 2016. One of his goals as director is to understand how games get people to learn in more effective ways, as well as to take action on sustainability and climate change. To that end, Lee's team developed *EcoChains: Arctic Crisis*. Self-published and available on Amazon, it is a multiplayer card game codesigned with Stephanie Pfirman, an environmental science professor at Barnard College, and arctic researcher. The project was part of a NSF grant on climate change education, and Pfirman was the principle investigator. (I met Pfirman backstage at the 13th Annual Games for Change Festival. She led the partnership that cosponsored the Games for Change Climate Challenge, which awarded a $10,000 prize to *ECO*, from Strange Loop Games.)

To play, you use cards to build food chains (or food webs) on top of a base of sea ice cards. Heavier weighing animals, like polar bears, require more sea ice cards to sustain them. When a player draws a carbon pollution event card, sea ice "melts," or leaves the player's hand, thus comprising the base of your food chain. Conversely, there are green energy action cards that restore sea ice. "When ice is melted, some of the species that rely on sea ice are threatened, then they migrate where the animal can survive," Lee explained. "If a suitable location can't be found, the animal perishes. The goal of the game is to keep as many animals as you can alive." Players earn points for sustaining species. "You feel the effects of climate change to learn the underlying process."

The goal of the NSF grant was to have players "feel" the experience of melting ice, and how climate change can have a major impact on arctic eco-systems. "We started with arctic because the effects of climate change are often the most dramatic," Lee said. Climate change is an urgent issue and there is a lack of effective education. "There is a need for more novel ways to raise awareness of climate change issues. We wanted to create a unique game that is accessible and flexible in use." EcoChains: Arctic Crisis can be played in classrooms, and there are lesson plans on its website (linked at the end of this chapter).

One of the design goals was to make EcoChains: Arctic Crisis fun to play and easy to learn, not chocolate-covered broccoli, not too overtly educational. Playing cards have a picture of an animal from the arctic. I asked Lee about the learning goals. He said:

> You learn predator-prey relationships. You also try to sustain the food chains. In the game, we promote values like stewardship and empathy as you try to keep animals, like polar bears, arctic cod, and walrus, alive. The game incorporates good science and we also consulted with arctic natives in Alaska, making the game is culturally responsive. The game also meets Next Generation Science Standards.

EcoChains: Arctic Crisis has been featured in a journal article, and it has been playtested at the American Museum for Natural History, the Koshland Science Museum, at classrooms, and at camps—including in Alaska. There are plans to translate it to native Alaskan languages, too.

EdGE at TERC

Technical Education Research Center (TERC) is a nonprofit that's been around for about 50 years. Its mission is to develop innovative science and math curriculum, with a technology focus. In 2009, Educational Gaming Environments (EdGE) was launched. EdGE develops learning games and then analyzes player data. The EdGE at TERC receives grant funds from the NSF. When I spoke to Jodi Asbell-Clarke, EdGE's Director, in March 2016, she told me about its games and click-data research.

It took a few years for EdGE to gather steam in the learning game market. Its first release, Martian Boneyards, ran for 4 months in a beta-test, called Blue Mars. The project, however, was ill-timed with the 2009 economic down-turn. Next came a proof-of-concept to measure scientific inquiry in an adult science mystery game. With the game, EdGE was able to study the 100 core players (out of 600 registered users) over a 4-month time span. The audience was homogeneous and affluent. "We found that females were one-third of the audience and they did two-thirds of the scientific inquiry—particularly later, during the data analysis and theory building phases," Asbell-Clarke said.

In 2011, EdGE started work on tablet games. Three games—*Impulse*, *Quantum Spectre*, and *Ravenous*—are still playable, and they are free. For each, there are two versions: one for the public, and one explicitly intended for research. The research version asks teachers to register their classes, and then students are automatically led to a pretest prior to play. After play, students take a posttest to measure learning outcomes. Additionally, EdGE collects "click data." "We were able to build data-mining detectors and learning analytics to be able to see not just how people did in the game, but how they played the game," Asbell-Clarke explained. "That's become very important on our research. These games are not teaching games."

Impulse was one of the games studied. The game involves balls inside a gravitational field, moving around. There are four different balls, each with a different mass. The goal is to get your ball to the goal without crashing into the other balls. "Nothing in there ever talks about Newton or Newton's Laws," Asbell-Clarke said. "There's no $F = MA$ [Newton's Law of Motion]—nothing like that. We collect the back-end data. We have been able to determine that people tend to treat the heavier balls different than the light balls. People strategically tend to let the ball float and not impart a force if it is not needed."

Physics concepts are learned through experiential play. Out of a textbook, it is abstract; however, in a game, teachers found that their students were picking it up intuitively. Asbell-Clarke continued:

> We did this study where there were 10 teachers in each three groups: 10 teachers in the control group, with their typical curriculum about Newton's Laws, and 10 teachers who recruited their kids to play the game outside of school, and then taught them the regular curriculum. And then the third group—the bridge group—10 teachers who had their kids play the game outside of class and then they would show a video clip from the game and ask what they did in the game. The kids would then articulate about not being around the heavier balls.

Asbell-Clarke explained that this allowed the students to build "an intuitive field," or an "implicit understanding," of the phenomenon of gravity. Now the teacher has something to leverage and draw upon when they teach a new concept. When the teacher uses words like force and motion, students have experienced each and can disseminate the relationship between those words.

The new version of *Zoombinis* is one of its latest games. It's a strategy puzzle game with roots dating back to the 1990s, the edutainment heyday. It had been on Kickstarter and there was a Facebook page, all leading up to its release. When I attended GLS 11, there was a pizza party to celebrate its launch! For the updated version, TERC at EdGE hired FableVision to develop it, along with the MIT Education Arcade's Scot Osterweil. He had been one of the original developers.

The goal of the new version was to keep the nostalgic base audience pleased, while iterating on game play. According to the EdGE at TERC's website that accompanies the game, players "solve fun and challenging puzzles and explore a strange land packed with memorable and quirky characters. Playing *Zoombinis* teaches and reinforces valuable life skills, including deductive reasoning, pattern recognition, hypothesis testing, and more." I observed its use in Steve Isaacs' video game and design class. His 8th grade students played on iPads and then wrote reflections about what they did. Asbell-Clarke's role with the *Zoombinis* was as a researcher, although she did contribute to design decisions. The team had very little disagreement. "It is the product we all wanted to see," Asbell-Clarke concluded.

Center for Games and Impact

Sasha Barab and James Paul Gee cofounded the Center for Games and Impact at the Mary Lou Fulton Teachers College at Arizona State University, in partnership with E-Line Media's Alan Gershenfeld and Michael Angst. The Center provides Impact Guides, which give "players, parents and teachers the tools to understand play, inspire reflection and stimulate transformation with the goal of building a more knowledgeable, responsible and empathetic citizenship" (2014). I had the opportunity to interview both Gee and Gershenfeld in the spring of 2014.

There are very few academic centers that study the full life-cycle research of actual products and continued services. Gershenfeld and his E-Line business partner, Michael Angst, along with Sasha Barab and Gee, discussed how there needed to be an alignment between game design, game mechanics, scientists, and good learning. "The Center was cofounded to integrate the thought process behind research, design, marketing, and distribution so that they become sustainable and can actually make an impact at scale, rather than result in just another research paper," Gershenfeld explained. "Research papers have been critical, but we've had years of them. We're trying to turn them into products and services."

The Center has a studio in Phoenix and a partnership with Arizona State University. The off-campus location is part of a joint venture with E-Line Media's Pathways Learning Project, tentatively called the Thrive Learning Platform. As of this writing, there are several projects going on in that space. Teachers can earn a certificate in Games and Impact from the Center. The web portal has Impact Guides for off-the-shelf games including *SimCity*, *Civilization V*, *Portal 2*, *Little Big Planet*, *Peacemaker*, *Journey*, and *Minecraft*. These are especially helpful for parents as well as teachers. In 2014, the Center introduced a new game, *Quest2Teach*. It is a role-playing game for preservice teachers. The video game features a variety of situations that a new educator might face.

Games Innovation Lab

Tracy Fullerton is the Chair of the Interactive Media & Games Division of the University of Southern California (USC) School of Cinematic Arts. She is also the Director of the Game Innovation Lab and author of *Game Design Workshop: A Playcentric Approach to Creating Innovative Games*, now in its third edition. I interviewed Fullerton as well as some of her research team. We spoke in March 2014. Her students' projects elicit more than fun—they often require introspection. Fullerton was the thesis advisor for Jenova Chen, whose company is expanding the emotional range people feel while playing games. Just about all of the members of Chen's company, Thatgamecompany, were students of Fullerton. The company's games include *flOw*, *Flower*, and *Journey*. Fullerton has also collaborated with Bill Viola, a MacArthur Genius grantee, on *The Night Journey*. The collaboration is an interactive game that has been exhibited in various galleries for the past 7 years. She described the game as "a spiritual journey."

Students at USC can earn a master's of fine arts degree in interactive entertainment and game design. Independent principal investigators choose research questions and then design a project. Next, they put a team together—along with the funding—to realize their intervention. All games in the Game Innovation Lab have a participatory design element between multiple designers. The process includes paper prototyping and iteration until the mechanics are worked out. Digital is the last step. Sometimes, games stay in the non-digital stage.

Marienta Gotsis, a researcher at the Games Innovation Lab, explained the creation process in more detail. "Games are the deliverable. That is a work of art. It may not always be beautiful, but it aspires to be," she said. In the end, a student's research project is an actual product. Because of the aesthetic component, there are different talents required at each stage from pilot to production. A systems thinker observes the paper-based version and then transposes that to a digital platform. A designer, on the other hand, thinks about the player's experience, not just the systems and mechanics. 3D digital artists, who are proficient in applications, are also required.

Research projects struggle with finding funding. Without a steady cash flow, it can be difficult to innovate. The graduation schedule presents another limitation: The master's degree takes 3 years. For education or health games, the process can be even slower. "You need to manage the iterative stages of production," Gotsis explained. "The sad part in research is when you don't have the money to go from what you want to make to actually making it. It can take years, even if you know it works. It's not like there is venture capital money and it becomes scalable for commercial use."

Thoreau in a Sandbox

In the classic book *Walden Pond*, author Henry David Thoreau attempted to balance a life of simplicity with a connection to nature. Fullerton's game is one of the first to be funded by the National Endowment of Arts in the category New Media Arts. *Walden, a Game* is "a simulation of Thoreau's experience of living." She explained, "There has always been a strong connection between play and making art." The act of making art can be seen as a game, or at least as a playful activity. Fullerton also pointed out many early examples of games as works of art, including surrealistic game environments.

Walden, a Game is an engaging way to teach 19th-century literature experientially. Thoreau's book seems readily adaptable to a digital simulation. The protagonist depends on four basics of life: food, shelter, fuel, and clothing. These elements became part of the mechanics of play. Players collect or grow food, find firewood and then chop it, mend clothes, and build shelter. Failure to do so affects the player's ability to survive. Visuals and sounds become gloomy when work becomes a grind. If too much time is spent on these tasks, the player's life experience "becomes dull and dismal." Fullerton continued, "If the player can sustain a simplistic existence, then he or she can spend time wandering the woods, enjoying occurrences of inspiration with the natural life of animals, plants, the sounds of the forest and even society in the distance." The challenges change with the seasons, too. It is fairly easy in summer, and then the difficulty levels up during the fall and winter months. Even in these "sparse seasons," some pleasures are presented, such as skating on Walden Pond. The game concludes with a celebration of the resurgence of spring. It is "experiential and poetic."

In 2014, Fullerton sent me video clips of the game; however, I have yet to play it. *Walden, a Game* has been a long project, and care is being taken with its release. Greg Toppo wrote about his playthrough in his book *The Game Believes in You* (2015). He wrote:

> Game play begins in summer and ends in spring, and it soon becomes clear that the amount of breathtaking scenery that the game generates moment-to-moment simply wouldn't have been possible on a home computer until recently. Nearly every item is "clickable," offering short descriptions of the pond's features, often in Thoreau's own writing. (Toppo, 2015, p. 169)

The game has the same underlying theme of *Walden Pond*: solitude, inspiration, and the sublime life. The challenge to Fullerton's team was how to achieve this in a game. When players find and collect pages of *Walden Pond*, the gain provides further insight into Thoreau's thinking. It took just a few hours for Toppo to complete the game. He then picked up Thoreau's book and read it again. It had new meaning for him. He found the book "more substantial and at times an angrier and funnier" (Toppo, 2015, p. 171).

Nutritional Education with *Virtual Sprouts*

Virtual Sprouts is a research project that brought together investigators from USC's medical school, school of education, school of engineering, and the world-famous film school. Nutritionists and other researchers also were brought in to help. The project was based on a real gardening program that was piloted in a Los Angeles elementary school. The garden was found to be just as useful in teaching nutrition as other metabolic interventions. It also hit multiple goals for education, including California's science standards. While putting a garden in every school is a lofty goal, realistically it is not feasible. Therefore, USC researchers created a digital gardening and cooking experience.

The alpha version (preliminary release) is being deployed into some schools. Researcher Marienta Gotsis explained how the team took a systems approach. She said, "Manage one thing and everything falls into place." In this regard, the core mechanic of gameplay is similar to that in *Reach for the Sun*, Filament's video game about mastering a plant's systems.

Virtual Sprouts is a first-person (perspective) role-playing gardening game. Students assist a gardener who is aspiring to be the top chef in a local contest. The goal is to help her cook and meet nutritional and taste standards. Gardening hints include "I'm craving protein" and "I'm craving sweets that are high in calcium." As the game progresses, the player is presented with healthy recipes. From there, he or she can grow an ingredient from scratch, such as garlic. The virtual garden experiences the four seasons, humidity, changes in sunlight, weeds, and other factors.

Once the plant is successfully grown, it can be harvested and brought to the kitchen. There is a pantry full of additional items to enable the player to make a wrap or a salad. The process includes a practical application of mathematics. Players need to think about making calculations as all ingredients are assembled. The feedback system assesses several dimensions of play, including the gardener's missions, how much sugar and fiber they used in recipes, and the quality of grown produce. Students can use augmented reality apps, with an iPad camera, to take a "selfie" photograph with the trophy.

The game was playtested with an after-school charity in December 2013. "Students were keen on replaying," Gotsis said. "The challenge is to fund a fully featured playable version." *Virtual Sprouts* comes with curriculum matched to California's teaching standards. "Teachers have limited time to cover curriculum. If they take time out, you have to make it up for them," she continued. Her team's goal is not to increase student's screen time; rather, they want to intervene and improve behaviors via short, meaningful, playful experiences. "You try a few times, and then come back to it." The teacher's lesson plan is the reinforcement activity. There are very few cooking and gardening games in Apple's App Store. Furthermore, the content is not connected to research. Gotsis explained that she sees a place for *Virtual Sprouts* as an eventual commercial release.

Adventurous Dreaming Highflying Dragon

Often times, researchers are in the third year of study, writing theses and looking for clinical interventions for projects. In this case, Marienta Gotsis connected a student investigator with a pediatrician and a psychiatrist. The deliverable, called *Adventurous Dreaming Highflying Dragon (ADHD)*, was a motion-controlled video game for children around age 11. The game is intended for those diagnosed with attention deficit hyperactivity disorder (ADHD).

Adventurous Dreaming Highflying Dragon plays on an Xbox Kinect, where the player is literally the controller. Kinect is a motion-sensitive camera that reacts to player movement. Gotsis wanted the game to be completely original. "Earning points can be too conventional, especially for kids," she explained. "The reward-oriented model is problematic. Whatever you're doing should be intrinsically engaging. Points don't matter after a certain point." In the game, students role-play as a clumsy dragon that can't fly. The goal is to earn the skill of flying.

As with most games, the player has an infinite number of opportunities to learn. First, the player is tasked with following a sequence of items, including yellow mushrooms, purple corn, and blue mushrooms. Next, the gamespace opens up to a large forest where many items are falling from trees. The challenge is to catch items in a sequential order. Gotsis remarked, "It is difficult to not get distracted and not catch everything that falls." Sequences and shapes increase in complexity, testing the player's memory. The second challenge has the player contorting his or her body—and then holding still—to stop cracks in a water tower. This, too, levels up, as more cracks appear in different locations. Gotsis laughed, "You have to be creative with poses to cover the cracks to heal the tower." The third task involves scratching off a cave wall to get to a gold nugget. It is both a visual-spatial challenge and a test of impulse control. The better the player gets, the smaller the nuggets become. Succeeding in all three tasks gives the dragon power to use its wings. While the game lacks the narrative of a commercial release, its core mechanics hold up. "The underlying mechanisms work for adults, too," Gotsis concluded. "Exercise and regulation can be transferred to other setting." *Adventurous Dreaming Highflying Dragon* is a game that puts sound educational research into practice. It is both fun and educational.

FutureBound

The process of getting into college is game-like: There is the arc of higher education and there are serious consequences. *FutureBound* turns those experiences into a game. It was collaboratively created by the Game and Innovation

Lab and the School of Education. Zoe Corwin, a professor at the School of Education, led the project, along with Tracy Fullerton.

There are actually four games in the series: *FutureBound*, *Application Crunch*, *Mission: Admission*, and *Graduate Strike Force*. The idea stemmed from a perceived lack of college counseling, especially in underserved areas. They used iterative design with a high school-aged audience, including students at game design camp. The team was interested in a solution that students would find engaging, that spoke their own language. The games help students to build and present themselves in the best light. There were real-world questions Corwin wanted to infuse in the game. Is it beneficial to join a lot of clubs and be spread thin, or to be a leader in just a few clubs? What are the differences between a technical school and a liberal arts college? The games are the ultimate role-playing adventure: aspirations for life. "We identified the moment—the tipping point—where kids go to college," Corwin explained. "Some kids were prepared for college and ready to go, but don't know the application process."

Tracy Fullerton elaborated further about how little many middle school students know about their futures. She said, "College and careers is a black box for many in middle school, how careers match up to challenges and aspirations." In *FutureBound*, the player is a middle school student haunted by a monster. The monster is fueled by fears and doubts. Fullerton explained, "The way you combat them is by powering up superpowers about career paths. You learn from characters about their passions and you use their powers." For example, soccer players use their powers to kick soccer balls at monsters. Players level up to attain more desirable careers. To become an airplane pilot or a neurosurgeon, you need to fight bigger monsters, attacking larger fears invading the school. The game is really about creating aspirations in an adventure game format, the core genre for that age group.

Two *FutureBound* games are geared directly to the application process: *Application Crunch*, a non-digital card game, and *Mission: Admission*, a Facebook game. *Application Crunch* is designed to help students complete college applications. It was not, however, intended to stay in its paper form. After paper prototyping and playtesting it with full classes, the team found the card-based game to be highly engaging. The playtesters did not want to stop playing and leave class. Therefore, Corwin's team decided to keep it paper-based.

Graduate Strike Force is targeted at a high school audience. The player evaluates colleges. Issues include weighing the cost of financial loans against the future opportunity the investment may—or may not—provide. Fullerton explained, "The world needs college graduates to fight monsters that are attacking us. Graduates need a range of skills and should be happy people not burdened by a lot of debt." The objective is to be part of the monster fighting force. Gameplay involves choosing schools, selecting financial aid packages, and seeing them through. Fullerton concluded, "If the player is depressed and burdened by debt, then they can't fight the robots attacking earth."

Corwin explained a three-pronged approach to the project's research. First are the qualitative components from observing students play, as well as from interviewing students. This is followed up with longitudinal interviews from students in their junior year of high school, then at the beginning of their senior year, and finally after they have applied to college. The idea is to see how the game affected their application process. The second prong is to perform quantitative pre- and posttests. Corwin said, "We test changes in efficacies of student's beliefs that they can go to college, as well as being able to afford college." Finally, there are the measures built into the game itself, such as knowledge about college. A straightforward example is in *Mission Admission*. When students play for the first time, they typically go to the shortest college application in the game. After playing the game repeatedly, students tend to review more options. There is observational data in the card game, too. If a player makes a mistake the first time by missing an application deadline, they often adjust their strategy for the next time, paying closer attention to scholarship dates.

Conclusions and Takeaways

University game labs are an excellent—and often, free or low cost—place to find games for learning. Some games intended for research projects are truly innovative. There are free and low cost games, and they are backed with research (always helpful when asking an administrator!). More and more universities are opening up game labs, so check them out online before the secret gets out!

Lesson Plan Ideas

Card Game Toolkit is a tool independent of the Games Research Lab from Lee. It is an excellent, free website to create card games or gamification tools. Anyone can create cards, as well as remix other people's creations—http://cardgametoolkit.com

EcoChain: Arctic Crisis: Middle school lesson plans—http://thepolarhub.org/sites/default/files/EcoChains-HS-Classroom-QuickGuide.pdf and high school lesson plans—http://thepolarhub.org/sites/default/files/EcoChains-MS-Classroom-QuickGuide_0.pdf

Citizen Science: Playable on BrainPOP, which posts all applicable standards—http://www.brainpop.com/games/citizenscience

Quandary: Ethical decision-making game. There is a PDF with mapped standards, as well as a teacher's guide with lesson plans—http://www.quandarygame.org

Games

ARIS location-based game and app—http://arisgames.org

Atlantis Remixed, Sasha Barab's science game—http://www.atlantisremixed.org

Citizen Science—http://www.gameslearningsociety.org/project_citizen_science.php

ChronoCards, a downloadable card game about history from the USC Game Innovation Lab. The first set is about World War I—http://www.gameinnovationlab.com/history

Dilemma 1944—http://ccbrumwell.wix.com/dilemma1944#!exploring-new-ideas/c380

Dow Day—http://arisgames.org/featured/dow-day

EcoChains: Arctic Crisis—http://thepolarhub.org/project/ecochains-arctic-crisis

EcoKoin mobile app about promoting sustainability—http://gamesresearchlab.com/ecokoin.html

FutureBound, Application Crunch, Mission: Admission, and *Graduate Strike Force*—http://www.futureboundgames.com

Jewish Time Jump—http://www.converjent.org

Play the Past—http://arisgames.org/play-the-past

Progenitor X, the zombies and health game—http://www.gameslearningsociety.org/px_microsite

Quandary, the award-winning game of interplanetary colonization—http://www.quandarygame.org

Quest 2 Teach, a role-playing game for preservice teachers—http://quest2teach.strikingly.com

The Radix Endeavor, MIT's science-themed, MMO game—http://www.radix-endeavor.org

Virulent, an educational health game—http://www.gameslearningsociety.org/project_virulent.php

Walden, a Game, to experience Walden Pond as Henry David Thoreau did—http://www.waldengame.com

The Yard Games are a series of free online science games from Field Day Lab—http://theyardgames.org

Zoombinis—http://zoombinis.com

Resources

American University Game Lab—https://www.american.edu/gamelab

Center for Games and Impact at Arizona State University—http://gamesandimpact.org

The CUNY Games Network—http://games.commons.gc.cuny.edu

EdGE at TERC—http://edgeatterc.com/edge

Games Research Lab—http://gamesresearchlab.com

Field Day Lab—https://fielddaylab.wisc.edu

Games and Innovation at the University of Southern California, headed by Tracy Fullerton—http://games.usc.edu

Games + Learning + Society Center—http://gameslearningsociety.org

Higher Education Video Game Alliance (HEVGA)—http://higheredgames.org

Learning Games Lab at New Mexico State University—http://learning-gameslab.org

Learning Games Network—http://www.learninggamesnetwork.org

MIT's Education Arcade—http://education.mit.edu

Play Forward—http://www.play2prevent.org/index.aspx

Reacting to the Past, Barnard College's game-based history program—https://reacting.barnard.edu

UC Department of Informatics, where Kurt Squire and Constance Steinkuehler relocated to in 2017—http://www.informatics.uci.edu

· 1 0 ·

MULTIPLAYER LEARNING

Each year my 7th grade students collaborate to create a "Virtual Student Constitution" on a wiki (a wiki is an online document that more than one person can edit). The idea for the project came from an article in the *Guardian* titled "Mob Rule: Iceland Crowdsources Its Next Constitution," which described how Iceland, in the process of recovering from a collapse of its banks and government, decided to use social media to get citizens to share their ideas for a new constitution.

My students are each given a laptop or an iPad and "meet" online (rather than face-to-face) in cooperative groups. Their task is to rewrite the school's student handbook—their "constitution." The Edmodo social network was the virtual meeting place. Although it has the look and feel of Facebook, it's private and secure. Edmodo has a feature called "Small Groups" in which side chats can occur. Students can have fun personalizing their pages with avatars; teachers can award digital badges on profile pages.

Students are given five student handbooks from middle schools around the state. Each group edits a portion of the wiki, which includes both text and talking avatars made using Voki. There is one wiki for each of my four 7th grade class sections. There can be several hundred edits over a 5-day period. The "game" began as students competed to control editing the wiki page—only one person can edit at a time. The mechanics of play are arguing, collaborating, and voting, all on content of interest to students—their hand-book. Following the project, students vote via interactive remote whether to ratify their Virtual Student Constitution wiki. After the vote, we compare the U.S. Constitution to Iceland's crowdsourced constitution.

Earlier in the school year, my students collaborated on an e-book that was eventually published and distributed in Apple's iBookstore. Each student worked with a partner to research information, gather copyright-friendly pic-tures, and create glossary terms about one of the 13 original American colo-nies. They used a variety of text and online sources for information. Students were taught about how Creative Commons and copyright law worked. A small group of students volunteered extra time during their lunch to create the over-all concept. It was decided that historical fiction would be the best vehicle to grab and hold the reader's attention. A few students also created original artwork for the lead characters—in this case, three magical, time-traveling unicorns. I scanned their drawings and added them to the "Gallery" widget. Once the book was completed, we submitted it for review to Apple. Our book is still available in the iBookstore.

What I constructed, using small groups and interest-driven learning, was essentially a multiplayer game. For example, the Constitution project used the mechanics of social collaboration (People Fun), frustration and relief (from wiki edits), and voting. When I interviewed media scholar Henry Jenkins in May 2014, he pointed out how simulations lead to deeper connections to content. He used the decades-old Model U.N. program as an example; it is an experience that has always been game-based. Jenkins said:

> It's a role-playing game where you simulate the activity of the United Nations. You just don't begin by playing; you do research, you read the U.N. charter, and you read up on the culture. You prepare to play the game. Coming out the other side, the best teachers have students report back to the school on what happened in the game. It becomes a springboard for writing and speaking activities. A very small part of the Model U.N. experience is the game. The other activities pull back into school's regimes. The game inspires young people to learn more deeply. That's really a better model for thinking about how games and play relate to each other.

In a 2012 video for Big Think, educational researcher John Seely Brown said, "I would rather hire a high-level *World of Warcraft* player than an MBA from Harvard." The very process of working in a guild, mentored by a team, is a valu-able career and life skill. Learning cooperatively is certainly a workforce skill.

Thanks to educators such as Spencer Kagan, cooperative, guild-like learn-ing has become more commonplace in schools. His Kagan Structures include

Jigsaw groupings and Round Robin discussions. This chapter compares project-based, problem-based, and inquiry-based learning to game-based learning. The truth is, each of these is not all that different from the others. The great news is that if you are familiar with any of the aforementioned techniques, then you are not too far from game-based learning. Be inspired by how games teach.

For this chapter I spoke with *Multiplayer Classroom* author Lee Sheldon, as well as Jim Bower, creator of *Whyville*, the first browser-based virtual world for learning. (I met Sheldon at the Games in Education Symposium in August 2014. This was almost 5 months after my interview with him. He was laughed and was amused when I told him that I put his interview in the cooperative learning chapter. My decision was based on the fact that his approach was effective with small groups.)

Cooperative Games

Mathematicians and game theoreticians know cooperative games as non–zero-sum games. Cooperative games are when "players can make enforceable agreements with other players" (Nasar, 1998, p. 96). No winner is required. Fundraising walks and crowdfunding websites are examples of cooperative games (Kim, 2012b; Kim, 2014b). They are win-win (as opposed to win-lose, like *Rock-Paper-Scissors*). No one really trains to win the Susan G. Komen Breast Cancer Walk the way they would the Boston Marathon (Kim, 2012b; Kim, 2014b). Most people run in most races simply to participate.

The genre of cooperative board games has a lot to offer classrooms. To win, everyone must work together to achieve a common goal. Cooperative board games have *social mechanics*, which force players to interact with one another. Examples for middle and high school students include *Pandemic, Forbidden Island*, and *Forbidden Desert*—all brilliantly designed by Matt Leacock. For younger learners, try *Count Your Chickens*, a number game published by Peaceable Kingdom.

Robot Turtles is a cooperative board game published by ThinkFun for young children. It uses coding logic as its core mechanic. In it, the parent or teacher plays the role of the computer and the child "programs" the Robot Turtle Card. The goal is to use directional movement cards (right, left, up, and down) to get across the board and past obstacles to the goal of the quest: the Jewel Card. I play *Robot Turtles* regularly with my son, who enjoys setting up the board's obstacles, which range from cards that represent ice blocks to castle walls. In early 2015, for an article for MindShift, I interviewed the game's inventor, Dan Shapiro. "It [*Robot Turtles*' creation] didn't come about because I wanted to teach kids to program," he said. "It came about because I wanted a fun way for kids and parents to interact."

Pandemic

In my 6th grade social studies classroom, I use *Pandemic* to teach students about the Columbian Exchange, the intentional and unintentional exchange of goods—and diseases—between Europe and the Americas in the Age of Discovery. During this pivotal time period, Europeans brought horses and wheat to the New World. In turn, corn and potatoes made their way to Europe. Just as the black plague traveled along the Silk Road, small pox washed up on American shores.

To play *Pandemic*, everyone must work together to stop four global disease outbreaks. There is sometimes a misconception with cooperative games: they are not games in which all players go home with a soccer trophy. Cooperative games are, in fact, quite competitive! The difference is that all players are on the same team, working to achieve a common goal. Either everyone wins together, or all is lost.

Figure 1. My 6th grade students at the *Pandemic* station during the Columbian Exchange unit. Photo credit: Lisa A. Galley, New Jersey Education Association.

The game board is an interconnected map of the world. World geography becomes situated in play. Students aren't memorizing locations on a map; they are using the map as a tool to solve problems. Also, in the game, players each take on roles with unique power-up abilities. "Dispatchers" can move other players anywhere around the world. "Medics" can cure all of the diseases on any city he or she moves to.

Meaningful role-play empowered my students. More from divvying up responsibilities, like assigning one student to be the note-taker and another to be the researcher, these roles had meaning. Each child had a power-up that the other did not. When I interviewed *Pandemic's* designer, Matt Leacock in 2015, he explained how roles "kind of turn everyone into superheroes." Next I asked about how he would design a lesson to be like a cooperative game. Leacock said:

> Everyone should have a common goal that they are aspiring to. Then you can play with that, like everyone has slightly different goals and that can lead to some interesting things. At the end of the day, it's about what are you trying to model. Are you trying to model the Silk Road, how it operates? Can you then put players in the roles of different people from the era?

There was one issue: up to four players at a time can play *Pandemic*. While the game is relatively inexpensive (especially online, using Amazon Prime, or at retailers that offer teacher discounts, like Barnes & Noble), I feasibly couldn't purchase 5 sets of the game! As a solution, I set up four learning stations in the classroom. The first station drew comparisons to current events: the Ebola outbreaks in West Africa nations. Here, I used BrainPOP resources, including the video on the outbreak and the related games on the site. The second station used resources from Stanford History Education's Reading Like a Historian curriculum. In it, students read and analyzed primary and secondary sources. In the third station, students took part in a PBS LearningMedia video lesson about the Columbian Exchange. The video concluded with an essay prompt. Because student choice leads to engagement, there was a choice on the topics to research, as well as the mode of delivery (essay, video).

Pandemic was the fourth station. Logistically, *Pandemic* takes about 35 minutes to play. This fit my school's bell schedule perfectly! I set up the board prior to students arriving, to streamline the process. The game's core mechanics of interconnected global cooperation supported the unit's learning goals: How the world changed after the Columbian Exchange. As a form of assessment, students wrote field journals, diary or blog entries written from the point of view of their roles. This facilitated knowledge from the game. Students who were Medics bragged on their ability to cure diseases. Social mechanics—actions that promote player interactions—made this game powerful as a teaching tool. Regarding social mechanics of board games, Leacock said:

> Naturally it's the very structure of a board game, you've got the board on a table with players encircling it. It forms a common space, a circle—a protected area of inter-action, where all the players feel safe within all of the confines of the rules. You're not just staring at a screen; it's not a solitary experience. With cooperative games, in particular, you're looking at the other players' faces just as much as the board. You need to communicate with each other. It forms a really wonderful medium to focus people in problem solving in a protected manner. It's a regulated problem-solving environment.

In December 2014, as Ebola spread through Western African countries, Pandemic Parties took place around the globe. Event participants played *Pandemic*—sometimes dressed as doctors—to bring awareness to the fight against the disease. To that end, Leacock and his wife launched a website to connect worldwide Pandemic Parties. I shared the news with my classes, which enabled them to make connections from the curriculum to the real world. Like the cooperative board game that inspired it, Pandemic Parties showed the benefits of working together to achieve a common goal. By early 2015, over $50,000 was raised to benefit Doctors Without Borders.

Kagan Structures

About every other week, teams of four students in my 7th grade social studies class play *Socratic Smackdown*, a gamified debate. To win, textual evidence must be used to support claims. The game builds argumentative thinking skills—a Common Core State Standard for English language arts. Mission Lab at the Quest to Learn school designed the game in collaboration with teacher Rebecca Grodner. Katie Salen, founding executive director of the Institute of Play, explained why the game is so engaging to play. We spoke in 2014. "When we see kids making arguments, debate, what situation can you put them in to arrive at that?" she began. "That's how you make games and map out the experiences."

In *Socratic Smackdown*, students debate in a "fishbowl." A fishbowl—with students playing a game together while others actively observe—is a cooperative learning strategy. Since the 1980s, Spencer Kagan, an expert on cooperative learning, has published several books on cooperative groupings. His Kagan Structures encourage student engagement. My personal favorite grouping is the Jigsaw, in which members switch out and rotate around the physical classroom. In a Jigsaw, "students are assigned a subpart of a classroom topic to learn and subsequently teach to others via reciprocal teaching" (Gee, 2007, p. 204). For example, in a group of three, one can be the note-taker, another can be the researcher, and the third would be the photographer, in charge of curating digital imagery. Kagan's books and websites state that there are about 200 different combinations. Four common groupings include:

- Rally Robin—In pairs, students alternate generating brief oral responses
- Timed Pair-Share—In pairs, students share with a partner for a predetermined time while the partner listens. Then partners switch roles
- Round Robin—In teams, students take turns responding orally
- Rally Coach—Partners take turns, one solving a problem while the other coaches, then partners switch roles. (Clowes, 2011)

Some groupings are better for certain activities. For example, Timed Pair-Share works well for anticipatory sets, or warm-up activities. The Round Robin arrangement is appropriate to discuss findings in inquiry lessons, while the Rally Coach ensures each member gets a turn to lead. Kagan has a magic number for optimal group size: four. Kagan favors teams of four because they "maximize and equalize active participation compared to any other number" (1998). The second best size is a pair (Kagan, 1998). The idea is to keep groups smaller and manageable, as well as even in number to promote equity. It can be helpful to have student desks arranged in a way that promotes cooperative learning.

Small groups are also desirable in the business world. Amazon founder Jeff Bezos nicknamed this dynamic the "two-pizza rule," where any team is small enough that two pizzas would be a large enough lunch order (Brandt, 2011). Building teams with players/students of varying abilities is a useful career skill. Business teams are often the same size as guilds communities. Multiplayer game guilds "can be made up of any number of players, depending on the common goals and play style that guild members decide upon" (Sheldon, 2012, p. 30). The next section reviews several anecdotes about how guilds and multiplayer learning work effectively together.

Lee Sheldon's Multiplayer Classroom Approach

One of the most effective examples of a game-like learning environment is Lee Sheldon's Multiplayer Classroom approach. In 2012, his book *The Multiplayer Classroom: Designing Coursework as a Game* was published. Sheldon's book reviewed the iterations his syllabus took in his game design course. His grading policy moved from percentages to Experience Points (XP), as in multiplayer video games. The higher a student scores, the more he or she advances, or "levels up." Unlike many professors, Sheldon doesn't deduct points for students who don't come to class; instead, he awards points for coming. "It's a positive," he told me. "I get almost perfect attendance. Colleagues think I'm crazy." His syllabus also includes "expansion packs," similar to purchasable downloadable content (DLC) such as extra maps. Sheldon and I initially spoke in March 2014 for this subsection; however, we have stayed in touch on social media.

Sheldon started his career as a television writer and producer. He wrote for *Star Trek: The Next Generation, Charlie's Angels,* and the long-running daytime soap opera *Edge of Night.* In 1994, he left television and began writing games. Eight years ago Sheldon entered the academic world, first at Indiana University; currently he is a professor of practice of interactive media and game development at Worcester Polytechnic Institute, in Massachusetts.

I interviewed Sheldon about his experiences in 2014. He pointed out to me that the trend of game-based learning isn't all that new. "Humans have been using storytelling and gameplay to teach for over a millennia," he said. "First and 2nd grade kids play games. In 3rd or 4th grade something happens and education gets 'serious'—multiple-choice questions and lecturing. We lost the ability to play and now we're fighting hard to get it back."

Sheldon's students are grouped in guilds. This arrangement was inspired by the role-playing game *World of Warcraft.* Grouping students can promote an intrinsic love of learning. Sheldon gave me an example of how this works. Sometimes he will add extra credit questions on exams that benefit an entire guild, rather than just the students who answer correctly. He explained, "If one person answers that question, everyone gets credit for it. It's not enough [credit] to change a slacker's grade from an F to a C. They try because they get peer acclamation for that. It's an intrinsic reward." This is an important lesson about what games can teach. It is an example of XEODesign's "fun" emotion of *naches,* or *kvell* (Yiddish for "pleasure or pride at the accomplishment of a child or mentee") (Lazzaro, 2004). There is a deep satisfaction felt when helping friends.

When students meet in Sheldon's physical classroom, they work in "zones." This arrangement is similar to stations or centers in kindergarten through grade 12 settings. Teachers sometimes arrange student desks to accommodate certain projects. Like all teaching, setting up a learning space is a personal preference. When organizing a class as a playspace, be cognizant of what works best for the student. I use conventional rows because most of my activities wind up taking place away from the desks and in stations around the room. Some of my colleagues configure their rooms differently, with desks paired together, or in a large circle. The classroom space is, in essence, the magic circle where play happens. Combining Kagan's preferred grouping with Sheldon's guild configurations suggests arranging desks in clusters of four.

I was curious to hear examples of how Sheldon teaches his college courses with a game-like narrative. Writing is so ingrained in his methodology that his classes are "episodes." Similarly, he refers to students as "players," sometimes using the words interchangeably. To Sheldon, narratives should not rely on cut scenes and conversation trees. He said, "I'm interested in environmental and nonlinear storytelling." When creating storylines for games and projects, don't assume it is the same as when writing for other media. This is an important tip in designing game-like (or problem-based and project-based, for that matter) activities. The game's narrative provides a frame for Sheldon to keep his students engaged.

Collateral Learning

There exists a balance between pedagogy and entertainment. Starting with curriculum creates boring experiences. On the other hand, focusing too much on engagement can leave little room for education. Sheldon has a name for this sweet spot: "collateral learning." According to Sheldon, "Collateral learning means that students learn in spite of themselves. They don't even know that they're learning." Movies and books teach collaterally. You may watch the World War II drama *Saving Private Ryan* and be moved emotionally by the story. In the process, you learn what happened when the Americans led the D-Day invasion of Normandy Beach. Teaching with narrative games is the same. The focus isn't merely on the act of learning; rather, there is a felt need to acquire the knowledge in order to progress in the story. Learning can be incidental if the learner is situated in an authentic setting (Lave & Wenger, 1991).

Sheldon's journey with collateral learning began at Indiana University. (His journey is detailed in the *Multiplayer Classroom*.) It began with a project sponsored by a grant from Robert Wood Johnson. The goal was to see the importance of student fitness and health simply from playing a game. "We didn't teach them anything, no food pyramids," he recalled. "I came up with a mystery of a professor that disappears, and then wild things happen. It ends with character being whisked away by a flying saucer." The activity had students solving puzzles and solving a mystery by running around the campus. Body mass index (BMI) tests showed that participants became healthier and fitter. "They got across the campus in less time than shuttle bus by walking; the collateral learning was sleeping in more and walking," Sheldon said. The smartphone game *Zombies, Run!* has a similar mechanic. Boasting a community of over 500,000, this fitness game puts players on missions collecting items while "outrunning" hordes of zombies. The app uses GPS and audio cues to motivate runners.

Sheldon next told me about "The Lost Manuscripts," a class in which students had to learn Mandarin Chinese in order to find the lost manuscript of a famous Chinese novel. Cultural exchange was part of the fiction, creating an immersive, game-based experience. The first few "episodes" (or classes) were in a lecture-style classroom. Then, for one of the classes, Sheldon had a woman burst onto the scene to engage in a heated argument with the learning designer. The dispute was in Mandarin, and took place just outside the room. Next, the learning designer (or as Sheldon told me, "a teacher playing the character of a learning designer") came back in and introduced herself to the students. Student interest about the conflict was piqued. They wanted to understand the disagreement. Sheldon next detailed further episodes of "The Lost Manuscript." He said:

> The class was supposed to go to Beijing (in the game-set classroom), following another group of students. The teacher informed the class that something went wrong with the first group and this class won't be going in 3 months—but in 2 weeks! Knowing it was a game accelerated their learning. For the next class, we moved chairs around like an airport, used an Xbox Kinect (sensor), and partition screens to create an information kiosk. The 1-hour, 50-minute-long class required students to clear customs, change currency, find their hotel at the kiosk, call the hotel, arrange transportation, and read signs in Chinese around the room, like "Restrooms," "Planes This Way," and "Transportation." They were originally told that someone would meet

them and guide them. When they arrived at the airport/classroom there was only a crumpled-up piece of paper saying, "Welcome Rensselaer Students"—with no sign from who would help them. Helping themselves, they got through it all in 30 minutes, by collaborating.

What Sheldon created was a live-action video game. He went as far as to hire native Mandarin-speaking actors to play customs agents, as well as other people in the airport. In video game parlance, they are called non-playable characters, or NPCs. Sheldon explained, "There was emergent gameplay going on. They solved all the puzzles I gave them, and they wanted to continue. That's what narrative brings: the desire to want to know what comes next. I just don't create scenarios, but ongoing narratives."

The final exam was a police investigation about where to find the lost manuscript. Sheldon used social media to have actors send tweets and messages to students. He said, "In the beginning, students were in four study groups of three each. There were four characters tweeting all of them. As the class went along, one person tweeted one group saying, 'Don't trust this other person. The manuscript is worth a lot of money; they are not going to preserve it, they're going to sell it.' Another one said, 'Don't trust that one.'" Sheldon used the narrative to split the loyalties of the students and the characters in the story. Students studied outside of class because the learning was meaningful—and fun. They weren't listening to lectures. Each class leveled up in challenge as in a video game.

Of course, hiring actors to engage with kindergarten through grade 12 students presents logistical and ethical challenges. A middle or high school teacher can, however, deliver a blended learning experience on an educational, social platform such as Edmodo, Schoology, or Moodle. Sheldon explained to me how his online course for Excelsior College included two extra student accounts controlled by the instructor and teacher's assistant. "They are the hint system in the game, driving discussion if it lags," he said. "Then they become part of narrative." The false student can also serve as a "docent," providing help, guidance, and assistance. A middle or high school teacher could tell students that the extra accounts are guest students from neighboring districts.

Sheldon worked on project funded by a National Science Foundation grant for teachers of engineering and science. The game's narrative is about "an extended Irish family who emigrated to a new land, only the new land is Mars. It's a family drama—*Downton Abbey* in outer space." Titled, *These Far Hills*, the objective is to get a biosphere up and running for others to follow.

By learning concepts from engineering and science, the student/players can move through the story. The lead character is a middle-aged woman with many children. Her father is her mentor. The story begins when the first child is born on Mars (the Mars setting calls to mind *Mars Generation One: Argubot Academy*, GlassLab's argumentation tablet game). Sheldon explained where collateral learning comes in. He said:

> You need to keep up with engineering necessary to keep up the biosphere. The father is getting stern with her, and then you learn he is dying and he won't live to see his dream. The father-child dynamic allows me to create a lot of emotion, which helps them to learn. The song "I'll Miss the Rain in Dublin," written by a guy in Saratoga, inspired the last scene. At the end, they make it rain inside the biosphere and then they see their father's grave outside on the red soil of Mars. Emotion draws the student into the learning.

Unlike a narrative in a typical problem-based learning unit, Sheldon's scenarios are ongoing (of course, college classes do not meet every day). He explained, "You prepare your syllabus and lesson plan, which is a design document. The narrative builds from class to class, with cliffhangers, so they [the students] want to come back." Sheldon teases out upcoming classes, or episodes, using social media. Games and stories are how humans remember things—not by memorizing lists of disconnected facts. The trick is creating a compelling enough storyline.

Whyville

Whyville was one of the first browser-based virtual environments. It remains popular to this day. Children continue to meet in Whyville to create and play together. Participants, known as "citizens," earn virtual currency, called "clams." The platform is free and it is a safe space for younger students to play.

I spoke with Whyville's founder, computational neurobiologist Jim Bower, in February 2014. He has been involved for many years in building computer models to figure out how brains work. He sees games as just one piece of the educational puzzle. He explained, "The core [idea] that kids love *World of Warcraft* or *Assassin's Creed* and therefore we can make it educational and 'win' is not true. It is much more complicated than that. Any teacher knows that." Bower prefers student-created environments instead of games designed to deliver content. He used the equal sign as an example of a concept that can be taught with a game. He explained:

They're [students] introduced to it in kindergarten or pre-K. Kids think the equal sign means the answer comes next. They don't understand that it is an expression of balance. They think of it the way computer scientists think of it: an output. But in math, it's a balance between left and right. Can you get all the way through math and not realize what an equal sign is? Sure. But can you build a higher understanding of math? No. Can you standardize test them? Sure, as long as the answer is on the right!

Bower wanted a "motif" to teach the mathematical concept of equality. "It should be obvious to a 3-year-old, but complex enough to be interesting to a college student," he stated. Researchers found it in a mobile, the decoration that hangs from ceilings and baby cribs. A mobile must be balanced— or equal—to hang properly. He explained, "With mobiles, you can go from addition, subtraction, multiplication, division, all the way up to systems of equations." The equal sign is the game mechanic of balance; the tablet game *Dragon Box* is a perfect example of using balance to teach algebra.

Publishers sometimes design games by looking at a textbook, or other traditional material, and asking, "Can we make a game that about that?" This is Bower's issue with most learning games. He said, "They take what's wrong with textbooks and replicate it in a game—which is simply ridiculous." In Whyville there are 150 to 200 different types of game-like activities, including ones that children invented themselves. Whyville also works with the Educational Development Center to get to the pedagogical structure that supports learning, not just content and skills (such as the concept of equality as balance, rather than the skill of arithmetic). Whyville focuses on building structures. This is the artifact that Bower finds missing in content-driven games. "Games are one form of play, but not the only form," he concluded.

Bower's connection from computational neurobiology to learning and education was brought together by simulation technology. His story began with a faculty position at the California Institute of Technology (Caltech) in 1984. He built a general-purpose simulation system for building models of the brain, called Genesis. It was designed to do research for graduate-level training. Because the entire field of neurobiology is theoretical, models and theory were important to understanding how things work. At Caltech he used his position to get involved in education, particularly "to explore simulation-based learning as a basis for young children to play with the dynamics of science." The challenge was to get science into schools, and then figure out how to get computers to engage students.

At this time, Bower founded the Caltech Precollege Science Initiative (CAPSI). He told me how, over the course of 17 years, CAPSI spent "about

$25 million to figure out how to get hands-on, inquiry-based, constructivist, kids-based science into public schools." He next began working with his friend, Alan Kay, an inventor of the original Apple Macintosh interface (Kay worked at the famed Xerox PARC project, where the graphical user interface (GUI) desktop was first developed). They talked about simulations for children and education. Working with Apple, they built the first virtual world for learning, in 1985. They installed it in the Los Angeles County library system. It was so successful that the librarians insisted it be taken out. Bower said, "The librarians complained that the Macs were blocking the card catalogue!"

In 1998, his Caltech program had seemingly run its course. In California there was a struggle between textbooks and hands-on science kits. Bower decided to end the project and to launch the company Numedeon. The following year, Numedeon started Whyville as an informal, broad-based educational site. It still has a fairly large number of registered users. Bower said that the number of registered users exceeded 7 million, nowhere near competitors such as Disney's *Club Penguin*. "We don't really care," Bower told me. "We're really figuring out how to work with real teachers, grow with students, bring best community practice to 5th grade classrooms, and make things holistic rather than one by one. It's very critical to the gamification business, how you replace an entire curriculum, not one piece."

Conclusions and Takeaways

Cooperative learning is basically a game. There is no need to reinvent years of proven research and practice. Like a game, projects should focus on the storyline and mechanics first. The learning will follow, and students will pick up knowledge collaterally. You can integrate technology without sacrificing the valuable time of students working together face-to-face.

Lesson Plan Ideas

Forbidden Island cooperative tabletop game that connects to plate tectonics—https://boardgamegeek.com/filepage/97639/summary-sheet-educators-connect-more

Lost at Sea: I begin each school year using team-building activities to model cooperative learning. In this survivalist lesson, individual students first rank items from a shipwreck by importance. The second step puts the student in a group to defend his or her position. Is fishing line more valuable item than a shaving mirror? The activity lends itself to inquiry-based learning common in history and science classrooms. This is an effective icebreaker; however, standards may not apply—http://insight.typepad.co.uk/lost_at_sea.pdf

Viral Video Commercials: The task is to educate and persuade others. Students will be able to do this by making a commercial. All projects will be created using either iMovie, Windows Movie Maker, or Animoto, a web-based application. Students in other class periods/sections should view the commercials and vote to see which was the most convincing. The class will be divided into teams, one per commercial. Social studies standards apply, as do Common Core State Standards for English language arts, pertaining to argumentation, apply. Frame around concepts in this TED Talk: https://www.ted.com/talks/kevin_allocca_why_videos_go_viral

Student Constitution: Your students have been nominated to attend the Virtual Constitutional Convention. They will help draft (write) a new Student Handbook. The Virtual Constitutional Convention will meet face-to-face in class, as well as online via Edmodo, or Today's Meet. Edmodo features virtual small groups, which I have found to be easy to manage. The class will be divided into groups. Topics should be common in all handbooks (e.g., dress code, electronic use policy). Each group will be responsible for drafting a topic from the Student Handbook. A 2/3 (66.7%) vote is required to ratify the final Student Constitution. Voting will take place in class. Social studies standards apply, as do Common Core State Standards for English language arts, especially those that pertain to argumentation. Each person in a group has a role and will be graded individually. Student roles include:

1. The Researcher—Responsible for reading different school student handbooks in the state, as well as your school's
2. The Writer—Responsible for the wording of the assigned topic
3. The Devil's Advocate—Responsible for coming up with scenarios that "punch holes" in the group's wording

Virtual Field Trip iBooks Project: Class-created interactive book to be submitted as a free iPad download in Apple's iBookstore. Using iBooks Author (a free Mac app), the teacher can compile each group's work into separate chapters (one per team). Creative Commons-licensed images of, for example, famous buildings, statues, or artifacts, can be included as an interactive gallery. Common Core State Standards for English language arts apply.

The Whyville Times: After young learners play in *Whyville,* have them read and summarize articles in the virtual community's online newspaper. Topics include Creative Writing and Entertainment. Common Core State Standards for English language arts apply—http://j.whyville.net/smmk/whytimes/index

Games

Hanabi is a cooperative card game with the goal of building a perfect firework display. Players can only look at others' cards—http://rnrgames.com/hanabi

Keep Talking and Nobody Explodes is a cooperative virtual reality game. Players print out a series of logic puzzles on paper. They solve it out loud while assisting a player who diffuses a bomb while wearing a virtual reality headset—http://www.keeptalkinggame.com

National Model United Nations, the long-running simulation—http://www.nmun.org

Zombies, Run!, a running game that puts players on missions collecting items and outrunning hordes of zombies—all while actually running!—https://www.zombiesrungame.com

Whyville, a vibrant virtual community for elementary students—http://www.whyville.net

Resources

Buck Institute of Education, resources for project-based learning—http://bie.org

The Corns Visit the 13 Colonies, my student's e-book in iTunes (free)—https://itun.es/i6gP67k

Is Game-Based Learning Assessment a Big Data problem? Lessons from Piles of Horse Manure, Whyville's Jim Bower's 2016 blog post on games and assessments—http://jamesmbower.com/blog/2016/05/is-game-based-learning-assessment-a-big-data-problem-lessons-from-piles-of-horse-manure

Kagan Online, resources for cooperative structures—http://www.kaganonline.com/index.php

Online Stopwatch, works great on an interactive whiteboard—http://www.online-stopwatch.com

"Project-Based Learning Explained," a short explanatory video—http://www.commoncraft.com/project-based-learning-explained-custom-video-project-bie

Lee Sheldon's archived edWeb webinar (free to view for a one-hour professional development certificate!) about the multiplayer classroom approach—http://home.edweb.net/the-multiplayer-classroom-education-in-play

· 11 ·

GAMIFICATION

I could drink coffee almost anywhere, yet I often frequent Starbucks. When I enter a store, I am greeted with the smell of freshly ground coffee and hipster music. The machines behind the counter are positioned to enable the baristas to face the customers. I can pay for my drink using the Starbucks app on my iPhone: All I have to do is shake the phone at the register. In exchange for purchasing coffee, I am awarded stars. The hope is that I level up from green stars to gold stars. The app includes other free rewards every week, such as a song from iTunes or a free app. There is even the fun mechanic of shaking my phone to pay. The store is filled with positive aesthetics, and I am moved along with a reward system (stars). Clearly there is more at work here than just a cup of coffee.

Visitors to websites and mobile apps may find progress bars encouraging completion of online profiles and badges to reward behaviors. This is known as gamification. Gamification is "interactive online design that plays on people's competitive instincts and often incorporates the use of rewards to drive action—these include virtual rewards such as points, payments, badges, discounts, and free gifts; and status indicators such as friend counts, re-tweets, leader boards, achievement data, progress bars, and the ability to level up" (Anderson & Rainie, 2012). Designer of apps often mix in game-like elements in unexpected places to create meaningful interactions. Social media is gamified; the "score" is based on shares, views, and "liked" activities. Should schools be gamified too?

Game scholar James Paul Gee spoke to me about two types of gamification in education. "Gamification is just extrinsic motivation," he began, in April 2014. "Or gamification is a way to try to motivate people by quest-based learning in the ways games are highly motivating. There really are two trends going on out there and battling each other, both of them popular. Unfortunately, our schools are mired in test prep."

Don't expect to add dice to a lesson, call it a game, and expect students' interest to be piqued. Gamification must be baked into lesson design. One approach is Amy Jo Kim's Social Action Matrix, which appropriated Bartle's Player Type Model to the social web. Kim has written extensively about the rise of cooperative games (e.g., *Draw Something*, *Words with Friends*) as being non–zero sum—everyone wins!

This chapter reviews how to implement gamification techniques that keep learning intrinsically engaging. A few gamification approaches are effective as stand-alone activities, like hiding Easter egg surprises in assignments or having students create their own digital avatars. I also analyze gamified learning management systems, which provide a digital game-like overlay to a classroom.

Meaningful Gamification

Meaningful gamification is "the use of gameful and playful layers to help a user find personal connections that motivate engagement with a specific context for long-term change" (Nicholson, 2014, p. 1). I asked game design professor in January 2016 to explain further. Nicholson coined the term. "Gamification is like the syllabus—a manipulation layer," he replied. "Game-based learning is when the game and content are integrated." There are six components, which Nicholson ranks in order: play is first and reflection comes last. The resulting "RECIPE" is a scrambled letter acronym. Nicholson's RECIPE for meaningful gamification is:

- Play—facilitating the freedom to explore and fail within boundaries
- Exposition—creating stories for participants that are integrated with the real-world setting and allowing them to create their own
- Choice—developing systems that put the power in the hands of the participants

- Information—using game design and game display concepts to allow participants to learn more about the real-world context
- Engagement—encouraging participants to discover and learn from others interested in the real-world setting
- Reflection—assisting participants in finding other interests and past experiences that can deepen engagement and learning. (2014, p. 4)

In January 2014, Filament Games's Dan White explained to me how all games include elements of gamification. White also shared the notion that education should already be intrinsically motivating. "There is a time and place for 'light gamification,' but I wouldn't lean too heavily with creating structures and systems that have students progressing because of extrinsic motivation," he said.

Richard Bartle, in March 2014, called the movement of gamification in education "a bandwagon." Not mincing words, he said, "the technical term for it is cheap psychological tricks." He then elaborated how gamification can be misappropriated. He said:

> If you design a game, you want [people] to play it because it's fun—not because you've written a Skinner Box and you're forcing them to play your game because you're using cheap psychological tricks. It means your game is not fun and you have to have another method. If you are a game designer, you want people to play because they like your game—not because you tricked them by giving them rewards. Imagine a machine, like a car, and it all has to work together. You say let's take the wheels off of this car and attach it to this plank of wood and call it "car-ification" and now you can ride around in this plank of wood. Kids would like that, but that's not car-ification, it's just playing with wood.

Bartle's point is that gamification should not be tacked on to learning. There are many games that function perfectly without traditional elements of gamification, like points and leaderboards. The popular mobile game *Monument Valley*—which won Apple's Game of the Year in 2014 and was featured on Netflix's *House of Cards*—is devoid of badges, points, and even a score. The only reward is to progress to the next M. C. Escher-like puzzle. Story-driven games, like *Her Story*, *Gone Home*, and *Life Is Strange*, rely on narrative to drive engagement.

There remains promise for meaningful gamification in education. When I spoke to Games + Learning + Society Center's Kurt Squire in January 2014 he said, "The devil's in the details on implementation." Schools already have structures and systems in place and may not necessarily need gamification.

"Gamification can be good or poor, like games themselves," he said. "There is a commoditization of it, like applying it to anything."

Gamifying may simply imply more interactive engagement from users. In March 2014 Jesse Schell explained that it really shouldn't come as a surprise that people would want to design products to be as compelling as some games. "Games have good qualities, games have good feedback, and games are very engaging," he explained. "Games make people satisfied about their progress, games make people feel good about themselves. I want people to feel those things."

Gamification Mechanics

School has notoriously slow feedback loops (from teacher to student and then back to teacher). It can often be the opposite of James Paul Gee's Explicit Information On-Demand and Just In Time Principle, in which "the learner is given explicit information both on demand and just in time, when the learner needs it or just at the point where the information can best be understood and used in practice" (2007, p. 226). Aside from issues with feedback, school can also be inequitable. The rich—who can afford to hire tutors—get richer.

In March 2014 I asked Jesse Schell about viewing school as a game. To a game designer, almost anything can be viewed as a game. Whether it is a well-designed game is another story. "The school system is set up as a game," he said. "Everything you do, you get scores. There's a leaderboard. We give out bumper stickers to parents that say, 'My Kid is an Honor Roll Student.' It is a game, just a badly designed game."

The elements detailed in this section should be used to deepen the journey or acknowledge "mile markers." It's not a pantry of ingredients. Taking pieces here and there from this list will not instantly turn your lesson plans into a game. I would not simply add a leaderboard; however, if it was done in the spirit of fun, it can be engaging. Adding a timer can make everyone in the room suddenly competitive, but that doesn't necessarily make it a fun or educationally sound game. BrainPOP's Kevin Miklasz remarked to me in 2016, "A good learning game is one that can be played *without* a timer." To be effective, allow student choice and use gamification mechanics around already meaningful activities, like in project-based learning units.

Leaderboards

Leaderboards, like badges, can encourage student iteration. Noticing the high score in a game, or your own score, triggers competition in many people (Bartle's Achiever type). Of course, not everyone is competitive; don't expect to engage every child with a leaderboard. Essentially a public scoreboard, when misused, the leaderboard can discourage children from trying (that's why grades aren't publicly posted). Instead, try using a leaderboard for nongraded game tallies. I regularly use a leaderboard when students play the discussion strategy game *Socratic Smackdown*, developed at the Quest to Learn school. I modeled mine after Rebecca Grodner's, the game's codesigner. Grodner is an 8th grade English language arts teacher at Quest. Individual scores are viewable on dry-erase boards. They are also tallied as part of a team score. The result became a cooperative—not competitive—game.

None of the *Socratic Smackdown* scores were used for grading purposes. It is important to emphasize to students that game scores are not grades. I explain the rationale to students to drive the point home. Using in-game assessments can stifle creative problem-solving in games. Simply put, the act of play itself cannot be graded—only learning outcomes after play should be assessed.

My advice is to create teams of equal ability. In *Socratic Smackdown*, stronger arguers can coach those who require more refinement and practice. Having a lower batting average on a champion team still makes everyone a winner! Figure 1 shows the leaderboard for one of the teams, I modeled on Grodner's example.

Team 1: Student	9/5/16	9/19/16	10/3/16	10/17/16	Total
John					
Sam					
Alexandra					
Allison					
Total					

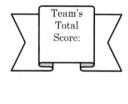

Figure 1. Team-Centered Leaderboard.

Badges

A classroom-based badge system can also serve as a scoring mechanism, as well as an artifact of achievement. Essentially a digital version of a Boy Scout or Girl Scout badge system, it can promote social participation. The core mechanic of social engagement is when people enjoy "shared activities" (Kim, 2012b; Kim, 2014a). Requirements to earn badges include social skills, such as sharing, expressing, and collaborating (Kim, 2012b; Kim, 2014a).

Aside from social dynamics, people play games together because it is fun. Fun can be categorized depending on the desired outcome (Lazzaro, 2009). Multiplayer games are engaging because the interactions stimulate People Fun (Lazzaro, 2009, pp. 40–46). People Fun mechanics includes the "social experiences of competition, teamwork, as well as opportunity for social bonding and personal recognition that comes from playing with others" (Lazzaro, 2004). Badges trigger People Fun by acknowledging the connections from working together. Badge issuance is an embedded assessment—an incremental check for understanding. Embedded assessments are built into educational activities and serve as part of the feedback loop of learning. This is not new to teaching, or mutually exclusive to game-based learning; many teachers already post mini-due dates and deadlines before a project is due. Formalizing embedded assessments adds feedback to students and for teachers, thus creating an iterative design loop.

Mods

Did you ever change a recipe? Perhaps you added a no-calorie sweetener instead of sugar? Maybe blueberries in a muffin mix instead of chocolate chips? That is called modding (short for modifying). It is my favorite gamification mechanic. Modding a game bends the rules and changes the system. Think about board games you played that came with a timer. Did you always use it? People have their own house versions of *Monopoly* and *Scrabble*. Part of the charm—and success—of *Minecraft* is that modding is part of the game experience. In fact, *Minecraft* is a mod of another game, *Infiniminer*. Learning should *matter* to the student. Therefore, students should be given an opportunity to customize their own learning.

It takes confidence in lesson planning to let students mod projects, directions, and even the rubric. When it's done correctly, students may show an increased ownership in their own learning. Bernie DeKoven said to me in

2014, "Freedom is an absolute necessity for the play to be meaningful and for the learning to be something the kids could truly internalize." As long as the student is meeting the learning objectives, why not give them freedom to pursue their interests in activities?

Avatars

I give students freedom to choose silly avatars in learning networks such as Edmodo. An avatar is "an online representation of a participant in a game or social network" (Sheldon, 2012, p. 30). Xbox, Nintendo, and PlayStation have toolsets to let players customize their online selves. There are several mobile apps that enable avatar creations. Morfo enables users to take a selfie and then turn their faces into an animation. From Nintendo, Miitomo lets anyone make a Mii, which is an avatar like those on Wii console games. On a smartphone, your virtual self can socialize with your online friends.

My students have created game-like presentations using Voki. Instead of classwork being posted on a bulletin board, work gets published online for a global audience. Voki offers a Classroom feature, which is private and teacher-controlled, and includes lesson plan ideas. The Voki for Education app is its mobile version. Simply tap and swipe to design an avatar. Then hit the record button to give it a voice.

Aside from the visual aspects of the avatars, Vokis can virtually speak in accents and languages. In a European Renaissance project, one of my students had Leonardo da Vinci tell his life story in Italian! Another student used a Shakespearean English translator on the website Shmoop to have the renowned playwright speak in an Elizabethan tongue.

Voki Classroom is game-like. When a student submits work, teachers can comment and offer them a chance to iterate prior to grading. The ability to approve or disapprove work turned fear of failure into a safe opportunity to retry. Using tools that promote self-expression gives students a sense of agency, mixed and with fun.

Game Geography

Games often use maps. Some, such as *Risk!*, attempt to be geographically accurate. Others are more abstract; Atlantic City's streets are not in a perfect square, as in *Monopoly*. *Battleship* plays on a grid, while *Settlers of Catan* takes place in regions. *Dungeon and Dragons*, which bears similarities to *Lord of the*

Rings, has a fantasy geography that develops as the game is played. Open-world video games are virtual worlds that players are encouraged to explore. *L. A. Noire* faithfully recreates almost all of Los Angeles during the late 1940s. Other games riff on historical accuracy, such as *Red Dead Redemption,* a fictionalized version of the American West and its borderlands with Mexico. Games with downloadable add-ons sometimes include maps. The war simulation game *Call of Duty* features several maps where multiplayer "capture the flag" tournaments take place.

Isn't it easier to understand a map after you've driven somewhere? In order to progress in the game, a practical, hands-on knowledge of geography develops. Mapping of game worlds is important to know because it *matters* to students who play these games. The *Assassin's Creed III* release in 2012 made my job teaching the American Revolution infinitely easier. My students knew exactly what the battlefield of Concord looked like because they experienced it virtually. The game puts its protagonist, Connor, at the foot of the famous bridge where British Redcoats were fought. (Connor is half-English and half-Native American and sometimes speaks in a Mohawk dialect; his real name in the game is Ratonhnhaké:ton.)

Teaching the "five themes" of geography (location, place, human-environment interaction, movement, and region) to children who barely venture out of town can be an arduous task. It can be too abstract for children to remember places they have never visited. I have trouble doing that myself. When I go away on vacation, the travel books I buy always make better sense when I read them after the trip has ended. To that end, consider creating simple board games with dice or spinners and small game pieces to have students "experience" traveling in the place you are teaching. Another option is a virtual field trip using Google Earth. Remember, engaging learners in virtual worlds is learning by simulation, which is learning by doing. This helps the knowledge "stick."

Easter Eggs

Near a computer? Go to Google's Image Search and type "Atari breakout" in the box. The search results will become a fully playable version of the 1980s Atari video game *Breakout.* What you just uncovered (thanks to my hint!) is an Easter egg. In an affinity group (online spaces of mutual interest), members share game "cheats." Cheats are not condoning cheating; rather, they can encourage the sharing of knowledge. They can help to uncover hidden challenges, known as "Easter eggs." (The game *Super Mario Bros.* was among the first to feature Easter eggs.)

Easter eggs provide "transgressive discovery: by bending the rules of the game in just the right way, the players get to see or experience something that more lawful players would not" (Salen & Zimmerman, 2003, p. 279). Warren Robinett is credited with subversively hiding the first Easter egg in the Atari 2600 game *Adventure*. He recalled the story in an essay featured in the book *The Game Design Reader* (2006). He wrote, "In this deviously hidden secret room, I affixed my signature, in flashing lights, 'Created by Warren Robinett.' I did this in the tradition of artists, down through the centuries, identifying themselves as authors of their own works" (Robinett, 2006, pp. 712–713).

Easter eggs empower the student to test the boundaries of the learning system. Uncovered Easter eggs can also be acknowledged with digital badges. For example, as part of a podcasting project I do, I award a "Magical Mystery Badge" once the student deciphers a backward recording. The student must figure out on their own how to use the tools available to decipher the recording. A hint, written in reverse, is part of the badge's description. Another way to hide Easter eggs is by using QR codes. QR codes are like bar codes that are read with a mobile device and take the user directly to a website or a picture. Easter eggs are common in movies, too. Disney's *Frozen* (2013) included characters from *Tangled* (2010). Try leaving some hidden surprises for your students to find in their learning journey!

Gamified Learning Management Systems

Many modern video games use sophisticated adaptive engines to automatically adjust the challenges based on player performance. Designers refer to the complicated mathematical algorithms coded into games as the Dynamic Difficulty Adjustment system. These adaptive algorithms have crossed over into computer-based learning. Dynamic Difficulty Adjustment in this setting is known as "adaptive learning," which attempts to create personalized learning environments for students. Often this may mean adaptive assessments. Challenges adjust as a student progresses through content.

Game designer Jenova Chen's master's in fine arts thesis, based on his game *flOw*, made a connection from games to education. (Chen's studio designed *Journey* and *Flower*, both for the PlayStation Network). His research showed that people can self-pace their challenges. In fact, many may desire that freedom. He also proposed more transparency in tests. Scores can add up the same way as in a video game—instantly and with no limit. Challenging students to perform better to beat their personal bests on assessments delivers an intrinsic satisfaction. He recommended:

1. There is no cap for the total score. Students can gain as much score as possible during the test period. Therefore, even top students can still challenge themselves every time they take the test.
2. Students should be able to see scores gained through each question and feel the joy of answering them correctly, which encourages them to do more.
3. The difficulty and the score of each question should be related. More challenge equals more reward.
4. Students should be able to sense the difficulty of each question and have the control to skip hard questions. (Chen, 2006)

There are a few learning management tools to create what Chen envisioned. They are not toolsets to design game; rather, they are digital applications that manage a classroom the way a massive multiplayer online (MMO) game would. The three discussed in this subsection apply elements from Lee Sheldon's multiplayer classroom, including replacing percentage grades with experience points (XP) that are earned—students start with a grade or score of zero and complete activities to earn the grade they desire. These systems also incorporate team dynamics and rewards for personalized achievements.

Rezzly

During field data collection for my dissertation, I observed Steve Isaacs and Peggy Sheehy deliver personalized, quest-based lessons with their middle school students. They each used 3D GameLab, which was rebranded Rezzly in November 2015. I spoke with Steve Isaacs in April 2016 about how he structures lessons in Rezzly. "What speaks strongly to me is the quest-based experience," Isaacs said. "I am trying to create a choice-based learning environment so the choices a student makes takes them further down the rabbit hole."

Isaacs teaches video game design; however, the way he populates Rezzly is helpful for any teacher who would want to replicate his successes. One quest a student may select is "Watch it, build it," in which they have to find a *Minecraft* video and then recreate the virtual structure in their account. That completed quest is then submitted to Isaacs, along with a written reflection about the challenges they encountered, the success they had, and how did they overcome these challenges. Also included is evidence: a link to a video. Isaacs continued:

> I can either approve the quest, or return it. If I need more depth and the reflection, there is a feedback loop for teacher to student, until students successfully demonstrate understanding. Then a new quest or branch opens, like to mod in Minecraft, then create your own. That would be three quests. They might diverge to a coding quest-line using Code.org or code academy to learning coding and computational thinking. My goal is to create a studio environment.

Isaacs is modeling his grading on how the game design industry actually works, with different career paths. Isaacs' quests enable students to take on the role of graphic artists or sound designer. "Kids earn XP [experience points] no matter the path, which translates to grade," he continued. "700 XP is an A+, but kids go far beyond that. They enjoy the quests and want to open up new quests." Gamification can be with points and badgers; for Isaacs, "The true power of gamification done right is when kids have choice and there is that autonomy in their learning pathways."

Chris Haskell, clinical assistant professor, Boise State University, cofounded 3D GameLab, which was renamed as Rezzly, in late 2015. I observed Rezzly's use in my dissertation research in both Peggy Sheehy's and Steve Isaacs's classrooms. I had met Haskell at several conferences over the years and I caught up with him to learn ideas about how teachers can use Rezzly to engage learners. We spoke in March 2016.

When 3D GameLab emerged on the scene, in 2009, it was the world's first game-based learning management system. It was originally built for universities. "We knew that game layers in big game MMOs, like *Star Trek Online*, *World of Warcraft*, and *EverQuest*, were really valuable," Haskell recounted. MMO games have a system in which experience is scored and can be used to level up player's avatars or purchase items. Players also earn badges, achievements, and awards after completing quests, many of which are individualized paths where meaningful choices are presented. "The quest structure was also a learning structure," he continued. "It was graduated, it was always situated, and it was relevant to the character and to the player. We said, wouldn't it be awesome if you could borrow that structure?"

At first, Haskell and his colleagues tried to bring this structure to their university's existing learning management system. What they discovered was that, at the time, they could not break from the "gradebook" method built-in to the system. They next wondered if they could build something new, from scratch. Haskell got to work sketching out how it could look. They then sent it off to programmers in India to build an alpha version. To the team's delight, it was functional.

3D GameLab was first used in a summer camp. Then, that fall, Haskell taught four classes in it. He immediately noticed students having a totally different experience. He recalled:

> The numbers stayed the same since then: a 71% success rate—A's B's C's in a col-lege class—to 93% A's! It was because we removed the punishment associated with when an activity is due. We gave everyone choice. It didn't matter when they had everything done, as long as it was done by the end of the course. In fact, the students actually completed it faster. A 16-week course took 14-and-a-half weeks. We were shocked!

Quest-based learning is mastery-based—students either get all the points or they are in the process of getting all the points. And they only get all the points if they meet the requirements. Midway through that first semester they realized they had something unique. They next raised money internally at the university, and then built the beta version, which is the core of what is there now. Eventually, demand grew. Because 3D GameLab was developed in the university, and because it was not attached to a grant, it was eventually spun off as an independent company.

Initially, when rolled out at the university, there was "tons of blowback" from other departments. Accusations of grade inflation were directed at Has-kell and his department. "The standard blowback was how could a class with a 93% success rate be rigorous?" Haskell explained. "Our team fired back saying how can a class with only a 71% pass rate be designed appropriately? This great debate was on campus." Haskell described the on-campus debate as "really cool," a healthy debate.

As it turned out, there were many start-up companies at with the words "game" and "lab" in it. This attracted companies that "patent, or license troll," claiming infringement on names. To avoid this, technology companies some-times choose strange, nonsensical words as corporate branded names. Hence, Rezzly, which is a nod to video game jargon of "rezzing," or creating something new.

Rezzly is built on choice, not extrinsic reward incentives. In the system, the student sees what he or she needs, while the teacher sees a graduated scaffolded approach to his or her curriculum. As opposed to teacher-facilitated, linear lesson planning, with this model, as with video games, students "do not need our permission to continue."

Haskell explained how Rezzly balances extrinsic and intrinsic motivation. In other words, in the system, badges do not replace grades; boss level battles are not tests rebranded with a game-like moniker. He said, "Once we give students choice, [teachers can] push that intrinsically. We don't care why [students] select one activity over another. In giving students three, four, or five different quests that they could do in a 45-minute class period, everyone can pick something they want to work on." In other words, it is not the tool that drives engagement; rather, it is the affordances for student choice that intrinsically motivate students to learn. Haskell continued:

> Students decide if they need 50 points to level up. Maybe they feel feisty and will pick the hardest thing to do. Or maybe they feel lazy today, so they pick the easiest thing. Then it becomes intrinsic. There may be [extrinsic] trappings we attached to it—XP, levels—but, when they choose what they're most interested in, it becomes an intrinsic conversation. Choice is the key.

Haskell gave me a detailed example of how a K12 teacher would use Rezzly. He told me how an 8th grade English language arts teacher in Nevada gives students the opportunity to read several books. Then she has quests associated with each of those books. When the student logs into Rezzly, it says: "Which of these eight books do you want to read?" If the student chooses to read Veronica Roth's *Divergent*, the teacher then awards them a series of rewards that is just for that book. Haskell explained, "Students still have the same expectations the other students have, getting to 2,000 XP and reading three books total. But, they get to choose what their curriculum will be about." In this structure, the first quests for students reading different books may be actually identical. Students may be asked to identify a list of characters or themes. Subsequent quests get specific to the book; however, the core questions are similar.

The teacher can also create a set of quests intended to remediate issues for some students. For example, some students may need to review the difference between mood and theme. Here, the teacher can offer extra curriculum that also has XP associated with it. Only the students who need—or want—that curriculum, will see it.

The teacher in this example took a single track of activities that she always used, and then she broke it into multiple tracks. Using Rezzly to design a quest-based system, she let students choose the vehicle that they would experience the curriculum in. She gave them meaningful choices.

Classcraft

With the look and feel of *World of Warcraft*, Classcraft is a gamified learning management system that has grown exponentially in classrooms. Two brothers, Shawn, based in Canada, and, Devin, in New York City, are the cofounders. Shawn has a bachelor's degree in physics and a master's degree in education, and he is the creative director. Devin is the designer.

Shawn, who is a self-described "closet gamer," grew up playing *Zelda*, *Final Fantasy*, and *World of Warcraft*, and also tabletop games like *D&D* and *Magic*. "I game a lot but am not super public about it," he said when we spoke in March 2016. Shawn wanted to bring the engagement from games to his students. In 2010, he "hacked a workable version" of a platform over a weekend, which, at the time, lacked graphics or advanced features. Basically, the early version managed the bookkeeping aspect of student XP and earned achievements. To reward students with points, however, additional coding was required.

The alpha version of Classcraft existed for 3 years as a side project for Shawn and his students. Then he and Devin refined it and launched it as a website for other teachers to use. "125,000 people came to the website on the very first day," Shawn recalled. "It was on the first page of Reddit gaming. We had 250,000 unique visitors to the website by the end of the first week. There were even more inbound e-mails from teachers looking for it to be a platform." At that time, there was no platform. At least, not yet.

After the media attention came, Shawn formally teamed up with Devin, "the guy behind how great it looks." They signed up their father, who is an experienced accountant, as the third cofounder. Classcraft officially launched November 2013, and the first product version was August 2014. Similar to a MMO game, in Classcraft, students play in teams, each taking on one of three role classes: warrior, healer, or mage. The teamwork mechanics are all based off of those roles. For example, warriors project power, while healers can restore lost hit points (HP represents virtual health scores). Mages have powerful spells to help each other, called powers. "MMOs have really figured out how to get significant collaborative work going—which is meaningful," Shawn explained. "The only way to get power back is from your teammates healing you."

Shawn describes Classcraft as being "like augmented reality, in a sense. It's a layer of a game that acts on top of teaching." Roles student teams take have a sense of immediacy and meaning. The game mechanics are related to the game or to real life." A teacher can customize it, too. Examples of real-life rewards from the game include being late to class, turning in an assignment a day late, or getting a hint on an exam. He continued. "The idea is that kids can level up and then can unlock amazing powers."

Real-world rewards are more than badges. Shawn's sense with badges is that children can get quickly disengaged because there is no meaning for them; there is no strong social value. It's not like an adult earning a badge from a fitness app that gets shared across social media. He explained:

> Students have real life things they want. Teachers can give XP for behavior, or whatever they want to encourage. We tell teachers, imagine you had a magic wand and you wanted kids to do a certain thing. What would it be? That's what XP is. Students get points for participating in class, helping other students, going online at night in the forum, defending a child who is being bullied. They then are rewarded and level up. They get more powers, or different gear for their avatar.

Instead of one point scoring system, which always goes up (e.g., earned XP and levels). Hit points are a separate scoring mechanism. Classcraft deducts hit points for negative things, like running late into class. If this occurs, a player's teammates can step in to heal, replenishing hit points. When healers they do that, they automatically gain XP. The game explicitly rewards using your powers to help other students on your team. This dynamic is what makes Classcraft more than a tracking system; it's really a game. Handing in homework early also generates XP. What's more, if a team hands homework in early, the entire team gets points. This incentive gets students to be cognizant of how their teammates are doing. "It's really powerful because it rewires social dynamics," Shawn said.

Aside from behavioral rewards, the system can be used for everyday formative assessments. Students can also team up to answer questions. "All of a sudden [formative assessments] become meaningful, because it counts to upgrade avatars," Shawn explained. "Because it counts for their team, they can help each other, prep each other. That has really piqued engagement."

Classcraft is optimized for Google Chrome browsers, and there is a Chromebook app, as well as iPhone, iPad, and Android app. It also works on the Firefox browser. In early 2016, Classcraft "deeply integrated" with Google. Student data can be imported from Google Classroom. Teachers can create class rosters now with one-click. After creating a class, the software, which fills the game with rules, examples, and recommendations, all of which a teacher can change.

There are also help videos, along with forums with an active community of teachers sharing best practices. Classcraft takes the active feedback from the community of teachers to make the platform better. There are also ambassadors—seasoned Classcrafters—who give talks about Classcraft. They get updated regularly on new features.

Shawn explained of the psychology behind how Classcraft can intrinsically motivate. Specifically, he explained how the system is centered on self-determination theory, "a modern approach to researching extrinsic and intrinsic motivation." He continued:

> Games hold a special place because they are internalizers of motivation. What starts
> out as external, becomes internalized. It starts extrinsic and then kids get into it on
> their own. They want to level up; they want to deck out their character. Students get
> used to working in a team, they like their teammates. All of a sudden, they do all of
> the things they're supposed to be doing—not just because they get caught up in the
> game, but also because they want to.

Shawn concluded by sharing anecdotes about students who helped others after school because they know how it will help them perform in the game. "Students exhibit the positive behavior in absence of the game, even when they move to a class that doesn't have it."

GradeCraft

GradeCraft is one of the newest game-based learning management tools. It was borne out of a college course on games and learning. It was cofounded by Barry Fishman and Caitlin Holman, at the University of Michigan. I spoke with Fishman, a professor of learning technologies in the School of Information and School of Education, in late March 2016.

Fishman is a learning scientist. In fact, he was one of the first learning scientists, having graduated from Northwestern in the program's first cohort. The discipline combines the study of learning with computer science and artificial intelligence, along with anthropology as a methodology. "The goal isn't just to study education, but to change it," Fishman said.

When we spoke, Fishman had just returned from a conference in Toronto, Canada. While there, he and Jane McGonigal met up and "talked about all the things that are wrong about the gamification movement. Then we talked about gameful learning, and about how to get this secondary term into broader use." According to the GradeCraft website, *gameful learning* uses game-design principles to create a more intrinsically motivating learning environment. Like Classcraft, it is framed around self-determination theory, which transfers control of learning to the student, giving autonomy and choice. Students can safely fail in GradeCraft, and then try again. The badges and achievement rewards are micro-credentials, marking "tangible progress." Fishman continued, contrasting the extrinsic incentives in gamification to being gameful. Gamification can be used as an instrument of control to get the learner or the player to do the thing that you want them to do, as opposed to asking what is it that learners want or need to accomplish. "Just re-labeling the midterm as a boss battle doesn't make it gameful," he said.

Being gameful is also about thinking beyond using *literal* games in the classroom. Well-designed games apply and leverage everything cognitive scientists have observed in the past half-century. "They just do it intuitively because they learned what is a good game," he explained. "School, by and large, does the opposite. School is designed as a terrible game, with all the wrong incentives aligned in all the wrong ways, so students feel like failure or struggle is not an acceptable part of the learning process."

As a college professor, Fishman has come into contact with many students who have yet to really experience failure. He continued, "It's all success, success, success, and the system is designed to keep channeling you upwards. Most real-world problems involve learning from failure. School doesn't welcome that. It also doesn't welcome autonomy." This observation echoes what Jesse Schell described earlier in this chapter: School is a poorly designed game.

GradeCraft started from James Paul Gee's work and McGonigal's work. Fishman next explained how self-determination theory is baked into Grade-Craft as a core design element. He said:

> We realized that self-determination theory was the best underpinning for what we were going for. We were trying to create classrooms that supported autonomy—people had to make meaningful choices for themselves, people had to have a sense of belonging, or relatedness. Students had to feel like they were part of something a little bigger than themselves, feeling like they were on a shared journey. There's a lot of ways to frame that.

As a learning environment, GradeCraft supports developing competence. "To me competence and autonomy are really related," Fishman said. "It's this notion that there are multiple entry points and multiple paths to get to the goals. If you're a strong writer, write. If you're a strong filmmaker, make movies. If you're a test taker, take tests."

Using GradeCraft has made students more accountable for their learning. It marks a departure in higher education where there is often a standard format for learning: lectures, problem sets, labs, papers, then a midterm and final. "I call it faith-based teaching. I've organized this material and I'm presenting it to you and I have faith that you're learning it somehow." GradeCraft, however, has multiple assessment points, which encourages "self-aware learners."

In other words, GradeCraft removes the penalty of losing grade points, which can never be recovered. Fishman called this "flipping the frame." Let's say in a typical class, graded out of 100%, a student earns an 85% on a midterm paper. The student might do better on the next assignment, but they will never again have 100%. "It's a losing game," says Fishman. Like Sheldon's multiplayer class, all students in a GradeCraft class start at zero, and then they earn points toward their goals in the course. GradeCraft makes the learning objectives clear, as well as what assignments are needed to meet those objectives.

Like Haskell, initially deploying 3D GameLab resulted with more students who earned A's. Also, like Haskell's experience, there might be concern about pushback regarding grade inflation. "But students worked really hard to get A's," Fishman explained. "They earn A's because they know they can. We make it brutally clear how to get to an A. When I made my class harder, the number of people who got A's doesn't go down. They see the A as a goal."

The centerpiece of GradeCraft is the Grade Predictor tool. Fishman previewed it for me at the Games + Learning + Society Conference in 2015. "You can game your plan for the course. You make a prediction about how you want your semester to go. When you get a grade back, your prediction changes into real points. Then you're invited to go back in to the system to see what you need to get back on track."

As of March 2016, more than 5,000 students at the University of Michigan have used GradeCraft. And it's grown beyond Fishman's department, to 15 different subject areas, with about 28 different instructors. GradeCraft is proving to be robust. Fishman concluded, "In most college classes, students walk in knowing what to expect: lectures, problem sets, a midterm, and might not start paying attention until week six." In a GradeCraft class, all experiences are different and students need to engage from the start; all learning environments are gameful.

Conclusions and Takeaways

Gamification is a trend in business and e-commerce that has entered the educational world. Some mechanics may work in the short term, while others tend to be extrinsic. Stories and quests are a better approach for school settings. Look into learning management systems that create a gamified platform. Gamification is the framework for gameful lessons—don't expect Rezzly, Classcraft, or GradeCraft to turn boring work into a fun game. What your students do must involve choice, freedom, and affordances for playfulness.

Lesson Plan Ideas

Game Map Cartography: Adapt a geography assignment to an authentic task of creating a game world map. Task the students to create a game-like map; include locations for fast travel and a key that features play to trade goods and Easter eggs. Mapping locations is useful for spatial thinkers. English language arts teachers can map out worlds in fictional literature (e.g., the districts that make up Panem in the *Hunger Games* books, Neverland, Middle Earth). The map should contain mathematical properties such as a grid and scale. Natural science standards can include the physical features in the map. Social studies and Common Core English language arts standards apply.

Geoguessr is a game that uses Google Maps. See the lesson plans on Graphite—https://www.graphite.org/game/geoguessr

Puzzle Challenge: One of the more straightforward methods for gamifying teaching is to throw in puzzle challenges. Many games have puzzles (e.g., *Portal, Tomb Raider*). Puzzles can be seen as practice for solving problems gradually. Make sure the mechanic fits the content, such as a letter puzzle in an English language arts game. Or try a science riddle about chemistry. Standards depend on discipline and content area.

QR and AR Scavenger Hunts: Classrooms and museums have begun to use mobile devices for scavenger hunt games. QR ("quick response") codes are the simplest to create. QR codes are essentially square-shaped bar codes that can be scanned with a mobile device camera. The code, read by a QR reader app, scans and launches a website or image. QR codes can be generated for free from any number of websites. The image can be saved and then pasted on a document. Some teachers copy small QR codes on worksheets to bring students directly to web content. An even more interactive idea is augmented reality (AR). Teachers and students can embed in everyday objects hidden images that can be viewed only with a tablet's camera. Aurasma is an AR app to launch an "aura," which can be a simple digital animation, audio, or picture. Standards depend on discipline and content area.

Socratic Smackdown: Institute of Play's non-digital argumentation game. Standards met include Common Core State Standards for English language arts, which are listed in the printable version of the game—http://www.instituteofplay.org/work/projects/print-play-games-2/socratic-smackdown

Talking Avatars: While not a game, creating talking avatars embodies something more powerful: Play. Using Voki to have students create real or fantasy likenesses. Both tools work well for students to present work. Standards depend on discipline and content area. There are Common Core-aligned lesson plans on Voki's website. Other Voki lesson plans, including rubrics, are on ReadWriteThink: http://tinyurl.com/7qnquqk

Games

Geoguessr geography gamified—https://www.geoguessr.com

Google's Atari *Breakout* Easter egg—http://goo.gl/PnBNw4

Rocksmith is a gamified approach that adapts to learner ability to teach guitar using a game console system or computer—http://rocksmith.ubi.com

Stagecraft foreign language puzzle game—http://ghost.playmationstudios.com/stagecraft

Resources

Answerables is a gamified learning platform with badges and student choice—http://answerables.com

Classcraft—http://www.classcraft.com

Easter egg directory—http://www.eeggs.com

Edmodo, the school-based social network to deliver quest-based instruction—https://www.edmodo.com

Epic Learning Academy, quest-based teacher professional development—http://edurealms.com/presentation-resources/epic-academy-game-inspired-professional-development

Gamification.co, resources and an annual conference on gamification—http://www.gamification.co

GradeCraft—https://www.gradecraft.com

Hyper Reality is a short film about augmented reality and gamification—https://vimeo.com/166807261

Miitomo is Nintendo's avatar app—https://miitomo.com/en

Morfo is another option for talking avatars in the classroom—http://www.morfoapp.com

Pixar's Easter eggs—https://youtu.be/jzWxue95WdU

Prezi presentations from Chris Haskell about Rezzly—http://prezi.com/user/haskell

Rezzly—https://portal.3dgamelab.org/ (Rezzly.com doesn't work)

Sight is another short film about augmented reality and gamification, also to the extreme—https://youtu.be/lK_cdkpazjI

Shakespeare Translator—http://www.shmoop.com/shakespeare-translator

Voki, to have students create talking avatars—http://www.voki.com

Zap Zap Math is a gamified math program, with games and a teacher dashboard—https://www.zapzapmath.com

· 1 2 ·

THE TEACHER AS DESIGNER

Lesson plans evolve over the years. I know mine have! They are constantly revised and iterated. I tweak what worked and what didn't, note how long activities actually took, and account for what was engaging for students to do. (If you are a preservice teacher, prepare for students to derail your best intentions!) That process—trial, reflection, and revision—is design thinking. The Institute of Play, which is a founding partner in the Quest to Learn school, defines design thinking as a "set of skills, competencies or dispositions relating to the highly iterative collaborative process designers employ when conceiving, planning and producing an object or system" (Institute of Play, 2014). James Paul Gee explains teaching as a design science, and as it relates to game design. When we spoke in April 2014, he said:

> What we've come to understand is that game designers are designing experiences that kids can have that can lead to learning. But so are teachers. I see teaching as a design act. You're designing good interactivity for learning. [Teachers are] doing something very similar to game designers. It doesn't mean you have to design a game. Good teachers have always been trying to design good experiences.

The real world isn't a "one-off" project, like a standardized test. Apps constantly have updates, and so should your lesson plans. Playtesting and iterating gives you, as lesson designer, the opportunity to tweak based on student feedback. I asked Gee to elaborate on how design thinking pertains to teaching. He stated:

> Teaching is a design process—if you let them [teachers] be professional. What we've done is deprofessionalize them by writing a script for them, by giving them a test booklet or a game or orders of what to do. Good teachers are designers of on-the-spot learning. Reflect on it, iterate, like game designers. Good teachers are also doing alpha testing and beta testing with their students. They're asking their students: Did that work? What worked? What didn't?

An "excellent teacher" meets the needs of all students by iterating their teaching style, even as the lesson unfolds (Hattie, 2012, p. 111). He or she "sees the learning through the eyes of the students" (Hattie, 2012, p. 111). In this chapter, game designers and teachers share tips about creating meaningful experiences for learners. I review how tools can be appropriated to turn lessons into games, as well common trappings to avoid. For example, Kahoot, which turns the class into a game show, can become a dressed up quiz, rather than a game. Teacher Stephanie Castle, as well as Kahoot's Jamie Brooker, offers a better way to use Kahoot, one that applies game mechanics.

This chapter opens with gamification classroom advice from teacher and author Michael Matera. He and I cohosted Ed Got Game together on the BAM Radio Network. The next subsections provide best practice ideas from BreakoutEDU's founder James Sanders, alternate reality game design from teacher Paul Darvasi, the use of commercial games in the classroom, and a lesson I codesigned, which was delivered as a text adventure story. The chapter concludes with advice from a game designer formerly of the Institute of Play. She talks about "exploding the game," a method the Institute uses to introduce and scale up its games.

Turning a Classroom into a Game

Over the years, Milwaukee, Wisconsin teacher Michael Matera constructed a very large game with his social studies students. Then in 2015, he wrote a book about it: *Explore Like a PIRATE: Gamification and Game-Inspired Course Design to Engage, Enrich and Elevate Your Learners*. The book is part of Dave Burgess Consulting's series of PIRATE books, which is an acronym for: Passion, Immersion, Rapport, Ask & analyze, Transformation, and Enthusiasm (Burgess, 2012). Burgess' book is very popular in teacher communities—it even charted on the *New York Times*' Best Sellers list. Like Matera, Burgess has a social studies teaching background. "He would go to the National History Conference and present *Teach like a PIRATE* before his book came out," Matera recalled, when we spoke in May 2016. "*Teach like a PIRATE* was inspirational and revitalized my teaching, pushing me to do what I love." At one of the conferences, Burgess approached Matera to write for him. "He wanted a manifesto on gamification in the classroom," Matera said.

Not all of the books published by Burgess's company are "PIRATE" books. Matera decided to write for the PIRATE series because of brand recognition. The books in Burgess' series have a loyal and expanding community of educators. "I really believe in the power of game-based learning and gamification," Matera explained. "I want to get it into the hands of most people. Because of the Like a PIRATE brand, there was a wider audience who could decide pick it up."

So what was it about gamification that Matera found so inspiring? "The things I love about gamification is that it is an amazing lens to amplify things, like project-based learning," he said. "Because of the challenge, the storyline—whatever the mechanics you throw into your [class] game, students are in it. Even when direct instruction gamified, it is better."

Ultimately, a game designer's job is to focus on the user's experience (or UX). Teachers, however, are not accustomed to thinking about student experiences. They already have many things to consider, like assessment models and technology integration. "Teachers are often not thinking about how students are doing as they move through the lesson," Matera explained. "The moment I started to gamify, the user's experience took center stage. I truly believe I became a better teacher because I was constantly thinking about their engagement. Are they motivated? Are they learning? Is it tailored to them?"

Matera described a gamified medieval times unit in his social studies class. For it, Matera created a website, the Roman Nobles, which is like a video game. Rather than text, images are hyperlinked (this can be done with most free website builders, like Wix or Weebly). If a student wants to go into the castle, they click the image of the castle. Inside the castle they will find doors, one of which leads to the map room. "When I told them the new unit is up, they knew there was a new link in the map room," Matera explained. "They're clicking all over, trying to find it. They know the map room starts them on their adventures."

In *Mario Kart*, Nintendo's popular go-kart race game, players sometimes see a mysterious box, the content of which contains a reward. That reward is never random; it is a power-up that will boost the player's ability, putting them back in their flow channel. Similarly, Matera has some catch-up mechanisms. "I had to put in some special things for this, because it's the last unit of the year," he said. The virtual medieval town also contains "sidequests," like a market to trade in.

Eventually students meet a king who talks about a secret society that students have heard about earlier in the game. Then they are given a hint: The last known location of this secret society is up a mountain. "The main town picture shows a mountain range on the side," Matera explained. "If they click around the picture they will find it. They then go on a complicated riddle, with some clues at the school and some online." Some students make it through the mystery and join the secret society. "Once in, there are many catch-up mechanisms for their houses [teams], which is huge! It was so fun." When Matera went to get coffee at recess, he observed students in the hall looking for quests and adventure paths. "All of this translates to a crazy pop in engagement. Now when I talk about the Dark Ages, these guys are excited. They're already clicked into class."

In *Explore Like a PIRATE*, Matera describes SAPS, which is an acronym for Status, Access, Power, and Stuff. "Stuff is the lowest part of motivation," he explained. "As teachers, we may toss out candy and bring in pizza. But that's the lowest. It is engaging and exciting, but not for long." Status includes power-ups, items to use in class (e.g., students can select the order they present a project). Access refers to a role-playing game component in which you are able to do something that others can't. Status is the number of points and badges students accumulate. "To me, the points, leaderboards, and badges are icing on a very complex cake. But without the cake, the icing doesn't work."

BreakoutEDU

When I spoke with game-based learning community expert Bron Stuckey in April 2016, BreakoutEDU kept coming up in our conversation. To Stuckey, BreakoutEdu is an excellent example of a gameful teaching practice. "I'm a huge fan," she said. "The Facebook group alone is a fantastic conversation about games. Teachers are getting back in touch with their creative side, which maybe some teachers—maybe a lot of teachers, have lost."

Later that same week, I contacted company founder James Sanders. BreakoutEDU is an escape room in a box. Increasingly popular, escape rooms are live action puzzle games. To play, you and your friends (or coworkers) are locked into a room and must work together to solve clues to escape. Games often blend live theater with cooperative play. You can play at home too: ThinkFun published *Escape the Room*, a boxed version, in 2016 (see link at the end of the chapter). The goal of a BreakoutEDU game is slightly different: to get past a series of locks to reveal the contents of a secret box. Published BreakoutEDU games align to various curricular topics, and meet Common Core and Next Generation Science Standards.

Sanders and I had spoken a couple of years earlier about ClassBadges, a digital badge website he started. Prior to his foray into educational technology and gaming, Sanders began his career as a social studies and English teacher. He also worked as a paid consultant for Google, curating for Google Play for Education, YouTubeEDU, YouTube Teachers, and YouTube for School. While advising Google, he started ClassBadges with his cousin Duncan Winter and educator Esther Wojcicki. In June 2013, Sanders took a position at the White House as a Presidential Innovation Fellow, part of Barack Obama's education initiative for postsecondary agenda.

When ClassBadges was sold to another company, Sanders moved on to BreakoutEDU in 2015. Each breakout game is open source. As of April 2016, there were roughly 140 teacher-published games on the website. Sixty percent of those games were in the "sandbox area," which is where anyone can submit a games. Games in the directory go through a formal review, including a video to explain the game. On the form to submit a game, teachers can choose a price to sell their game. "If you want to sell your game, it's like selling an app in the App Store—you can," Sanders explained. "To date, no one has taken us up on that." In June 2016, former Presidential Innovation Fellow, Adam Bellow, became BreakoutEDU's first CEO.

There are an estimated 7,000–10,000 kits "out in the wild." Sanders estimated that 40% are ones his company built and shipped. "The other 60% are from open source that other people built. We're going to take a census to get a snapshot of the community, what they teach, and where they are in the world." It is a voluntary assessment of how BreakoutEDU kits are being used.

The website freely shows what is included in the kit, and links each item to Amazon, for any purchases done à la carte. You can even brand it using the company logo. Games typically require a physical component, like pulling on a lock to check a puzzle's solution. "You put that math solution into a lock," he continued. "If it doesn't open, then you have feedback and you have an urge to go back to look at your work again."

Sanders walked me through a BreakoutEDU game he designed. It serves as a model of what a meaningful experience can be. Called *Time Warp*, it is an introduction to the history of communication. The game's main character is Vint Cerf, one of the founders of the Internet. The first puzzle the players encounter uses hieroglyphics. The team then has to translate ancient Egyptian into corresponding alphabet letters. Next they translate those letters into numbers (in this case, A = 1, B = 2, and so on). The resulting answer is the four-digit password to a lock on the box.

Later in the game, players work with Incan forms of communication: quipu knots on colored strings. The red string has four knots, green has two, and blue has four, which results in the next lock's code: 424. At that point, players discover a blacklight in the box, along with a small slip of paper. Shining a blacklight reveals Morse code, which opens yet another box.

Eventually players arrive at a password-protected website. Once signed in, players see a picture of Cerf, who asks the players to e-mail him. (Sanders set up a dummy website and e-mail account.) The automated reply contains a video with the formula $E = MC^2$ hidden in it. Players must algebraically balance the equation to get the final password.

Figure 1. Students working together in a BreakoutEDU game. Photo by Arlee Hall, Technology Teacher, Donald E. Suburu School, Bakersfield, CA.

Sounds complicated, I know. But it is also fun. If students are stumped, there are hint cards. The hint system was modeled on those in live action escape rooms. "A hint is not the answer, but a clue or prompt from the teacher-facilitator," Sanders explained. "The facilitators have to be aware of how to play the games. This gives teachers an opportunity to work with students."

In a few instances, teachers use rewards as a goal, like putting candy or a prize in the box. Gamification expert Scott Nicholson has voiced his opinion and worked with Sanders about ways to steer the community to make games with better intrinsic motivations. As stated earlier, the community is the shining star of BreakoutEDU. This is where Sanders shares best practice ideas with the community. As of February 2017, Facebook page had over 19,000 members. The page is a virtual sounding board where people share ideas, and it is divided into content discipline subgroups. "It is our most valuable asset right now," Sanders said. "There are 10–20 posts a day in which teachers share success and failures. We're still trying to figure this out. We are pleasantly caught off guard by the interest." BreakoutEDU can be an effective tool to gamify your class. "The magic comes when that tool is in the hands of a great teacher," Sanders said.

Blind Kahoots

Kahoot is a wildly popular tool that enables teachers to create a quiz-style game show. Playing classroom *Jeopardy!*, however, is clearly not as immersive of an experience of *Minecraft*. So where does a teacher-led Kahoot fit into a game-based classroom? Are there best practice models?

To play Kahoot in a classroom, the teacher generates a quiz game on the website GetKahoot.com. Students are then directed to another website: Kahoot.it, where they are prompted to enter a code to join the class game. In the game, questions are prompted in real time on a projected screen. Answer choices are on the participant's devices.

When I perused Kahoots that teachers shared, I found mostly quizzes dressed up as games. The addition of a timer and dramatic score to a quiz does make it game-like, but is that educationally sound? Was I seeing the best that the Kahoot teacher community had to offer? I reached out to Jamie Brooker, one of its cofounders via Skype in early April 2016.

Launched in 2013, it took just 3 years for Kahoot to amass 27 million monthly active users. "They [the community of users] are the content creators," Brooker explained. "They choose to use it the way they want to use it.

I compare it to Twitter. You have 140 characters and you choose how to use it. We're a platform like that. How you choose to use it is your own choice." So perhaps I was judging Kahoot the way some judge social media. My Instagram feed can be celebrity gossip or photos uploaded from NASA's account. Any platform that encourages shared content is at the mercy of its users. "Going to market with a simple game format of question, image, and video often gets misinterpreted," Brooker continued. "They [teachers] are not necessarily using it wrong. They're just not using to its deepest potential."

One of Kahoot's core design decisions was to not put questions and answers on the player's mobile devices. "We want to encourage people to look up, to have social interactions in the classroom," Brooker said. He then explained why I saw so many quizzes. He said:

> Initially, no one is going to use a new product in its deepest way, because that requires an investment in time. You don't know the value then. Teachers use Kahoot commonly for reviewing. What becomes disruptive is when copycat products come in the market, which don't have the same pedagogy. This puts us in the wrong conversation, as review quizzes.

So how does one use Kahoot to its "fullest potential?" Are there best practices models to replicate? As it happens, there is. One of its star users, Stephanie Castle, came up with an idea she called "Blind Kahoots." "She really thinks like a game designer," Brooker stated. "She designs games to introduce completely brand new concepts to students."

Castle is a teacher at the United Nations International School in New York City. When she saw how new topics could be introduced using Kahoot, the game literally changed for her. She told me about how she designed her quizzes to be game-like. "Sometimes you hit upon something that changes how the learning takes place," she said, when we spoke in April 2016.

Each Blind Kahoot deals with a topic the students have never seen. Like level design in video games, Castle orders questions in such a way that student knowledge builds, and gets scaffolded. Students learn through failure in the mini-lessons between Castle's questions. Then she assesses them on what she just taught. Castle explained:

> I tell the students, "You're going to take a Blind Kahoot and I'm not going to tell you anything prior to it. I'm going to ask that you look at each question. You probably will know absolutely nothing about the first question." I call that a leveling question. It levels the playing field. That first question is a complete guess. Then, in between each question, you, as a teacher, illustrate why the correct answer is right. You give

feedback in between. The student then knows that new questions refer to previous questions. The follow-up questions are based on previous questions.

In her biology class, Castle may ask a leveling question about mitosis, and then explain the fundamentals across about chromosomes and homologous pairs. She sometimes shows and slides in between questions, too. "You should go from zero on the blind questions to close to 100% on the reinforcing questions, when you look at the data afterward," she said. "They should take what you tell them and apply it to the question afterward. When you go through the Kahoot, you alternate between the blind and reinforce."

A typical Blind Kahoot lesson for Castle has 20 questions. First, it is the cycle of blind and reinforcing questions. After student responses demonstrate that they can put concepts together, she levels up the challenge. In the second set of 10 questions, she has students put those concepts together. "I call those compound reinforcing questions. You put two ideas together. You gradually build up the level of difficulty."

When executives at Kahoot heard about what Castle was doing, they visited her class to film her. They also invited her to speak on their panel at South by Southwest Education (SXSWedu) in 2016. "Most of our users don't see Kahoot as a learning game," Brooker said. "They see it as putting a bunch of questions together, playing it to review content already taught. But Castle uses it as a game. She thinks about how the experience unfolds, and how players learn as a consequence of that."

Teaching with Commercial Games

Using a commercial, off-the-shelf (COTS) game doesn't necessarily mean that a teacher implements *Assassin's Creed: Unity* to teach about the French Revolution. It could just mean using the simple card game *Guillotine*, which happens to be set during the same time period. In my research, expert game-based learning teachers tended to use game that they themselves play. They also used games that were open-ended, with affordances for playfulness. Then they created qualitative assessment strategies, which included reflection questions.

Zack Gilbert is one such game-playing teacher. When we spoke in spring 2016, Gilbert recounted when he learned that he had attention deficit hyperactivity disorder (ADHD) at age 30. When he found out, his affinity for gaming made sense to him. "I played golf, and I was pretty good," he said. "It was a space where I could zone everything out and concentrate. We played tabletop games, like *Axis and Allies*, until 2 o'clock in the morning. I was fully engaged in what I was doing at the time." Those were vivid memories for Gilbert. Not only was he in his state of flow, he was emotionally engaged with games.

As a tech savvy teacher, Gilbert is comfortable when his students try different things. "I'm better at thinking on the fly than having everything organized and mapped out," he said. Gilbert uses COTS games, which include board games and digital games, which he discovers in his free time. He also teaches with content-specific games designed by Filament. "I'm the gaming teacher," he said. One commercial game Gilbert loved was *Civilization III*, which he had been playing at home in the mid-2000s. He continued:

> I realized this is totally what I teach. All the learning targets are in this game. People would say, it's not historically accurate, and I would say great! Then students could compare and contrast it. Why did you choose to build the Great Wall of China in Rome? You're on a peninsula; do you need a wall?

Gilbert turned his master's degree project to be about games and long-term memory, using *Civilization*. Next came support from his school administration and his university. "I wanted to do it so badly, I paid for it [licenses for *Civilization*] myself," he recalled. "I have 20 licenses, but only have 15 computers that can actually run it." State Farm Insurance, which is headquartered in Bloomington, Illinois, donated several computers to his class.

Gilbert also uses Euro-style board games, which have multiple ways to start and win. Board games are technology free and are social experiences for students. For example, he has his students play the settlement game *Catan*, which has a trading mechanic. There are many expansion packs available, including ones for colonial America. During play, he constantly assesses student decisions. "They know I'll ask them to demonstrate or show how this connects back to our targets," he said. "I am constantly asking questions. How does the board relate to geography? Is it accurate to the geography of Europe? Why did you trade there?"

Similar to Gilbert, New York teacher Peggy Sheehy uses COTS video games (she uses games from BrainPOP and Filament, too). In my dissertation research, I observed Sheehy's 6th grade humanities students learn about *The Hobbit* by experiencing their own hero's journey while playing in *World of Warcraft*. Her use of the game to teach was detailed in Greg Toppo's 2015 book *The Game Believes in You: How Digital Play Can Make Our Kids Smarter*. When Sheehy and I spoke in November 2015, she told me how the WoWin-Schools project [a *World of Warcraft* curriculum by Lucas Gillispie and Craig

Lawson] had about 13 schools participating. "Many of them went over to *Guild Wars 2* because *World of Warcraft* is too expensive," she said. "Not just the expansions, but the game itself [*World of Warcraft*] is subscription-based. *Guild Wars 2* is a one-time buy and you're done."

Sheehy frames her class around Joseph Campbell's hero's journey. Her students read about Bilbo Baggins' journey in *The Hobbit*, and play quests in *World of Warcraft*. As students play, they write in a journal on Google Docs. Students also write about their own hero's journey in life. "We use *Journey* [another game about the hero's journey]," Sheehy explained. "In *Journey* they are writing a running account of who the person is, where are they going, why are they going there, what are they encountering. And yet, they are playing the game."

Alternate Reality Games

Paul Darvasi is an expert in alternate reality games, as well as pervasive games. He defines a pervasive game as a game that takes place in the real world. It is not necessarily a treasure hunt or riddle system of patterns. "But it is non-linear," he explained. "It could involve actors, meeting people to get clues. It mixes digital and real-world elements and is played in physical space. Alternate reality games are a subset of pervasive games."

Darvasi teaches high school English in Toronto, Canada. His students' use of the video game *Gone Home* became part of my dissertation research. I contacted Darvasi again in early May 2016 with specific questions about two alternate reality games that he had designed over the years: *Blind Protocol*, which is about online privacy, and *The Ward Game*, a school-set version of Ken Kesey's novel *One Flew Over the Cuckoo's Nest*.

Although I had read about *The Ward Game* on his blog, questions lingered about the students' player experience. On the first day, students arrive to class thinking that they are beginning a unit on privacy and surveillance. "I introduce the class with a TED Talk video that focuses on privacy and surveillance," Darvasi began. "Then, all of a sudden, I get a phone call. I pick up my phone and look somewhat disconcerted. Then I pause the video and leave the room."

While Darvasi is out of the room, the video starts to play again. Then the video flashes a message, which prompts students to check their e-mails. Students are informed that they are in contact with an unknown entity known as

"Horace," which could be a person or an organization. Horace then instructs them to perform a series of tasks in order to reach the next level. Down the rabbit hole they go!

Students next go around the school looking for the clues that Darvasi planted for them. This eventually leads to a cache of documents with further instructions. "It is a combination of puzzles, the physical space of the school, narrative, and game mechanics," Darvasi explained. "Each is in conjunction with the other in order to create an immersive environment."

The underlying objective of *The Blind Protocol* is cyberwarfare, privacy, and surveillance in an online world. Every thematic element builds into that. In subsequent game levels, students build a database of articles, websites, and resources related to the topic on online privacy. Based on that research, the next gate opens, tasking students to present PowerPoints, white papers, or videos on their findings. The entire game is embedded with the typical elements of a research project, in which data are gathered and then presented. "They were introduced to the game very playfully," Darvasi explained. "They've gone through a research phase, then they move into a production phase."

Instead of grades, students get paid in Bitcoin [the virtual currency of the web]. At that stage, students also learn that the process they have been put through also occurred to others, at an undisclosed location. "Now they are pitted competitively against each other," Darvasi said. "They use their Bitcoins to buy 'protocols,' which allow them to open windows into their opponent's geographical location. Whoever uncovers the other team's location first, wins the game."

Darvasi was delivering his curriculum as a nonlinear story. It is entirely likely that he was influenced by the way the video game *Gone Home* tells a story with found items. After all, every fall Darvasi has his students play it in class. "You can tell a lot of stories by being the archaeologist or the investigator," *Gone Home's* designer Steve Gaynor told me early in 2015. "*Gone Home* is a clear demonstration of how much the narrative process happens in your head, as opposed to on the page or on the screen." Interested to learn more, I asked Gaynor how he would teach a history class using a nonlinear narrative to engage students. He said:

> Start by thinking of a linear story. Then ask, what is the story you want the pieces to point to? What is it you want the audience to be able to reconstruct? If they don't reconstruct it perfectly or in the way that you initially pictured it, you have to be able to lead them to a place that is satisfying, a place that supports their interpretation of what the pieces mean. You could make a little story, a soldier or minuteman in

the Revolutionary War. Then students find a hat with a bullet hole in it, a letter from a boy to his mother stating that he is going to join the war, a patient log from a field hospital that has that boy's name on it with his injury, and then an obituary. You found all these things and then you can spin it out from there? Who was this soldier? Why was he killed? Once you have that simple story spine—that kernel of a story about this kid who decided to join the American Revolution and was killed in battle—now I can create all of this evidence about who he was, why he joined, all of the circumstances for the battle he was in, and the repercussions it had.

Available on computers and mobile devices, *Her Story* is another game with a nonlinear story. From Sam Barlow, creator of the horror game *Silent Hill: Shattered Memories*, it is set in the 1990s (like *Gone Home*). You play as a police detective tasked with reviewing hours of interrogation footage on VHS tapes. The clips all pertain to the wife of a missing man. I am not sure if the game has a "win-state"; you simply keep searching the videos, digging for more information. All of the whodunit theories are in the player's head; there are no points or badges to be found. *Her Story* is a low cost and simple entry point into the world of nonlinear storytelling. When I played, I observed a tattoo on the interview subject's shoulder. I typed in "tattoo" to see if other clips mentioned it. Two did, one with an explanation. The tattoo was an apple and a snake. The other clip mentioned a name that was a palindrome. Guessing "Eve," I searched more clips. And down the rabbit hole I went!

Aside from using *Gone Home* or *Her Story* as digital models, check out Darvasi's blog post (linked at the end of this chapter) about the resources he uses, like QR code generators and digital documents that can be password-protected. "Look over materials, like those on my website," he suggested. "Look at what other [game-making] teachers are doing and ask: What can I do as a novice?" One idea is to start with a weeklong activity. Then, based on that, add elements to make it more complex. "Start small at a manageable level and then take some risks."

Text-Based Adventures

Back in 2014, when I initially interviewed Erin Hoffman-John about creating *SimCityEDU*, I discovered that she had a deep connection to text adventures, also known as interactive fiction. Hoffman-John, a published fantasy writer, started her career building the text-based, multiplayer *DragonRealms* in 1999. "Interactive fiction is a pet thing of mine," she said. "I've got text-based gaming really deep in my brain." Delivering reading and writing lessons with interactive fiction is an engaging alternative to traditional methods. This section reviews authoring tools that you can use to draw students into content areas.

When Hoffman-John led her team at GlassLab in prototyping *Mars Generation One: Argubot Academy*, her team playtested a text-based version of the experience (it was codenamed *Hiro* at the time). She used Inform7, a free downloadable authoring tool, to prototype *Mars Generation One*. Inform7 has an "all natural language interface" that includes visual story maps. Hoffman-John told me that the resulting code was like reading "a strange book—but it is readable!" During playtesting, the focus group displayed an unexpectedly high degree of enthusiasm and engagement with the text world. Hoffman-John recalled:

> What really shocked me was, when we tried this game with about 20 kids in a library, they loved the text-based prototype. It was astonishing. It was so sparse and simple, but the kids have never seen a text-based game before. They actually said, "I never played a game like this; it's completely new." A text-based game immediately causes close reading. I've heard from English language arts teachers that they struggled to get kids to close read. Within minutes of the prototype, their spelling improved—it had to in order to enter in commands. I think there's a lot there.

Richard Bartle's Player Type Model (described in Chapter 3) was specifically intended for multiplayer games in this genre. In Bartle's game design course, he puts 30 students together in one room and has them play a text adventure together. His students are doing something else besides play; they are learning how to spell, create commands, read, and visualize locations, all things they wouldn't ordinarily do. They are thinking and they are learning. Bartle noted, "It's not something people play every week, but it's a tool in your toolbox."

In interactive fiction, the player is not reading from the first-person point of view; rather, the reader *is* the protagonist, making choices that have consequences. Furthermore, in a role-playing game, the player makes decisions based on the perspective of someone else. Interactive fiction challenges the writer to apply logic. The genre of interactive fiction is sometimes abbreviated as "IF," which has a double meaning: interactive fiction, and the logic command "if-then." Interactive fiction depends on verb-noun statements from players (e.g., "Open door."). In *parser-based* interactive fiction games (those built with Inform 7, for example), there is typically a "command prompt," an open invitation to type responses. For example:

You can see an apple and a plant here.
>Take apple.
Taken.
>Eat apple.
You eat the crunchy apple.

Text-based gaming has its roots going all the way back to the 1970s. The paper-based classic *Dungeons & Dragons*, created by the late Gary Gygax, a legend in geek lore, required a Dungeon Master to run the game by describing the world. The player's character's fate depended on the roll of multisided dice. *Dungeons & Dragons*'s core mechanics, Dungeon Master-led adventures and random die rolls, were readily adaptable to become text-based computer games. The first title was Infocom's *Adventure* (1975). Other text-based games followed, including *Zork* (1980) and *Ultima* (1981). Douglas Adams, author of *The Hitchhiker's Guide to the Galaxy* (1984), created a text-based adaptation of his own book. It is still playable online (it is linked at the end of this chapter). The wide proliferation of Internet-connected computers brought large numbers of players together in multiuser dungeons (MUDs). This style of game declined in popularity in the late 1990s with the advent of graphic-based virtual environments, such as the massively popular *World of Warcraft*, which have thousands of participants interacting together.

This genre has resurged and still has many fans. In fact, branched stories are still a part of many modern video games. Telltale's *The Walking Dead* (2013) and *Minecraft: Story Mode* (2015) relies on threaded, multiple-choice, decision-making mechanics to advance in the story. Even blockbuster console video games, like *Fallout 4* (2015), have players converse with non-playable characters (NPCs, which is computer-controlled) using branched conversation trees.

Hoffman-John and I decided to take my students back in time to the signing of the Declaration of Independence. We both saw the clear educational connection to reading, writing, typing, spelling, and geography. Hoffman-John initially set up a wiki for us to work asynchronously (she lives in California; I am in New Jersey). We also spoke via Skype every Thursday afternoon. Our interactive fiction game was called *Chronicles of the Time Society: Independence*. Below is our text adventure's original narrative frame:

You are a member of the elite Time Society, a secret international organization that protects the timestream of the universe. In your time it is 2253, but you have been given a mission to travel back to the summer of 1776 and ensure that the Declaration of Independence is successfully signed. One of the signers has fallen ill, and you must take his place in history. Good luck, Inspector!

There were several considerations we discussed. For example, when in the year would I was teaching about the Declaration of Independence? How long would the whole experience be? It could run for multiple days or a single class. Our initial conversations pertained to the major insights I wanted students to come away with, and possibly any key figures I'd want them to encounter. Another issue was the setback penalties for losing the game, also known as "fail states." An example in a board game is falling down the chute in *Chutes and Ladders*. Feedback from making wrong choices can reinforce what the player needs to do the next time they play. In an e-mail to me, Hoffman-John explained the complications of building a threaded history game. She even bounced ideas off of Michael John, her then colleague at GlassLab (and future husband). Hoffman-John wrote:

> There are tons and tons of dependencies that all had to come together in order to make the Revolution happen. So we [Michael John and Hoffman-John] netted on this expression of "history is fragile," which can be experienced through game mechanics. But what that would mean is designing lots of different failure states and then messaging what happened as a result of that failure state. Then in each of these cases, we would actually cause them to lose the game and get bounced back to the Time Society (where they could try again). There, they'd experience the alternate history that happened as a result of this not happening. It's a way in which narrative could be especially powerful because we could convey in just a couple of paragraphs a whole alternate world that emphasizes how rare our particular history is.

Playing a text-based game can easily seem more like work than play. After all, close reading and typing are part of the mechanics. Therefore, *Chronicles of the Time Society: Independence* was playtested with my students. Playtesting allowed Hoffman-John and me to not to lose sight of the conceptual take-away. For example, we noticed students spending a considerable amount of time exploring colonial Boston. The learning objective was to convey the frustration and helplessness colonists felt from being taxed by King George, not a geography lesson. My students concluded each round of play by anonymously answering questions on a Google Form. Below is the text of the survey used to assess the early iterations of the game:

> *Thank you so much for helping us playtest this game! Your comments will be extremely helpful in making the game better. It's still very early, so we know there are a lot of things we can improve. Please don't hold back in your criticism!*

- *What grade are you in?*
- *Who do you think this game is for?*
- *What age group? 5th, 6th, 7th, 8th grade? Other?*
- *If you kept playing, what do you think would happen next?*
- *How would you describe this game to a friend?*
- *How would you describe this game to a teacher?*
- *If your teacher considered playing this game in class, how would you describe it?*
- *What did you want to do that you couldn't do?*
- *What do you think you learned?*
- *What do you think video games could teach in school?*
- *What kinds of games do you play in school?*
- *If you played another level, what level would be most exciting to you: Independence Hall (Philadelphia, where the Declaration was signed), George Washington at Mount Vernon, or John Adams in Boston?*

In the end, we decided to create separate missions. In the Time Society headquarters, players choose canisters. The first world, described in this section, was the "Chase Canister." A future economic mission was planned, but never completed. We intended to give students the feeling of frustration from being taxed without having government representation; however, time got the best of us!

I would recommend adding playtest questions such as the ones above, in addition to formative assessments such as exit tickets. This creates a feedback loop of "what works" and brings students further into the learning conversation. The next section details how to roll out, and then "explode" a game. This technique can be particularly effective for both digital and non-digital games, as it levels up challenges and asks students to critically think like a designer.

Exploding the Game

I spoke at length with Shula Ehrlich, of the Institute of Play in January 2014. She designed games for the Quest to Learn school, in New York City. Mission Lab is the Institute of Play's design studio situated within Quest to Learn. The team works collaboratively with teachers. They meet once or twice a week to develop a curriculum and to develop games to be used in the classroom. Most of the original games are non-digital, and often involve cards, dice, and/or game boards. Ehrlich told me that they "really like paper-based because teachers and students can modify the games; digital is a black box to most people."

Teachers with little to no background knowledge of game design can modify or adapt a non-digital game more easily than a video game. Paper-based games have a low barrier to use, allowing for iteration from year to year. Ehrlich described the process:

> We call it exploding the game. Stretching out the capacity of the game as a teaching tool. I think it's more powerful than playing a game once. The important thing is what surrounds a game. It's not one discrete thing you play and that's it. A game is situated in a larger learning trajectory. There are lessons before, related activities, and a period of rolling out pieces of the game.

Ehrlich gave an example of "exploding a game." She described the 7th-grade math game *Absolute Blast*. It is a card game about rockets that teaches the concept of absolute value. In the game, every player has three rockets and needs the highest absolute value to shoot into space. It teaches adding, subtracting, multiplying, and dividing integers, as well as negative and positive numbers. Ehrlich explained:

> To explode it, the teacher rolls out a simplified version: just one rocket instead of three. You only play the cards on your own board, not others. This gets students acclimated to the rules, the basic structure of the gameplay, and math concepts. Then there is more teaching and related activities, and then back to the game, which becomes more complicated. After that the kids reflect until, finally, the full version.

Once a game is exploded, Quest teachers—like other educators—assess student learning. The teacher gives the class a piece of paper with a picture of a frozen game state and asks, "What would you do in this scenario? What would each player do in this scenario? Explain your reasoning." Here the teacher is asking the student to reflect on game strategy as well as underlying skills. Both are higher-order challenges; the game-related question puts the learning in an authentic context. Ehrlich summed it up concisely: "We think of exploding the game as before gameplay, during gameplay, and after gameplay."

Conclusions and Takeaways

Teaching is a design science. You should not be writing lesson plans just because you are made to do so, simply to follow the curriculum. See the lessons through your students' eyes. Be mindful of fun and engagement. This chapter essentially presents the teacher as a game master (or dungeon master, like in *Dungeons & Dragons*). You run the game, whether it is an alternate reality game, playful direct instruction lesson (e.g., Blind Kahoot), or a commercial game you bring to students. As you rollout games, use student focus groups to gauge learning. A text-based game may be fun for some, but not for all. Like a game designer, it is best to playtest lessons, gather feedback, and then iterate.

Lesson Plan Ideas

Absolute Blast: Mission Lab's absolute-value math game for grades 6 through 8. Common Core State Standards for mathematics apply—http://www.instituteofplay.org/work/projects/print-play-games-2/absolute-blast

Escape the Guillotine is a digital breakout lesson from Tom Mullaney about the French Revolution—https://sites.google.com/site/escapeguillotine

Mystery Skype!—https://education.microsoft.com/ConnectWithOthers/Play-MysterySkype

Phylo: The biodiversity trading card game. The website includes free printable rules and cards. Standards met include Next Generation Science Standards—http://phylogame.org

The Ward Game is Paul Darvasi's alternate reality game about Ken Kesey's classic novel *One Flew Over the Cuckoo's Nest*—http://www.ludiclearning.org/2016/01/17/the-ward-game-how-mcmurphy-mcluhan-and-macgyver-might-help-free-us-from-mceducation

World of Warcraft in School curriculum, which ties the MMO game to the hero's journey in books like *The Hobbit*—http://wowinschool.pbworks.com/f/WoWinSchool-A-Heros-Journey.pdf

Games

80 Days is a choice-based mobile game based on Jules Vernes' book *Around the World in 80 Days*—http://www.inklestudios.com/80days

A Dark Room is a text-based game about resource management—http://adarkroom.doublespeakgames.com

Catan, the popular Euro-style board game that teaches economic concepts, like resource management—http://www.catan.com

Dixit is a commercial card game that teaches storytelling, perfect for an English language arts class—http://en.libellud.com/games/dixit

Educational Text Adventure Games—http://textadventures.co.uk/games/tag/educational

Escape the Room—A boxed board game version of an escape room http://www.thinkfun.com/products/stargazer

Her Story is a nonlinear police procedural playable on mobile devices—http://www.herstorygame.com

How to play *Pokémon*, rules that are easily adaptable to any paper-based game—http://howtoplay-pokemon.com/howtoplay-pokemon-page04

The Hitchhiker's Guide to the Galaxy, playable interactive fiction cowritten by Douglas Adams, author of the original book—http://bbc.in/1m0bFfi

Journey—http://thatgamecompany.com/games/journey

Lifeline is an interactive story about a stranded astronaut. The sequel takes place with a lost hiker stuck in whiteout conditions. Both use push notifications (including on Apple Watch) to tell a text-based story. Consider having students play and then journal about it, perhaps paring *Lifeline: Whiteout* with Jack London's *The Call of the Wild*—http://www.bigfishgames.com/daily/3mingames/lifeline

The Room is an award-winning puzzle game for mobile devices. Playing it is an easy and low cost way to understand the engagement behind a BreakoutEDU game—http://www.fireproofgames.com/games/the-room

StoryCubes are dice adorned with pictures, which are excellent story prompts—https://www.storycubes.com

Syrian Journey: Choose Your Own Escape Route is BBC's interactive story about the Syrian Refugee crisis—http://www.bbc.com/news/world-middle-east-32057601

Time Society Chronicles: Independence!—http://timesocietygame.com

To Be or Not To Be, Shakespeare as choice-driven, interactive fiction—http://store.steampowered.com/app/324710

Minecraft: Story Mode is an episodic game that features a threaded storyline—https://www.telltalegames.com/minecraftstorymode

Resources

Amazon's Echo is a web-enabled speaker, featuring Alexa—its built-in virtual assistant. Try out the Baker Street Experience, a Sherlock Holmes radio play that is also an interactive fiction story. From Schell Games, it's free—https://www.schellgames.com/games/the-baker-street-experience. Or have students design their own Alexa Skill (Amazon's name for the Echo's app ecosystem)—https://developer.amazon.com/alexa-skills-kit

Blind Kahoot—https://getkahoot.com/blog/the-art-of-blind-kahoot-ing and https://getkahoot.com/blog/unveiling-the-magic-introducing-new-topics-with-kahoot

BreakoutEDU—http://www.breakoutedu.com

BreakoutEDU explained by a teacher to her elementary school class—https://youtu.be/C0SUvkpgJqo

Ciphers on Khan Academy, to learn for ARG codes and hints—https://www.khanacademy.org/computing/computer-science/cryptography/crypt/v/caesar-cipher

Down the Rabbit Hole: How To Turn Your Class into an Alternate Reality Game blog post from Paul Darvasi—http://www.ludiclearning.org/2015/08/19/down-the-rabbit-hole-how-to-turn-your-class-into-an-alternate-reality-game

Explore Like a PIRATE, from Michael Matera—http://explorelikeapirate.com

Games As, Institute of Play's exercises to get educators to imagine use of games in the classroom. Katie Salen recommended this a starting point for teachers—http://www.instituteofplay.org/work/projects/games-as-guide

Kahoot—https://kahoot.it

Kahoot Guide to Creating & Playing Learning Games—http://bit.ly/1PgXHVT

Inform7, interactive fiction authoring tool that uses "natural language"—http://inform7.com

Locks, an app from BreakoutEDU—http://bit.ly/LOCKSapp

Peeking behind the locked door: A survey of escape room facilities (2015) is a white paper about escape rooms from Scott Nicholson—http://scottnicholson.com/pubs/erfacwhite.pdf

Text Adventures, interactive fiction authoring tool—http://textadventures.co.uk

John Fallon's blog—https://thealternateclassroom.org

Teaching with Alternate Reality, an interview with John Fallon from myself and Steve Isaacs—http://www.bamradionetwork.com/game-based-learning/3689-gbl-teaching-with-alternative-reality

QR Code Generator—https://www.the-qrcode-generator.com

· 1 3 ·

THE STUDENT AS DESIGNER

When Zack Gilbert was teaching J. R. R. Tolkien's *The Fellowship of the Ring* to his 5th graders, students played a simple game. It was designed by one of his students' parents. To play, you randomly select a card and then set it out along the story's timeline. "Did the event happen after they left the Shire?" Gilbert recalled, when we spoke in May 2016. The game then led to an organic class discussion.

Next, something interesting happened. "I showed them the game and then they created cards from other books," he continued. "They mixed up the cards and tried to put them back in order." The timeline game Gilbert's class played was similar to the commercial game *Timeline*, published by Asmodee. Sold at many retailers, there are decks of *Timeline* for different historical eras. Similarly, BrainPOP's *Time Zone X* is a timeline game connected to its library of informational animated content. Both Asmodee's and BrainPOP's timeline games are a model that can be easily replicated and then hacked, or changed, by students.

Like Gilbert, I try to engage students by using the "game as model," in which students play a game a lot, and then remix it, modify it, or wholly redesign to make something original. One foray into this is when I have my students play the commercial, off-the-shelf party game *HedBanz* and then critically analyze its core mechanics and system. Basically a mash-up of *charades* and *20 questions*, players put a plastic ring on their head, and then affixed it with an image-adorned index card in front. Players then sit in a circle and deduce what is on their heads. Maybe you're a tomato, or a unicorn. After playing a few times, students make their own deck of cards about class vocabulary.

This chapter reviews different approaches that engage students with design thinking, user empathy, and systems thinking—all 21st-century skills. What's more, designing games situates well in a project-based learning environment. One model is to hold a game jam in your class with students. The content you teach can become the jam's theme. This chapter begins with iterative design, and continues with models of game jams in and out of formal school settings.

Iterative Design

The iterative design cycle is a process in which designers ideate (brainstorms) based on a need (or design challenge), and then prototype. That model is usertested, which involves feedback from focus groups. Next, it is iterated, or revised, and then tested again. This may seem like a never-ending process, and it is. Think about the apps on your phone and why there are updates. Good design always follows the iterative cycle. This cycle is increasingly common in STEM labs, too.

Tracy Fullerton, director of the University of Southern California's Game Innovation Lab, wrote the textbook *Game Design Workshop*, now in its third edition. Paper prototyping and iterative design is something that The Game Innovation Lab has done for over a decade. Many academic institutions use the methodology to create innovative games. In March 2014, I asked Fullerton how teachers could apply techniques such as paper prototyping and iterative design in the classroom. She pointed out how similar the process was to constructivism, or learning from doing. "It's a version of constructivist education, more focused on systems thinking than just making," she said.

Erin Hoffman-John explained the design process when GlassLab made its first tablet game, *Mars Generation One: Argubot Academy* (2014). We spoke in 2014 about how the app was originally prototyped on trading cards, and then as a text-based adventure before it was coded as a digital video game. The mechanic of argumentation was modeled on *Pokémon* card duels, which were first worked out using paper. "For the argument game [*Mars Generation One*], we did a paper prototype," she explained. "We got cards, played *Pokémon* to get the feel for what would work, the phases of battle. We also paper proto-typed the map exploration."

After researching paper prototyping, I was inspired to create a student game design center in my classroom. I purchased inexpensive plastic drawers and filled them with different game components. The station currently con-tains several inexpensive items:

- Dry erase spinners
- Dry erase whiteboards
- Plastic poker chips (for game tokens—not gambling)
- Novelty eraser caps (useful as game pieces)
- Different sizes of blank index cards
- Color folders, to be used as game boards
- Hourglasses
- Toy money
- Graph paper
- Rulers
- Several sets of dice—and not just six-sided.

Playtest questions with focus groups follow prototyping. Game mechanic and design questions should be avoided in favor of assessing the overall experi-ence, such as what made the game fun (Schell, 2008, p. 401). Questions may include: If the game has physical pieces to manipulate, are they age-appropri-ate? Who should be playing this game? There was a case in my class when stu-dents were playing an online social studies simulation game and soon enough, it was discovered that the game had an interactive that could be randomly clicked until the correct answer was revealed. The core mechanic should have been a puzzle, but became an exercise in trial and error. This impasse became a teachable moment as students critique a game.

Blind playtests are effective to ensure that a designer need not be present to direct play. It can be difficult to observe a player struggling to understand a function and resist intervening. But game play should feel natural and intu-itive. I ask students what direction Mario moves in *Super Mario Bros.* The answer is left to right. Then I ask students what direction they read on a page. I observe many "a-ha moments" as students realize the answer is the same.

Hoffman-John told me that she has witnessed less experienced game designers get so wrapped up in their games that they fail to see how someone couldn't play them in a certain way, the "right way." "I've noticed that there is a tendency to draw too many conclusions on the basis of a single playtest, and also to overweight confusion in playtesting," she said. "You learn eventually what to pay attention to. It's an intuitive skill you build up over time. You have to ask questions like: 'What did you think just happen? What did you expect to happen? How is this making you feel? What does this remind you of?' Those kinds of questions can be more effective than: 'Is this confusing? Does this make sense?'"

The Institute of Play publishes a free, downloadable *Q Design Packs for Games and Learning Design* that includes playtesting forms for the classroom. Students reflect on whether the game was fun and challenging, and remark on the clarity of the rules (Institute of Play, 2014). Student learning becomes more active when playtesting. They look for bugs and glitches while problem solving within the game's system. They also know that their feedback has a real effect of a game's final outcome. "Kids feel like they become collaborators because they know it [playtesting] is important," Hoffman-John explained. "They get more highly engaged in the learning if they're invested."

In my class, I grade the artifacts, not the finished products. This can be difficult for some students, especially those who are really good at the game of school. Students work to meet a design challenge and are given chances to iterate, but not for an unlimited time. The games that students make will likely not be perfect, which is the point. I follow the lead of middle school teacher Steve Isaacs, who has his students write daily designer diaries. These reflections become the formative assessments.

Literally meaning "after death," a postmortem gives designers a chance to discuss what worked and where they came up short. A postmortem occurs after a creative project concludes. It is typical in the game designers and film-making fields. Pixar cofounder and president Edwin Catmull shared the company's design process in *Creativity, Inc.* (2014). Design and technology intersect at Pixar, where computer-animated favorites such as *Toy Story* and *Finding Nemo* come to life (Steve Jobs was the CEO of both Pixar and Apple, both companies known for design). Upon completion of each project, the team conducts a postmortem. Catmull and coauthor Wallace listed five reasons why this is fundamental to the creative process:

1. Consolidate what's been learned
2. Teach others who weren't there
3. Don't let resentments fester
4. Use the schedule to force reflection
5. Pay it forward. (2014, pp. 216–217)

Postmortems go beyond reflection. An important postmortem question is, How easy was the game to master? Prototyping, playtesting, and reflecting with postmortems can enable students to understand the interconnected relationships of parts of a system. Game-based learning can be used to give students a deeper understanding of content. Putting a student in front of an educational video game does not accomplish this. True learning with games involves a thorough analysis of how games teach (Gee, 2007). This can include how to make games, which puts design and systems thinking into practice.

Game Jams

Like improvisational theater, game jams center on a theme. Game jams challenge participants to create a game in a short period of time. It has commonalities to competitive cooking TV shows—like the Food Network's *Chopped*, or Bravo's *Top Chef*, in which chefs are given design constraints (e.g., only use certain provided ingredients). Next, chefs prepare meals in a limited timeframe. Finally, a panel of experts judges the results using a rubric. Similarly, game jams are framed around a design challenge. They are, in effect, a game about making a game.

Game jams have grown in popularity across college campuses. Of note is the annual Global Game Jam. In 2014, the White House followed this model, hosting an Education Game Jam. Developers, educators, students, and academics were invited to participate. GlassLab Game's *Battleground 538* (2015) was prototyped at the White House jam, and was eventually published for iPad. The game's goal (linked at the end of the chapter) is to amass enough delegates to win the presidency.

Moveable Game Jam

In 2015, I collaborated on the Moveable Game Jam initiative, a series of student game jams in the New York City area. The Hive Digital Media Learning Fund at the New York Community Trust supported the game jams, and it took place at different locations—hence, moveable. Participants included the Institute of Play, the Museum of the Moving Image and Mouse.org, an after-school student STEM program. In 2016, Games for Change received the grant from Hive to run four more Moveable Game Jams as part of its Student Challenge program (for more on Games for Change, see Chapter 16). Kevin Miklasz, who began the Moveable Game Jam, transferred and updated documentation into the Moveable Game Jam Guide. The document is an excellent resource for anyone who replicates a game jam afterschool, or in a classroom. Games for Change is the initiative's lead partner, led by project director Sara Cornish. I am the co-project coordinator.

The 2016–17 events took place at the Andrew Freeman Home in the Bronx, the Museum of the Moving Image in Queens, the Brooklyn College Community Partnership in Brooklyn, and at the New York City Library in Manhattan. At each of the four events, Mouse, Global Kids, CoderDojo NYC, Institute of Play, Spazecraft, Brooklyn College Community Partnership, and Museum of the Moving Image led the breakout sessions. For more on, check out the blog post *Moveable Game Jams Hosted with HIVE Partners in the Bronx and Queens for NYC Students*, on Games for Change's website: http://www.gamesforchange.org/studentchallenge/2016/11/21/10569.

The first Moveable Game Jam I volunteered at was cosponsored by the Institute of Play. It was hosted at the Quest to Learn school in New York City. The event began in the school's library, with a brief warm-up. First, components of a game—goal, rules, components, core mechanics, and space—were reviewed. Next, teams were challenged to make a game using the space of the library. Participants were given constraints, which included only using hands, feet, or paper as a game component. The rules were open to student choice. After time lapsed, teams shared out their games, which included paper airplane races and hide-and-seek remixes.

At this point, everyone was given a review of the breakout sessions that were planned throughout different classrooms. Some were digital, while others were tactile. The participants remixed musical chairs, adding in the challenge of balancing a book on your head during play. In one room, students used grid paper and pencils to draw video game levels. The pictures were captured with an iPad using the *Floors* app. Each drawn level became an actual video game in the app! Other rooms included a mobile game making website, and a Sphero robotic ball obstacle course race. The event ended with time to share out designs with other peers, and parents. Kids who started the day as strangers left as friends.

A few months later, I facilitated a game jam day for teachers and students at the A. Harry Moore School at New Jersey City University. The school serves students from ages 3 through 21 who have low-incidence disabilities, many of whom are in wheelchairs. I used Moveable Game Jam materials, and recorded the experience on the Guide. That day focused on the playability in everyday objects. After all, play is what occurs within the structure of a game.

For the opening session, I screened a BrainPOP's video about video games. Next, students engaged in a hands-on task: to play with cups, ping-pong balls, string, and duct tape. The challenge for students was to make a game out of everyday objects. I used the Institute of Play's *Find Play in Things* (linked at the end of the chapter) as a resource. A cup would no longer serve its intended purpose for drinking water. Instead, it became a basketball hoop, a phone (attached to a string), or a hat! Tactile and kinesthetic learning, paired with game-like activities, was the theme of the day.

Teachers facilitated the small group activities. Regarding playfulness, we used ThinkFun's *Compose Yourself* game to compose symphonies. *Compose Yourself* does for music composition what Scratch does for coding—it removes the symbol barrier. To play, arrange transparent cards in any direction. Each card is adorned with music notes, and has a code at the bottom. When the code is entered into a computer, music plays! Students could print out their songs too, on sheet music.

I ran the Makey Makey station, the kit that hacks a computer's keyboard. Attaching an alligator clip to Makey Makey and a low-conductive object—in this case, Play-Doh—turns the object into an input device. A tap on the glob of moldable clay is like hitting the space bar! In the room, I preloaded games that worked using keyboard clicks. Upon entering the room, one young girl said, "This is all weird!" She did not understand why I used Play-Doh with a computer. After learning basic circuitry, and after she got her hands on some clay, she was soon customizing her own video game controller. By the day's end, as she left the room, she proclaimed, "This was fun!"

The game jam model doubled well as a game-based learning professional development day. Rather than sit-and-get training, teachers and volunteers actively participated. They were excited, imagining how the design tools used could support their students' learning. Using a game as a model works well in a project-based learning classroom, too. It affords students a chance to engage deeply in learning content. Next, I review social deduction and interactive fiction writing tools, which work well in a classroom game jam. Both can be used to deliver content in any discipline.

Climate Game Jam

In the spring of 2016, I took part in organizing Climate Game Jam: Water. Organized by Peg Steffen from the National Oceanic and Atmospheric

Administration (NOAA). It was a follow-up event to 2015's Climate Game Jam. Steffen runs the games page on NOAA (http://games.noaa.gov), which uses digital games to teach children about climate issues. The topic of water was part of a White House announcement on Building a Sustainable Water Future.

Climate Game Jam: Water was hosted at several locations around the country. I volunteered at the event hosted at BrainPOP's headquarters, in New York, which was run as a Moveable Game Jam. Themes specific to this game jam included: changing precipitation patterns, freshwater supply and sources, ocean acidification, polar issues, human use of water and marine/freshwater ecosystems. There were also different game categories: hack this game (remix from a template), paper prototype, analog game, basic digital game, and advanced digital game.

As in other Moveable Game Jams, participants at the New York site first deconstructed a common game: *Tic-Tac-Toe*. Then, in small groups, they "hacked it," changing the rules in the game. Some made the added letters other than X's and O's, while others added randomness using dice. Then the group split up into one of two rooms, one that used Scratch as the authoring tool, and one with Twine, to write interactive stories.

Figure 1. Students at the Climate Game Jam: Water, hosted at BrainPOP. Photo by Sanda Balaban.

At the conclusion of the game jam, everyone presented finished games. The share-outs helped focus participants to complete their prototypes in the time allotted. The results were quite clever. Some hacked a Scratch game, changing the goal to be about saving arctic wildlife. The interactive stories were also unique and imaginative. One team made a game about maintaining a pollution-free lake. They embedded memes [captioned, viral images from the Internet] in the stories, driving the message home. It was a fun day for students, educators, and several BrainPOP game designers to learn about climate change and water issues together.

Social Deduction

The game jam approach has been transformative in my teaching practice. In 2015, I used the model to teach my students about the Salem Witch Trials among the Puritans in 17th-century New England. First students played the social deduction card game *One Night Ultimate Werewolf*, created by Ted Alspach. Widely available in stores, as well as online, the game can be played in less than 10 minutes and up to 10 players participate. *One Night Ultimate Werewolf* is a variant of the summer camp game *Mafia*, which is played with a deck of playing cards. In the game, there are villagers and mafia roles. Played over several rounds, the villagers have to root out the mafia. This takes place over several rounds of players closing their eyes and then trying to guess who is on which team. *Mafia* creates "play activities that are almost entirely social" (Salen & Zimmerman, 2003, p. 468).

Over the years this game's mechanics were part of Looney Labs' card game *Are You a Werewolf?* The issue with *Mafia* and the Looney Labs version is that once a player is eliminated from the game, there is nothing left for that person to do. I spoke with Alspach in the fall of 2015 about his game and our class project. As it turned out, he had played both *Mafia* and *Are You a Werewolf?* about a decade ago. He expressed a similar frustration.

In 2007, Alspach picked up the game *Ultimate Werewolf*, which solved the player elimination problem by adding in more roles to the card. Each role had a prescribed action, which made play more engaging. Then he played a Japanese version called *One Night Werewolf* from Akihisa Okui. It had three roles: a werewolf, villagers, and a robber. "I saw this and I liked the idea that your role can change," Alspach said. "It was pretty compelling. The idea of who am I?" Alspach's company, Bezier Games, licensed it, and he went to work adding in new roles.

One Night Ultimate Werewolf takes place over just one round (hence, one night), and it is played in a circle around a table. Players then randomly select a role card from a deck. Each card has an action that is taken during the "night," which is when all players close their eyes. In the middle of the table are three extra cards, turned face down. Using a free mobile app, one by one, each role is instructed to wake up (open their eyes). They then are told to take their action. Werewolves acknowledge one another. The Troublemaker swaps other player's cards. Other actions include peeking at cards or switching cards from the center pile. Once the night-round ends, everyone is instructed to wake up. And then the fun begins! The group is given 5 minutes to lie, bluff, and accuse others of being a werewolf. After time runs out, players vote on who they believe actually is the werewolf. A false accusation that "kills" a villager means that the werewolf wins.

The Troublemaker role card played a key role during Alspach's play-testing. In One Night Ultimate Werewolf, the Troublemaker "wakes up" (opens his or her eyes) after the werewolf does. The action is to switch other player's cards, which casts doubt over everyone's true identity. "It was the one role that has made the game go from fun to incredibly compelling. Now, anyone—with the exception of the Troublemaker—can be a werewolf, regardless of what they started as. There is now a level of uncertainty. Who is the Troublemaker, and do I believe them?" The Troublemaker role is what differentiates One Night Ultimate Werewolf from other social deduction games. It adds a level you normally don't often get in games: Who am I? It's rare in a game that you don't know yourself what team you're on. "For some people that can be oft putting and chaotic, but that's part of the game," Alspach said.

After playing, I ask students how they felt being accused. The core mechanic of bluffing also aligns with my learning goal: historical empathy for those accused in the Salem Witch Trials. Next, students took part in a warm-up game jam. They first had to make a "state of being" game, using worksheets from the Institute of Play. The goal is to use tabletop game materials, such as dice and graph paper, to design a game that gave the player an emotion or feeling. Teams chose a state of being: jealousy, anger, happiness, or frustration. Then they had one day to make a game about it, and then write out the rules for others to follow. The next day, students played and discussed the effectiveness of their creations.

The following day was the main assignment: change *One Night Ultimate Werewolf* to be about the people in Salem. Students were instructed to have all actions take place in one night. Aside from selecting roles and actions, a script with a wake-up order would be required. Deciding a wake-up order required playtesting and peer feedback. For resources, I mixed in different levels of texts, from graphic novels to above grade level material, including Arthur Miller's *The Crucible.* I wanted to challenge students to playfully read in their zone of proximal development.

I asked Alspach how he would make his game Salem Witch-themed. Going further, I recorded his response, playing it back for each of my classes. I also showed students Alspach's various Kickstarter campaigns, in which he raised funds to publish and sell his games. "I've watched some Salem-related movies," he said. "There have been a couple of films where people are like, maybe I did do this? Maybe somehow I am indirectly involved in witchcraft and maybe they're right? That adds to the uncertainty aspect. You're not 100% sure if you are innocent of what they are accusing you of."

Experiential learning from the game brought meaning to students. Many selected Abigail Williams as the Troublemaker because she instigated the witch accusations. Student groups also layered additional core mechanics to their games. One team added a judge role for the accused to plead their cases. Another added the John Hale card, giving certain players the ability to force others to reveal their cards. John Hale was a notable witch accuser.

In the end, there was a sense of intrinsic pride among students. By the end of the game jam project, many called out to their peers in class, "Who wants to play our game?" Aside from social studies, using werewolf card games can cross over to other content areas, too. For example, a science teacher can have students change the roles to be red blood cells and a pathogen (instead of villagers and werewolves, respectively). Social deduction also works well in English language arts classes, in which character webs can come alive.

One Night Ultimate Werewolf is not the only social deduction game to play. Try *Spyfall*, which has a similar bluffing mechanic. In *Spyfall*, each player gets one role card. Instead of a night-round, players simply ask questions of other players, hoping to root out the spy. Students can easily change the role cards to fit characters from a play or novel, or historical figures. And, like *One Night Ultimate Werewolf*, arguing using claims is a Common Core standard that can be met in a fun and playful setting.

Interactive Fiction Writing

Interactive fiction is game-like reading and writing. It is, essentially, a digital version of Choose Your Own Adventure books. This section discusses easy-to-learn tools to write and publish branched stories. There are more complex tools, like Inform 7, which was discussed in the previous chapter. The learning curve for Inform 7 is a bit steep—beyond my personal zone of proximal development! That was why I worked on the *Chronicles of the Time Society: Independence* with Erin Hoffman-John—a professional game designer.

inkleWriter is an authoring tool that works right in a computer browser. It is easy-to-follow and features a walk-through tutorial. inkleWriter won Best Website for Teaching and Learning from the American Association of School Librarians in 2013. Fledgling interactive storywriters can share links to their stories or even export to Kindle devices. I used inkleWriter in 2015 with 6th grade students. Each wrote a tale set in medieval Europe. One girl wrote a story about a knight that rewarded the reader only when chivalrous choices were selected. Here's the link to her story, which took just one day to complete: https://writer.inklestudios.com/stories/m3r3.

In 2016, I branched out (pun intended!) and used Twine, another free interactive fiction tool. This time I used it with my 7th grade students. Open source and completely free, Twine has been around for a few of years. Chris Klimas created it. My students used the online version, Twine 2.0 (there is a downloadable version, too). The goal of the project was to enable students to engage deeply with content in a meaningful manner. Having students author their own versions of interactive historical adventures was the next step.

For some strange reason, middle schoolers at my school (and elsewhere, I'm sure!) are obsessed with Illuminati conspiracy theories. The narrative shell I used was student-inspired: I presented the project as a design challenge to students. Rather than having students retell historical events, I encouraged them to blend in elements of conspiracy theories. In fact, George Washington once wrote a letter warning his friend about the Doctrines of the Illuminati. The document, which is available on the Library of Congress website, was shared when I rolled out the game-based project. Upon seeing it, several exclaimed, "Illuminati confirmed!"

Each Twine, each node, or page, is mapped onto a canvas, like a concept map. To write a node, or page, in Twine, double-click on a box to enter the text you want. To create a branch from that node, put your choices within a double set of brackets (on each side) to make that section of text turn into a hyperlink:

Up ahead you see [[a red door]] and [[a blue door]].

When the story "plays," the text in the double brackets becomes blue, like a hyperlink on a website. Clicking red door or a blue door jumps to another node in the story map. And that's it. From there, students add more and more choices, branching outward. You can also loop back by using the same word again in the double brackets. For example, adding [[red door]] later in the story would link back to the original node associated with the red door. This means that students applied logic-based statements to in their nonlinear storylines.

Using the Twine Guide wiki as a resource (also linked at the end of this chapter), students copied and pasted in HTML code to add images. To embed a picture, first search online for a picture and copy the link. Next, paste the link into a single line of HTML code. The code goes just after the text they wrote in a box:

<img src="*Link of image.jpg*" width="500" height= "300">

Embedding sounds is just as straightforward. I directed students to visit Sound Bible, a website of sound effects we use when podcasting. Search for a sound, and then right click to "copy link." Next, paste the link into a line of HTML code. Below is an example, with a link pasted from a Sound Bible audio file:

<audio src=http://soundbible.com/grab.php?id=1265&type=mp3 autoplay>

Historical empathy through role-play was a theme in the finished projects. One student put the reader in the role of Paul Revere without mentioning who he or she was until the conclusion. Making the same decisions as Revere did in his famous 1775 ride results in the win-state outcome. Another student built in level design, ramping up the decisions from a single choice per node to complex dilemmas. The player took on the role of a simple farm boy in Saratoga who got swept up into the turning point battle of the Revolution. Yet another story took place at the Valley Forge encampment. The reader, who takes the role of a young soldier, interacts with quartermasters, as well as France's Marquis de Lafayette and Prussia's Baron von Steuben. The student used Google Translate to add choices in French and German, to intentionally confuse the reader, just as a boy soldier may have been bewildered at Valley Forge.

When the project ended, several children told me that this project "was actually fun"—something I don't normally hear after students read and write in class. Completed Twine files were shared from a DropBox account or from a free hosting website (http://www.philome.la). Using Twine with my 7th grade class, and inkleWriter with 6th grade, challenged my students to close read and think logically, as well as to have empathy for historical figures. It reinforced student's systems thinking and designing thinking skills; the interconnections were thoughtfully mapped out and user experiences are considered.

Interactive fiction situates reading in an authentic learning context; the story becomes the mechanic. Like fan fiction, there is a low barrier to entry. The participatory culture provides feedback and celebrates exemplary work. There is also an active online community of practice, with discussion forums about game design and story ideas. There is even an annual interactive fiction writing competition to celebrate exemplar works.

Participatory Design

As I put together notes for this book, I designed a unit called *Revolutionary War Games*, about America's independence. In it, I tried to apply only "fun" game mechanics, such as role-play, guessing, and arguing. Prior to finalizing everything, I focus grouped the activities with students. After all, what I find engaging is likely not what a child may want to do. The narrative shell put the student in the role of a game designer trying to win the exclusive rights to create content for an Independence Day festival. I set up four stations—or "quests"—around the classroom and divided the class into equal groups. Each station also included feedback questions for students about their experiences.

The first three quests were fairly straightforward to complete. One station used *Minecraft: Pocket Edition* on iPad. The task was to build a Revolutionary War fort, take a screenshot, and then write a description. Using *Minecraft* was the students' idea. The second station was a remix of *HedBanz*. Students researched war heroes, drew pictures on blank index cards, and played together as a group. The third quest, the badge design station, took the least amount of time to complete. Using a simple website, students created achievement awards for Revolutionary War figures, as if they were designing a video game. Captions had to integrate the cause-and-effect loops required to win the badge. Students were quite creative in their badge design. One soldier was awarded the "#braveman" badge for his heroism on the battlefield. The badge art depicted *The Wizard of Oz*'s Cowardly Lion—after he was awarded his regalia. The most involved quest to complete was the board game maker station. I advised students to split into two groups at that station. They could modify the directions and the rubric, which simply scored student-created artifacts (e.g., game board, chance cards). Students were directed to brainstorm their favorite mechanics in games they like. Upon completion, they playtested the other group's game and completed a playtest form.

While the project looked fun on paper, the playtest questions I asked exposed some issues. First was timing: Badges took about 2 days to finish, while the board game took about 5. The *HedBanz* remix station's research took up more class time than I anticipated. A flipped learning approach—with research being done from home—may have worked better. Also, *Minecraft* took some students longer to learn than others. I could have "seeded" environments to create the same starting landscape (*Minecraft* randomly generates how worlds look, which can take time to customize, depending on the fort). There was a behavioral issue, too. One student "joined" other virtual worlds and set buildings on fire. I had to enforce a "no griefing" rule, gamer-speak for shaming losers; it's the digital version of bad sportsmanship.

In April 2014, I explained the project to James Paul Gee. I was worried the bumps in the road would affect student learning (almost all students tested well and enjoyed the activities). I was relieved to hear him agree with my game-inspired—rather than game-based—approach. "You're doing it right because you're putting the things into a larger system of multiple activities and multiple modalities and then it becomes a learning system," Gee remarked. "You're not just putting a digital game in there." He was referencing his Multimodal Principle, in which "meaning and knowledge are built up through various modalities (images, texts, symbols, interactions, abstract design, sound, etc.)—not just words (Gee, 2007, p. 224). Teaching with games requires an enormous amount of teacher-led reflection to facilitate students in making connections. Gee elaborated why students should be in the learning conversation. He said:

> You should be testing with your students. You're incorporating them as consumers or players and you're treating your audience with respect. Students increase their ownership, just like how people beg to be beta testers in new games. They get ownership, which means they are co-designing with you. Game designers need alpha and beta testers. Game designers, unlike teachers, aren't isolated and alone. They design and iterate together all the time. They do postmortems. They have conferences where they compare designs. Imagine a game developer conference where teachers are

treated as designers. We're never going to get there until society treats teachers more as professionals, with more respect.

After the *Revolutionary War Games* project concluded, I gathered student feedback to ascertain what students found was fun to do. Should stations be merged or eliminated in the next iteration? What I didn't do was expect my students to pass from section to section seamlessly. By showing students that each activity is a work in progress and that feedback matters, I created a culture of codesign. Teaching is a design science, and learning is a conversation. In 2016, I kept the *Minecraft, HedBanz,* and badge station intact. The board game station topics became the interactive fiction game jam described earlier in this chapter, using the same curricular resources. While the game-based project took longer to complete, it was fun for students, and it brought meaning for the course content.

Conclusions and Takeaways

Video games are paper prototyped or built in text-based worlds prior to final release. Teachers should look to use early versions of games, or make their own. Paper games are easier to modify. Students should design games, too. Teaching one another and peer reviewing becomes more engaging when someone is playing your designed object. Plus, it is a Common Core State Standard and a 21st-century skill—of course, you only get one shot to take a standardized test!

Learning is an iterative process. Students should be your codesigners, completing the feedback loop of learning. Student interest may be piqued further knowing that a lesson, game, or project is being playtested and that their opinions count. Be sure to use playtest forms with students and have them beta test each other's projects. It is okay to ask students if a lesson felt more like work than play. You may be surprised with some of the responses. The student is the target player/learner; effective student-centered learning should be a conversation. Have a postmortem with students—not just other staff members.

Lesson Plan Ideas

Argumentation Card Game Jam: The mechanics of the party game *Apples to Apples* has been remixed in several games, including *Cards Against Humanity,*

Superfight, and *Metagame*. Challenge students to design two decks of cards on a unit you are covering in class. Then have groups play one another's decks. Use the rules to *Superfight*, which are easy to follow—http://bit.ly/1AggKFZ

Community Talks: Quest to Learn hosted a TEDx Talk event—so can your students! The Institute of Play's Mission Pack, created for wellness education, can fit other curriculum standards—http://www.instituteofplay.org/work/proj-ects/mission-pack-tedx-questschool. Clips of Quest to Learn presentations serve as effective exemplars—http://www.ted.com/tedx/events/7172. Or try Ignite talks, which are 5 minutes in length and restricted to 20 PowerPoint slides—http://igniteshow.com. Standards met include Common Core State Standards for English language arts.

Illuminati Confirmed! Students write interactive fiction set in a time period incorporating conspiracy theory fictional elements (think: *Assassin's Creed*, whose motto "History is our playground"). Students can choose inkleWriter or Twine, as well as their story topics. Finally, students should each peer test other stories and compare and contrast what actually happened.

Make your own timeline game, includes free printable templates for students to use from BrainPOP's *Time Zone X*—https://educators.brainpop.com/printable/create-your-own-time-zone-x-game-cards

Poké Cards—Have students use http://www.mypokecard.com/en to design *Pokémon* cards about a topic in your class. Then have students play their games. Here are the rules: http://www.pokemon.com/us/pokemon-tcg/rules

Witch Hunt Game Design Challenge—Students are game designers tasked with making a Salem Witch Hunt card game. In groups, play the tabletop card game *One Night Ultimate Werewolf* or *Spyfall*. Next, students remix the role cards using historical people from Salem (e.g., Sarah Good, Reverend Cotton Mather), or characters from a novel play. Students should playtest another group's, and then iterate (redo) to make it better (more fun, more interesting, more fair).

Games

Apples to Apples has terrific social game mechanics for classrooms—http://www.mattelgames.com/en-us/apples-to-apples/index.html

Battleground 538, started at the White House Education Game Jam, this is GlassLab's finished product—https://www.glasslabgames.org/games/B538

Coup (The Dystopian Universe) is a social deduction game with a bluffing mechanic—http://amzn.com/B00GDI4HX4

HedBanz, the reverse charades party game that is easy to modify with standard sized index cards—http://www.hedbanz.com

Metagame is a party game codesigned by *Rules of Play* coauthor Eric Zimmerman, along with Colleen Macklin and John Sharp. Decks and expansion packs on different themes can be purchased or downloaded—http://metaga.me

One Night Ultimate Werewolf—http://beziergames.com/products/one-night-ultimate-werewolf

Ozobot is a toy robot that students can hack—http://ozobot.com

The Resistance is a terrific multiplayer social deduction card game—http://www.indieboardsandcards.com/resistance.php

Superfight is an argumentation card game—https://www.superfightgame.com

Sphero is another toy robot, controlled by iPad. There is a BB-8 *Star Wars* robot too!—http://www.sphero.com

Spyfall online—http://spyfall.crabhat.com

Spyfall social deduction board game—https://www.cryptozoic.com/spyfall

Timeline games from Asmodee—https://www.asmodee.us/en/games/timeline

Resources

Episode is a popular interactive story app on mobile. Anyone can contribute a story on computer and then share it—https://www.episodeinteractive.com

Find Play in Things, from the Institute of Play, is an effective way to start a game jam—http://beta.gamek.it/challenge/find-play-in-things

The Game Crafter, a website to create prototypes of board, card, and dice games. Templates are available to create booklets, game pieces, boards, tiles, shades, and more—https://www.thegamecrafter.com

Global Game Jam, marathon sessions of collaborative game design—http://globalgamejam.org

Harlowe Manual with Twine tips—https://twine2.neocities.org

Hooked is a new app to write chat stories—http://www.hooked.co. Here's an example three of my students wrote about colonial New York: http://bit.ly/2ivm4B5

inkleWriter, the free and easy-to-use interactive story tool—www.inklestudios.com/inklewriter/education

Storium is a collaborative interactive fiction tool—https://storium.com

Twine—http://twinery.org

Twine Guide—http://twinery.org/wiki/twine2:guide

The White House Education Game Jam—https://www.whitehouse.gov/blog/2014/10/06/white-house-education-game-jam

Zulama's game jam resource page—http://zulama.com/resources/game-jam-resources

· 1 4 ·

MAKING DIGITAL GAMES

Similar to constructivism's tenet of "learn by doing," the theory of constructionism can be summed up as "learn by making." Seymour Papert pioneered
this learning theory. His seminal book *Mindstorms: Children, Computers, and
Powerful Ideas*, first published in 1980, detailed constructionism and the kid-
friendly programming language Logo, created by his MIT lab. In the preface to
Mindstorms, Papert stated, "a modern-day Montessori might propose, if con-
vinced by my story, to create a gear set for children" (1993, p. xx). Programming to Papert was not about the language, but rather the toolset to create a
working system.

Expectations for widespread school adoption of the "Logo Turtle," a
small, programmable robot, were promising at the time. I remember using
Logo for Apple II in the early 1980s, but it seemed like a novelty compared to
the BASIC language taught in schools. In 1993, MicroWorlds was released,
integrating the language with robotic-controlled interlocking LEGO bricks.
About a decade later, "a new Logo programming environment called Scratch
emerged from the Lifelong Kindergarten Group at the MIT Media Lab" (Logo
Foundation, 2011). Papert's vision is still strong today in today's Maker movement. The LEGO-robot collaboration lives on with Mindstorms, a top seller
that uses advanced tablet applications to program movements. Scratch, the
digital animation and game design tool, is a descendant of Logo.

This chapter reviews a variety of applications available that teach game creation at an early age without requiring prior knowledge of how to code. Many of the tools use a click-and-drag interface, while others use interlocking bricks, similar to LEGO bricks, to create programming instructions. It begins with the National STEM Video Game Challenge, an initiative that celebrates innovative games made by youth.

The National STEM Video Game Challenge

The National STEM Video Game Challenge began in 2010 and it has grown in size each year. Alan Gershenfeld, the cofounder of E-Line Media and a board member of the Cooney Center, described to me how the idea came to fruition. "We approached the White House and said we would raise the money privately," Gershenfeld recalled, when we spoke in 2014. "Then we showed research about why making games fit Obama's Educate to Innovate Challenge."

The STEM Challenge, as it is often called, takes place across schools, libraries, museums, and cultural centers across America. Allison Mishkin is its research and program manager. Her background is in the social sciences of the Internet, particularly pertaining to child development. She worked to scale up and expand the program. We spoke in May 2016.

At age 14, Mishkin had been obsessed with *The Princess Diaries* books. Then she had an opportunity to meet Meg Cabot, the author. Soon enough she was working with Cabot and HarperCollins to create an online book club for teenagers. "Seeing thousands of teenagers use the Internet to define their identity was powerful," Mishkin recalled.

Inspired by this, Mishkin went on to design her own undergraduate major, focusing on the social implications of computer sciences. In particular, she studied how the design of games teaches children certain values. "If you give a kid a learning game about math they learn about math," Mishkin explained. "But what about the interactions on the screen? Other than the concrete learning objectives, what do the interactions have to teach about their social emotional skills?" Later Mishkin became a Google Fellow, and earned her master's degree from Oxford University in social science and the Internet. She is currently a PhD candidate at Oxford University, and works as a data analyst at BrainPOP and the Cooney Center. The Cooney Center brought her on to lead the research, documentation, and evaluation of the impacts of the STEM Challenge.

Speaking to Mishkin, you can tell how passionate she is about getting kids to create games. "Because they see themselves as creators, rather than consumers, their image of themselves changes and they get more motivated," she said. "Their self-esteem grows. They're better working with teams because they're so excited about what they are working on." Also when children code games, they learn systems thinking principles. "This is really valuable for their STEM progression. Through creative exercises, you can empower kids with social emotional development in a way that a traditional classroom might not necessarily teach."

Lexi Schneider won the STEM Challenge in 2013. She was 16 years old at the time, winning in the Game Design Document category. Schneider was also a soccer captain and active in her school's band. She did not see herself as a game designer. As it happened, Schneider's brother was making a game. So she decided to as well. Schneider liked art and realized that games were, in fact, kind of like art. Her animated game eventually won the Challenge that year. Inspired by the win, she learned how to code, reentered the Challenge as a high schooler, and won again! "She viewed the STEM Challenge as a motivator," Mishkin said. "The Challenge has a lot of different entry points, so we can interact with you wherever you are on the game design pathway."

Olivia Thomas won the 2016 Challenge. She got into games because she loved to read, particularly Nancy Drew mystery books, video games, and art. (*Nancy Drew: Codes and Clues*, a story-based app with a programmable robot dog was released in 2016. The press release mentioned Thomas as an inspiration!) To Thomas, games were another way of telling stories. "She liked creative writing and decided to tell a story using Gamestar Mechanic," Mishkin explained. "She viewed games for the many purposes they have."

After winning the Challenge, Thomas was invited to the White House Science Fair. She has since toured Schell Games, and even rang the company's gong (fun fact: both Filament Games and Schell Games have a large gong!). "She used her win to give back to her community," Mishkin said. "She created a program in her hometown of Boise to teach girls in her community. For the winners it doesn't stop when they win, it becomes a motivator." Thomas entered college in the fall of 2016.

As part of the STEM Challenge, there is a grant to design sustainable learning ecosystems in Pittsburgh. "We led sessions at the Carnegie Science Center and at the Carnegie Museum of Art," Mishkin said. "The groups that showed up to each were different, even though the workshops were the same." Some kids felt they belong in a science museum, while others identified with being at an art museum. As a result, the team offered a different experience at the locations. "Students could recognize a pathway for themselves. If a girl likes art, we suggest an interactive art activity, or to create a game design document. The idea is to get you really excited by getting you to view game design as an artistic expression."

My middle school students have used game design tools, like those in the STEM Challenge, to create projects about historical events. As mentioned in Chapter 13, they designed interactive fiction stories with Twine. Once, during the Twine project, I stopped the class to announce, "Guess what? Everyone here is coding!" After all, embedding images into Twine required students to copy and paste, and then hack (change) a line of HTML code. "I hate coding," one girl responded. When I inquired why, she said, "I don't see the big deal about having Anna turn three times to meet Elsa." The student was referring to a *Frozen*-themed puzzle in an Hour of Code activity. When I shared this anecdote with Mishkin, she expressed a similar concern with the STEM Challenge. "There are certain words that have become really loaded, like coding." She continued:

> Because of TV shows like *The Big Bang Theory*, when you think of scientists, the roles we have to look up to are non-empathetic characters. Kids can't look up and say, "Hey they're like me!" Coding sounds like you are at your computer working alone. Software development is actually team-based and collaborative. Kids also don't see the amount of creativity inherent in coding. The STEM Challenge sees entry points for kids who see themselves as "gamers," another loaded word. When you say gamer, and you think of a guy in his basement drinking orange soda, glued to his Xbox. It is important to show kids that coding means many different things. It's about trying to weave coding and systems thinking skills into different types of activities. Every kid can then realize what they are passionate about has a connection to coding, digital literacy, and game design.

Many activities on the Hour of Code website are puzzle-based. While fine for some children, it can quickly become rote and boring. As a response, MIT Media Lab's Mitchel Resnick, along with David Siegel, wrote a blog post in late 2015 about how coding applications, like Scratch, are best used as tools for self-expression. Resnick and Siegel wrote:

> We are strong proponents of children learning to code, but we have concerns about the motivations and methods underlying many of these new learn-to-code initiatives. Many of them, motivated by a shortage of programmers and software developers in industry, focus especially on preparing students for computer science degrees and careers, and they typically introduce coding as a series of logic puzzles for students to solve.

> We co-founded the Scratch Foundation in 2013 to support and promote a very different approach to coding. For us, coding is not a set of technical skills but a new type of literacy and personal expression, valuable for everyone, much like learning to write. We see coding as a new way for people to organize, express, and share their ideas. (2015, para. 2)

Mishkin launched Code Like a Girl in 2016, which held its first conference weeks before we spoke. For the conference, they brought together about 500 girls from New York City (NYC) area public, private, and charter schools. "The focus of the conference isn't to teach you how to code," Mishkin said. Instead, it is to teach about what being a professional developer looks like on a day-to-day basis. "The goal was to create a safe space and to empower girls to break the barrier bit by bit."

Some girls in attendance already knew how to code. Others signed up because they heard that the conference keynotes included Jocelyn Leavitt (cofounder of Hopscotch, featured later in this chapter) and TV's Mindy Kaling (*The Office* and *The Mindy Project*). Minerva Tantoco, the former Chief Technology Officer for NYC was the third keynote. "She [Tantoco] gave a great analogy," Mishkin said. "Technology is no longer a bigger piece of the pie; it is the plate that holds the pie together."

Digital Design Tools

The National STEM Video Game Challenge website is a terrific entry point for teachers of all content subjects who seek to teach using game design. This subsection includes digital tools that use coding to support self-expression, thus promoting interest-driven learning. The authoring tools in this section give students a chance to code, as well as to be creative in design. Many use a drag-and-drop interface, which is a simplified way to code. By interlocking LEGO-style digital bricks, students can create original games, or remix others shared in a community of practice.

Gamestar Mechanic

Gamestar Mechanic was launched in the late 2000s and is now published by E-Line Media (it was cocreated by E-Line Media and the Institute of Play, originally funded by the MacArthur Foundation). Robert Torres, formerly of the Gates Foundation, used it for his doctoral dissertation about systems thinking. At the time, he was working at the Institute of Play, one of Gamestar Mechanic's partners.

When E-Line Media purchased Gamestar Mechanic, it focused on teacher discoverability, or "bottoms-up," word-of-mouth marketing. Gershenfeld explained, "There was early efficacy in the classroom with teacher-to-teacher recommendations." Due to its ease of use and well-run ecosystem, the platform keeps growing. "We're in 7,000 to 8,000 schools and after-school programs," he elaborated. "It's purely bottoms-up, and I think we're going to see that grow significantly. There is an entire curricular service, there are also tools to create games, there's a community that we run, and there is also a flexible, modular curriculum."

To help teachers implement the tool, the Institute of Play published a Gamestar Mechanic Learning Guide (linked at the end of this chapter). Users of Gamestar Mechanic can also take a course in game design, or just freely play. Classes are offered online as well as in local and regional programs. The tool itself is gamified and quest-based, with levels, challenges, and missions unlocking as users proceed. There are also badges to accumulate. According to the website's portal, there are more than 250,000 user-designed games. Gamestar Mechanic is an excellent tool to encourage design thinking, systems thinking, and problem-solving. There are deep discounts available to educators and classrooms and a virtual store to purchase game add-ons.

Hopscotch

Hopscotch is a visual coding app tailor-made for mobile devices. According to its iTunes page, children can program "characters to move, draw, and collide with each other, and use shaking, tilting, or even shouting at the iPad to control them." It uses a visual coding language. Unlike many of the Hour of Code activities, Hopscotch is not based on puzzle challenges. Hopscotch's "Community" is where ideas are exchanged. Practical applications of math are deeply ingrained in the shared Community projects. One example is the Sydney Opera House, featuring flying robots that trace out the famous Australian landmark. By clicking "Edit," the angles and directions that were coded become revealed. It is intuitive and easy to use.

I spoke with Jocelyn Leavitt, the CEO and cofounder, in May 2014. The company's philosophy is constructionism—to use technology as a creative tool for expression. "The whole idea is children teaching computers, rather than computers teaching children." The interface is similar to Scratch, the coding tool influenced by the constructionist work of Seymour Papert.

Leavitt has a background as a social studies teacher. Originally from Hawaii, she worked at the Dalton School in NYC. Her interest is in experiential education. "I was influenced by the indigenous people in Hawaii and the way project-based learning figured into indigenous education," she stated.

Hopscotch's cofounder, Samantha John, whom Leavitt met through mutual friends, had an engineering background. Both shared a passion about women in software. They discussed how there were not enough female engineers in the software field. Leavitt explained, "We were passionate about building a toy that we would have been passionate about growing up with. We saw that a lot of our friends were software engineers with similar backgrounds: white, male, and nerdy growing up." Many engineers began programming for fun when they were in middle school. Leavitt continued, "We wanted to get girls to have the same experiences. We saw huge potential for a mobile programming language with the iPad becoming more popular."

I asked Leavitt how they market the app to girls as well as boys. It can be tricky and it may appear that you are pandering to your audience if you adjust the look of a toy traditionally made for a boy. Leavitt explained the process:

> We deliberately tried to make it not overly girly, to make it gender-neutral. Early on, we made decisions to make it feel welcoming and opening to girls. For instance, the basic things like choice of colors. We went back and forth with designers five to six times. The initial set of illustrations looked too boyish; we wanted it to appeal to girls too. I took the app into the classroom to have kids play with it. I asked the boys and girls, "Do you think it's an app made for boys, an app made for girls, or unisex?" All the girls said it was an app made for girls and all the boys said it was unisex. That perfectly illustrates the line we're trying to walk.

Hopscotch seeks to get all children to build their own software, even those who do not consider themselves to be engineers. By creating a gender-neutral experience, every user becomes empowered. Leavitt elaborated, "At the end of the day, being able to build your own computer programs and your own software is deeply empowering. It's kind of an extension of human capabilities." Middle school was the chosen target group because research showed that children at this age are more able to grasp coding concepts. The app is designed for informal learning (outside of school); however, it is frequently used in the classroom. Information is not tracked due to the intended age of users. As a result, Hopscotch relies on anecdotal data from pictures and stories teachers send in.

The company's first foray into coding began in 2011 with *Daisy the Dinosaur*. Its very simple interface enabled young children to control an animated dinosaur. *Daisy the Dinosaur* teaches coding by challenging children to make Daisy perform tasks. Hopscotch was launched about a year later. The business model is now focused solely on the Hopscotch app. Simply put, Hopscotch has more power. Leavitt said, "We saw things that worked in *Daisy*, but wanted to move on." Because people still enjoy and find utility with *Daisy*, it remains Apple's App Store.

Designing in Hopscotch is completely open-ended, like a sandbox. Similar to Scratch, there is a toolbox of commands and functions. Leavitt explained the company's approach to me. "We don't do a ton of hand-holding," she explained:

> Teachers recognize Hopscotch's value as a tool. We have a shared community, kids upload projects, games, and apps. Other kids take inspiration from what they can make or do. We see a lot of games. Kids like to play the thing they made and see other kids enjoy the things they made. We wanted a toy for the iPad because of the form factor and it made a lot of sense to have a touch screen interface for a visual programming language.

After playtesting, Hopscotch discovered that many students went home and continued their projects on their own time. It is very driven by how testers—both children and adults—use the program. Leavitt said the reception was very positive. She said, "Kids really are delighted when they discover they can make their own things. It is empowering when they have an idea for a game or something they want to make and they can do it."

The Hopscotch's interface is easy to use. There are "Rules" that can be assigned to characters. Each rule creates new "Abilities." Hopscotch is an engaging tool to create content on a tablet that takes advantage of a mobile device's motion sensors. Animations can react from being tapped, tilted, or shaken. Its broad appeal may inspire a future engineer—boy or girl!

Scratch

Scratch descended from the Logo language. According to the MIT Media Lab, Scratch is intended to help "young people learn important mathematical and computational ideas, while also gaining a deeper understanding of the process of design." No knowledge of Flash, Java, or other actual coding is required; programming commands are embedded in color-coded bricks. Each brick is assigned a function. A blue one might say, "turn 15 degrees" or "move 15 steps." Logic statements (if-then) are on yellow bricks. Certain bricks snap into place with others, creating an interlocking computer language. When everything is assembled, simply click the green flag icon to see if the project works.

Scratch has a large and active user base. There are shared projects that range from animations to complex games. You can create, remix, and publish, as well as learn informally via its participatory community. Scratch has a "See Inside" feature that enables anyone to "open the hood" and view the bricks that were used in a particular project. I have found this feature to be an effective teaching tool for new users. It is empowering to see students make simple changes and then have the ability to call the project their own.

My 6th grade social studies students remix video games using Scratch. Each is assigned to research a topic—in this case, medieval Europe. The remixed game should fit the theme. Examples ranged from a trivia game to a role-playing adventure about a baker's guild. I use a flipped classroom approach, giving the class links to YouTube tutorials for students to view from home, saving face-to-face class time for projects. I recommend the "I do, we do, you do" approach, modeling the app first on an interactive whiteboard. I keep my direct instruction to a minimum. This approach can motivate students to seek out additional how-to videos in informal learning spaces (e.g., the Scratch community, more in-depth YouTube videos). A brief self-reflection essay is also part of the assignment. The idea is for students to explain how their game relates to their researched topic.

A collaboration between MIT Media Lab, led by Mitchel Resnick, and the DevTech group at Tufts University, cofounded by Marina Umaschi Bers, ScratchJr was released in 2015. The interface is optimized for tablets, and the target audience is young children. Differing from the web-based version, ScratchJr has a horizontal design grammar. In other words, the interlocking bricks click together like a sentence, read from left to right (Scratch, on computers, is "read" vertically). There is also a PBS KIDS ScratchJr app, which features characters from children's shows that run on public television. There is a terrific book from Bers and Resnick aptly titled, *The Official ScratchJr Book* (see book link at the end of the chapter). I use it with my 6-year-old son to familiarize him with concepts on constructionism (incidentally, both Bers and Resnick were students of Seymour Papert). The book does not teach coding; rather it shares fun projects, like digital animations, games, and stories, which *use* coding.

In 2016, Scratch 3.0 was released. For those keeping track (nerds like me!), Scratch 1.0 was a free, offline download, and Scratch 2.0 was web-based.

The latest iteration is a partnership with Google's Blockly (visual interlocking blocks that works like Scratch), called Scratch Blocks. Scratch Blocks will work with LEGO WeDo 2.0. Creating a line of Scratch 3.0 code can control LEGO robotics (Nguyen, 2016).

Teaching coding is like implementing other educational technologies. It should be integrated into the curriculum, not used as an add-on. As with a game, students are quite adept at figuring out Scratch as they go. Many get "lost in the moment" of design, similar to what happens when building in *Minecraft*. There are helpful resources for teachers on the ScratchEd page, including remix and project ideas for all disciplines. Rubrics are also available.

GameMaker: Studio

Mark Overmars, a professor from the Netherlands, originally created the authoring tool GameMaker: Studio. He eventually sold it to YoYo Games, which has scaled up its use. More and more schools are using it because it is robust, yet easy to use.

To learn more about GameMaker: Studio's classroom implementation, I met up with Steve Isaacs, a computer teacher at William Annin Middle School in Basking Ridge, New Jersey. We spoke in July 2014. Isaacs teaches video game design to 7th and 8th graders. He has spoken about teaching with GameMaker: Studio at several conferences, including the Serious Play Conference. Isaacs and a former student published the book *GameMaker Programming by Example* in 2016. It is about using GameMaker Language (GML).

Isaacs started using GameMaker: Studio in his classroom over 15 years ago. It wasn't originally intended to be a teaching tool; he was an early adopter. As a result, Isaacs began to aggregate and develop his own resources, including video tutorials. A few years ago, Isaacs started sharing his tutorials on Twitter. YoYo Games's CEO took notice and commented on his postings. Isaacs was seen as the perfect conduit to get GameMaker: Studio into students' hands. Isaacs, along with Mark Suter, an Ohio-based computer technology teacher, worked with YoYo Games to create a "Learn" section on its site.

Like many authoring tools in this chapter, GameMaker: Studio has a drag-and-drop interface. It's an easy entry point to teach about game development. Each clickable object has a "conditional statement" (e.g., if clicked, then go left—the classic "if-then" programming logic couplet). Objects are programmed as "events" or "actions." Users can then define the actions that sprites (movable objects), rooms, sounds, and backgrounds have. For example, *if* a sprite collides with a wall, *then* it stops. "It's very intuitive," Isaacs said. "It's structured in a way that a programmer would think. It's a great introduction to computer science in an unintimidating manner." Advanced students can eventually code in GML.

To get a sense of game mechanics, Isaacs has students try out games from different genres. "I give a little bit of instruction and a lot of support," he said. "I show the kids the basic syntax of how typical things work, like adventure-type games. I give a number of 15-minute demo lessons. My goal is that they understand how things work, and then go the online community. I don't want their games to look like my demo." Isaacs's methodology describes my (unintentional) first experience using Scratch. I showed the basics of Scratch to my class; many went to YouTube, from home, to learn more. Isaacs's approach whets students' appetites to lead them to learn informally, from the community.

Isaacs's students first prepare a "road map" to plan their games. This occurs before using GameMaker: Studio. They fill out a simplified version of a professional design document. Doing this serves to help students map out their games, as well as to keep the assignments authentic. Next, students write up the game's narrative storyline and character outlines, describing physical attributes and abilities (e.g., strong fighter, enemy). Then students sketch out the level design, scoring mechanisms, and win/loss scenarios.

As in a professional studio, an iterative design approach works best. Isaacs encourages a lot of peer testing. "The goal is to provide constructive, concrete feedback," he explained. "What would make your game better?" Middle school students can be prone to telling others how to play their game. To remedy this, Isaacs assigns a student to watch the playtest. He elaborated, "I have to tell kids to 'sit on their hands' and not help. Students watch their game played through someone else's eyes. At that age, students think that something is obvious to do because they planned it. If it's obvious to the designer, it may not be obvious to the player. If five people go left when you want them to go right, then they have to go back and iterate."

GameMaker: Studio is currently Windows-only; however, projects can be easily ported (exported copy) to other platforms. Isaacs's students have published games for Mac, iOS, Android, and HTML5. The tool is available as a free download, with paid add-ons. The Learn section is constantly growing, as is its community of practice. GameMaker: Studio is an effective tool to engage students in the iterative design process of game creation. "The point of entry is low, but the potential is huge!" Isaacs concluded.

Tynker

Tynker is a coding tool accessible on computer browsers and tablets. It offers an entire suite of instructor tools, including a teacher dashboard and an online grade book. Harnessing a Vygotskian approach, Tynker scaffolds learning, moving from interlocking bricks to more advanced concepts such as syntax-driven programming. Tynker offers a Starter Pack with lesson plans and project ideas.

I interviewed Krishna Vedati, Tynker's CEO and founder, to learn more about what differentiates it from other visual coding apps. Vedati has been a technology entrepreneur for more than 15 years. Each had something to offer, but they were not built as systems of self-learning. Some applications, such as Scratch, rely on a community of practice, in which users learn from shared projects. Tynker is gamified as an adaptive learning tool. Each task is presented as an increasingly complex puzzle. This avoids the need to incorporate an open online community where outsiders can critique projects. After all, in a school there are privacy concerns. "Even with all of the social options available, many students simply opt to work with one or two of their own friends," Vedati explained, when we first spoke in March 2014.

Vedati hoped to bring technology skills to students in a fun way. The answer was to build a game-like structure to promote progress. Tynker's gamification techniques work because its puzzles function as part of a larger system of learning. Vedati explained, "In our case, the underlying mission is to teach programming, then gamify." Challenges include fixing a robot and saving a puppy. "Kids become immersed and emotionally involved. We've learned a lot from that," he continued. Vedati observed his two children consuming media from mobile devices. He felt that they needed to become creators and makers of media. "My kids are 10 and 7 and—if you ask them—programming is not on top of their minds," Vedati said. "Fun is."

"Tynker" was chosen as the product's name. "Kids like to tinker with things," Vedati stated. (Vedati told me that the word "tinker" was hard to acquire. The misspelled moniker was chosen to convey a spirit of fun.) Many of the teachers who use Tynker have no programming experience, which makes their feedback valuable. The company visits classrooms several times a week. It also tests with parents and offers online courses, giving parents a full view of their children's progress.

The built-in tutoring system constantly tests. It observes how fast students solve adaptive puzzles, what and how many blocks are required to execute a series of commands, and how many steps and tries are required. Higher-level tasks challenge students to reverse engineer (figure out how a project works). And like other coding tools, Tynker can be integrated into any discipline. It can be used in project-based science classes (experimentation), in math (fractals), and art (digital animation). Tynker can teach 1st and 2nd graders mini-animations, and science and engineering to students in middle grades. There is even an *Angry Birds*–style physics challenge. "Be creative—with programming as the glue," Vedati stated.

In upper grade levels, Tynker becomes a JavaScript language that can be used to build complex apps. Students sequence, create conditions, loops, and combinations, and build simple Turing machines. "We take them from where they don't know anything, give them computational thinking skills, and then make them build complex things to transition to mainstream programming," Vedati explained. "Visual programming is a starting point."

In 2016, Tynker integrated its coding language with objects in the real world. "It's designed as a maker platform," Vedati explained, when we spoke in June 2016 at the International Society for Technology in Education Conference. Using Tynker, students can now program Parrot drones, Sphero and Ollie robots, Makey Makey electronic circuit kits. "We extended the curriculum to include makerspaces and STEM. So when students make mobile apps, they can now program toys and robots. They can make robots dance."

Conclusions and Takeaways

Digital game design applies systems thinking and design thinking skills. It is a practical application of math and science, along with the humanities. There are dozens of apps for student to create digital games. Visual coding languages are compelling because they apply constructionism, or learning by making. Some tools are click-and-drag, while others use interlocking blocks. Some coding sites use games and puzzles to teach, creating a community of practice in the classroom. Others use an open canvas and an online community.

Lesson Plan Ideas

DIY Assistive Game Controllers: Makey Makey is an electronics kit that came on the market in 2013. With it, ordinary objects become input devices for a computer. The website features bananas played as piano keys and Play-Doh used as a *Super Mario Bros.* game controller. The possibilities of do-it-yourself (DIY) game controllers are truly limitless! Switch interfaces are commonly used in assistive technology. Review the AbleGamers Foundation's Game Accessibility Guidelines to learn more about remapping keyboards. WASD and arrow keys are common in PC-based games. Because the keys are so close together, a disabled person would have difficulty being precise—even when using a keyboard overlay. The AbleGamer Foundation's Game Accessibility Guidelines—http://www.includification.com; Makey Makey—http://makey-makey.com

The Foos is a kid-friendly coding game with diverse characters. From CodeSpark, it can be played on almost any platform. There are puzzles and drag-and-drop level editors. Check out the curriculum guide and extension activities—http://thefoos.com/coding-resources-for-you

Gamestar Mechanic Learning Guide: Lesson plan ideas are suitable for any content area. Coding is a tool, not the lesson—http://www.instituteofplay.org/wp-content/uploads/2011/02/Gamestar_Mechanic_Learning_Guide_v1.1.pdf

Get Ready with Ready: Combining a Scratch-like interface with Unity 3D, lesson plans for creating games like *Air Hockey* and *Flappy Bird* are in its curriculum—http://www.getready.io/educators

Hour of Code Lessons: Standards depend on the discipline and content area—http://csedweek.org/learn

Level Editors: The mobile game *Badlands* has a level maker—http://frogmind-games.com/badland. And Teach with Portals includes lesson plans to design *Portal* puzzles—http://www.teachwithportals.com

The Official ScratchJr Book is filled with lesson ideas that use coding as a tool for self-expression—https://www.nostarch.com/scratchjr

Scratch Lesson Plans: Rather than start from a blank page (or, literally, from scratch), why not remix an existing project on Scratch? Go to http://scratch.mit.edu and then select "Explore" or "Search." Find and test a game (some projects are partially completed; it is important to test functionality and whether a game is fun prior to remixing). Click "See Inside" to view the blocks that made the program (it's like checking under the hood of a car). Next, click "Remix." The Scratch team has templates at http://Scratch.MIT.edu/ users/scratchteam and the ScratchED community of shared content—http://scratched.media.mit.edu/resources

Tynker courses are available for multiple disciplines and content areas—https://www.tynker.com/courses

Games

Blockly from Google, which will be part of Scratch Blocks—https://developers.google.com/blockly

CodeMaster board game—http://www.thinkfun.com/products/code-master

Colorless, Olivia Thomas' 2016 National STEM Video Game Challenge winning game, built with Gamestar Mechanic—http://bit.ly/25lFM7W

Gamestar Mechanic, systems thinking games and game design tools from the Institute of Play and E-Line Media—http://gamestarmechanic.com

GameMaker: Studio, an authoring tool to create games. Prices range from free to professional—https://www.yoyogames.com/studio

GameSalad, a game creator for mobile, downloadable for free—http://gamesalad.com

Goldie Blox, a non-digital game marketed to teach STEM skills to girls—http://www.goldieblox.com

Hopscotch, coding with color-coded blocks, made for a tablet—http://www.gethopscotch.com

MaKey MaKey projects on Scratch—http://scratch.mit.edu/studios/230629/projects

Nancy Drew: Codes and Clues is an app that has the famous girl detective code a robot puppy to help her get out of "sticky situations." Coding is embedded in the story—http://www.herinteractive.com/nancy-drew-codes-clues

PBS KIDS ScratchJr—http://pbskids.org/apps/pbs-kids-scratchjr.html

Robot Turtles, a board game with tiles and illustrated cards to teach programming and coding logic to early elementary school children. The turtle was inspired by Logo—http://www.thinkfun.com/robotturtles

Scratch, to play, remix, and create games and digital animations—http://scratch.mit.edu

ScratchJr, early childhood coding on iPad—http://www.scratchjr.org

Sploder, to test and create arcade games. There are four categories of design: Retro Arcade, the Platform Creator, the Physics Puzzle Maker, and the Classic Shooter, a space game. There is a Parents/Teacher page and community comments can be switched off to keep the learning environment more restricted—http://www.sploder.com

RPG Maker game design tool—http://www.rpgmakerweb.com

Unity, a professional-grade game-rendering tool—http://unity3d.com

Resources

The Able Gamers Foundation, gaming for people of all abilities—http://www.ablegamers.com

Black Girls Code—http://www.blackgirlscode.com

Boy Scout Game Design Workbook, by David Mullich—http://boyslifeorg.files.wordpress.com/2013/03/gamedesign.pdf

Code.org, a nonprofit that offers cross-curricular support to teachers—http://code.org

Code Like a Girl—https://codelikeagirlnyc.dalton.org

A *Different Kind of Coding*, blog post from Mitchel Resnick and David Siegel—http://bit.ly/1TnWRbS

GameKit, from Institute of Play, featured challenges and ideas to create and mod paper-based games, which is an effective opening activity for a game jam—http://beta.gamek.it

Designer Journey blog post from student Olivia Thomas, winner of the 2016 National STEM Video game Challenge—http://stemchallenge.org/featured/olivia-thomas-a-video-game-designers-journey-to-the-white-house-science-fair

GameMaker Programming by Example, book by Steve Isaacs and Brian Christian—https://www.packtpub.com/game-development/gamemaker-programming-example

Hour of Code during Computer Science Education Week—http://code.org/educate/hoc

Includification, game accessibility PDF from AbleGamers—http://www.includification.com/AbleGamers_Includification.pdf

Logo Foundation, the little turtle that started it all—http://el.media.mit.edu/logo-foundation

MaKey MaKey kit—http://www.makeymakey.com

National STEM Video Game Challenge—http://www.stemchallenge.org

Remake Learning, the afterschool initiative in Pittsburgh—http://remake-learning.org

· 1 5 ·

GEEKING OUT AND EARNING BADGES

Educator Rafranz Davis is an advocate for interest-driven learning. When we spoke in April 2016, she talked about how gaming is just one of many interests that youth have. "Learning is different in terms of what a kid is interested in," she said. "We need to understand that not every kid is interested in games. We also have to broaden our definition of gaming and talk about how the design of games incorporates so many aspects of what kids are interested in."

Davis shared a story about working with her district's robotics team. She was amazed as she listened to students talk about what their passions were and how it translates into their robotics team. Some of the team members were deeply invested in gaming. Specifically, they played the card game *Magic: The Gathering*. Because of this, they wanted to program games into their club's robot. Other kids on the team who were into art, music, and writing wanted to apply those interests. At the center was the robot.

Games are designed in such a way that they can incorporate the multiple interests of children. When a company like BrainPOP designs a game, each person on the team has a specific role. There are designers, coders, researchers, artists, and more. "We don't talk about that stuff," Davis said.

"We need to provide multiple platforms besides just designing a game." She continued:

> When I think about passion-based learning I think about what kids' interests are. There are kids with creative interests, and kids who are history buffs, science buffs, and English buffs. How can we bridge a way to explore all of the things that they are care about, in a way that is authentic to them to apply it? For some it is gaming. And gaming is not just designing the game—it's all of the elements that make up the game. We have to bridge to all the parts that other kids are interested in. We have to create that space for that to happen. It's a challenge we need to do.

This chapter describes communities of practice for students who "geek out" in passion-driven gamer culture. Fans generate and remix content within affinity groups and participatory cultures. Also in this chapter is a discussion of best practices pertaining to digital badges. As a system of micro-credentials for achievements, digital badges have potential in mapping out a student's personal learning pathway.

Affinity Spaces and the HOMAGO Framework

Communities of practice relating to games feature apprenticeship learning, in which members analyze and interpret information together. A community of practice is one in which "members of a group have multiple levels of participation" (Lave & Wenger, 1991, p. 98). Members share hypotheses, and demonstrate scientific thinking. Regarding gamer communities, discussion topics are often authentic, "even though the worlds themselves are fantasy" (Duncan & Steinkuehler, 2008, p. 543). Game communities support "social knowledge construction" among its participants (Duncan & Steinkuehler, 2008, pp. 540–541). Of note are *World of Warcraft* communities. Its fan wikis and discussion boards feature apprenticeship learning, from novice to master (Black & Steinkuehler, 2009; Duncan & Steinkuehler, 2008). Because players of *World of Warcraft* are passion-driven, adolescent boys who participate in its communities—including those who struggle with reading in school—were observed reading text "up to eight grades above their ability with 94–99% accuracy" (Steinkuehler, 2011, pp. 12–13).

Connected Learning's Mizuko (Mimi) Ito's HOMAGO Framework describes how one follows his or her interests and moves from apprentice to participant in community of practice. HOMAGO means "hanging out, messing around, and geeking out." It is the continuum of experiences in which youth are exposed to something, become interested in something, and then get to the point where they are actively sharing their work and knowledge with their peers to create a community of practice (Ito et al, 2009).

I have observed the HOMAGO Framework in the student technology club that I advise. Students decided to attend the club and were given choice about what activity to pursue. This represented freedom to hang out and to mess around. Then they were "geeking out" about how to survive in *Agar.io*, the game where you gobble up floating blobs, and in *ROBLOX*, a *Minecraft*-like multiplayer world. I observed a 6th grader's affinity toward digital art. She had spent hours on Pixilart, a social network for artists. In particular, she made dozens of fan art pictures inspired by one of her favorite video games, *Undertale*. A pixilated role-playing game, *Undertale* puts players on a silly adventure.

Pixilart is an example of affinity space. Slightly different than a community of practice, an affinity space focuses on the place where members meet; communities of practice pertain to group affiliation (Gee, 2005). Within this affinity space, the student became a master pixel artist. She even takes requests from other community members (taking requests is a feature on the website) to design artwork. At 12 years old, she already amassed a digital art portfolio!

Game-Related Fan Fiction

In *Convergence Culture: Where Old and New Media Collide* (2006), Henry Jenkins described "fan fiction," or "fanfic." This genre of participatory writing refers to "any prose retelling of stories and characters drawn from mass media content" (Jenkins, 2006a, p. 285). Jenkins analyzed "participatory" fan communities such as FanFiction.net and the unofficial Harry Potter fan site MuggleNet. Video game-themed fan fiction is a popular subgenre on FanFiction.net. A casual search of the "Games" subsection showed thousands of stories, mostly for *Pokémon*, *The Legend of Zelda*, *Mass Effect*, and *Assassin's Creed*. There were some intriguing fan-created historical fiction stories about the game *Civilization*. I wondered how game-related fan fiction would work in my classroom.

I decided to combine fan fiction with a character web, thus mashing up storytelling with the dynamics of systems thinking (everything is interconnected). I constructed *The Assassin's Creed: Renaissance Character Web Project*, a project-based learning unit. Students were tasked to add Renaissance-era characters to the video game. Titles in the series have featured Leonardo da Vinci, Niccolò Machiavelli, Nicolaus Copernicus, several popes, and members of the Borgia and Medici families. Also included in the game are "databases," in which players are given historical information about people and places from the time period. The unit was tied to historical fiction, which can make history more "real" and relatable to middle school students. The culminating activity was to create a functioning fan fiction wiki of characters, similar to the *Assassin's Creed* wiki: http://assassinscreed.wikia.com.

When I launched the project, I informally asked my students to tell me if they had ever written or read fan fiction. Only a few hands went up—although most said that they had heard of it. When I interviewed Henry Jenkins in May 2014, I asked about the state of fanfic's current popularity (remember, *Convergence Culture* came out in 2006). "Sixth grade is the earliest that people engage in fan fiction," he said. "Most people I talked to were in high school or older; a high percentage in my grad school have read or written it."

Jenkins coined the term "participatory culture." This is the situated learning space where "fans and other consumers are invited to actively participate in the creation and circulation of new content" (Jenkins, 2006a, p. 290). Participatory cultures are relatively easy to join. When a new member creates content by, for example, posting game footage on YouTube, other members offer feedback. Jenkins has done experiments bringing fan fiction around canonical literature into the classroom. "I think all of the tools are there," he explained. "The challenge is to get young people to make connections. People learn outside of school. Some of these activities may not be valued in the classroom."

I asked Jenkins for advice on using game wikis as a teaching tool. For example, *Assassin's Creed* is rated M for mature content, mainly due to violence. Students weren't playing the game in school; however, they were engaged in remixing its content. Jenkins told me about the ethics of participatory culture practices. Not every educator can see the value in a child's hobbies, including cartoons, comic books, and video games. Some student interests may not be perceived as "appropriate" by teachers. Jenkins explained:

> Teachers can't simply invite it [student's interests and hobbies] in and then impose their own hierarchy on the behaviors that young people choose to be involved with. In many ways, it has to do with the ethical environment within the classroom, as much—or more—than the specific activities that form a participatory culture. It should be a safe space. A safe space isn't just defined by the way we normally use that term, like sexual issues or gender issues. It also has to be culturally safe, so kids don't

get put down for the popular culture they like, or the activities they engage with. Teachers should keep an open mind and look at the ways that those can be valuable sites of learning and be meaningfully connected to the classroom.

Jenkins discussed a book he coedited, *Reading in Participatory Culture* (2013), which "described instructional activities we developed around remix in a participatory culture." It was shaped by the work of Ricardo Pitts-Wiley, an African-American playwright who got incarcerated youth to read *Moby-Dick* by getting them to rewrite *Moby-Dick*—essentially, creating fan fiction. Jenkins said, "These are kids who are reading below grade level [and] not just at risk—already in prison. They read a book that the school system generally saw as too difficult to teach because of its complexity."

Pitts-Wiley had students write fan fiction characters, thus remixing *Moby-Dick*. He asked them to imagine what these characters would be like in the 21st-century and they transformed *Moby-Dick* from a story about the whaling trade to a story about the drug trade. "It becomes [about] a gang leader bent on vengeance at the expense of dealing drugs," Jenkins explained. "And the question of the story is, how far will a young crew follow into the mouth of hell and vengeance when they recognize that it's going to lead into their own destruction. It's very important to introduce these kinds of remix activities because it not only teaches kids to read critically, but to read creatively." It was *Grand Theft Auto V* meets Herman Melville.

Intramural eSports

For the uninitiated, Twitch is a streaming video service in which users watch others play video games. And it is a huge business. In August 2014, Amazon purchased Twitch for $970 million dollars. SuperData Research (published in an article on Quartz's website) reported that in 2013, "71 million people watched other people play video games" (Mirani, 2014). This is almost twice the viewership of the 2013 Major League Baseball World Series (Mirani, 2014)! Electronic sports, or eSports, are clearly popular.

To some it might seem boring to watch other people play video games. Isn't it more fun to play than to watch? eSports is not unlike watching players face off in a *chess* tournament. The World Series of Poker is another tabletop game televised as a spectator sport. The most watched eSports are multiplayer online battle arena (MOBA) games, in which "teams of five players compete to strategically attack an enemy team's guarded base" (Magdaleno, 2014). In other words, the games are like an online version of *Capture the* Flag, the classic summer camp game about defending your team's base.

League of Legends, Counter-Strike, and *Dota 2* are three of the more team-based eSport games. In fact, ESPN 3 has televised *Dota 2* championships. In 2016, the University of California at Irvine began to offer a *League of Legends* eSports scholarship (Kollar, 2016). Like basketball or soccer scholarships, "it will be offered to 10 students for up to four years at UC Irvine. As students with the scholarship graduate or leave the college, the school will offer the scholarship to new students in their place" (Kollar, 2016, para. 8).

eSports is also making its way into after-school programs. Super League Gaming launched in October 2015 with a *Minecraft* league. Held in 74 movie theaters across the country, teams played for 6 weeks, competing for scholarships. Super League Gaming turned *Minecraft* into a cooperative-style game, in which players work together to solve a problem. In the United States, High School Starleague offers a guide for after school club leagues. Started in 2010, it recommends using games rated T, for Teen, by the Entertainment Software Ratings Board (ESRB), including *Minecraft, Dota 2, League of Legends, Starcraft 2*, and *Hearthstone*. If you are thinking of starting an afterschool gaming club, consider eSports.

Publishing Game Reviews

Teachers can have students contribute to game-based communities of practice, including wikis, blog posts, and discussion forums. In a game-related affinity space, members may engage in complex discussions, including problem-solving in the game's system (Duncan & Steinkuehler, 2008). I observed this in my dissertation research, which brought me to three classrooms of teachers who frequently use games as part of their pedagogical approach. Each tapped into gaming communities, which are passion-based and interest-driven.

When students in Steve Isaacs's video middle school class make a video game on Gamestar Mechanic or Scratch, they post comments on other's games. "They reflect on what they completed, the successes, and the challenges, as well as what they want to accomplish the next week," Isaacs told me in April 2016. "They then share with an authentic audience. Talking about short-term goals keeps students in tune with time management." His students also write game reviews, which are posted online in gamer forums. "If a kid just writes, 'This game is good,'" I draw them in to see what details other game reviews include, like mechanics, customization, playability, aesthetics, and

GEEKING OUT AND EARNING BADGES

graphics," he said. "Kids then understand what to focus on, and how thorough reviews need to be."

As class assignments, Isaacs has students publish tutorials on the website SnapGuide. He also has students write comprehensive backstories on games, including the non-playable characters. Similarly, 5th grade teacher Mark Grundel has students write about the characters on *Ultimate Werewolf's* role cards. "The writing process is huge in game design," Isaacs continued. "There is a narrative embedded in games. Stories are crucial component. When I ask kids to recount a storyline, and then realize they need to play that part as a designer."

Toronto-based high school English teacher Paul Darvasi also has students write about games. His class close reads the nonlinear, story-driven game *Gone Home*, which stands in as a substitute for a literary text. He then uses assessment strategies that are actually traditional: students write responses and give presentations about the game. "The game is framed by reviews, which is consistent with gamer culture," Darvasi told me in late 2015. "Then they give fairly elaborate presentations on specific topics. Because video games are predominantly a visual experience, it allows them to translate the visual elements to their audience." To this end, his students take screenshots from moments in the game and later use them in PowerPoint presentations. They also answer questions, which ask them to make claims and use screenshot evidence as support. Finally, students publish reviews of *Gone Home* for an authentic audience on game review websites. Aside from *Gone Home*, this approach can fit other narrative games, like *Minecraft: Story Mode*, *Life Is Strange*, or *The Stanley Parable*.

Machinima

In a project-based learning unit, I had students use games and game design tools to author video presentations. To frame why we were doing the project, I showed the class Kevin Allocca's TED Talk, *Why Videos Go Viral*. According to Allocca, videos go viral because they are shared on social networks by "tastemakers," or trendsetters. They also are created in a community of participation, and have an element of unexpectedness, which can often be humor.

Some students led recorded tours of *Minecraft* worlds using Bandicam or Camtasia as the screencast tool. They also erected signs, which described what was there, and added in music and narration. Editing was done in iMovie or MovieMaker. Very little direct instruction was required from me. Using game footage to tell digital stories is called "machinima," a portmanteau of "machine cinema."

In that class, another student remixed the animated "Nyan Cat" viral video. In the video, a digital cat flies in the air, as electronic music pulsates in the background. Allocca mentioned it in his TED Talk. First the student searched "Nyan Cat Simulator" on Scratch (MIT's free game design tool) and then hacked the code by using the "See Inside" feature. She added in facts from her research topic, which popped up sporadically. This was the first time she ever coded using Scratch. To her, coding was about self-expression and social sharing. To me, this project was about teaching students move past consuming digital media to become content creators.

The genre of machinima was first known as "*Quake* films," after the 1996 first-person shooter. Players began to use *Quake*'s world as a filmmaking platform. Machinima predates Let's Play and has grown to become a popular niche with its own YouTube and Xbox Live channels, and even an annual film festival. *Anna* (2003) was one of the first notable films. Its story "deftly employs pathos to engender an emotional relationship between the viewer and the life and death of a single flower" (Luckman & Potanin, 2010, p. 141).

The rise of machinima occurred at the same time as the growth of massively multiplayer role-play games. Multiplayer worlds give players free time to explore and interact. *Halo*'s setting and characters were used to create comedic stories for the series *Red vs. Blue*. More recently, *Seedlings* followed the adventures of characters in *Minecraft*'s blocky world.

Machinima can be an engaging tool for students. Shakespearean plays, historical events, or anything else that can be told using film can be created as machinima. The book *DIY Media: Creating, Sharing and Learning with New Technologies* (2010) suggested several activities using machinima in the classroom. Students can create a "music video, social commentary, advertisement, drama, or comedy" (Luckman & Potanin, 2010, pp. 155–156). There is an EduMachinima fest at the International Society for Technology in Education (ISTE) Conference, which celebrates students who remix game content as a new media.

Let's Play Videos

As of early 2017, Joseph Garrett (AKA Stampylongnose, or Stampy Cat) had almost 34 million subscribers to his channel. He specializes in a trend called "Let's Play," a variation of machinima that is more commentary-based than story-driven. According to the website Let's Play Archive, people post "screen-shots of themselves playing various old fondly-remembered video games (such as *Oregon Trail* and *Pokémon*) and include their own humorous commentary."

YouTube can be a competitive marketplace—not just for attaining popularity, but also for commerce. When I searched for "*Minecraft*" on the video streaming service, I got more than 150 million results. (One could argue that YouTube is a game; the scoreboard is the total number of sub-scribers and views.) Videos of games help market video games. *Minecraft* has never used traditional advertising such as television commercials. Instead, Let's Play boosts the grassroots following for the game (Goldberg & Larsson, 2013, p. 147).

Jordan Maron—also known as CaptainSparklez—is another YouTube celebrity. In 2017 he had more than 9 million subscribers! The more view-ers that watch CaptainSparklez's Let's Play posts, the more monetized rev-enue Maron earns. Maron's tips on how to play even made their way into a book from Scholastic, *Minecraft: Essential Handbook* (2013). Paul Soares, Jr., who also contributed to the book, hosts several *Minecraft* shows on YouTube from the perspective of a father and a gamer. For more kid-friendly *Minecraft* YouTube stars to view, check out the Resources at the end of Chapter 8.

Let's Play is a way for students to reflect and share what they have learned from problem-solving in video game worlds, as well as to explain what they have created in sandbox games (e.g., *Minecraft*). Let's Play gives students a meaningful space to demonstrate knowledge. Also, the ability to teach and to explain information in an engaging way can make one highly marketable in today's global economy. Job interviews, as well as business meetings, are often conducted via videoconferencing tools including Skype and Google Hangouts.

One of my former students had his father record his *Minecraft* project sim-ply by holding a smartphone camera in front of the computer screen! More advanced users may opt to try screencasting tools—software that records what plays on a computer's screen. There are many options for recording soft-ware, including Bandicam. Keep in mind that screencasting video games can make a school-issued computer lag in performance and speed. It can work better to use lower power, browser-based screencast tools such as Screencast-O-Matic. For tablets, simply take a screenshot (on an iPad, hold the power button and the home button simultaneously). Then import the image into a word processing app—or even iMovie—for postproduction and written reflection. Having students record *Minecraft* worlds is a meaningful authentic assessment.

Modding

In 2013, a young man named Alexander Velicky created an immersive world known as Falskaar. It was an expansion of Bethesda Game Studio's medieval-themed *Elder Scrolls: Skyrim* (2011). He employed over 100 people to record dialogue and to assist in its development (Birnbaum, 2013). Velicky, however, was not an employee of Bethesda—he was a fan creating a "mod," or modification. The Falskaar mod was one of the largest fan-made expansions of all time. It is, in a way, a love letter to the world of *Skyrim*. Of course, it can also be said that the mod was Velicky's résumé to become employed by Bethesda. That plan worked, too—well, sort of. Eventually, Velicky did get a job as a game designer, but he did not take a position with Bethesda. Instead, he formally began his game design career with a competitor, Bungie, maker of the original *Halo* games.

Velicky is part of a large and vibrant community of game "modders." They create and share content for reasons other than the promise of a career in game design. Many, as it would seem, simply love the craft of game design. Video game modding is an extension of hacker culture, whereby "closed" content is opened for all to access (Salen & Zimmerman, 2003). The book *Rules of Play* categorized different types of game mods:

- *Alterations* change the representational or interactive structures of a game
- *Juxtapositions* place unlikely elements together in the same game space
- *Reinventions* more radically redesign the structure of a game. (Salen & Zimmerman, 2003, p. 569)

The Falskaar mod falls under the category of reinvention, adding to the world in the same way a fan fiction adds content to books without the author's direct consent. The other categories, alterations and juxtapositions, are also common in modding and remixing cultures. Fans began to mod digital games because the barriers to entry were lowered as the technology improved.

The history of modding dates back to the early 1990s. Two decades ago, hackers realized that game data were saved in a separate file location than its game engine. Each is built on a framework, like a car's chassis. Examples of game engines include the Unreal Engine, Frostbite, Source, and Unity 3D. The Unreal Engine runs games from competing publishers, such as Warner Brothers Interactive Entertainment's *Batman: Arkham City* (2011) and 2K Games's *Bioshock: Infinite* (2013). A helpful analogy is to think of the engine as an application and the game as a dependent file. The application Microsoft Word is stored on one part of a computer's hard drive, while its documents are saved elsewhere, perhaps in folders. Discovering this file-application relationship meant that fans could mod games. Early mods ranged from changing rules, such as having unlimited weapon ammunition, to adding levels.

The first "viral" mod was Justin Fisher's *Aliens TC*, a remix of *Doom* ("TC" stands for "total conversion," alluding to the complete overhaul of the game's content). *Aliens: TC* was inspired by Fisher's love of James Cameron's film *Aliens* (1986). *Doom* was one of the first 3D game worlds. It was considered to be shockingly violent at the time it was released. It lacked a story structure; the player was dropped in a maze filled with dangerous enemies. The simple mechanic of survival lends itself to artistic modification. Its code was also freely accessible and shared over the emerging Internet. Because *Doom* was a PC game, its code was created separately from its engine. *Doom's* creator, iD's John Carmack, reportedly made the data open and easily accessible (Carmack currently is the Chief Technology Officer for Oculus Rift, the virtual reality company). Basically, he embraced hacker culture. Hackers and modders nicknamed *Doom's* engine a "WAD," meaning "Where's all the data?" ("5 Years of Doom," n.d.). Like modifying a Word document, *Doom* modders simply needed to locate the outside data to make game customizations.

One idea to bring modding into the classroom is through discussion and reflection. For example, in 2014, a mod of *Civilization V* was released to coincide with the FIFA World Cup. It used the nation-building game as a platform to teach about the alleged bribery that takes place when cities vie to host the soccer tournament. The mod, called *FIFA World Cup Resolution*, placed values on migrant workers and cheap laborers as pawns for corrupt nations. Another lesson-ready option is to have students remix games on Gamestar Mechanic or Scratch. They can modify the rules or the scripts. Modding games is a gateway to coding.

Micro-credentials and Learning Pathways

Digital badges in game-based learning recognize the achievement of mastering content or a skill. A digital badge system has three interconnected participants: "the issuer, the earner, and the displayer" (Mozilla Foundation and Peer 2 Peer University, 2012). In a video game, the computer has a clear algorithm that determines when a goal is met and a badge is granted. In the classroom, as opposed to a video game, the teacher is the issuer and the student is the earner. Many website tools are available for teachers to create virtual classrooms, complete with predesigned badge artwork. It is not necessary for a student to accumulate badges in a linear fashion. He or she may—or may not—decide to earn badges in any sequence, even after an activity has ended. Logging onto Khan Academy's Learning Dashboard is helpful example of how this works. On Khan, you will see an integrated badge system geared for self-paced learning at the middle and high school levels.

In the 2014–15 school year I tried digital badges with my middle school students. I began with good intentions, having students codesign badges, which included achievements to discovering errors on websites or turning in work early. It was a total and epic failure. It's not that the class or myself didn't have fun with it, nor did it fail as a motivator. The problem was that students just didn't care. They had apathy to the entire system. Perhaps it was because I had used a standalone website to issue badges. Students never logged in to check or share their displayed badges. If they won a badge, they often did not know it.

As it turned out, digital badges for K12 students are different than those in video games. To learn more, I asked an expert in the field: Noah Geisel. We spoke in March 2016. Geisel is a high school and middle school Spanish teacher, based in Aurora, Colorado. In 2013, he won ACTFL National Language Teacher of the Year. In addition to teaching, Geisel delivers educational technology professional development, and he is the founder of the #BadgechatK12 Twitter chat. He also implemented a district-wide badge system at Aurora and organizes the national Digital Badge Summit.

My first question pertained to my student's disinterest in their earned badges. I wasn't sure what to do. If I put badges on a learning management system, like Moodle, it becomes an extrinsic motivator, a grade. "In the design process, ask, is the badge earner going to care about this?" Geisel began. "It takes time and effort to credential young people. If students don't care, it's not worth badging."

So how can teachers get students to care about badges without it becoming an extrinsic motivator? Geisel first explained the idea of equivalence. Earned badges in one teacher's class often do not carry over to another's. Digital badges in school are not longitudinal. "Badges that are really awesome in one classroom have no carry over meaning in the next classroom," he said. "Students don't value it when they move classrooms or grades, or if they transfer to a different school." Geisel recommended teachers coordinate and work together, to set egos aside and to consider the "value proposition of the badge, with equivalence built in."

Geisel starts with areas of commonalities, like the ISTE educational technology standards, which are cross-curricular, or the P21 Framework for 21st-century skills. In the Aurora Public School District, teachers framed badges around five 21st-century skills, as prescribed in the Colorado state standards. These included collaboration, critical thinking, information literacy, invention, and self-direction. Each skill can be earned in any content area and grade, from Spanish class to physical education class. On a more granular level, Geisel reviewed what each strand should look like at each grade level.

There are valuable skills that are not mutually exclusive to content areas. In Aurora, these became "Journey Badges" and "Summit Badges." The idea is that learning is a journey, which eventually leads to a summit. At the K12 level, badges are not rewards in a game—they are micro-credentials. In science class, a student who achieves invention skills gets noticed and credentialed. "Part of the idea is not to compete with grades, we intentionally avoid it," Geisel said.

In the approach to digital badges, there are two camps. One is to implement badges using the lens of gamification, as a reward, like in a game. The other is to use badges to micro-credential students, like what Aurora does. "The skills that really matter for colleges—and, more important employers—are invisible on transcripts," Geisel explained. "They are also really difficult to verify on a resume. Are you responsible? Having an A in AP biology doesn't tell me that. Are you collaborative? Are you a critical thinker? Can you create something from scratch? Are you a lifelong learner? Do you read things when nobody's looking?" Micro-credentials are effective when they are linked to evidence. Geisel continued:

> There's a huge part of student's narrative about who they are as achievers. Micro-credentials fill in that gap. That digital component is that evidence can be attached, so there is a validation component. LinkedIn's recommendations are kind of a joke. Writing on a resume "I am collaborative" is not verifiable. With a digital badge we can attach evidence—all of a sudden, that credential is verifiable. I don't have to take [the applicant's] word for it. I can click on her badge, view her evidence, and see that she has demonstrated that on this occasion, she has a skill set I'm seeking as an employer. Attaching to evidence gives meaning for the outside audience.

With most gamification models, the audience for earned badges is the student, their peers, or possibly their parents. Using a digital micro-credential lens, the audience is transformed. The audience is outside the walls of schools or school district. "You're going to share this with colleges or employers, when you're trying to convince someone to hire you," Geisel said. "There's a broader audience."

Thousands of students earned open badges in Aurora over the past few years. To design badges, Geisel recommended the website Badge Canvas Digital Me (linked at the end of this chapter). The district adheres to Mozilla's Open Badges Initiative (OBI) specifications spelled out by Mozilla's working group. "It [Badge Canvas Digital Me] asks you to think about the audience, who will validate the badge?" Geisel said. "Our Journey Badges fit a pathway to Summit Badges. Any system with leveling needs pathways, how badges connect."

The Summit Badges are where Geisel focuses time and energy now. His team signed up local employers to be endorsers. "Students can apply for a badge endorsed by a local employer," he said. An informational literacy Summit Badge could include a ride-along with the TV production crew to Coor's Field to conduct behind-the-scenes tour of a Colorado Rocky's baseball game. "The value proposition is that we recognize your asset and lend the weight of social capital of our brand for this badge endorsement."

At Aurora, badges are not part of a gamified system; rather, they are a micro-credential identifying smaller steps students take as lifelong learners. Locally, in a classroom, teachers have options about badge delivery. They can manually issue a badge and attach the evidence. Or teachers can e-mail a claim code to the student. When the student clicks the link, they must attach the evidence, and then the teacher clicks to approve it. It is the evidence piece that adds value, making students care.

Conclusions and Takeaways

Gamers learn and participate together in online communities of practice. This is an example of situated learning. Placing students in authentic settings (e.g., eSports, machinima, and modding communities) can teach skills not ordinarily taught in schools. Doing so gives students an opportunity to engage in storytelling that interests them. Furthermore, it turns students into creators of digital content, rather than consumers.

Learning in a digital informal setting is often personalized. This is a result of adaptive algorithms that can automatically predict and level up learning.

No technology can replace a teacher. Digital badges are an increasingly common approach to certify personalized learning. They create visible career and college pathways. Badges exist in some city programs, museums, and cultural centers. To be most effective, intrinsic learning must come first and then be acknowledged with a digital badge.

Lesson Plan Ideas

Design a Badge System: Digital badges are used in games and websites to acknowledge accomplishments. Students can design a badge system for a historical figure's life. Mix in geo-location badges (such as those awarded on mobile apps such as Foursquare, Yelp, and Facebook location "check-ins") with badges for achievements. For example, what badges would George Washington earn? For checking in at Valley Forge (geo-location badge), attacking the Hessians? The badge should have a spirit of "fun" in its title (e.g., for George Washington—"Un-merry X-mas, Hessians!") and a few sentences describing how the badge is issued (e.g., for George Washington, mention what he would need to accomplish to earn the badge; in this case, for leading an attack on the Hessians after crossing Delaware). Steps to complete the project: Go to www.MakeBadg.es; type the label for the badge's name; find a clip art image appropriate for the badge, save it and upload it to MakeBadges; download the completed badge; add it to a document with a caption.

Game Critic: Preview articles on *Game Informer* magazine's website and have students write their own reviews of their favorite video games. The reading level may be higher than you think! This lesson meets Common Core State Standards for English language arts. Common Core State Standards for English language arts apply.

Game Wikis: Construct a project-based, character web project. It should be framed around creating additional characters for an existing (or invented) video game series via downloadable content. The culminating activity is uploading the student-created character pages on a wiki. Common Core State Standards for English language arts apply, as well as whichever discipline and content area this activity is modified to fit. Here are links to my student's finished wiki pages: farber7th.pbworks.com/ACRen1 and farber7th.pbworks.com/ACRen2

"*Me-chinima*": iMovie for Mac or a green screen iPad application, like Do Ink, which enables students to use any footage as a backdrop. Be sure to use a green screen (fabric or poster paper works, too) behind the student. Next, add in game footage on the application's film editor.

Modding 2048: The popular number sliding game and mobile app can be played for free online—http://gabrielecirulli.github.io/2048 (*2048* has a core mechanic closely resembling *Threes!*). Students can mod their own version—https://www.udacity.com/course/ud248. Udacity, the online class provider, suggested making a mod using U.S. presidents. A better mod is one that fits the mechanic of combinations and/or geometric math with content, such as chemical bonds in the *Isotopic 256* remix—http://jamesdonnelly.github.io/Isotopic256—and *Circle of Fifths*, which teaches musical progressions—http://calebhugo.com/musical-games-interact-with-sound/2048-circle-of-fifths

Spec Scripts: Many video games feature cut scenes, or short interludes between levels. Students can act out cut scenes from games relating to content. As an exercise in transmedia storytelling, students can create a "spec script" using the characters and situations from a game. This is a popular genre on fanfiction.net, where users write and share episodic stories. Common Core State Standards for English language arts apply, as well as whichever discipline and content area this activity is modified to fit. Preview samples for appropriateness—https://www.fanfiction.net/game

Viral Videos: You will create viral marketing campaign using concepts from the TED Talk: *Why Videos Go Viral*: https://www.ted.com/talks/kevin_allocca_why_videos_go_viral. Students should screencast a game (like *Minecraft* or use the record function built into Scratch. Step-by-step is here: http://scratched.gse.harvard.edu/stories/new-scratch-feature-record-project-video) video using humor, hashtags, or other trends that go viral. Videos should be posted on YouTube.

Walkthroughs: Write a walkthrough of a game you play. Or create a walkthrough about an original game. Like Steve Isaacs' class, use SnapGuide for students to publish work. Common Core State Standards for English language arts apply, as well as whichever discipline and content area this activity is modified to fit.

Games

Aliens TC—http://www.moddb.com/mods/aliens-tc/downloads/aliens-tc-full

Dota 2, massive online battle arena game—http://blog.dota2.com/?l=english

Doom mod from co-creator John Romero, published in 2016—https://www.dropbox.com/s/2x2ee3ı51986dkt/c1m8b.zip?dl=0

Falskaar Mod for Skyrim—http://www.nexusmods.com/skyrim/mods/37994

FIFA World Cup Host Resolution Mod for Civilization V—http://steamcommunity.com/sharedfiles/filedetails/?id=286563387

Galactic Hot Dogs is a virtual world game on Poptropica, as well as a free, episodic virtual world from Funbrain. A graphic novel with text, it is an engaging work of transmedia storytelling—http://www.funbrain.com/galactichotdogs

Kongregate Game Community (be sure to review game appropriateness first)—http://www.kongregate.com

League of Legends, massive online battle arena game—http://na.leagueoflegends.com

Steam Workshop, a place to share and play fan-created mods—http://steamcommunity.com/workshop

Undertale is a role-playing game with a loyal community of practice, which extends to fan art on websites like Pixilart—http://undertale.com

Resources

Anna, the award-winning machinima film—http://youtu.be/bKEr5RRKoO4

Badge Canvas Digital Me—http://www.digitalme.co.uk/badges

BadgeChatK12—www.BadgeChatK12.com

Bandicam, a popular screencasting tool specializing in *Minecraft* videos—http://www.bandicam.com

Board Game Geek, the ultimate non-digital gamer community—http://boardgamegeek.com

CaptainSparklez *Minecraft* Let's Play channel—www.captainsparklezblog.com and http://www.youtube.com/user/CaptainSparklez (preview videos for content appropriateness first)

Camtasia screen recorder—http://www.techsmith.com/camtasia.html

Confronting the Challenges of Participatory Cultures, by Henry Jenkins et al.—http://mitpress.mit.edu/sites/default/files/titles/free_download/9780262513623_Confronting_the_Challenges.pdf

DeviantART, fanart (fan-made art) and "cosplay" (portmanteau of "costume play")—http://www.deviantart.com

Digital Badge Summit—http://badge.aurorak12.org/

FanFiction.net's game-related stories—https://www.fanfiction.net/game

FRAPS Game Capture screencasting tool—http://fraps.com

HASTAC, digital media learning—http://www.hastac.org

High School Starleague, resources to start an eSports after-school club—http://hsstarleague.com

IGN community: video game cheats, walkthroughs, wikis, and guides—http://www.ign.com

Khan Academy's Learning Dashboard—http://www.khanacademy.org

League of Legends after school eSports club—http://promo.oce.leagueoflegends.com/en/high-school-clubs/teacher-resource.html

Let's Playlist, wiki of game developers friendly to LP producers—letsplaylist.wikia.com

Let's Play Guide for Newbies—http://letsplay.wikia.com/wiki/LP_guide_for_newbies

MakeBadges, design your own badges. It's easy for students to use, too—http://www.makebadg.es/badge.html#

Machinima—https://www.machinima.com

Major League Gaming—http://tv.majorleaguegaming.com

OpenBadges, learning pathways portal from the Mozilla Foundation—http://openbadges.org

Pixilart is a social community of pixel art, much of which is game-related—http://www.pixilart.net

Real-Life Mario Kart, fan film of Nintendo's Mario Kart, in the real world—http://youtu.be/-h4zTEwgCpQ

Red vs. Blue, machinima in the virtual world of *Halo*—http://www.youtube.com/show/redvsblue

Screencast-O-Matic, screencasting tool for Let's Play videos—http://www.screencast-o-matic.com

SnapGuide is where students can publish step-by-step guides—https://snapguide.com

Source Filmmaker (SFM), a free, robust machinima tool—http://www.source-filmmaker.com

Super League Gaming—www.superleague.com

T Is for Transmedia: Learning through Transmedia Play, Cooney Center report, with an introduction from Henry Jenkins—http://www.joanganzcooneycenter.org/publication/t-is-for-transmedia

Twitch, video gaming as a spectator sport—http://www.twitch.tv

Wikia—A wiki for movies, film, video games, and other popular cultural topics—http://www.wikia.com

· 1 6 ·

GAMES TO CHANGE THE WORLD

Social impact games are a genre that seeks to affect positive changes in society through play. These games are not necessarily designed for teaching; rather, the goal is to enable players to have empathy about social issues. As a social studies teacher, I have found that they are effective in putting students into authentic, problem-solving scenarios. In some instances, students discover that there may be no solution to certain problems.

One of the first social impact games, *Darfur is Dying* has a message that still resonates today. My students virtually forage for water while outrunning the militia, as well as see daily life in a refugee camp. In *Quandary*, they encounter ethical dilemmas, or quandaries. To play, you assemble a team to colonize a new planet. Other social impact games to play in a classroom include the web-based *The Migrant Trail*, which puts players in two roles: a border patrol agent, and then as a migrant. All of these games have enjoyed recognition from Games for Change.

Game designer Jesse Schell refers to the social impact or serious games as "transformational." His studio, Schell Games, moved from creating only entertainment titles to creating both educational and transformational games. To Schell, transformational games are "designed to change a person." When we spoke in 2014, he elaborated:

I like the term better than "serious games," which is a broken term. I've been prosely-tizing a bit that serious games imply a serious goal: If you are having fun, you're doing it wrong. I'm from an entertainment background; entertainment is a serious business. From the realm of art or entertainment, saying their work isn't serious is insulting. The goal isn't to be serious, but to transform people. Most of the design failings of transformative games happen when they spend too much time on the game's content, or the information they want to come across, and not enough on how they want to transform a person.

An example of a transformational game is *Half the Game*, published to raise Americans' awareness of international women's rights. It is based on a docu-mentary that detailed the oppression of women in some developing countries. Related to the Half the Sky movement, the United States Agency for Inter-national Development (USAID) released three mobile games: the family-planning awareness titles *9-Minutes* and *Family Choices* and the digestive health game *Worm Attacks*.

This chapter details how to integrate social impact games. Each tran-scends the genre of first-person shooters and is an immersive, deep experience. I sat down with several developers, and I also had the opportunity to speak on a panel at the Games for Change Festival in 2016. I share that experience, as well as the meaningful games that were showcased. After all, a successful game delivers its message through both aesthetics and mechanics.

Mary Flanagan's Tiltfactor

Pox: Save the People is a simple board game in which "infected" red poker chips need to be surrounded by "vaccinated" blue chips. Aside from the tabletop version, it is also available for free for iPad. *Pox* is a product of Mary Flanagan's Tiltfactor studio, at Dartmouth University. In the game, the core mechanic actually serves a dual role: as a player's actions and as a device to carry a mes-sage. Playing *Pox* elegantly teaches the importance of vaccination circles.

Flanagan is an artist, a game designer, a professor, and a leader in the space of social impact games. In 2014, MIT Press published her book *Values at Play in Digital Games*. She won the Vanguard Award at the 13th Annual Games for Change Festival in 2016 for her contribution to the field. We spoke in April 2016.

Flanagan grew up in a household that played all kinds of games: Atari 2600 console games, family board games after dinner, and at family gatherings. "Everyone knew their role, even when we were socially awkward," she said. "It can be a framework for conversation." In graduate school, Flanagan studied film. Soon after, she was designing interactive learning games for a company that made content for Discovery Channel's website. She began to wonder how people were actually learning from the games the company made. How much serious content can fit into a playful space? "This predated user research and games and learning, in the early 1990s," she said.

Flanagan started Tiltfactor in 2003, while at Dartmouth. The lab is her way of continuing to ask deep questions about games, as well as a space to create new models about the social impact of games. Flanagan used to think that playing transformational games had to about serious topics, with the goal of either raising awareness or starting conversations. "I guess this is still valid, but lately I've been thinking about transformation or psychological change the players may have and collect evidence on that," she said. "There are some interesting things that emerge in formal research studies you would never get as a research designer watching a playtest." In other words, watching a player's reaction and gathering playtest feedback paints an incomplete picture of whether one's view on a social issue is affected. She continued:

> When you do a psychological study, what you think is going on is not going on. What goes on in our minds is not what we always share with each other. Or it may take time to process, or it may be processing in our minds. For example, things like social biases and stereotypes, which may be meta-level things, are not necessarily a topic of social change. When we think about poverty, race, gender, class, or any ways that people categorize each other or treat each other unfairly, this kind of happens everywhere. It's how bullying happens, how people are graded, funded—it's such a foundational thing. I've been focusing on the unconscious processes. For me a social impact game is what's the evidence of social change. How do you document social change? What are the big picture shifts that happen with players to make the world a better place?

Going beyond playtest feedback, Tiltfactor asks these big questions. For example, how does the act of playing become the meaning in the game? "As opposed to reading a text, enacting a mechanic that has a meaningful message is really hard to do," Flanagan explained. "The trick is to not message so much with a game."

To illustrate her point, Flanagan played Tiltfactor's card game *Buffalo* with me over Skype. A name-dropping game for ages 16 and up, large groups of people can play at the same time. In the game you have two cards with descriptions on them. The goal is to name someone real, living, or dead who matches the criteria on the set of cards. *Buffalo* is a transformational game that doesn't condescend with its messaging. "Many people are actually willing to buy interventions for their family," she said. *Buffalo* is available commercially, at retailers including Barnes & Noble. "It has to be fun as a game first."

First, she drew two cards: "punk" and "doctor." Simultaneously we responded House, the cranky doctor from the eponymously named Fox television show. Next came "Hispanic" and "student." She offered the cartoon character Diego. Then we drew "stunning" and "movie director," with Angelina Jolie being an obvious answer. But then came "Iranian" and "private investigator." We were stumped—we were "buffaloed." When a player is buffaloed, they must add two more cards to their deck. Adding cards continued until we can find a combination emerges from the cards in hand. The act of picking and choosing from those cards becomes a point of discussion. The more difficult it gets to arrive at a combination, the more points the player can earn. We finally pulled two cards from our growing hand: "lunatic" and "bully." We both selected politicians.

The conversation is actually the game. "The game operates on dual levels," Flanagan explained. "When you don't know an Iranian private investigator, you Google it at the conscious level. This leads to an unconscious reworking pathways of how stereotypes are made." *Buffalo* is actually a game about expanding social identity complexity, which is *how* people stereotype one another. Because psychologists can measure people's social identity complexity, players can be tested on their biases before and after play. Another way to measure people's biases is the universal orientation scale, which *Buffalo* plays into. Flanagan continued:

> At the gym the other night, I saw women's college basketball on TV. There were "fun facts" about the players, like "I'm also a figure skater" or "I am a part time chef." Social identity complexity is the stereotype is that it is okay that they play sports, but they also do something else. It's the dumb jock stereotype. If I tell you I am an artist, but I then tell you I really like roller derby and I trade stocks on weekend, the combinations change your stereotype model of an artist who maybe wears a beret and listens to jazz.

Expanding people's social identity complexity is one way to get rid of stereotypes. "Playing *Buffalo* for 20 minutes lowers racism and starts this conversation," Flanagan said. "No one ever thinks it's a pedagogical game when they pick it up. They think it's a fun party game." For Flanagan, this is the way "games for change" need to go. "The game shouldn't need to run in a supervised or managed situation (like a school). It should be 'out in the wild,' with families. It needs to stand on its own to embody that conversation."

Awkward Moment is another commercially sold card game from Tiltfactor. It shares an *Apples to Apples* mechanic. To play, you share awkward stories from your life. "I got gum stuck in my hair," Flanagan began. "I waved to my friend, then I realized it was a stranger. It's about dork moves." Mixed in the *Awkward Moment* card deck are serious topics, like a girl who is teased and called a terrorist because of her last name. "We studied and mixed in the offensive with the dorky," she said. "Then we ask what would you do?" *Awkward Moment* is geared to middle school. There is also a grown-up version, called *Awkward Moment at Work*.

Flanagan next shared an unpublished study from Gina Roussos, a graduate student in Yale University's Social Psychology program. It pertained to the online poverty simulator *Spent* (linked at the end of this chapter). In it, players take on the role of a homeless person presented with a series of difficulty choices. "It turned out that playing *Spent* did nothing to increase empathy. It actually lowered empathy for those who were already empathetic," Flanagan explained. "It was flat or lowered empathy." Players didn't see characters; rather, they saw hard choices. According to Roussos, the author of the study:

> The experience of playing a game differs from the experience of watching a film or reading a book. When I'm playing a game, I feel like I have complete control over my outcomes. I click on Door A instead of Door B, and I find a treasure chest full of jewels. I found that treasure because I choose Door A. This feeling of control over one's outcomes is called personal agency. The belief that people in general have personal agency is a central component of the American ideology called meritocracy, and it's highly correlated with anti-poor attitudes. (2016, para. 6)

In other words, *because* there were choices, playing the game made empathetic people less empathetic. "There is a sense of promise because it's a game," Flanagan said. "We transfer onto poor people that they have choices." Roussos has since verified this after observing a group watch game play, thus pushing aside agency over decisions. "When people merely watch a screen recording of this game, they show all of the effects the game creators intended— more empathy and more liking. Watching the game removes that feeling of agency, letting the effects of perspective taking shine through" (Roussos, 2016, para. 1).

The value of using games to teach empathy is in the discussions mediated by a teacher. To this end, teachers and students can use Tiltfactor's *Grow-a-Game* (free on iPad or as a printable via downloadable PDFs). It was developed along with the *Values at Play* book. To play, draw from the different suites of values (e.g., honesty) and games (e.g., checkers) and then brain-storm ideas. Like *Buffalo*, the idea is to start conversations about larger val-ues. Let's say you draw a value card that reads "sustainability and access to basic goods." Then you draw a game card. "I got the video game *Portal*," Flanagan said. "How would I change *Portal* to support this value? Would I add in a trading mechanic?" Breaking mental models is how the game encour-ages original ideas. "Human values are used as an innovation tool," Flanagan continued. "It's a great start for people nervous about working with games in the classroom."

Mission US

For the past few years, my students have played *Mission US: For Crown or Col-ony*, set in pre-Revolutionary Boston. That first mission came out in 2008—ancient history in the educational gaming market. The second title, *Flight to Freedom*, was about the Underground Railroad, and has met with some con-troversy (discussed later in this section). That mission unfolds on the perilous trip runaway slaves took to the free Northern states. In *A Cheyenne Odyssey*, the player takes on the role of Little Fox, a young Native American boy. The team collaborated with advisors from the Northern Cheyenne Reservation to create an authentic experience. More recent missions include *City of Immi-grants* and an upcoming exploration of the Dust Bowl and Great Depression.

 Mission US games are simple to roll out in a class and works in a com-puter browser. Students can create usernames and passwords without e-mail addresses or personal information. The purpose of the accounts is to create a save point for play to continue from home. By talking to teachers, the *Mission US* team discovered the need for smaller games that don't take long to play. A 40-hour game isn't feasible for a teacher who is required to teach 350 years of American history. Everything is playable on a computer's browser, and no downloads or installations are required. *Mission US* has videos to help teach-ers implement the game.

 I met with the series' design team, David Langendoen and Spencer Grey, both partners at Electric Funstuff in New York City (Grey has since left the firm). Our interview took place in May 2014. I also met with Leah Potter. She was previously with the American Social History Project and now works at Electric Funstuff. Also in attendance were Bill Tally and Jim Diamond from the Education Development Center's Center for Children and Technology, and Jill Peters and Chris Czajk from Thirteen/WNET, part of the Corporation for Public Broadcasting. Peters's role is to connect all of the pieces of the *Mission US* projects together, especially with fundraising.

Mission US games focus on social history, rather than political history. They are not just about specific events, but also about the experiences people had. Unlike the game *Civilization*, which remixes history, *Mission US* has a rule that what has happened cannot be changed. The choices must then involve a character's personal interests. These include emotional decisions and romantic involvements. Causal loops grew in complexity with every added mission in the series. *Mission 1* is the simplest, with the smallest number of cause-and-effect loops. For example, angering a character can result in a lost round. The short-term penalty is to scrub an outhouse, followed by a quick return to the main storyline. *Mission 2*, set during the Civil War, is more sophisticated and features a badge system. The badges you earn tell a story at the end. In *Mission 3*, there are even more options in dialogue and actions, including ethical choices. Players can decide whether to be brave. For authenticity, the reward system is based on the virtues of the Cheyenne people, such as bravery and generosity. The payoff for taking chances is delayed. In the Battle of Little Big Horn, survival is heavily dependent on whether the player was wise, brave, or generous. *Mission 4* is about immigration in New York, and *Mission 5* is about the Dust Bowl and the Great Depression.

The Education Development Center conducted research and evaluation on *Mission US* games. It studied students' prior knowledge and assumptions about history and gameplay. The goal was to see where games fit in a classroom that has multiple layers of expectations. The *Mission US* curriculum serves to connect player decisions to historical events. The kind of history a game covers determines the causes and effects it can present. What would a young person's perspective be? What kind of actions could a teenager take? The major national events in the *Mission US* games happen in the background of the narrative. (Conversely, in *Assassin's Creed III*, the player rides along with Paul Revere and is at the Boston Massacre. So much U.S. history is intertwined with game missions that the game was criticized as being like *Forrest Gump*.)

Langendoen explained how *Mission 3* was originally to be about the railroad expansion. The issue was player agency. Is the player a 14-year-old Irish surveyor or a teenage Chinese immigrant? What actions could he or she realistically take? Player agency is also a concern when trying to elicit emotions such as empathy. It was at that moment that the Native American theme was chosen. A 12-year-old Cheyenne boy character gives players more freedom and choice. Teachers should consider agency when designing an authentic project-based learning activity.

Games empower people—often more so than real life can. This helps to make the experience fun. A player's character may be more skilled or luckier than others. In a historical game, however, power needs to be balanced with realism. In *Mission 1: For Crown or Colony*, the design team initially assumed that the player would want to be a Patriot. This notion turned out to be a misconception; not everyone in colonial Boston wanted to get involved in a revolution. The team decided to intentionally make the lead character, Royce, a little dislikable. Constance, the Loyalist (a colonist siding with Britain) was more sympathetic. She was introduced as she searched for her lost dog. Narrative storytelling built empathy for her character. (The team pointed out that there was a real newspaper clipping from the time about a missing dog. The primary source document is included in the game.)

Students project themselves onto characters. The teacher must "unpack" these experiences. "The game without the conversation about what happened diminishes the experiences," Langendoen explained. "The *Mission US* games are really conversation starters." Then he shared how teachers assess student progress in *Mission 1*. "They ask the class: How many have had tea with Constance?" This is a reference asking who went against the political affiliations of the time. Remember: Royce is a Patriot and Constance is a Loyalist.

The game teaches consequences by gamifying personal choices. I asked the design team about "fail states"—the consequences from losing in the game. Langendoen explained that there was controversy over losing due to the fact that class times are typically brief. Starting over from scratch isn't feasible in a 40-minute bell schedule. In *Mission 1*, consequences mean Royce has more chores to do. After that, the player can keep going.

In *Mission 2: Flight to Freedom*, the player is Lucy, a slave. In parts of that game the designers *wanted* students to fail. The design team told me in 2014 that they wanted to elicit feelings of frustration. The escape from the slave plantation must be difficult to do the first time. About 75% of players failed the first time. The game then "rewinds" the player to the start to try again. When they initially playtested, an unintended issue occurred: Students weren't resisting—ever. More feedback was added, along with a badge system to relay the message that choosing resistance is an acceptable choice. Also in that mission, Lucy has opportunities to sabotage her master's dress, which has consequences a few steps later.

Although *Mission 2* was released in 2012, it garnered controversy in 2015 when teacher Rafranz Davis authored a blog post about the "gamification" of slavery. "The slave mission was built on the idea that users could 'understand what a real slave felt' while walking around in Lucy's shoes," she wrote. "Unfortunately this is also where the game failed because one cannot simulate the emotional scars of slavery" (2015). Davis' post went viral. WNET—Electric Funstuff's producer—responded with an editorial. Published on EdSurge; the response cited several social historians who advised the design of the game. The statement read:

> The mission portrays enslaved African Americans with agency and personal power (even when social, economic, and political power was non-existent), and as central actors in their own destinies. Our goal is for all students to develop a greater respect for African Americans' struggle and African American history as a part of American history. Although we regret to hear that some people have found the game to be problematic, we stand by it. (Specter, 2015)

Of course, the game is not intended to be "fun." In this case, the lesson is not about the game, but the discussions that follow (similar to Mary Flanagan's *Buffalo* and *Awkward Moment*, described earlier). When my 7th grade students played *Mission 1: For Crown or Colony*, it was part of a learning trajectory. (By virtue of the curriculum, we never play *Mission 2*. The American Civil War is covered in the 8th grade.) First students played the game. Play was followed by whole class discussions and written reflections. Then they played *Chronicles of the Time Society: Independence*, the text adventure I codesigned with Erin Hoffman-John (see Chapter 12). Finally, students had an opportunity to choose battles in the American Revolution, and then write about those events using a choice-driven story tool, like Twine (see Chapter 13). I do not depend on a video game to teach historical empathy. Similarly, I would never assume that player agency in *Spent* informs empathy for the poor. The power of teacher is to contextualize the game. So, yes, Davis has a point, but so does the team at Electric Funstuff and WNET. Games should not run a class—the teacher should.

Never Alone (Kisima Ingitchuna)

E-Line Media is a company with diverse connections: Alaska native leaders, game designers, and learning scientists (from Arizona State University and the Center for Games and Impact). Other partners include the social impact game *Half the Sky* and the video game authoring tool *Gamestar Mechanic*. It also cosponsors the National STEM Video Game Challenge (discussed in Chapter 14). I spoke with Alan Gershenfeld, the cofounder of E-Line Media, in May 2014. "E-Line Media's service leverages game design, game mechanics, and other learning modalities," he said. "It's not like we just build games. We also build ecosystems, services, creating communities around games used for trajectories."

E-Line began working with the Cook Inlet Tribal Council in Anchorage, Alaska. The Council formed Upper One Games. The Council was seeking to change education by infusing its values of resiliency into comprehensive prod-ucts. It is a partner in *Never Alone (Kisima Ingitchuna)*, a puzzle game about Iñupiat folklore. *Never Alone* won an award for best game at the 12th Annual Games for Change Festival, in 2015.

I played *Never Alone*, along with my son, on our Xbox One. A side-scrolling platform game (like *Super Mario Bros.*), it is a hero's journey tale that weaves in the oral legends on the Iñupiat people. According to myth, northern lights in the arctic night sky can kidnap people. As a result, the Aurora Bore-alis is one of the enemies in the game. As challenges are achieved, recorded video interviews with the Iñupiat are unlocked. There is a cooperative mode; one player can be the heroine, Nuna, while the other can play as the arctic fox. Like other role-playing games (*Pandemic*, the board game, or the LEGO video games), each player has a power the other does not. Only the arctic fox can jump, and Nuna has the ability to throw the bola, a traditional Iñupiat weapon made of a rope and balls.

In June 2016, *Never Alone: Ki Edition* was released ("Ki" is Iñupiaq for "Let's Go!"). It is a mobile version of the console and computer game, scaled for tablets and smartphones. Nuna and her fox are in this version too, which now has a touch screen interface. And, like the original version, cultural insight videos can be unlocked along the Nuna's hero's journey. The mobile version is available in several languages, which enables the Cook Inlet people to share their stories with more of the world.

Papers, Please

Set in 1982, *Papers, Please* shares the visual aesthetics reflect games from that era. It is playable on computer and iPad. In the game, you assume the role of immigration officer at the border of a fictional Communist country, Arstotzka. Rules for immigration—including requiring entrance tickets and passports—constantly change, or level up, until mastery is reached. Player decisions in *Papers, Please* are not black or white. Ethical quandaries are front and center. You can accept bribes or let in "less desirable" immigrants. When I first played, my character was repeatedly penalized for allowing immigrants with falsified documents to enter. Penalties led to me not being able to cover my rent or heating bill, which resulted in my character's wife, son, uncle, and mother-in-law getting sick. I was eventually jailed for unpaid debts and my family was sent away.

When students play video games, they project themselves onto characters. The teacher's role is to contextualize and facilitate discussions on story content *and* game decisions. *Papers, Please*'s "mature content" can be toggled off to make the game more appropriate for school settings. As with any media, it is best for teachers to preview materials first. For a deeper understanding of the interplay of ethics and video games, I highly recommend viewing Nick Fortugno's Well Played talk about *Papers, Please*: http://youtu.be/kQR3xh-C9hJA. After viewing it with your class, facilitate a discussion about morals and dilemmas.

Gone Home

A commercial, off-the-shelf game, *Gone Home* has won several awards, including recognition from *Entertainment Weekly*, *USA Today*, *Polygon*, and *PC Gamer* (*Gone Home*, 2014). It won the Game of the Year award at the 11th Annual Games for Change Festival. *Gone Home* is a single player, "interactive exploration simulator," set in 1995 (*Gone Home*, 2014). It includes a simple point-and-click interface, similar to the computer games played during that time period (e.g., *Myst*). The game's narrative begins in the middle of the night, during a storm. Players take the role of Katie Greenbriar, who returned home from a year backpacking in Europe. She is greeted with a note on a locked front door. Once inside, the house appears suddenly abandoned—frozen in time, all family members nowhere to be seen. What follows is a deep exploration of the house, piecing together clues about the whereabouts of the Greenbriar family. With the mood and tone of a horror game, the story is actually about a family's dysfunction.

Teacher Paul Darvasi uses the game as a text, similar to how a book or film would be studied. In November 2015, he told me how he created assessments that "in line with the typical high school lit class—but with some adjustments to honor, or to acknowledge, the fact that it is a game, and not a work of literature." The entire unit was housed on the school's learning management system; the game was installed on each student's computer. Darvasi created Word documents for students, which asked them to record game interactions and provide supporting screenshot evidence. The in-game screenshots later becomes the unit's culminating activity, which are student-led presentations. Each student had a subtopic: character tracking; 1995 archeology; video game references; and *riot grrrl* references—which prompted students "to consider why Sam [the protagonist] was drawn to a west-coast feminist punk movement" (Darvasi, 2014). Each of his lessons includes traditional formative assessments, like completion of charts and answers to open-ended questions. For more on Darvasi's implementation and assessment strategies, see the links and resources at the conclusion of this chapter.

Life Is Strange

Like *Gone Home*, *Life is Strange* is a narrative-driven game that can be read like a traditional text. Set in a private art school in the northwest, the player takes on the role of Max Caulfield, a budding photographer. Caulfield has a mysterious power to rewind time. When she does, there is a ripple effect on subsequent events. The game covers complex topics, like bullying, teen suicide, and fleeting friendships. The mechanics include puzzles, but mostly interactive fiction conversation trees. Players are presented with a series of multiple-choice responses that either have innocuous results or deeper consequences. Much of the game plays like a movie, and an emotional soundtrack drives it all. *Life is Strange* is one of the best video games I have ever played. It is more of an experience than a game, one that sticks to you long after it concludes.

There is coarse language and some difficult themes; however, it is so powerful that I would be remiss to not recommend it. Play first. Consider securing permission slips from parents. While the game is rated M for "mature" language and content, keep in mind that there are comparable young adult books. I would use this game with older students, at least in high school. The game takes place over five episodes, which can be downloaded individually or purchased together. *Life is Strange* has a loyal community, which shares fan art and stories about issues pertaining to adolescence. In 2016, publisher Square Enix (the independent French studio DONTNOD designed it) partnered with the Parent Advocacy Coalition for Educational Rights (PACER) for an anti-bullying campaign (hashtag #EverydayHeroes, a reference to the photography contest in the game).

That Dragon, Cancer

Video games can engage with more emotions than just fun and thrills. One of the most moving games in that respect is *That Dragon, Cancer*. It is a game that "acts as a living painting; a poem; an interactive retelling of Ryan and Amy Green's experience raising their son Joel, a 4-year-old currently fighting his third year of terminal cancer" (Green, 2014). Joel succumbed to cancer on March 13, 2014, before the project was completed. According to a feature article in *Wired* magazine:

> Green's idea to make a videogame about Joel came to him in church, as he reflected on a harrowing evening a couple of years earlier when Joel was dehydrated and diarrheal, unable to drink anything without vomiting it back up, feverish, howling, and inconsolable, no matter how Green tried to soothe him. He had made a few games since then and had been thinking about mechanics, the rules that govern how a player interacts with and influences the action on the screen. "There's a process you develop as a parent to keep your child from crying, and that night I couldn't calm Joel," Green says. "It made me think, 'This is like a game where the mechanics are subverted and don't work.'" (Tanz, 2016, para. 8)

That Dragon, Cancer is emotionally arduous to play. At the 13th Annual Games for Change Festival, Nick Fortugno led a "Well Played" critique on his experience playing the *That Dragon, Cancer*. He noted that, because of the game's topic, not too many people have actually played the game. As the father of a 6 year old, it seemed too jarring for me to play. Early in the game you must console Joel from crying. Nothing works; all of the interactions in the game have no consequences. The game is also the subject of a documentary, *Thank You for Playing*. It is an empathy-art game about the most serious of topics.

Games for Change Festival

Since 2004, Games for Change has sponsored a festival in New York City. Its mission is simple: to catalyze social impact through digital games. Games for Change is a relatively small nonprofit. Its philosophy is that games—like other art forms—can be more than just for entertainment. Games for Change celebrates artistic achievement in video games the way the Sundance Film Festival does for independent films. Previous keynote speakers have included Supreme Court Justice (and iCivics founder) Sandra Day O'Connor, former

Vice President Al Gore, and Valve Corporation founder Gabe Newell (Valve published *Portal 2* and runs the Steam platform). When there, Newell announced Teach with Portals, the initiative to bring the physics puzzler into the classroom.

I spoke with Asi Burak, former President of Games for Change, prior to attending the 11th Annual Festival, in New York City. We spoke prior to the festival, in March 2014. Games for Change stemmed from the Serious Games Initiative. (Burak, like Schell, told me that he does not care for the moniker "serious games.") The first event, about a decade ago, had about 40 people in attendance. It was held in Washington, D.C. The past few years have seen an increased profile. The current Advisory Board and the Board of Directors members include James Paul Gee, Jane McGonigal, and Ken Weber from Zynga.org.

Before Games for Change, Burak helped develop the game *Peacemaker* (2007). It was an early example of a social impact game designed for general consumption, not necessarily for use in schools. *Peacemaker* is essentially two games, with two different points of view: Israeli and Palestinian. "It was powerful, depending on if you are part of the conflict," Burak explained. The game used real footage from the news, licensed from Reuters. Upon its release, Burak observed how teachers used it with discussion and how it became part of a larger program. He recalled, "Very early I saw games as piece of a larger concept, not a stand-alone." *Peacemaker* cost over half a million dollars to produce, and it can be played for hours. Schools in the West Bank may avoid discussing politics in class, but they do play games. "The game provides a safe environment," he continued. "Kids talk about the role-playing element, like, 'what I did when I was the Israeli prime minister.'"

Burak stepped down after 5 years as president in 2015, handing the reigns over to Susanna Pollack, who had been the vice president of partnerships and special projects. He is still very much a part of Games for Change, curating the Neurogaming and Health track, which was added to the Festival in 2016. The other tracks in the 13th Annual Festival included the Civics and Social Issues Track and the Games for Learning Summit. The 14th Annual Festival added a 4th track to its 2017 line-up: the VR for Change Summit.

Games for Learning Summit

The Games for Learning Summit started in 2015. It took place the day prior to the 12th Annual Games for Change Festival. Cohosted by the U.S. Department of Education, and sponsored by the Entertainment Software Association and Microsoft, that first event mixed together teachers, game developers, government officials, and students. Held at New York University, I was fortunate to be one of the 200 people invited. Many of the people I spoke researching this book were in attendance, including two of the keynote speakers: game designer Jesse Schell and educator Rafranz Davis. While there, I attended several breakout sessions. One was from Ubisoft, which discussed how its *Assassin's Creed* games and the World War I-set *Valiant Hearts* could be used in history classrooms. Other sessions included *Minecraft*, *Angry Birds* in physics classrooms, GlassLab's psychometric analytics, and BrainPOP.

In 2016, the Games for Learning Summit formally became fully integrated into the 13th Games for Change Annual Festival. Now held at The New School's Parsons School of Design, in Manhattan, the Entertainment Software Association was again a partner, and Sara Cornish curated the speakers. It included talks from members of the White House and the Department of Education, the Mayor of New York City's office, and companies like Unity, Code.org, PBS, the Institute of Play, and BrainPOP. Although there was a separate track for learning games, there was an overlap in content. Like other educators in attendance, I sat in on multiple sessions from all three tracks.

Eric Huey, the senior vice president for government affairs the Entertainment Software Association, and Richard Culatta, formerly from the White House Office of Educational Technology, framed the Festival's breakout themes. And like the Summit the year prior, Eric N. Martin, Policy Advisor at Office of Science and Technology Policy, was in attendance. Martin is sometimes nicknamed the White House games czar. Bethesda game studio founder Christopher Weaver led the first keynote, which focused on the psychology of why challenges in games are leveled, and how learning gets scaffolded. Magic Leap's Chief Game Wizard Graeme Devine led the second keynote, speaking about the potential for "mixed reality" in the classroom. Mixed reality blurs virtual reality and augmented reality—"photons, instead of atoms," he said. In fact, virtual reality and empathy were recurrent themes in both days of the Festival.

Representing an actual real-life classroom teacher—"atoms, not photons," I joked—I participated in the "Computer Science for All: Putting Students in the Driving Seat" panel. Also on the panel were Michael Preston, New York City's Director of Computer Science, and Debbie Marcus, Computer Science for All's director at the New York City Department of Education, and Minerva Tantoco, New York City's (now former) Chief Technology Officer, who served as moderator. Echoing my conversation with Allison Mishkin, of the

National STEM Video Game Challenge, we discussed where game design fits in a project-based learning classroom. We also discussed multiple entry points to computer science education, and how "computer science," "coding," and even "games" are loaded words, each carrying a different meaning that could detract youth from participation. Because students are creating an interactive system, computer science and game design supports deeper learning. After all, computer science isn't just programming!

Because there were three concurrent tracks, it was impossible to attend every session. Thankfully, Games for Change recorded all of the sessions and uploaded them to YouTube. The Festival is a true idea forum; it is also a great space to network with thought leaders. For example, there was an Industry Circle panel moderated by Mark DeLoura, the organizer of the White House Educational Game Jam. It featured Playmatics' Margaret Wallace, Filament's Dan White, BrainPOP's Scott Price, and Schell Games' Jesse Schell, and the discussion shared ideas on how to get good learning games to students' hands. Greg Toppo led a panel on violence in video games. Other sessions included Minecraft Education director Deirdre Quarnstrom, along with teachers Steve Isaacs and Chris Aviles, showing the new toolsets in *Minecraft: Education Edition*, and the Institute of Play and BrainPOP debuting *Meaning of Beep*. The Office of Educational Technology's Katrina Stevens moderated a panel about children's games (e.g., Toca Boca, CodeSpark, and PBS Kids). And there was a session from AbleGamers about "includification," a guideline for designers for gamers who have disabilities.

The 13th Annual Games for Change Festival included an awards ceremony, hosted by Jesse Schell. *Dragon Box: Numbers* won Best Learning Game. This was the first time that there was a category specifically for learning. Other Best Learning Game nominees included *Mission US: City of Immigrants* and *NOVA's Evolution Lab*, a puzzle game about evolution. *Life is Strange* took home the most awards: Game of the Year, Most Significant Impact, and the Games for Change and Mashable (the online blog) People's Choice Award. *Block'hood* won Best Gameplay, and *That Dragon, Cancer* took home honors for Most Innovative Game.

Perhaps the biggest announcement at the 13th Games for Change Festival came from Sid Meier, the creator of the *Civilization*. For the past 25 years, there have been several iterations of the *Civilization* series. Each is a historically set turn-based strategy game. Meier sat down with Games for Change president Susanna Pollack, Collective Shift's (GlassLab's parent) Connie Yowell, and Take-Two Interactive Software's Strauss Zelnick, to announce

CivilizationEDU. Expected for release in 2017, GlassLab will create a teacher dashboard and an analytics engine, similar to its *SimCityEDU*. Regarding where the "EDU" fits in Meier's commercial game, fun and learning come first. In fact, both intertwined, deeply embedded in the design decisions of *Civilization* games. Meier told Pollack:

> I kind of make a distinction between education and learning. I think learning is a component in almost every video game. When you're playing *Tetris* you're learning how to fit some squares together. You're always expecting to get better. And that really requires learning. Learning is a part of any video game experience. That's why people play—to get better. People play to get that sensation of getting better.

CivilizationEDU brings Kurt Squire's landmark research using *Civilization III* one decade earlier (see Chapter 1) full circle. His students played *Civilization* because it "1) provided a framework tying together world geopolitical history; 2) gave fluency with a model that is useful for analyzing world history on broad time scales; and 3) inspired revisiting, tinkering, and socializing" (Squire, 2011, p. 28). In other words, students were put in an experience that was meaningful, not just fun. This builds on Meier's definition of games as being a series of interesting decision. And it is these interesting decisions that drive players to *want* to continue to learn.

The Games for Learning Working Group was founded at the second annual Games for Learning Summit, part of the Games for Change Festival, with support from the Entertainment Software Association (ESA). The group is made up of leaders in the game-based learning community. Games for Change acts as the convening organization, bringing the group together on a quarterly basis to map the sector and road ahead; identify opportunities to engage, educate, and empower key stakeholders such as funders and developers; and shape the growing learning games market. Members of the group include leaders from Ubisoft, The White House, U.S. Department of Education, Filament Games, USC Game Lab, Magic Leap and Unity.

Final Words on Game-Based Learning

So what is it about games that have drawn together so much interest from passionate people? I asked Mitch Weisburgh, from Academic Business Advisors, for his opinion. In addition to educational technology entrepreneurship, Weisburgh has helped launch Edchat Interactive, a teacher professional development platform. To Weisburgh—like many others I spoke to—game-based learning really came down to one thing: *student agency*. When done right, games—like projects—enable students to take charge of their learning goals. "When the students and teachers have voice to choose what they are doing, the learning is deeper and better," Weisburgh explained, in April 2016. "Whether it is a game or a project—which is two sides of the same coin—you want to set things up so students see a problem they want to solve, and then they learn something in the process. Highly motivated, self-directed learning is the best kind of learning."

As you bring games to your students, keep in mind their experiences. Your lessons should be constantly iterated, like a game, based on their feedback. After all your students are your playtesters. The lessons you design, with or without games, must be meaningful and need to include a sense of playfulness. Remember to assess learning outcomes—not how students play, or if whether they win, or not. With story-driven games, have students "close read" and critically analyze the narrative, assessing with your own qualitative and quantitative instruments, just like you would using other media in a class (e.g., novel, film). For commercial, off-the-shelf games, after playing yourself, think about the core mechanics, as well as the game's theme and narrative. Can you align the mechanic to content in your curriculum? And importantly, remember teacher Marianne Malmstrom mantra: "Follow the learning!" See what play patterns students do and follow that.

Conclusions and Takeaways

Social impact games push the envelope of entertainment. As the medium matures, so should the content. That is, themes shouldn't become more adult; rather, a deeper range of player emotions, such as empathy, need to figure in the games. Try implementing games from sites such as Games for Change, and other portals that feature social impact or transformational games.

Lesson Plan Ideas

Gone Home in the classroom resources can be viewed on Paul Darvasi's blog. Here's the first of several posts (I also observed his use of the game to teach in my dissertation research)—http://www.ludiclearning.org/2014/03/29/annotating-the-foyer-towards-a-close-playing-of-gone-home

Grow-A-Game, brainstorming cards to create kindergarten through grade 12 social impact games, available using paper cards or on iPad—http://www.tilt-factor.org/game/grow-a-game

Mission US: Lesson plans for the social studies interactive. This lesson meets English language arts Common Core State Standards—http://www.mission-us.org

Push/Pull Immigration: Have students first play *Mission US: City of Immigrants*, followed by *The Migrant Trail*, which is based on a PBS documentary, *The Undocumented*. It presents a first-person journey through Arizona's desert borderlands. Play as an undocumented immigrant and then as a border patrol agent. Both are free. I put students in these experiences before our 13 American Colonies project, in which they had to recruit settlers to their colonies—http://theundocumented.com

Well Played: Classroom Edition: Each year the Games for Change Festival and the Games + Learning + Society Conference features a "Well Played" series of talks. The talks are based on the *Well Played Journal*, published by Carnegie Mellon University Entertainment Technology Center. The talks are essentially live walkthroughs of games given by designers not associated with the production of the titles. This style of analysis is like hearing authors read and discuss their favorite books with an audience. Common Core State Standards include English language arts, especially those pertaining to "explain."

Republica Times is a game about bias in the media, created by Lucas Pope, the designer of *Papers, Please*. See the educator lesson plans from Graphite—https://www.graphite.org/game/the-republia-times

Way is a social learning game. See lesson plans from Graphite here—https://www.graphite.org/game/way

Games

1979 Revolution: Black Friday is story-driven, with multiple-choice conversation trees. Like *Life is Strange*, the protagonist is a photographer. Pictures taken in the game are juxtaposed next to actual photos from the revolution. Set in Tehran, Iran, during 1978 and 1980, it is a political dystopian thriller—http://inkstories.com/1979RevolutionGame

Awkward Moment—http://www.tiltfactor.org/game/awkward-work

Ayiti: The Cost of Life, a social impact game about poverty in Haiti—http://ayiti.globalkids.org/game

Buffalo—http://www.tiltfactor.org/game/buffalo

Data Dealer, a web-based game that raises awareness about online privacy concerns—https://datadealer.com

Dig Rush, from Ubisoft and Amblyopia, is a game to treat lazy eye disorder—http://blog.ubi.com/dig-rush-announced

Dumb Ways to Die is a series of games about being safe around trains—http://www.dumbwaystodie.com

EyeWire, a massively multiplayer online game from MIT to map neurons in the human brain—http://eyewire.org

Gone Home, the first-person exploration game about the horrors of ordinary life—http://www.gonehomegame.com

Half the Sky, the social game for women's rights, playable on Facebook—https://www.facebook.com/HalftheGame

The Migrant Trail. Tied to a documentary, this game lets players assume the role of a migrant or a patrol agent—http://theundocumented.com

Mission US—http://www.mission-us.org

Nightmare: Malaria, a social awareness game about malaria—http://nightmare.againstmalaria.com

Papers, Please—http://papersplea.se

Peacemaker. Play as Palestine or Israel—http://www.peacemakergame.com

Pox: Save the People—http://www.tiltfactor.org/game/pox

SuperBetter, on Jane McGonigal's (author of *Realty Is Broken*) site, launched after she recovered from a concussive injury—https://www.superbetter.com

Never Alone—http://neveralonegame.com

Papo & Yo. According to the developer's website, players "will need to learn to use Monster's emotions, both good and bad, to their advantage if they want to complete their search for a cure and save their pal"—http://www.wearemi-nority.com/papo-yo

Save the Park, designed by Schell Games for Games for Change to bring awareness to U.S. National Parks—http://www.gamesforchange.org/savethepark

Sea Hero Quest is a mobile game designed to fight dementia—http://www.seaheroquest.com/en

Start the Talk, a game developed by the U.S. Substance Abuse and Mental Health Services Administration to help parents discuss underage drinking with their children—http://samhsa.gov/underagedrinking

The Stanley Parable, a first-person "nonviolent" exploration game—http://www.stanleyparable.com

That Dragon, Cancer, Ryan Green's tribute to his son, Joel—http://thatdragoncancer.com; and the documentary, *Thank You for Playing*—http://www.thankyouforplayingfilm.com

Third World Farmer, a simulation game—http://www.3rdworldfarmer.com

Valiant Hearts: The Great War is a mobile game set in World War I France. It plays like an interactive graphic novel—http://valianthearts.ubi.com

This War of Mine—http://www.11bitstudios.com/games/16/this-war-of-mine

Uplifted, the "happiness" game—https://itunes.apple.com/gb/app/uplifted/id582248097

Xenos, the English language learning game—http://www.xenos-isle.com

Resources

Brené Brown on Empathy is an animated video on YouTube that describes the oft-confused difference between empathy and sympathy—https://youtu.be/1Evwgu369Jw

Cathedral is the Radiolab show featuring Ryan and Amy Green of *That Dragon, Cancer*—http://www.radiolab.org/story/cathedral

Classcraft's extensive blog reporting on 2016's Games for Learning Summit—http://www.classcraft.com/blog/g4c

Critical Play, Mary Flanagan's TEDx Dartmouth Talk about games as art—http://www.dartmouth.edu/~tedx/maryflanaganvideo

EdChat Interactive for online teacher professional development—http://www.edchatinteractive.org

A Father, a Dying Son, and the Quest to Make the Most Profound Videogame Ever, in *Wired* about *That Dragon, Cancer*—http://www.wired.com/2016/01/that-dragon-cancer

Follow the Learning, Marianne Malmstrom's blog and website—http://www.followthelearning.com

Impact with Games: A Fragmented Field is a research report led by Games for Change and the Michael Cohen Group, presented by advisory board chair and Games for Change cofounder, Benjamin Stokes. It is available for free online—http://gameimpact.net

Games for Change—http://www.gamesforchange.org

Games for Learning Summit's 2015 talks—http://bit.ly/1WcmJI3

Games4Ed is a weekly Twitter chat (hashtag: #Games4Ed). It is an extension of the Games4Ed nonprofit organization—http://www.games4ed.org

Games for Health—http://gamesforhealth.org

Playmatics is where Margaret Wallace and Nick Fortugno develop serious games, museum games, and entertainment titles—http://playmatics.com

Tiltfactor, Mary Flanagan's social impact game design studio—http://www.tiltfactor.org

Well Played Journal. Volumes are accessible for free and feature in-depth analysis of video games—http://press.etc.cmu.edu/wellplayed

Values at Play, adding human values into games—http://valuesatplay.org

Zynga.org, where the social gaming giant meets the social good—http://zynga.org

REFERENCES

The AbleGamers Foundation. (2014). Retrieved July 28, 2014, from http://www.ablegamers. com

Abt, C. C. (1987). *Serious games*. Lanham, MD: University Press of America.

Allocca, K. (2011, November). Why videos go viral. Retrieved June 11, 2016, from https:// www.ted.com/talks/kevin_allocca_why_videos_go_viral?language=en

Almond, R. G., Mislevy, R. J., & Steinberg, L. S. (2003). On the structure of educational assessment. *Measurement: Interdisciplinary Research and Perspective, 1*(1) 3–62.

Anderson, J., & Rainie, L. (2012, May 18). *The future of gamification*. Retrieved January 19, 2014, from Pew Internet & American Life Project website: http://www.pewinternet.org/ Reports/2012/Future-of-Gamification.aspx

Apter, M. J., & Kerr, J. H. (1991). *Adult Play*. Amsterdam: Swets and Zeitlinger.

The art of video games. (2012). Retrieved December 24, 2013, from Smithsonian Institute website: http://americanart.si.edu/exhibitions/archive/2012/games/

Assassin's Creed III wiki guide. (2014). Retrieved January 18, 2014, from IGN website: http:// www.ign.com/wikis/assassins-creed-3/Animus_Database

Backyard engineers: A case study. (2015). Retrieved from Filament Games website: https:// www.filamentgames.com/case-learning-games-measurable-results-seen-playing-back-yard-engineers-0

Badges. (2014). Retrieved January 19, 2014, from Mozilla Wiki website: https://wiki.mozilla. org/Badges

Baer, R. H. (2005). *Videogames: In the beginning*. Springfield, NJ: Rolenta Press.

Bartle, R. (1996, April). *Hearts, clubs, diamonds, spades: Players who suit MUDs*. Retrieved July 22, 2013, from http://www.mud.co.uk/richard/hcds.htm

Bateman, C. (Ed.). (2009). *Beyond game design: Nine steps towards creating better videogames*. Boston, MA: Charles River Media/Cengage Technology.

Bauer, M. I., Corrigan, S., DiCerbo, K, Hao, J., Hoffman, E., John, M., … von Davier, A. (2014). *Psychometric considerations in game-based assessment*. New York, NY: CreateSpace Independent.

Bernstein, J. (Producer). (2015, December 9). Five ways you can use Minecraft to teach math. *Ed got game*. Podcast retrieved from http://www.bamradionetwork.com/game-based-learning/3606-five-ways-you-can-use-minecraft-to-teach-math

Bernstein, J. (Producer). (2016, March 28). GBL: Differentiating and extending learning with games. *Ed got game*. Podcast retrieved from http://www.bamradionetwork.com/game-based-learning/3791-gbl-differentiating-and-extending-learning-with-games

Bers, M. U., & Resnick, M. (2016). *The official ScratchJr book: Help your kids learn to code!* San Francisco, CA: No Starch Press.

Birnbaum, I. (2013, July 16). Behind Falskaar, a massive new Skyrim mod, and the 19-year-old who spent a year building it. Retrieved July 19, 2014, from *PC Gamer* website: http://www.pcgamer.com/2013/07/16/behind-falskaar-a-massive-new-skyrim-mod-and-the-19-year-old-who-spent-a-year-building-it/

Bisz, J. (n.d.). The five simple game mechanics. Retrieved July 8, 2014, from Composition Games for the Classroom website: http://joebisz.com/compositiongames/Composition_Games_for_the_Classroom.html

Bjork, S., & Holopainen, J. (2006). Games and design patterns. In K. Salen & E. Zimmerman (Eds.), *The game design reader: A rules of play anthology* (pp. 410–437). Cambridge, MA: MIT Press.

Black, R. W., & Steinkuehler, C. (2009). Literacy in virtual worlds. In L. Christenbury, R. Bomer, & P. Smagorinsky (Eds.), *Handbook of adolescent literacy research* (pp. 271–286). New York, NY: Guilford

Bodrova E., Germeroth, C., & Leong, D. J. (2013). Play and self-regulation: Lessons from Vygotsky. *American Journal of Play*, 6(1). (pp. 111–123)

Bodrova, E., & Leong, D. J. (2003). The importance of being playful. *Educational Leadership*, 60(7), 50–53.

Bogost, I. (2008). The rhetoric of video games. In K. Salen (Ed.), *The ecology of games: Connecting youth, games, and learning* (pp. 117–140). The John D. and Catherine T. MacArthur Foundation Series on Digital Media and Learning. Cambridge, MA: MIT Press. doi:10.1162/dmal.9780262693646.117

Boss level at Quest to Learn: Connected learning in a public school. (n.d.). Retrieved December 17, 2013, from Connected Learning website: http://connectedlearning.tv/case-studies/boss-level-quest-learn-connected-learning-public-school

Boyle, A. (2013, January 20). 10 most important board games in history. Retrieved December 22, 2013, from Listverse website: http://listverse.com/2013/01/20/10-most-important-board-games-in-history/

Brandt, R. (2011, October 15). Birth of a salesman. Retrieved December 14, 2013, from the *Wall Street Journal* website: http://online.wsj.com/news/articles/SB1000142405297020391 4304576627102996831200

Bronson, P., & Merryman, A. (2009). *New research: $13 Christmas gifts = 13 point gain in kids' IQ.* Retrieved June 11, 2016, from http://www.nurtureshock.com/IQLeaps.pdf

Brown, J. S. (2016). How World of Warcraft could save your business and the economy. Retrieved June 11, 2016, from http://bigthink.com/videos/how-world-of-warcraft-could-save-your-business-and-the-economy-2

Burgess, D. (2012). *Teach like a pirate: Increase student engagement, boost your creativity, and transform your life as an educator.* San Diego, CA: Dave Burgess Consulting.

Byrd, C. (2016, January 8). 'Life is strange' Passes the Spielberg test for video game as artform. Retrieved May 19, 2016, from The Washington Post website: https://www.washingtonpost.com/news/comic-riffs/wp/2016/01/08/life-is-strange-passes-the-spielberg-test-for-video-game-as-artform/

Caillois, R. (2001). *Man, play, and games* (M. Barash, Trans.). Urbana, IL: University of Illinois Press. (Original work published 1961)

Caillois, R. (2006). The definition of play: The classification of games. In K. Salen & E. Zimmerman (eds.), *The game design reader: A rules of play anthology* (pp. 122–155). Cambridge, MA: MIT Press. (Original work published 1962)

Calendar, S. (2016, June 1). 5 assessment strategies in learning games. Retrieved June 10, 2016, from https://www.filamentlearning.com/blog/5-assessment-strategies-learning-games

Campbell, J. (2008). *The hero with a thousand faces* (3rd ed.). Novato, CA: New World Library.

Cassell, J., & Jenkins, H. (2000). *From Barbie to Mortal Kombat: Gender and computer games.* Cambridge, MA: MIT Press.

Catmull, E. E., & Wallace, A. (2014). *Creativity, Inc.: Overcoming the unseen forces that stand in the way of true inspiration.* New York, NY: Random House.

Center for Games and Impact. (2014). Retrieved January 18, 2014, from Arizona State University: Mary Lou Fulton Teachers College website: http://gamesandimpact.org/

Chen, J. (2006). *Flow in games.* Retrieved January 4, 2014, from http://www.jenovachen.com/flowingames/flowing.htm

Chen, J., Lu, S.-I., & Vekhter, D. (n.d.). Zero-sum games. Retrieved January 13, 2014, from Game Theory website: http://www-cs-faculty.stanford.edu/~eroberts/courses/soco/projects/1998-99/game-theory/index.html

Clowes, G. (2011). *The essential 5: A starting point for Kagan Cooperative Learning.* San Clemente, CA: Kagan Publishing.

Common core homepage. (2015). Retrieved from http://www.corestandards.org

Conklin, A. R. (2016, July 25). Time to leave: Fed up with political climate, game pioneers abandon UW-Madison. Retrieved July 29, 2016, from Isthmus website: http://isthmus.com/news/news/fed-up-with-political-climate-game-pioneers-abandon-uw/

Cook, D. (2006, October 23). *What are game mechanics?* Retrieved from Lostgarden website: http://www.lostgarden.com/2006/10/what-are-game-mechanics.html

Crair, B. (2010, December 13). Brenda Brathwaite: Holocaust game designer. Retrieved December 24, 2013, from the *Daily Beast* website: http://www.thedailybeast.com/articles/2010/12/13/brenda-brathwaite-holocaust-game-designer.html

Creative Learning Exchange. (2013). Retrieved November 22, 2013, from http://clexchange.org

Csikszentmihalyi, M. (1990). *Flow: The psychology of optimal experience.* New York, NY: Harper & Row.

Darvasi, P. (2014). *Prologue: A video game's epic-ish journey to a high school English class.* Retrieved from http://www.ludiclearning.org/2014/03/05/gone-home-in-education/

Darvasi, P. (2015). *Pursuing quests: How digital games can create a learning journey.* Retrieved from MindShift website: http://ww2.kqed.org/mindshift/2015/12/04/pursuing-quests-how-digital-games-can-create-a-learning-journey/

Davis, R. (2015, February 17). Because slavery should not be edtech gamified #slavesimulation. Retrieved May 19, 2016, from Rafranz Davis website: http://rafranzdavis.com/because-slavery-should-not-be-edtech-gamified-slavesimulation/

DeBarger, A. H., Dornsife, C., Rosier, S., Shechtman, N., & Yarnall, L. (2013, February 14). *Promoting grit, tenacity, and perseverance: Critical factors for success in the 21st century.* Retrieved January 31, 2014, from Office of Educational Technology website: http://www.ed.gov/edblogs/technology/files/2013/02/OET-Draft-Grit-Report-2-17-13.pdf

DeKoven, B. (2013). *The well-played game: A player's philosophy.* Cambridge, MA: The MIT Press.

De Lisi, R. (2015). Piaget's sympathetic but unromantic account of children's play. In J. Johnson, S. Eberle, T. Henricks, & D. Kuschner (Eds.), *The handbook of the study of play* (pp. 227–237). New York, NY: Rowman & Littlefield.

Diamond, J. M. (1998). *Guns, germs, and steel: The fates of human societies.* New York, NY: W. W. Norton.

Doom WAD. (n.d.). Retrieved July 19, 2014, from Wikipedia website: http://en.wikipedia.org/wiki/Doom_WAD

Doty, M. (2013, December 10). Play "Frozen" find-it! Discover all the Easter eggs in Disney's blockbuster. Retrieved December 10, 2013, from Yahoo Movies website: http://movies.yahoo.com/blogs/movie-news/play-frozen-discover-easter-eggs-disney-blockbuster-170605113.html

Duncan, S., & Steinkuehler, C. (2008). Scientific habits of mind in virtual worlds. *Journal of Science Education & Technology, 17*(6), 530–543. doi:10.1007/s10956-008-9120-8

Dunniway, T., & Novak, J. (2007). *Game development essentials: Gameplay mechanics.* Clifton Park, NY: Thomson Delmar Learning.

Dweck, C. (2006). *Mindset: The new psychology of success.* New York, NY: Random House.

Dweck, C. (2015). *Carol Dweck revisits the "growth mindset."* Retrieved from Education Week website: http://www.edweek.org/ew/articles/2015/09/23/carol-dweck-revisits-the-growth-mindset.html

Eberle, S. G. (2014). The elements of play: Toward a philosophy and a definition of play. *American Journal of Play, 6*(2), 214–233.

Ekman, P. (2007). *Emotions revealed: Recognizing faces and feelings to improve communication and emotional life* (2nd ed.). New York, NY: Owl Books.

Ebert, R. (2010, April 16). Video games can never be art. Retrieved December 24, 2013, from Roger Ebert's Journal website: http://www.rogerebert.com/rogers-journal/video-games-can-never-be-art

Ebert, R. (2005, June 24). Ebert's walk of fame remarks. Retrieved July 11, 2016, from http://www.rogerebert.com/rogers-journal/eberts-walk-of-fame-remarks

E-Line Media. (2013). Retrieved December 10, 2013, from http://elinemedia.com

Essential facts about the computer and video game industry. (2016). Retrieved June 8, 2016, from The Entertainment Software Association website: http://essentialfacts.theesa.com/Essential-Facts-2016.pdf

Farber, M. (2015, January 16). Gone Home: A video game as a tool for teaching critical thinking skills. Retrieved June 10, 2016, from http://ww2.kqed.org/mindshift/2015/01/16/gone-home-a-video-game-as-a-tool-for-teaching-critical-thinking/

Farber, M. (2015, April 1). Three games about viruses that teach interconnectedness. Retrieved June 10, 2016, from http://ww2.kqed.org/mindshift/2015/04/01/three-games-about-viruses-that-teach-interconnectedness/

Field study results: Mars generation one. (2015, February 20). Retrieved from GlassLab Games website: http://about.glasslabgames.org/wp-content/uploads/2014/08/ResearchMGOFull.pdf

Field study results: Ratio rancher. (2015, May 14). Retrieved from GlassLab Games website: http://about.glasslabgames.org/wp-content/uploads/2015/06/Ratio-Rancher-Field-Study-Results.pdf

Filament Games. (2014). Retrieved January 17, 2014, from http://www.filamentgames.com/

Fishman, B., Plass, J., Riconscente, M., Snider, R., & Tsai, T. (2014a). *Empowering educators: Supporting student progress in the classroom with digital games part I: A national survey.* Ann Arbor, MI: University of Michigan.

Fishman, B., Plass, J., Riconscente, M., Snider, R., & Tsai, T. (2014b). *Empowering educators: Supporting student progress in the classroom with digital games part II: Case studies.* Ann Arbor: University of Michigan.

Framework for 21st Century Learning. (2015). *About us.* Retrieved from Partnership for 21st Century Learning website: http://www.p21.org/about-us/p21-framework

Frum, L. (2012, October 19). American history unfolds in "Assassin's Creed 3." Retrieved January 18, 2014, from CNN website: http://www.cnn.com/2012/10/19/tech/gaming-gadgets/assassins-creed-3-history

Games and Learning. (2014). Retrieved January 21, 2014, from Games and Learning website: http://www.gamesandlearning.org

Games and Learning Society. (2013). Retrieved November 2, 2013, from http://www.gameslearningsociety.org/index.php

Games for Change. (2014). Retrieved January 18, 2014, from http://www.gamesforchange.org

Garner, D. (2011, October 12). After a quarter-century, an author looks back at his Holocaust comic. Retrieved May 28, 2016, from http://www.nytimes.com/2011/10/13/books/metamaus-by-art-spiegelman-review.html?_r=0

Gee, J. P. (2005). *Good video games and good learning*. Retrieved December 14, 2013, from http://www.jamespaulgee.com/sites/default/files/pub/GoodVideoGamesLearning.pdf

Gee, J. P. (2007). *What video games have to teach us about learning and literacy* (rev. ed.). New York, NY: Palgrave Macmillan.

Gee, J. P. (2010). Video games: What they can teach us about audience engagement. Retrieved April 17, 2014, from *Nieman Reports* website: http://www.nieman.harvard.edu/reports/article/102418/Video-Games-What-They-Can-Teach-Us-About-Audience-Engagement.aspx

Gee, J. P. (2014, August 14). What are James Paul Gee's favorite games? Retrieved from edSurge website: https://www.edsurge.com/news/2014-08-14-what-are-james-paul-gee-s-favorite-games

Gibbs, J. (2011). *Player agency, critical states, and games as formal systems*. Retrieved from Gamasutra website: http://gamasutra.com/blogs/JoeyGibbs/20110713/89809/Player_Agency_Critical_States_and_Games_as_Formal_Systems.php

Goldberg, D., & Larsson, L. (2013). *Minecraft: The unlikely tale of Markus "Notch" Persson and the game that changed everything*. New York, NY: Seven Stories Press.

GradeCraft. (2016). Retrieved June 11, 2016, from https://www.gradecraft.com

Gray, P. (2014a). *Free to learn: Why unleashing the instinct to play will make our children happier, more self-reliant, and better students for life*. New York, NY: Basic Books.

Green, R. (2014). About the game. Retrieved April 18, 2014, from *That Dragon, Cancer* website, http://thatdragoncancer.com/

Grundberg, S., & Hansegard, J. (2014, June 16). YouTube's biggest draw plays games, earns $4 million a year. Retrieved June 18, 2014, from the *Wall Street Journal* website: http://online.wsj.com/articles/youtube-star-plays-videogames-earns-4-million-a-year-1402939896

Gushta, M., Mislevy, R. J., Rupp, A. A., & Shaffer, D. W. (2010). Evidence-centered design of epistemic games: Measurement principles for complex learning environments. *Journal of Technology, Learning, and Assessment*, 8(4). (pp. 1–48).

Harris, B. J. (2014). *Console wars: Sega, Nintendo, and the battle that defined a generation*. New York, NY: It Books.

Herr-Stephenson, B., Alper, M., Reilly, E., & Jenkins, H. (2013). *T is for transmedia: Learning through transmedia play*. Los Angeles, CA and New York, NY: USC Annenberg Innovation Lab and the Joan Ganz Cooney Center at Sesame Workshop.

Jenkins, H. (1992). *Textual poachers: Television fans & participatory culture*. New York, NY: Routledge.

Gone Home. (2014). Retrieved from http://www.gonehomegame.com/

Hattie, J. (2012). *Visible learning for teachers: Maximizing impact on learning*. London, UK: Routledge.

Heft, H. (1988). Affordances of children's environments: A functional approach to environmental description. *Children's Environments Quarterly*, 5(3), 29–37.

How to do a Let's Play. (2014). Retrieved January 18, 2014, from WikiHow website: http://www.wikihow.com/Do-a-Let's-Play

Huizinga, J. (1955). *Homo ludens: A study of the play-element in culture*. Boston, MA: Beacon Press. (Original work published 1938)

Hunicke, R., LeBlanc, M., & Zubek, R. (2004). *MDA: A formal approach to game design and game research*. Retrieved December 30, 2013, from http://www.cs.northwestern.edu/~hunicke/MDA.pdf

Impact guides. (2014). Retrieved August 30, 2014, from The Center for Games and Impact website: http://gamesandimpact.org/impact-guides/

Inform. (2014). Retrieved January 10, 2014, from http://inform7.com

Institute of Play. (2014). Retrieved April 27, 2014, from http://www.instituteofplay.org/about/context/glossary/

Interactive Fiction Community forum. (2014). Retrieved January 10, 2014, from http://www.intfiction.org/forum/

Interactive Fiction Competition. (2014). Retrieved January 10, 2014, from http://www.ifcomp.org

Ito, M. (2010). *Hanging out, messing around, and geeking out: Kids living and learning with new media*. Cambridge, MA: MIT.

Jackson, S. (2010, February 2). PBS's *Frontline* airs *Digital Nation* tonight. Retrieved January 19, 2014, from Spotlight on Digital Learning & Media website: http://spotlight.macfound.org/blog/entry/pbss-frontline-airs-digital-nation-tonight/

Jenkins, H. (2006a). *Convergence culture: Where old and new media collide*. New York, NY: New York University Press.

Jenkins, H. (2006b). Reality bytes: Eight myths about video games debunked. Retrieved May 14, 2014, from the Video Game Revolution website: http://www.pbs.org/kcts/videogamerevolution/impact/myths.html

Jenkins, H., & Kelley, W. (Eds.). (2013). *Reading in a participatory culture: Remixing Moby-Dick in the English classroom*. New York, NY: Teachers College Press.

Juul, J. (2003). The game, the player, the world: Looking for a heart of gameness. In M. Copier & J. Raessens (Eds.), *Level up: Digital Games Research Conference Proceedings* (pp. 30–45). Utrecht, The Netherlands: Utrecht University. Retrieved from http://www.jesperjuul.net/text/gameplayerworld/

Kagan, S. (1998). *Teams of four are magic!* San Clemente, CA: Kagan Publishing.

Kelly, K. (1994, January). Will Wright: The mayor of SimCity. Retrieved December 10, 2013, from *Wired* website: http://www.wired.com/wired/archive/2.01/wright.html?pg=2&topic=&topic_set=

Kent, S. L. (2001). *The ultimate history of video games: From Pong to Pokémon and beyond: The story behind the craze that touched our lives and changed the world*. Roseville, CA: Prima.

KerbalEdu. (2013). Retrieved December 10, 2013, from http://www.kerbaledu.com

Kim, A. J. (2012a, September 14). The player's journey: Designing over time [Blog post]. Retrieved December 29, 2013, from Amy Jo Kim website: http://amyjokim.com/2012/09/14/the-players-journey-designing-over-time/

Kim, A. J. (2012b, September 19). Social engagement: Who's playing? How do they like to engage? [Blog post]. Retrieved April 8, 2014, from Amy Jo Kim website: http://amyjokim.com/2012/09/19/social-engagement-whos-playing-how-do-they-like-to-engage/

Kim, A. J. (2014d, April 8). The player's journey. [Blog post]. Retrieved August 30, 2014, from Amy Jo Kim website: http://amyjokim.com/2014/04/08/the-players-journey/

Kim, A. J. (2014e, June 11). The co-op revolution: 7 rules for collaborative game design. Retrieved August 30, 2014, from Slideshare website: http://www.slideshare.net/amyjokim/the-coop-revolution-7-rules-for-collaborative-game-design

King, E. M. (2011). *Guys and games: Practicing 21st century workplace skills in the great indoors* (Doctoral dissertation). Retrieved from ProQuest Dissertations & Theses Full Text; ProQuest Dissertations & Theses Global. (Order No. 3488741) http://search.proquest.com/docview/917951417?accountid=12793

Kohn, A. (1999). *Punished by rewards: The trouble with gold stars, incentive plans, A's, praise, and other bribes* (1999 ed.). Boston, MA: Houghton Mifflin.

Kohn, A. (1997). Why incentive plans cannot work. In S. Kerr (ed.), *Ultimate rewards: What really motivates people to achieve* (pp. 15–24). Boston, MA: Harvard Business School Press.

Kollar, P. (2016, March 30). University of California, Irvine announces a League of Legends scholarship. Retrieved May 23, 2016, from Polygon website: http://www.polygon.com/2016/3/30/11330776/league-of-legends-university-california-irvine-esports-scholarship-riot

Koster, R. (2005). *A theory of fun for game design*. Scottsdale, AZ: Paraglyph Press.

Kyttä, M. (2004). The extent of children's independent mobility and the number of actualized affordances as criteria for child-friendly environments. *Journal of Environmental Psychology, 24*, 179–198.

Lave, J., & Wenger, E. (1991). *Situated learning: Legitimate peripheral participation*. Cambridge, UK: Cambridge University Press.

Lazzaro, N. (2004, March 8). *Why we play games: Four keys to more emotion without story.* Retrieved April 20, 2014, from XEODesign website: http://www.xeodesign.com/xeodesign_whyweplaygames.pdf

Lazzaro, N. (2009). Understanding emotions. In C. Bateman (ed.), *Beyond game design: Nine steps toward creating better videogames* (pp. 3–48). Boston, MA: Charles River Media.

Learning Games Network. (2014). Retrieved January 17, 2014, from http://www.learninggamesnetwork.org

Let's Play Archive. (2013). Retrieved December 10, 2013, from http://lparchive.org

Logo Foundation. (2011). What is Logo? Retrieved January 19, 2014, from http://el.media.mit.edu/logo-foundation/logo/index.html

Lorenzsonn, E. (2016, July 27). Departure of UW scholars spells the end for influential video gaming research group. Retrieved July 29, 2016, from The Capital Times website: http://host.madison.com/ct/news/local/departure-of-uw-scholars-spells-the-end-for-influential-video/article_bca79e1e-7f1f-5542-84d5-5b9178444c70.html

Lorenzsonn, E. (2017, January 3). *New UW video games institution will get in GEAR Tuesday.* Retrieved January 4, 2017, from The Capital Times website: http://host.madison.com/ct/business/technology/new-uw-video-games-institution-will-get-in-gear-tuesday/article_dc8fc18b-14a3-5152-9ccc-dc562c0b7207.html

LP guide for newbies. (2014). Retrieved January 18, 2014, from Wikia website: http://letsplay.wikia.com/wiki/LP_guide_for_newbies

Luckman, S., & Potanin, R. (2010). Machinima: Why think "games" when thinking "film"? In M. Knobel & C. Lankshear (eds.), *DIY media: Creating, sharing and learning with new technologies* (pp. 135–160). New York, NY: Peter Lang.

Magdaleno, A. (2014, July 18). ESPN's "Dota 2" broadcast is a giant leap for e-sports. Retrieved July 19, 2014, from Mashable website: http://mashable.com/2014/07/18/esports-dota-2-espn/

Makebadges. (2014). Retrieved January 19, 2014, from http://www.makebadg.es/badge.html#

MaKey MaKey. (2014). Retrieved January 17, 2014, from http://www.makeymakey.com

Matera, M. (2015). *Explore like a pirate: Engage, enrich, and elevate your learners with gamification and game-inspired course design.* San Diego: Dave Burgess Consulting.

McGonigal, J. (2010, February). *Jane McGonigal: Gaming can make a better world.* Retrieved January 18, 2014, from TED website: http://www.ted.com/talks/jane_mcgonigal_gaming_can_make_a_better_world.html

McGonigal, J. (2011). *Reality is broken: Why games make us better and how they can change the world.* New York, NY: Penguin Press.

Milton, S., Soares, P., & Maron, J. (2013). *Minecraft essential handbook.* New York, NY: Scholastic.

Mirani, L. (2014, April 3). Last year, 71 million people watched other people play video games. Retrieved April 5, 2014, from Quartz website: http://qz.com/195098/last-year-71-million-people-watched-other-people-play-video-games/

Montessori, M. (2012). *The Montessori method.* New York, NY: Renaissance Classics. (Original work published 1912)

Moseley, A., & Whitton, N. (2014). *New traditional games for learning: A case book.* New York, NY: Routledge/Taylor & Francis Group.

Mozilla Foundation and Peer 2 Peer University. (2012, August 27). *Open badges for lifelong learning.* Retrieved July 22, 2013, from MozillaWiki website: https://wiki.mozilla.org/images/5/59/OpenBadges-Working-Paper_012312.pdf

Muncy, J. (2016, June 17). 1979 Revolution: Black Friday: Gripping adventure game puts you in the Iranian Revolution. Retrieved June 19, 2016, from Wired website: http://www.wired.com/2016/06/1979-revolution-black-friday/

Nasar, S. (1998). *A beautiful mind: A biography of John Forbes Nash, Jr., winner of the Nobel prize in economics, 1994.* New York, NY: Simon & Schuster.

NationStates. (2014). Retrieved January 23, 2014, from http://www.nationstates.net

NewSchools Venture Fund. (2014). Retrieved July 29, 2014, from http://www.newschools.org

Nguyen, M. (2016, June 9). The next generation of Scratch. Retrieved June 11, 2016, from https://medium.com/scratchfoundation-blog/the-next-generation-of-scratch-d83426eb9ca9#.qbhrk7doc

Nicholson, S. (2014). A RECIPE for Meaningful Gamification. In T. Reiners & L. C. Wood, L. C. (eds.), *Gamification in education and business.* (pp. 1–20). Cham, Switzerland: Springer.

Nicholson, S. (2015). *Peeking behind the locked door: A survey of escape room facilities.* White Paper available at http://scottnicholson.com/pubs/erfacwhite.pdf

Norman, D. A. (2013). *The design of everyday things* (Rev. and expanded ed.). New York, NY: Basic Books.

Papert, S. (1993). *Mindstorms: Children, computers, and powerful ideas* (2nd ed.). New York, NY: Basic Books.

Parker, I. (2013, March 26). Improv, robots, parkour and more: Boss level at Quest to Learn. Retrieved December 17, 2013, from Institute of Play website: http://www.instituteofplay.org/2013/03/improv-robots-parkour-and-more-boss-level-at-quest-to-learn/

Parlett, D. (2005). Rules OK, or Hoyle on troubled waters. Paper presented at the 8th annual colloquium of the Board Game Studies Association, Oxford, 2005. Retrieved December 14, 2013, from http://www.davpar.eu/gamester/rulesOK.html

Piaget, J. (1962). *Play, dreams and imitation in childhood.* New York, NY: Norton Library.

Piccione, P. A. (1980, July/August). In search of the meaning of *Senet. Archaeology,* 55–58.

Pike, J. (2015, September 25). *Use Minecraft to teach math.* Retrieved from ISTE website: https://www.iste.org/explore/articleDetail?articleid=558&category=In-the-classroom&article=

Playful assessment with BrainPOP. (2016, April). *BranPOP educators webinars.* Podcast retrieved from https://educators.brainpop.com/video/playful-assessment-brainpop/

Poundstone, W. (1992). *Prisoner's dilemma.* New York, NY: Doubleday.

Puentedura, R. (n.d.). SAMR model. Retrieved June 11, 2016, from https://sites.google.com/a/msad60.org/technology-is-learning/samr-model

Q Design Pack Games and Learning. (2013). Retrieved from http://www.instituteofplay.org/wp-content/uploads/2013/09/IOP_QDesignPack_GamesandLearning_1.0.pdf

Resnick, M., & Siegel, D. (2015, November 10). A different approach to coding: How kids are making and remaking themselves from Scratch. Retrieved June 10, 2016, from Medium website: https://medium.com/bright/a-different-approach-to-coding-d679b06d83a#.q2m4k25hm

Robinett, W. (2006). Adventure as a video game: Adventure for the Atari 2600. In K. Salen & E. Zimmerman (eds.), *The game design reader: A rules of play anthology* (pp. 690–713). Cambridge, MA: MIT Press.

Roussos, G. (2015, December 7). When good intentions go awry: The counterintuitive effects of a prosocial online game. Retrieved May 19, 2016, from Psychology Today website: https://www.psychologytoday.com/blog/sound-science-sound-policy/201512/when-good-intentions-go-awry

Rufo-Tepper, R., Salen, K., Shapiro, A., Torres, R., & Wolozin, L. (2011). *Quest to learn: Developing the school for digital kids.* Cambridge, MA: MIT Press.

Salen, K., & Zimmerman, E. (2003). *Rules of play: Game design fundamentals.* Cambridge, MA: MIT Press.

Sandseter, E. (2009). Affordances for risky play in preschool: The importance of features in the play environment. *Early Childhood Education Journal, 36*(5), 439–446. doi:10.1007/s10643-009-0307-2

Schell, J. (2008). *The art of game design: A book of lenses.* Amsterdam: Elsevier/Morgan Kaufmann.

Senge, P. M. (2006). *The fifth discipline: The art and practice of the learning organization* (rev. ed.). New York, NY: Doubleday/Currency. (Original work published 1990)

Shear, E. (2014, August 25). Letter from the CEO. Retrieved August 30, 2014, from Twitch website: http://www.twitch.tv/p/thankyou

Sheldon, L. (2012). *The multiplayer classroom: Designing coursework as a game*. Boston, MA: Course Technology/Cengage Learning.

Shuler, C. (2012). *Where in the world is Carmen Sandiego? The edutainment era: Debunking myths and sharing lessons learned*. New York, NY: Joan Ganz Cooney Center at Sesame Workshop.

Shute, V. J. (2011). Stealth assessment in computer-based games to support learning. In S. Tobias, & J. D. Fletcher (Eds.), *Computer games and instruction* (pp. 503–524). Charlotte, NC: Information Age Publishers.

Shute, V. J., Ventura, M., & Torres, R. (2013). Formative evaluation of students at Quest to Learn. *International Journal of Learning and Media, 4*(1), 55–69.

Sosnick, E. (2016, May 26). Medium. Retrieved June 7, 2016, from http://The end of the yellow brick road

Specter, K. (2015, February 18). In support of 'flight to freedom', one of many ways to teach history. Retrieved May 19, 2016, from EdSurge website: https://www.edsurge.com/news/2015-02-18-in-support-of-flight-to-freedom-one-of-many-ways-to-teach-history

Spiegelman, A. (1986). *Maus: A survivor's tale*. New York, NY: Pantheon Books.

Squire, K. (2011). *Video games and learning: Teaching and participatory culture in the digital age*. New York, NY: Teachers College Press.

Steinkuehler, C. (2011). *The mismeasure of boys: Reading and online videogames* (WCER Working Paper No. 2011–3). Retrieved from University of Wisconsin–Madison, Wisconsin Center for Education Research website: http://www.wcer.wisc.edu/publications/working-Papers/papers.php

Suits, B. (2006). Construction of a definition. In K. Salen & E. Zimmerman (Eds.), *The game design reader: A rules of play anthology* (pp. 172–190). Cambridge, MA: MIT Press.

Sutton-Smith, B. (1997). *The ambiguity of play*. Cambridge, MA: Harvard University Press.

Takahashi, D. (2013, May 5). Valve's experimental psychologist discusses sweat detection and eye-tracking for games. Retrieved December 30, 2013, from Venture Beat website: http://venturebeat.com/2013/05/05/valves-experimental-psychologist-discusses-sweat-detection-and-eye-tracking-for-games/

Tanz, J. (2016, January). A father, a dying son, and the quest to make the most profound videogame ever. Retrieved June 7, 2016, from http://www.wired.com/2016/01/that-dragon-cancer/

Teacher Gaming. (2013). Retrieved December 8, 2013, from http://www.teachergaming.com

Tolkien, J. R. R. (2012). *The hobbit, or, there and back again* (75th ed.). Boston, MA: Mariner Books, Houghton Mifflin Harcourt.

Toca Boca. (2013). A digital toy or a game—what is the difference? Retrieved January 23, 2014, from Toca Boca website: https://tocaboca.desk.com/customer/portal/articles/564124-a-digital-toy-or-a-game---what-is-the-difference-

Toppo, G. (2015). *The game believes in you: How digital play can make our kids smarter*. New York, NY: Palgrave Macmillan Trade.

Toppo, G. (2015, April 14). Sandra Day O'Connor's post-court legacy: Civics games. Retrieved July 11, 2016, from USA Today website: http://www.usatoday.com/story/news/2015/04/14/oconnor-civics-games-legacy/25505871/

Victor, B. (2011, March 10). Explorable explanations. Retrieved May 19, 2016, from Worry Dream website: http://worrydream.com/ExplorableExplanations/

Von Neumann, J., & Morgenstern, O. (2007). *Theory of games and economic behavior*. Princeton, NJ: Princeton University Press.

Vygotsky, L. S. (1997). *Educational psychology* (R. J. Silverman, Trans.). Boca Raton, FL: St. Lucie Press.

Vygotsky, L. S. (1978). *Mind in society: The development of higher psychological processes*. Cambridge, MA: Harvard University Press.

Walther, B. K. (2003, May). *Playing and gaming reflections and classifications*. Retrieved from Game Studies website: http://www.gamestudies.org/0301/walther/

We want to know. (2016). Retrieved June 11, 2016, from http://wewanttoknow.com

What's next? Researcher James Gee on teaching children with games. (2013, September 3). Retrieved June 11, 2016, from http://www.gdconf.com/news/whats_next_learning_researcher/

White, D. (2014, January 3). Building educational games that get used in schools. Retrieved January 8, 2014, from *Gamasutra* website: http://www.gamasutra.com/blogs/DanWhite/20140103/208005/Building_Educational_Games_That_Get_Used_in_Schools.php

Zoombinis. (2015). Retrieved June 10, 2016, from https://external-wiki.terc.edu/display/ZOOM/The+Game

INDEX

Colin Lankshear & Michele Knobel
General Editors

New literacies emerge and evolve apace as people from all
walks of life engage with new technologies, shifting values
and institutional change, and increasingly assume 'postmod-
ern' orientations toward their everyday worlds. Despite many
efforts to take account of such changes, educational institutions largely remain out of touch with the range of new
ways of making and sharing meanings that increasingly mediate and shape the lives of the young people they teach and
the futures they face. This series aims to explore some key
dimensions of the changes occurring within social practices
of literacy and the educational challenges they present,
with a view to informing educational practice in helpful
ways. It asks what are new literacies, how do they impact on
life in schools, homes, communities, workplaces, sites of
leisure, and other key settings of human cultural engagement, and what significance do new literacies have for how
people learn and how they understand and construct knowledge. It aims to challenge established and 'official' ways
of framing literacy, and to ask what it means for literacies
to be powerful, effective, and enabling under current and
foreseeable conditions. Collectively, the works in this series will help to reorient literacy debates and literacy
education agendas.
    For further information about the series and submitting
manuscripts, please contact:

            Michele Knobel & Colin Lankshear
            Montclair State University
            Dept. of Education and Human Services
            3173 University Hall
            Montclair, NJ 07043
            michele@coatepec.net

    To order other books in this series, please contact our
Customer Service Department at:
            (800) 770-LANG (within the U.S.)
            (212) 647-7706 (outside the U.S.)
            (212) 647-7707 FAX

Or browse online by series at:
            www.peterlang.com